Techniques for Teaching Law 2

Techniques for Teaching Law 2

Gerald F. Hess
GONZAGA UNIVERSITY SCHOOL OF LAW

Steven I. Friedland
ELON UNIVERSITY SCHOOL OF LAW

Michael Hunter Schwartz
WASHBURN UNIVERSITY SCHOOL OF LAW

Sophie Sparrow
UNIVERSITY OF NEW HAMPSHIRE SCHOOL OF LAW

CAROLINA ACADEMIC PRESS
Durham, North Carolina

ISBN 978-1-59460-750-9 (alk. paper)
LCCN 99-61099

Carolina Academic Press
700 Kent Street
Durham, NC 27701
Telephone (919) 489-7486
Fax (919) 493-5668
www.cap-press.com

Printed in the United States of America

This book is dedicated to:

My extended family of teachers — partner, children, grandparents, mother, brother, sister, aunts, uncles, and cousins — Gerry Hess

My grandmother, Ethel, for her love, dedication to her family, and egg creams. — Steve Friedland

My daughter Samantha because students like you make me want to be a better teacher. Thank you for the inspiration — I hope that, for the rest of my life, I emulate your success in being a dedicated learner, a loving friend, a caring sibling, and, in every imaginable way, a wonderful daughter.— Michael Schwartz

Chris — thanks for all the support, laughter, and love — Sophie Sparrow

Contents

Contents by Contributor

Preface

This book is designed for legal educators who want to improve their teaching and their students' learning. The first chapter presents foundational principles of learning and instruction as well as insights from students. The remaining twelve chapters address topics such as classroom dynamics, technology, questioning, discussion, collaborative learning, experiential learning, feedback, assessment, and continued development for teachers. Each of these chapters starts with an introduction summarizing the basic ideas that underlie the topic and follows with classroom-tested exercises, approaches, material, ideas and insights from veteran teachers. Although *Techniques for Teaching Law 2* follows a format similar to the first *Techniques for Teaching Law* (1999), all of the content and ideas are new.

We intend this book to be a resource for all law teachers. New and experienced teachers will find pedagogical principles relevant to all levels of law school education. Our book includes ideas for legal educators who teach doctrine, theory, skills, and values in traditional classroom courses, clinics, externships, and academic support programs. There are many innovative and challenging exercises from which to choose.

A central feature of *Techniques for Teaching Law 2* is the collection of 160 ideas and exercises contributed by dedicated law teachers who have tested them with their students. We realize that not all of these ideas will appeal to all teachers, but we hope that the variety of approaches in these contributions will provide inspiration for any teacher. We greatly appreciate all of the thoughtful legal educators who contributed their insights and exercises to our book.

While many people played important roles in making *Techniques for Teaching Law 2* a reality, one person deserves special mention. We are indebted to Robbie McMillian, the Program Coordinator for the Institute for Law Teaching and Learning, for her outstanding work managing a project that included 100 authors and four editors and doing a copy edit that led to 1000s (literally) of corrections and improvements in the manuscript.

Gerry Hess, Steve Friedland, Sophie Sparrow, Michael Schwartz
May 2011

Techniques for Teaching Law 2

Chapter 1

Learning Theory, Student Perspectives, and Teaching Principles

This chapter is a primer that addresses the research on how students learn, students' perspectives on law school, and what makes for effective teaching. Fundamental principles of teaching and learning summarized in this chapter are reflected in the ideas and techniques presented in the rest of the book.

A. How Students Learn

Educational psychologists, instructional designers, and teachers from all disciplines have produced a vast literature on learning. This chapter focuses on three learning theories particularly relevant to law teachers: cognitive learning theory; constructivist learning theory; and self-regulated learning theory.

All learning theories assume that a primary goal of education is for students to achieve competency or mastery. In the law school setting, significant learning has occurred when students are able to solve a previously unseen problem by using applicable legal knowledge, skills, and professional values.

Cognitive Learning Theory

To transfer learning from an old setting to a new one, students must store their learning in an organized, meaningful, and useable way. Hundreds of pieces of information reach students' senses every moment. At any point during a class session, students are hearing what we and their peers say, hearing each other's clicks on their laptops, seeing what's on their computer screens, looking at slides we project on a screen or words we write on the board, feeling how hard their chairs are and how cold the classroom is, and smelling each other's colognes and soaps. The information registers in our students' senses for a brief moment. Humans can attend, however, to only a few of these pieces of information. The process of choosing a focus is known as "selective attention." The learning process is short circuited if students decide to pay attention to their email, their social interactions, their breakfasts, the hardness of their chairs, or their doodling, instead of attending to learning the skills, values and knowledge we are teaching.

If students do pay attention to their learning, it passes into their working memory. Students' working memory can retain only a small amount of learning and only for a short time. When students do something *active* to store their learning in a meaningful way, the information becomes a part of their long-term memory. For this reason, cognitivists were the first to emphasize the crucial importance of engaging students in active learning activities, in which students cannot simply sit and listen but must do something to mentally process concepts. If students are writing about the concepts, discussing them with a peer, applying them to a problem, or figuring out how concepts relate to each other, students are engaged in active learning.

The most common way students store new learning is by making connections between the new learning and what they already know. Other ways students store new learning include mnemonics, rehearsal (practicing recall, such as self-testing using flashcards), and elaborations (which include paraphrasing difficult concepts). The more deeply students think about what they are learning, the more likely they are to remember and use it.

The brain organizes long-term memories in hierarchical structures called "schemata." A schema is like the folder systems in computer operating systems that allow users to create folders and sub-folders and sub-sub-folders. These hierarchical systems allow users to readily remember where they can find any document they need.

Humans can store a single concept or set of concepts using more than one schema. For example, law professors can recall the case analysis process in abstract, generalized terms as a set of mental steps or through the many contexts in which they themselves have performed the skill. Storing learning in multiple schemata as opposed to storing learning in a single schema, improves recall—either because it strengthens the memory trace (the mental processes involved in gathering previously-learned concepts) or because it creates more mental paths to the learning.

Schemata, however, are not only analogous to operating system folders. Schemata also are like entire computer programs in that the organized material includes structures that reflect how to perform skills. Thus, most adults who can play a musical instrument, such as the piano, have developed a schema for performing all the mental and physical steps involved. In addition, schemata are like theories in that they allow us to make predictions and to draw inferences.

But storing learned skills and knowledge in schemata isn't enough. To analyze a problem, students must recall what they have learned and use that learning to interact with the environment in some way. In law school, this last step involves recalling cases, rules, and policies, and then generating an oral answer to a classroom hypothetical, writing a full analysis to a legal writing problem, or answering a timed essay test. In law practice, it includes interacting with a client, other parties, a judge, another attorney, and colleagues, taking risks, making complex decisions, and drafting pleadings, briefs, contracts, wills and other legal documents.

Constructivist Learning Theory

Constructivists focus on the process required for new learning to become a permanent part of who the students are. Three learning principles derive from constructivist research. First, learning is a matter of constructing an interpretation from an experience. When students engage with materials in an active way and reflect on the process, they develop personal understandings. Those personal understandings, having been entirely generated within the student's mind, stay with the student. Thus, significant law student learning only can happen if the law professor provides the students with opportunities to develop such interpretations, to figure things out for themselves.

Constructivists also emphasize the importance of real-world experiences. Students learn when their opportunities to construct understandings are authentic, such as when their learning is anchored in a realistic context. Thus, law professors who situate their teaching of doctrine, skills, and values in law practice problems, whether simulations or actual client issues, provide students the authenticity they need to construct meaningful understandings.

Finally, constructivists emphasize the role of social interaction in learning. Students engage in crucial mental activity when they negotiate meaning and seek to synthesize their personal understandings. The hundreds of studies demonstrating the superiority of cooperative learning groups compared to all other teaching methods support this assertion. These groups are effective because they allow students to obtain access to multiple perspectives with respect to a problem or issue and thereby develop the more complex approaches and understandings required to address complex problems.

Self-Regulated Learning Theory

Self-regulated learning is the process by which successful students manage their learning process. According to the research, self-regulated learners typically possess the following qualities:

- Students who are self-regulated learners actively control their behavior, motivation and thinking process when engaging in academic tasks.
- They view academic learning as something they do rather than as something that is done to or for them.
- They believe academic learning is a proactive activity, requiring self-initiated activities.
- They are interested in the subject matter, well-prepared for class, and ready with comments, questions, ideas, and insights.
- They look for problems and try to solve them.
- They seek opportunities for practice and feedback and also create such opportunities.
- They are willing to fail or admit a lack of understanding.
- They are driven to rectify failure and construct understanding.

Self-regulated students engage in a three-phase learning cycle: they engage in a planning phase, an implementation phase, and a reflection phase.

The planning phase consists of all the thinking the student does before engaging in a learning task. It includes four principle activities: deciding what to learn; predicting success; setting mastery goals; and developing a strategy to achieve the goal.

The first step in the planning stage is for students to decide what to learn. Self-regulated learners base this decision on their reading of the course material and classroom discussions, rather than relying exclusively on the class notes or outline of a peer or on a supplemental resource, such as a commercial outline.

The second step, predicting success, invokes the concept of "self-efficacy." Students with high self-efficacy do better on academic tasks because their belief that they can learn enables them to persist when they encounter difficulty, their persistence increases the likelihood of success, and those successes increase the students' self-efficacy.

The self-regulated learner then sets a goal, a specific, desired outcome, for the task. Expert self-regulated learners generally set mastery learning goals, goals that emphasize learning the material as well as possible rather than achieving high grades.

The final step of the planning process involves students in devising and tailoring a strategic approach to achieving the goal. When selecting strategies, students plan the appropriate study techniques and decide where, when, with whom, and for how long they will study.

The implementation phase is much simpler—the self-regulating student executes the plans made in the planning phase. One key to successfully implementing the student's plan is for the student to maintain focused attention. The other key to successfully implementing the planning phase is self-monitoring. Successful self-regulated students continually monitor whether they understand what they are supposed to be learning. Students who re-read a paragraph of an opinion to make sure they understand the author's point or who brainstorm a hypothetical that either proves the author wrong or confirms the author's assertion are engaging in self-monitoring. Monitoring learning allows the student to modify her chosen learning process, while it is ongoing, if the learning or studying process is not working as well or as quickly as desired.

The reflection phase begins when students evaluate how well and how efficiently they have learned. After evaluating their performance, self-regulated learners develop attributions about the causes of their results. An attribution is an explanation for why the student performed well or poorly. Self-regulated learners are much more likely to attribute failures to correctable causes—such as not working hard enough or selecting ineffective learning techniques—and to attribute successes to personal competence. These attributions lead self-regulated learners to try again and to try harder when they fail. Finally these students brainstorm about how they can adjust and improve their learning processes in the future.

B. Students' Perspectives

Students bring varied perspectives to law school based on their preexisting knowledge, attitudes, cultural backgrounds, and school and work experiences. Students' perspectives change during law school. While most first-year students are deeply engaged in their courses, upper level students may focus their attention on practice experiences outside of the classroom. Students' perceptions of law school are shaped by what they are taught (legal doctrine, theory, skills, and values), how they are taught (lecture, Socratic, discussion, simulation), and the affective domain (teachers' and students' attitudes, feelings, and motivation).

When students with diverse perspectives are asked about what will assist or impede their learning in law school, they offer critical insights. Two major themes that emerge from student comments are discussed below: (1) the learning environment; and (2) teaching methods.

Learning Environment

A positive teacher-student relationship is a critical part of an effective learning environment. After completing a study of students at the UNLV and University of Colorado Law Schools, Professor James Levy concluded that healthy teacher-student relationships are essential to promote student learning. "When it comes to teaching, it is not enough that law professors be experts in their fields, possess skill in Socratic instruction, or know how to use classroom technology to the best effect. Just as important, if not more so, is that professors understand how much their classroom relationship with students influences whether or not students learn." On the other hand, "An ineffective law school instructor is more concerned with scaring and embarrassing students, and less concerned about whether students are actually learning." As one student stated: "Professors who are degrading to individuals or classes of persons are not appreciated." (Levy 98). Another student noted: "I guess the single most important piece of advice I would give to a brand new law professor is to do whatever it takes to create a positive learning environment where people aren't afraid to speak up." (Institute for Law Teaching and Learning).

Many students find the law school environment to be problematic. Studies have shown that, while all graduate students enter graduate school with the same levels of depression, anxiety and substance abuse, law students are the most miserable by the end of their first year. These studies have found that the legal education process itself serves to promote these adverse psychological reactions. However, the studies also have found that acknowledging students' stress, valuing students for their contributions and questions in and outside of class, and empowering them to control their own learning, ameliorates some of the negative effects and helps both their learning and their self-confidence.

When asked about the specific actions teachers had taken to create a positive environment, students offered helpful suggestions.

- "[The teacher] made you feel like your opinions were valuable ... she didn't necessarily have to agree with you, but she wanted you to make the point." (Institute for Law School Teaching and Learning).
- "Create an environment where [the students] will feel comfortable, where they will feel validated and not made to feel small, like they're not worth being in an institution.... I tend to learn better from professors that I respect and create that environment and make me feel that I can contribute to the profession." (Institute for Law Teaching and Learning).
- "[The teacher] took me step by step through the process and not just once or twice but we went over and over it until I understood it. And that wasn't the first time that he had done it. He had been available plenty of times." (Institute for Law School Teaching and Learning).

A teacher's passion and enthusiasm for the subject matter can go a long way in helping students learn and can provide a model for the students. As the saying goes, enthusiasm is contagious. Teachers who make it clear that the subject matter, such as the Rule Against Perpetuities, is not their favorite, create obstacles for their students.

Many students also appreciate teachers' humor and humanity. It is possible to augment the class discourse with humor, but it is more effective if the humor is not directed at students or others. A professor's self-deprecation often serves as a platform for a laugh and invites students to feel more comfortable in the classroom. Knowing that the professor—who has misplaced his/her glasses again—is human makes a difference. As one student put it:

> [W]hen a professor exhibits an air of humaneness toward his or her students it just goes a long way in the student's heart, especially a first-year student, toward feeling like the professor is in the classroom not only to teach the students the law but to welcome them into the legal profession. And the professors that exhibited that air by and large motivated me to work the hardest in their classrooms. (Institute for Law Teaching and Learning).

A final aspect of the learning environment is teachers' expectations. Students yearn for teachers to provide clear expectations and then teach class sessions and give exams that reflect those expectations. As Professor Paul Bergman noted: "Like many entering law students today, I came to law school with the understanding that its purpose was not to teach me rules, but to teach me how to think like a lawyer. This puzzled me because we seemed to spend a lot of class (and exam) time on rules. And I was never sure if or when I was thinking like a lawyer." Or as a student put it: "[If] a teacher can articulate what they expect of the student ... and then follow through with that through the whole course and through the evaluation, they're a better teacher." (Institute for Law Teaching and Learning).

Teaching Methods

Classroom methodology gets students' attention. Students appreciate transparency and organization, such as learning how a class or course is organized. This notion was reflected by a student in the following way:

> I tried a little experiment the other day in one of my favorite classes: I asked my professor her rationale behind the way in which the course topics had been ordered.... She openly and honestly explained why the course was ordered the way it was, acknowledging the order may seem counterintuitive, but explaining why it's really quite logical. She also acknowledged areas that could have been ordered in some other way and told us candidly she made the call because the call needed to be made, but that didn't mean this way was either the correct nor the only way it could have been done. And I thought, "My God, Toto, look! A question ... an answer ... a rationale!!!" (Sigler 2/23/08).

Many professors use a form of the Socratic Method, creating a dialogue by questioning students in class. The Socratic Method itself does not create stress in law students. If done in a belittling or negative manner, however, students take away a negative impression, no matter how well-conceived the questioning process is. Students who are fans of the Socratic Method value having to be prepared because they may be called upon, appreciate the opportunity to practice articulating arguments and responding to questions, and enjoy hearing from a greater range of students. Critics note how intimidating the Socratic Method can be and how it does not engage most of the class.

- "[T]he Socratic Method is a really good individual learning tool, but unfortunately not everyone gets to participate in that dialogue, and I find myself thinking about, well, maybe I should sit and balance my checkbook, I'm not getting anything from this." (Institute for Law Teaching and Learning).
- "[T]here is a place for the Socratic Method. It's a question of whether it's applied with some humanity and whether you allow the student to maintain some dignity." (Institute for Law Teaching and Learning).

Law students have been in school for years. They have a wealth of information about their perspectives on teaching and learning. When asked how we can help them learn, law students emphasize variety, engagement, and collaboration.

Students express great preference for teachers who use a wide variety of teaching methods.

- "[A] mix of lectures, discussions, and group work is effective for me because the class is broken up and not as monotonous. Too much of one method makes my mind wander ..." (Institute for Law Teaching and Learning).
- "The more variation you bring to a class the more interested ... I stay. When it's just strictly lecture I tend to have a habit of drifting in and out." (Institute for Law Teaching and Learning).

- "Give your students as many opportunities to learn in different ways as you can." (Institute for Law Teaching and Learning).

Students also prefer learning activities that actively engage them in the learning process. They prefer to learn by acting like lawyers and not like note-takers.

- "I need to do, in order to learn ... I am usually most interested and motivated by how things work in the 'real world,' and in trying to apply or use theories in a practical way ..." (Institute for Law Teaching and Learning).
- "Absent active participation, I am likely to be precluded from offering vital input on a subject, which creates boredom and disinterest." (Institute for Law Teaching and Learning).

Students recognize the deleterious effects of the law school competitive model and report that they learn a lot by working with each other and appreciate the break from competition that peer collaboration provides.

- "[T]his focus on grades ... drives every student off into their own separate world. And I think it's detrimental to learning ..." (Institute for Law Teaching and Learning).
- "Working in small groups facilitated discussion not possible in larger groups, and let all of us truly express ourselves without fear of being wrong or sounding dumb." (Institute for Law Teaching and Learning).
- "Cooperative exercises and role playing are very useful ..." (Institute for Law Teaching and Learning).

If you ask, your students can offer their own insights about what you can do to improve their learning. As one student said so eloquently: "Listen. Listen. That's all."(Institute for Law School Teaching and Learning).

C. Effective Teaching

Teaching can be characterized as excellent only if that teaching produces significant student learning. Teacher behaviors that facilitate significant student learning fall into three categories: (1) intellectual groundwork; (2) attitudinal approach; and (3) teaching practices.

Intellectual Groundwork

Intellectual groundwork, at which many law teachers excel, includes all the things law teachers do to ready themselves intellectually to feel like authorities in their fields. Intellectual groundwork includes expertise, clarity, and preparation.

An essential foundation of good teaching is subject matter expertise. To teach well, we need to understand, at a deep level, doctrine, theory, policy, practical application, thinking skills, performance skills, ethical issues, and professionalism.

Clarity in law teaching is *not* about "spoon-feeding" or "dumbing-down." Instead, it is about providing structure and effectively communicating complex ideas, skills, and professional values. Several practices help us communicate more clearly in and out of the classroom, including roadmaps, closure, examples, visuals, and manifested openness to student questions.

Teachers and students benefit when they are clear about what should be learned, how that learning will take place, and how students will demonstrate their learning. Effectively designing courses to address these topics includes : assessing students' existing strengths and weaknesses; establishing expectations for student attendance, preparation, participation, and behavior; planning teaching methods, exercises, and assignments, both in and out of class; selecting print and electronic resources that will support the teaching and learning activities; pacing the course rather than letting the clock or the calendar determine speed or content; designing opportunities for give students feedback throughout the course; and, of course, determining how to assess and grade student performance.

A parallel set of issues informs designing individual class sessions. Designing effective class sessions includes: assessing where the students are at this point in the course in terms of their understanding and skills; selecting two, three, or four concepts or skills that students should learn or practice in the class session; deciding what students should do outside of class to prepare; planning what students will do during class; consciously choosing how the session will begin and end; and planning opportunities for learning and to give students feedback about their learning.

Effective teachers are not only prepared and organized; they are flexible, too. Planning need not lead to rigidity. In every course, and many individual class sessions, opportunities present themselves to explore a concept in more depth, weave in professionalism, engage students in practicing lawyering skills and values, and build on students' insights and skills.

Attitudinal Approach

How teachers think about their students has an enormous influence on student learning. Adopting the attitudes described below, including respect, high expectations, support, and passion, can help a teacher succeed in motivating students to work hard and learn complex knowledge, skills, and values.

Mutual respect among students and teachers is fundamental to a healthy teaching and learning environment. Respect should go in three directions: teacher to students, students to teacher, and students to students. Classrooms that feature humiliation, intimidation, or denigration lead many students to withdraw from participation and learning. However, classrooms that leave students feeling valued and admired encourage students to grow.

Here's a brief list of behaviors that foster respect.

- Learn your students' names. Call students by name in and out of the classroom.
- Learn about your students' experiences and goals. Have students introduce themselves by completing a short questionnaire in class or online.
- Value students' time. Law students, like their teachers, lead busy lives. Start and end class on time. Keep appointments with students. Respond to email from students.
- Be inclusive. We motivate students when we make them feel welcome and when we try to tie their learning to their personal and professional interests.
- Model respect. Respect is more about what we do than what we say. It is how we treat students, colleagues, and staff on a daily basis.

Teachers' expectations greatly affect students' learning. High, realistic expectations lead to more student achievement; low expectations result in less student learning.

Five attributes of teacher expectations affect student motivation and learning: clarity; quality; achievability; uniformity; and credibility. Clarity requires us to define our expectations for both ourselves and our students. Quality means we need to emphasize quality rather than quantity. No course can teach all of the skills and knowledge students need to develop; consequently, we should emphasize the critical skills, values, and knowledge and accept we cannot teach everything. Achievability means our expectations should challenge students to stretch themselves and to do their best work while accounting for our students' current level of development and the demands of professional practice. Expectations are uniform if we communicate that we believe every student can attain a high level of achievement. Finally, our expectations are credible if we impose high expectations on ourselves. Perhaps the best way for teachers to inspire students to excellence is through modeling. We should have high expectations for ourselves. We should show, day after day, that we are diligently seeking continuous improvement in our professional practice.

A supportive teaching and learning environment should accompany respect and high expectations. We should demonstrate our commitment to helping each student succeed in law school. A supportive environment is built upon teachers' attitudes, availability, and trust.

One set of common descriptors of exemplary teachers focuses on their attitudes toward students: "helpful," "caring," "concerned," and "encouraging." Another group of attributes of effective teachers is "available," "accessible," and "approachable." Student-faculty contact outside of formal class time is associated with students' motivation, satisfaction, and active involvement in their own education. An operating assumption that reflects our trust and support is that "there is a good faith explanation for students' behavior." When we communicate our faith in students, most will reciprocate with faith in us.

Students regularly identify teachers' passion or enthusiasm as the most important ingredient of effective instruction. Our passion can inspire, energize, and motivate our students. Passion includes both excitement about the subject matter and excitement about student learning. Be direct. Tell students what you love about teaching at your school, about your joy in working with students, and about your fascination with the subject matter. Celebrate success in the classroom. Provide positive reinforcement when students produce insight, solid analysis, or creative thinking. Teachers' nonverbal behaviors associated with enthusiasm include movement (away from the podium and out into the classroom), gestures, facial expressions, and smiling.

Teaching Practices

How you teach matters. Certain teaching practices have consistently been correlated with greater, more in-depth student learning. Those practices are variety, active learning, collaboration, and formative feedback.

We can inject variety into many aspects of our teaching—identifying variety in learning objectives, teaching and learning methods, materials, and assessment instruments. Students express distinct and varied preferences in terms of teaching modalities; consequently, variety can manifest a teacher's respect for students, support, and passion for student learning. More importantly, different types of teaching methods and materials are appropriate to achieve different objectives. Lecture may work well to transmit information, but collaboration produces deeper and more robust learning of problem-solving skills. Finally, variety can keep students' interest and sustain their motivation throughout a course.

Students learn from active and passive methods. Students learn passively when they listen to a presenter who organizes and conveys information. Active learning occurs when students engage in more than listening. Law teachers employ many types of active learning techniques: Socratic dialogues, discussions, writing exercises, simulations, computer exercises, and real-life experiences in externships and clinics. Active learning is particularly effective in achieving four types of core goals of legal education: thinking skills, understanding concepts, lawyering skills, and professional values.

Two types of collaboration enhance teaching and learning in law school. The first is cooperative learning, where students work in pairs or small groups in or outside of class. Research shows that cooperative learning fosters: (1) more student learning and better academic performance, especially when the task is complex and conceptual; (2) development of problem solving, reasoning, and critical thinking skills; (3) positive student attitudes toward the subject matter and course; (4) closer relationships among students and between students and teachers; and (5) students' willingness to consider and their appreciation for diverse perspectives.

The second form of collaboration is teacher and student teamwork in making course design decisions, including decisions about course coverage, teaching methods, and, even assessment methods. Giving students a voice in course design is supported by the literature on learner-centered teaching, adult education theory, and, in particular, empirical research on motivation and performance in college and law school. Student involvement can increase students' intrinsic motivation and positive attitudes.

Feedback is a critical element of teaching and learning. Formative feedback, i.e., feedback designed to improve learning, is an essential part of the learning loop. Students engage in learning activities, demonstrate their learning in writing, orally, or behaviorally, and then get feedback on how to improve their performance and, perhaps even more importantly, their approaches to learning. Effective formative feedback has four characteristics: specific; corrective; positive; and timely. Teachers should articulate *specific* criteria for student performance and give students feedback based on those criteria. *Corrective* feedback identifies weaknesses in student work and provides strategies for improvement. *Positive* feedback identifies the strengths upon which students can build. *Timely* feedback comes relatively soon after student performance and gives students an opportunity to improve before their performance is evaluated for the purpose of assigning grades.

Formative feedback is essential for teachers' continued development as well. To make appropriate adjustments during a course, we need to get feedback from students about their learning. Classroom Assessment Techniques, simple five-minute exercises in which we ask students to anonymously summarize what they have learned, identify areas of confusion, or evaluate teaching methods and exercises, can give us that feedback. Further, for continuous improvement of our teaching practice, we can engage in self-reflection and gather input from students, consultants, and colleagues.

References

- Susan B. Apel et al., *Seven Principles for Good Practice in Legal Education*, 49 J. Legal Educ. 367 (1999) (eight articles applying the seven principles to legal education).
- Ken Bain, What the Best College Teachers Do (2004).
- Paul Bateman, *Toward Diversity in Teaching Methods in Law Schools: Five Suggestions from the Back Row*, 17 Quinnipiac L. Rev. 397 (1993).
- Paul Bergman, *Thinking Like a Lawyer*, Elon Univ. Sch. of Law, Ctr. for Engaged Learning in the Law Blog, (May 21, 2008, 3:20 PM), http://blogs.elon.edu/cell-blog.

- Lila A. Coleburn & Julia C. Spring, *Socrates Unbound: Developmental Perspectives on the Law School Experience*, 24 Law & Psychol. Rev. 5 (2000).
- Steven Friedland & Gerald F. Hess, Teaching the Law School Curriculum (2004).
- Steven Friedland, *How We Teach: A Survey of Teaching Techniques in American Law Schools*, 20 Seattle U. L. Rev. 1 (1996).
- Barbara Glesner-Fines, *Fear and Loathing in the Law Schools*, 23 Conn. L. Rev. 627 (1991).
- Barbara Glesner-Fines, *The Impact of Expectations on Teaching and Learning*, 38 Gonz. L. Rev. 89 (2003).
- Mitu Gulati, Richard Sander & Robert Sockloskie, *The Happy Charade: An Empirical Examination of the Third Year of Law School*, 51 J. Legal Educ. 235 (2001).
- Bethany Rubin Henderson, *Asking the Lost Question: What is the Purpose of Law School?*, 53 J. Legal Educ. 48 (2003).
- Gerald F. Hess, *Heads and Hearts: The Teaching and Learning Environment in Law School*, 52 J. Legal Educ. 75 (2002).
- Gerald F. Hess & Steven I. Friedland, Techniques for Teaching Law (1999).
- Ann Iijima, *Lessons Learned: Legal Education and Law Student Dysfunction*, 48 J. Legal Educ. 524 (1998).
- Interviews by Paula Lustbader, Laurie Zimet and Gerald Hess with 67 students from seven law schools. (comments taken from 16 hours of video recorded interviews).
- Lawrence Krieger, *Institutional Denial About the Dark Side of Law School, and Fresh Empirical Guidance for Constructively Breaking the Silence*, 52 J. Legal Educ. 112 (2002).
- *Law School Survey of Student Engagement*, http://lssse.iub.edu/ (data gathered from 140,000 law students in the US and Canada from 2004–2009).
- James Levy, *As a Last Resort, Ask the Students: What They Say Makes Someone an Effective Law Teacher*, 58 Me. L. Rev. 49 (2006).
- Deborah Maranville, *Infusing Passion and Context into the Traditional Law Curriculum Through Experiential Learning*, 51 J. Legal Educ. 51 (2001).
- Douglas D. McFarland, *Students and Practicing Lawyers Identify the Ideal Law Professor*, 36 J. Legal Educ. 93 (1986) (based on a survey of a small group of volunteer law students).
- Ruth Ann McKinney, *Depression and Anxiety in Law Students: Are We Part of the Problem and Can We Be Part of the Solution?*, 8 J. Leg. Writing Inst. 229 (2002).
- Suzanne Segerstrom, *Perceptions of Stress and Control in the First Semester of Law School*, 32 Willamette L. Rev. 593 (1996).
- Michael Hunter Schwartz, Expert Learning for Law Students (2d ed. 2008).
- Michael Hunter Schwartz, Sophie Sparrow & Gerald F. Hess, Teaching Law By Design: Engaging Students From the Syllabus to the Final Exam (2009).
- Kerri Sigler, *Legal Ed: A View From the Cheap Seats*, Elon Univ. Sch. of Law, Ctr. for Engaged Learning in the Law Blog, (Feb. 17, 2008, 2:44 PM), http://blogs.elon.edu/cellblog.
- Kerri Sigler, *Beneath the Stamp of Preeminence: A Student's Take on the Big Blue Books*, Elon Univ. Sch. of Law, Ctr. for Engaged Learning in the Law Blog, (Feb. 25, 2008, 2:55 PM), http://blogs.elon.edu/cellblog.

- Kerri Sigler, *The Great & Mighty Oz: (or: The Rationale Behind Your Course*, ELON UNIV. SCH. OF LAW, CTR. FOR ENGAGED LEARNING IN THE LAW BLOG, (Feb. 23, 2008, 2:52 PM), http://blogs.elon.edu/cellblog.
- Alan A. Stone, *Legal Education on the Couch*, 85 HARV. L. REV. 392, 406–07 (1971).
- David J. Walsh & Mary Jo Maffei, *Never in a Class by Themselves: An Examination of Behaviors Affecting the Student-Professor Relationship*, 5 J. EXCELLENCE C. TEACHING 23 (1994).

Chapter 2

Materials

Materials include both print and electronic resources that students will use outside of class or that students and teachers will use during class. Examples of materials include readings, websites, pictures, videos, computer exercises, handouts, PowerPoint slides, objects, and items written on the board or a flip chart.

Materials serve four basic functions:

1. Achieve objectives. Just as objectives drive the choice of instructional activities and feedback, they also inform the selection of materials. The primary function of materials is to facilitate student learning of the content, skills, and values that are the focus of the course. In some instances, in fact, materials can produce learning that occurs entirely outside the classroom, freeing up classroom time for those learning activities for which a live teacher is essential.
2. Guide student preparation. In many instances, teachers create or assign materials to help students prepare to participate in a meaningful way during a class session.
3. Support learning activities. Materials can and often are used to support the learning activities that take place during class sessions. For example, handouts on which students write ideas or take notes assist students in retaining focused attention and provide information, hints and cues to guide their classroom work.
4. Facilitate feedback. Except for feedback that happens spontaneously during class, feedback depends on material, quizzes and rubrics, for example.

The four functions of materials provide guidance on the process law professors can use in choosing materials. The key to making optimal choices regarding materials is identifying and understanding the relationship between a proposed set of materials, the learning objectives the professor seeks to accomplish, the learning activities by which the professor hopes to achieve the objectives, and the feedback mechanism the professor chooses to assess his and his students' success. Different class objectives, instructional activities, and feedback mechanisms call for different types of materials.

In addition, as is true with respect to all aspects of teaching, the key to sustained success is being systematic and reflective. Choices are systematic when they are conscious predictions about likely learning effects that are grounded in research on teaching and learning or learning theory, in our understanding of our students' needs, and in our expertise in our subjects. Choices are reflective when, each time we use materials, we consciously evaluate their efficacy in achieving our goals in selecting them.

Several additional considerations apply, regardless of the type of material. Effective materials are selective, variable, focused, and interactive.

Selective

For virtually any topic or skill we teach, we could find thousands of pages of text (e.g., cases, statutes, articles) along with websites, pictures, and videos. Consequently, for every class session, we are choosing a tiny slice of the available material. What considerations should guide those choices? First, we should select the material that is most relevant to our class objectives. In an ideal casebook, most of the cases, statutes and materials focus on the core objectives we hope students will learn; even the best casebooks, however, sometimes include materials that, while interesting and useful, are not optimal uses of our students' time and effort. Second, we should limit the material we assign to students to a reasonable amount. We believe that the traditional guideline of two hours of student preparation for each hour of class is reasonable. If we expect students to read, brief cases, and generate responses to problems, a sixty-page assignment is not reasonable for a one-hour class. Instead, we can require the most relevant twenty pages and alert students to supplemental material that they can explore if they want to broaden or deepen their understanding. Another possibility is to convert the unassigned cases to problems. In that way, we can refer interested students to the unassigned cases.

Selectivity applies to our use of materials during class as well. Research shows that students will copy verbatim anything we write on the board or project on a screen. The words or diagrams we write and project go directly into our students' notes. So we should be thoughtful about those words and images. Less is more. A few key phrases or a clear, simple flow chart will aid student learning more than a board covered with our writing or slides jammed with text.

Variable

Variety in materials is a virtue for several reasons. In modern life, we get information from both print and electronic sources. Our class materials should reflect that reality. We miss opportunities to enhance our teaching and our students' learning if we march through the casebook without incorporating relevant stories, documents, and images. Further, variety makes our classes more interesting. Each time we shift material in the classroom, we grab attention. When we distribute a handout, project a picture, show an object, or run a short video, most students are or become alert and therefore stay on task. However, most students' attention will wane if we proceed through a dozen slides or show a forty-minute video. In addition, different students will respond more favorably to different types of materials. Some students hone in while reading and briefing cases. For other students, a picture really is worth a thousand words. Some students learn deeply through a CALI lesson, while others need to work with real documents, such as contracts, wills, and pleadings.

Focused

One way to facilitate student preparation for class is to provide questions about the material before class. These questions allow students to focus their preparation, just as a lawyer prepares for the issues that will be central to a motion hearing. We will ask many other questions in class as well, just as judges ask lawyers questions in court. We can provide the advance questions to students in writing via a supplement, webpage, email, or a handout.

We can use focus devices in both handouts and in material we prepare for use in class. For example, we can focus students' attention in handouts and on slides through text boxes, font changes (e.g., bold, italics, underlining), symbols, and color. Bullets, indentation and numbering allow us to break material into chunks that facilitate student remembering. Blanks or open boxes in charts can provide context, promote curiosity, and, later, stimulate memory. Most of these focus devices apply to material we write on the board during class as well.

Interactive

Much of the material we assign to students is designed for students to read, such as cases, statutes, and articles. Likewise, materials we use in class are often intended for students to read or view, including slides, handouts, pictures, and diagrams. This type of material is valuable for presenting doctrine, policy, analytical frameworks, and theory to students. To maximize the effectiveness of material in achieving class objectives, we should look for ways to make materials interactive as well.

Simple techniques can add interactive features to many types of materials.

- Readings. The most passive use of readings is to simply assign pages. We can encourage more active reading by giving students focus questions (discussed above) or by asking students to do something with the reading, such as brief a case, apply a statute to a problem, or synthesize the law and policy from the material assigned for the previous several classes.
- Videos. Short video clips relevant to the class objectives can be powerful teaching and learning tools. Videos are readily available on websites such as www.youtube.com. Books such as *Reel Justice* describe portions of movies that illustrate doctrine, skills, and values. We can make the clips even more effective by providing students with questions or problems to focus their attention.
- Slides. Presentation software, such as PowerPoint, allows us to produce slides that transmit information and images to students. These visual aids are helpful to many students. On the other hand, if we use slides extensively and the slides do no more than present information, many students will become passive receivers. We can change this dynamic by including interactive slides, that is, slides with questions, problems, quizzes, and hypotheticals designed to facilitate active student engagement in the classroom.
- Whiteboards, flip charts, and projectors. These basic tools excel at supporting discussions. We can easily capture student contributions to class discussions on the whiteboard, a chart, or a document projector.
- Word processing software. We can accomplish the interactive aspects of presentation software and whiteboards by projecting a document on a screen in word processing software. The document can include questions, problems, quizzes, and hypotheticals. We can capture student contributions during class discussion and send the document to students after class if we desire.
- Diagrams, flow charts, and tables. These tools, which education experts refer to as graphic organizers, can be excellent devices to organize concepts and illustrate the interrelationships among ideas. Better yet, we can provide students with partially completed or blank diagrams and tables, and have them complete them before or during class.
- Handouts. We can accomplish many of the functions of materials with handouts, distributed in either paper or electronic form. Handouts can include readings, pictures, questions, problems, hypotheticals, quizzes, rubrics, flow charts, and

diagrams. The interactivity of a handout we design for use during class depends in part on how we incorporate white space. Studies have compared the learning results of (1) students given the professor's notes; (2) students given a bare-bones outline into which they can take notes; and (3) students given nothing. The students in group (2) learned more than the students in groups (1) and (3), and the students in group (1) and (3) learned at about the same level. The mental effort students have to use to listen for what to write in the blank space combined with the hierarchical structure that provides a schema for understanding the material explain why the students given the bare-bones outline learned more.

Any choice of materials involves uncertainty. Choosing materials to facilitate learning is not unlike any other problem-solving activity; a professor can make smart, justifiable choices regarding materials, and the materials can still prove unsuccessful. In some instances, materials that have been wildly successful for years may, without warning, lose some of their efficacy. Consequently, it is crucial that you evaluate your materials each time you use them, reflecting on their effectiveness in achieving the objectives for which you selected them.

References

- Walter O. Dick, Lou Carey & James O. Carey, The Systematic Design of Instruction (6th ed. 2005).
- Steven Friedland & Gerald F. Hess, Teaching the Law School Curriculum (2004).
- Gerald F. Hess & Steven I. Friedland, Techniques for Teaching Law (1999).
- Michael Hunter Schwartz, Sophie Sparrow& Gerald F. Hess, Teaching Law By Design: Engaging Students From the Syllabus to the Final Exam (2009).
- Patricia L. Smith & Tillman J. Ragan, Instructional Design (3d ed. 2005).
- Roy Stuckey et al., Best Practices for Legal Education: A Vision and a Road Map (2007).

Juggling Failure & Success

Athletes often talk about the mental side of their jobs. But professors rarely discuss the physical aspects of theirs. Should we strive to make our lessons sound in body as well as in mind?

I usually keep my actions in the classroom simple. I speak; I listen; I write. Sometimes I wrestle with a remote control to show a video clip. I avoid things I can't do. I don't have a stentorian voice that could "fill the room," as Professor Kingsfield (*The Paper Chase*) demanded of his students, so I don't try. I don't emulate my high school teacher who once tore a Manhattan phone book in two to make a point. (Why should I? I don't even remember the point.) And although I occasionally quote lyrics from popular music, I always turn down requests to sing.

Still, I sometimes ask a little more of my body. I once thought I had reached the pinnacle of physical professing by throwing balls to students. To help teach analysis and synthesis, I have often done an exercise that uses balls to represent cases. The premise is that the Glashausser Supreme Court has held public schools liable to children for injuries caused by throwing footballs in gym class because footballs are dangerous. As undangerously as possible, I toss other balls—a tennis ball, a golf ball, a Nerf football—to students acting as judges in various courts and ask them to examine the facts in light of our burgeoning body of law and decide each new case.

The exercise stimulates the class and simulates the common law. It teaches that principles are elastic, that the legal relevance of a particular fact (such as a ball's shape, weight, or material) is usually debatable, and that *stare decisis* notwithstanding, results can therefore be unpredictable. It also teaches that laptops are not built to withstand foul balls; accidents can make classes sound neither in mind nor in body, but rather in tort.

This past semester, I decided to build on the ball exercise by trying a new physical feat—juggling. Throwing I can do; my neighborhood Whiffle ball team (don't ask) was a juggernaut. But my innate ability as a juggler? Naught.

In an article published in *The Law Teacher*, a fellow law teacher once urged us all to try learning something for which we have no talent. With a book as my guide, I practiced and became reasonably competent at handling three balls evenly. I tried uneven juggling, which involves throwing one ball higher than the others, and learned how to do it, if not fluidly. So far, so mediocre. Once I added a fourth ball, no amount of repetition helped. Occasionally I could delay the inevitable fall for a few seconds, but I did not come close to mastering the skill. The book made juggling look easy, but for me, it was not.

Even if I was not ready for the circus, though, I thought I might be able to handle the classroom. To introduce students to the art of advocacy, I took out three balls and named two of them after precedents; the third represented our facts. I juggled the three balls evenly, pointing out that in objectively analyzing our case we would compare it to others and examine relevant similarities or differences from various angles.

Having concluded that one of the two precedents helped our case and one hurt it, I then switched into argument mode. I explained that I would highlight the "good" case and minimize, but not ignore, the "bad" one. To illustrate, I started juggling unevenly: I launched our case and the helpful precedent high in the air for all to admire, while I shifted the third ball quickly from one hand to the other to soften its impact. I told the students that although I felt reasonably comfortable with balanced juggling, as they did with objective analysis, uneven juggling was trickier—as was advocacy.

Not having dropped any balls, I could have quit while I was ahead. I had not planned to go for the jugular. But someone asked the juggler to go further: "Can you do four?" I didn't stop to do what law professors do—think—about the risk of failure. If I had, I would have realized that the idea sounded, well, insane. Instead, emboldened by the enthusiastic crowd, I found myself mindlessly grabbing another ball.

I told the class how adding another case to the mix could make my argument more thorough and persuasive. The more cases one tries to juggle, the harder the task, but the more impressive if one pulls it off. I tried, and it worked—for about five heartbeats. Then I fumbled all four balls, before I had the chance to throw some higher than others, and the demonstration was over.

As for juggling, I had failed. But the reaction of the class told me I had succeeded at teaching. First and foremost, the students understood the point of the exercise and saw the distinctions between objective analysis and advocacy. The second piece of feedback was more fortuitous: they told me how much they had appreciated my willingness to take a risk and challenge myself by reaching for something a bit beyond my grasp.

I responded by telling them that dropping the ball is not all bad. By trying, stretching, and falling short, we pave the road for improvement, whether as professors or as practitioners. As new lawyers, I continued, they might feel intellectually overwhelmed and physically overtired by their caseloads. Of course, they would not take on work they were not capable of handling competently. But even within the realm of ethical behavior, I stressed, they would face great challenges. My advice—which I hope sounded only *intelligent*—was to take a deep breath, merge the body with the mind, and start juggling.

Alex Glashausser
Washburn University School of Law

Rules for Monica (and for Lina)

In teaching both Contracts and Legal Method and Writing, I have noticed that two features of the law school experience can impede learning: the law itself and the near panic that sweeps through the first-year class as their first set of final examinations approaches. It may seem odd to identify the law itself as an obstacle, but we profess to use the cases and statutes in our first-year courses primarily as vehicles for teaching techniques of legal method and analysis rather than as a comprehensive source of a body of law that students must master. Whether we really practice what we preach on that score is debatable in light of our common preoccupation with "coverage" in nonskills courses. Nonetheless, an occasional diversion to nonlegal cases can be justified if they teach something about the law and legal method through metaphor or analogy.

Moreover, if the nonlegal context is familiar and universal, the students can quickly bring their personal experiences to bear on the problem and can focus all their attention on the lessons of legal method, without being distracted or confused by the introduction of complex and unfamiliar legal rules. Once they gain confidence in addressing ambiguities in the holdings of cases in a nonlegal context and understand what it means to synthesize those holdings, first-semester students can apply their newly formed conceptual frameworks to more complicated and unfamiliar cases dealing with elusive legal concepts such as consideration and causation.

This relatively nurturing approach is especially welcome about a month before the first set of finals, when students are furiously outlining course material in preparation for examinations, or desperately trying to comprehend what it means to outline course material. At that time, they very much appreciate a workshop that ties together key concepts of legal method and shows how the concepts relate to future success on examinations. And their anxiety is greatly reduced if we can use a familiar, nonthreatening, nonlegal setting to demonstrate the relationships between case analysis, case synthesis, outlining, and exam taking.

One such demonstration is described in my article, *Using Classroom Demonstrations in Familiar Nonlegal Contexts to Introduce New Students to Unfamiliar Concepts of Legal Method and Analysis*, 7 Leg. Writing 37 (2001). That article describes in detail a workshop, 60 to 90 minutes in length, in which a classroom instructor can lead students through an overview of case analysis and synthesis, outlining, and essay exam taking. Through a grant from the Institute for Law School Teaching, I also produced an accompanying video, in which a mother and a daughter act out the "cases" that form the basis for parental rule making regarding the daughter's evening social activities.

The video, *Rules for Monica*, presents four scenes, or cases, in which (1) the daughter, Monica, either arrives home after an evening social outing or requests permission to participate in a social outing; and (2) her mother, Carmen, reacts to the daughter's actions or requests. In the first scene, Carmen reacts negatively to Monica's return from a football game and pizza. From Carmen's statements, it is fairly plain that Carmen is concerned as a general policy matter about Monica's sleep and her studies and that Carmen believes that Monica has violated some curfew rule. But what precisely is the holding, and what rule governs Monica's future actions? Did Monica misbehave by going out for pizza after the game or because she "hung out" at the pizza parlor after finishing her pizza, or did she displease her mother simply by returning after some previously unannounced, bright-line curfew, such as 11 p.m.? Carmen's statements are ambiguous, allowing some debate about the precise meaning of her ruling.

By intermittently viewing the video and pausing it for discussion, students quickly learn that new cases, presenting Carmen's reactions on slightly different facts, help to clarify the ruling in the first case and add new dimensions to Carmen's initial rulings. By the time students have analyzed and synthesized all four cases, they end up with a policy rationale that is implemented with a two-part rule, qualified by an exception. Some students also read between the lines and infer that Carmen's rules are really driven by her concern for Monica's safety in unsupervised settings and not by her expressed concern for Monica's ability to get enough sleep and finish her homework.

What should students do with these policies, rules, and illustrative cases? The video encourages them to outline the material, organizing the outline around the rules, and then to illustrate each rule with a brief summary of one or more cases. Even if students have only enough time to begin such an outline, an instructor's example on an overhead projector can drive the lesson home.

Finally, the video invites the instructor to distribute an essay examination that presents new facts raising now familiar issues about Monica's social outings. Armed with the rules in the sample outline and with the analytic reasoning and policy considerations presented in the previous cases, students can present reasonable arguments both for and against the proposition that Monica violated Carmen's rules in the cases presented in the examination. Following the brief examination period of 10 minutes or so in which students can at least analyze the problem and outline their answers, the instructor can lead the class in discussion about the question.

After this workshop, most students seem to feel a bit less anxious about examinations and better prepared to study for them. Students may also understand more concretely that the examinations will not ask them to simply recall particular legal rules or facts that they have studied, but will invite them to apply analytic skills to recognize issues and arguments and to apply past lessons to novel facts, sometimes requiring attention to underlying policies when interpreting and applying specific rules.

An updated version of this exercise, *Rules for Lina*, is described in my book, LAW SCHOOL EXAMS : PREPARING AND WRITING TO WIN 49-52, 121, 153-54 (Aspen 2007). In *Lina*, the first two cases establish that Lina can come home at late as 11 p.m. if she informs her mother of her activities, by cell phone if necessary. The third case, however, establishes a firm curfew of midnight, regardless of notice of activities, and the fourth case adds an exception to the midnight curfew for important family activities. *Rules for Lina* is a bit easier to use, because it provides a clearer distinction between the policies motivating the mother's rulemaking and the rules themselves.

If you would like a copy of the video or a written guide to either of the exercises, email me at charles.calleros@asu.edu.

Charles Calleros
Arizona State University, Sandra Day O'Connor College of Law

Drawing on Nonlegal Experiences to Bring Home the Law

This past summer, I was a new teacher in a new city at a new law school preparing a new course in Fundamentals of Health Care Law. Like all new faculty at my university, I dutifully attended faculty orientation at the start of the school year, a little bit peeved that it would take a full day away from my preparation time for my courses. Little did I know that from what I saw as a necessary but inconvenient distraction would come one of the most effective teaching tools I employed during the year.

As part of the orientation, we received information about our benefits, including health insurance options. Like many employers, the university offered several different health plans to its faculty, ranging from extremely comprehensive, but with restricted choice of providers, to less comprehensive, but with more choice of providers. The benefits office representative did a masterful job of explaining the benefits to us in half an hour. As a lawyer who spent many years representing health care providers in payment disputes with various insurers, I knew that, with regard to health insurance, "the devil is in the details." When disputes about coverage or payment for a particular treatment or illness arise, it is the fine print of the insurance contract that most often determines the outcome. Therefore, I planned to take the health plan information home and study it assiduously for a day or two.

However, most of my fellow new faculty members made their selections right then and there, without reading the fine print, or even most of the large print, in the information in front of them. I realized that, if these consumers of health care, who are among the most well-educated people in the country, made these decisions off-the-cuff, then virtually all American consumers of health care, including the students taking my Fundamentals of Health Law class, make these decisions in the same manner. I determined that my students would not only read the cases in the casebook about the consequences of not reading the fine print, but would be faced with making the choices that far less well-informed people must make on a daily basis. In some cases, these choices can make the difference between life and death, or between life with comfort and life with extreme poverty.

My students and I plunged into the statutory and regulatory maze that applies to health care financing, delivery, and access. The students read about people seeking experimental treatments for life-threatening conditions, the insurers' refusals to pay for such treatments, and the resulting inability of these insureds to receive the treatments. The students read about insurers' concerns about the lack of proof that such treatments are effective and of the insurers' inability to fund basic health care for most people if they funded unproven treatments for the few. They read about the tensions between consumers, health care providers, and insurers that underlie the American health care delivery system. But to bring these issues home for them, I drew from my experience and observations during my new faculty orientation.

I requested that the university benefits office send me the health insurance brochures that were presented to new faculty at orientation. When I told them the purpose of the request, they were thrilled to be involved in the teaching process. I created six characters for the class to play, all of them in different family and health-status situations. The characters I created included a single young man with no health problems and a small income, who liked to engage in high-risk activities (rock climbing, snowboarding, etc.); a single mother of three who had recently moved into town, with a moderate income, one child with chronic diabetes, a doctor in another town that she really liked, and no prior health insurance; and a 55-year-old married woman with an upper-middle-class income, two children in college, and a 50-year-old husband who suffered from severe depression and was not working.

The class was divided into groups, and each group became one of the characters. During the next class session, each group received the health plan information I received from the benefits office. I gave the students the short talk that the university had given the new faculty about the health plan choices. The students had 30 minutes to review the information and decide which plan their character would choose. Each group then had to present their choice to the class as a whole and explain why they had made the choice. This activity led to an interesting class discussion regarding the financial, personal, and health care consequences of these decisions and the possible legal consequences of making these choices should a coverage dispute arise, a new illness appear, or an existing illness worsen.

When I asked for feedback on the exercise, the students were uniformly enthusiastic. Many of the younger students had never had to choose a health plan and were quite surprised at trade-offs they were forced to consider and the difficulty they had in choosing a plan. Even students who had chosen health insurance for themselves and their families in the past found that their concerns were quite different now that they had studied some of the legal consequences of making these choices. The students believed that this experience would help them be more understanding practitioners, more sympathetic to their clients who faced such dilemmas, and, not least of all, better consumers of health care themselves.

I plan to repeat the exercise next year. The university benefits specialist has graciously and enthusiastically accepted my invitation to do the "benefits talk" to my class in conjunction with this exercise. The exercise illustrates the value of remembering that lawyers operate not just among other lawyers, but in the wider world as employees, consumers, and family members. The experiences we have outside of the context of the practice or study of law can be valuable sources of teaching material for law students who also operate in that wider world. We need to draw on those experiences and resources that are available outside of the context of the law school to bring the law home to our students—not just to make them better lawyers but to make them understanding practitioners, family members, and community leaders.

Vickie Williams
Gonzaga University School of Law

Law as a Crossword Puzzle

I love crossword puzzles. I enjoy working out the solutions, piece by piece. I can even see an analogy to the law in crossword puzzles. The law develops piece by piece, case by case, statute by statute, regulation by regulation, until it is one interrelated whole.

So, on the second day of my Wills and Trusts course, I assign a crossword puzzle. My goal is nothing as lofty as leading students to the realization that law in its entirety can be viewed, and learned, like a crossword puzzle. Rather, my goal is much more mundane. The assigned material is vocabulary and history, what law professors typically assign as background reading. I do not like to assign material that I do not cover in class. It sends a signal to the students that this material is not important. But in this case it is. The vocabulary of the law helps us communicate and informs us of important underlying concepts. In Wills and Trusts, the language also tells the history. Moreover, I believe that active learning is more efficient. If students "do," they remember. The exercise fosters co-operation and confidence, requiring all students to participate, and it therefore also helps establish my expectations for the rest of the semester.

The exercise is relatively simple, although it takes some preparation on my part. I create a grid (using the table feature in WordPerfect) and fill it in with as many of the words from the reading as possible. Crossword puzzle fans realize that this is not as easy as it first appears, because many of the words are long, and creating a pattern where they intersect without colliding is difficult. I am never able to get all the legal words that I want into the puzzle, but I do manage to insert a reasonable number of them. I then finish off the puzzle with "normal" words that will assist the students in solving the puzzle. I then test my creation on family members, friends, or staff to catch the inevitable errors. Although it creates additional work, I construct a new puzzle each year so that my students cannot acquire the answers from prior classes.

On the syllabus, I simply assign the text pages and tell the students to bring a pencil to class. The first year or two, this created a sense of unease among the students. I allow students to work alone or in groups of two or three, but all books and notes must be closed. These rules require all students to participate in the exercise and force students to rely on their colleagues for answers. I allow students approximately 35 to 40 minutes to complete the grid, circulating through the room to determine when a reasonable

ACROSS

1. **system of descent and distribution**
7. **evidence of ownership**
10. negative word
11. trees are made of this
12. conceal
14. **where decedent lived**
18. opposite of WNW
19. **leave personal property by will**
21. gun an engine
22. before (poetically)
23. notice in a newspaper (short form)
25. forbid
27. **arrangement where individual or corporation holds property for the benefit of others**
29. **last will and __________**
32. lavatory (British slang)
33. place in Congress
34. **document disposing of property at death**
36. **person acquiring real property in intestacy**
38. narrated
41. **see 26 down**
42. **support paid to widow at common law**
43. **passes to survivor (3 words)**
47. member of a western Native American tribe
48. often person in 36 across
49. **see 26 down**
51. small
52. **system where eldest son inherited the land**

DOWN

1. **acquire property through intestacy**
2. din
3. female sheep
4. therefore
5. in the direction of
6. notice in a newspaper (short form)
7. tease
8. prefix meaning three
9. **person appointed to carry out terms of a will**
13. **to give real property by will**
14. owed
15. A___ the fields we go
16. ____ West
17. burn slightly
20. the LSAT is one
24. many lectures are this
25. piece of sports equipment
26. **with 41 and 49 across person acquiring personal property in intestacy**
27. prefix meaning three
28. therefore
30. **this happens to property when the decedent leaves no heirs or next of kin**
31. urban mode of transportation
35. in this direction
37. group of bones
38. also
39. guided
40. _____ Scott
41. young fox
42. lair
43. type of woman's shoe
44. the abominable snowman
45. crave
46. garden implement
50. **paid to attorney**
51. us

I N T E S T A C Y T I T L E
N O W O O D W R X
H I D E D O M I C I L E
E S E B E Q U E A T H C
R E V X E R E A D U
I I B A N T R U S T
T E S T A M E N T R L O O
S E A T X W I L L R
C X T D
H E I R T O L D K I N
E I D O W E R I
P A Y A B L E O N D E A T H
U T E S O N D O F
M T N W E E
P R I M O G E N I T U R E E

number have completed the essential words. Then I "debrief" by going through the class, student by student, asking for the answers. At the end, everyone will have completed his or her puzzle and learned the terms.

Students enjoy this exercise because it is novel. The students who do not enjoy crossword puzzles are few and far between. Because it is not graded, or even collected, students are willing to take risks. This exercise works well at the beginning of the semester and it might work in a review session.

The lesson I learned from this exercise is to be adventurous and try something different. By the third year, students are tired of the same old case analysis and Socratic Method. They will learn more if the material is presented in different ways. The other lesson I have learned is that students react positively to this exercise because *I* enjoy it. They are willing to take the risk of something new because of my enthusiasm. So when you try something different, make sure it is something that *you* like.

Stephanie J. Willbanks
Vermont Law School

How Buffalo Creek Can Keep Your Legal Writing Class from Being a Disaster

Nothing can replace real-life experiences. Yet as a legal writing professor it is difficult to make a writing assignment realistic and still accomplish all my pedagogical goals. I found using the book *The Buffalo Creek Disaster,* by Gerald Stern, helped me replicate real life without sacrificing any of my course objectives. In fact, using the book actually had unexpected benefits for the students and myself.

The Buffalo Creek Disaster is attorney Gerald Stern's easy-to-read narrative detailing his representation of the survivors of a horrible coal mining accident in West Virginia in the 1970s. The plaintiffs sued a major coal company after one of the company's slurry dams broke, destroyed entire towns, and killed more than 120 people.

How I Used the Book

I used *The Buffalo Creek Disaster* as the basis for my graded assignments during the fall of 2000 and for the first persuasive writing assignment in the spring of 2001. During the first week of class I asked the students to read the book. It is straightforward and written for a broader audience than law students, so it is both easy to understand and a nice variation from the traditional casebook reading. I then showed the class an Appalshop documentary of the disaster. This video gave vivid detail to the images in the book. The students also were able to see and hear their "clients."

Closed Memo

Piercing the corporate veil was the topic for the closed memo. In the real case, the plaintiffs' attorney wanted to show there were enough ties between the Buffalo Creek Mining Company and its parent company, Pittston Inc., to sue Pittston directly. Because I gave the assignment fairly early in the fall semester, I provided the applicable case law that resolved the issue. Students needed to analyze several factors as part of a balancing test, making it a perfect exercise for first-year students. Students used the book to find the facts that were relevant to this issue. I liked this approach better than the typical pre-packaged memo from a hypothetical senior partner who has done all the fact investigation for the case because facts are never presented to a practicing lawyer in such neat packages.

Open Memo

The open memo addressed whether bystander plaintiffs with no physical injuries could recover damages for their psychological trauma under the tort of intentional infliction of emotional distress (IIED). The students went outside West Virginia to find authority that would support this claim because there was no case directly on point. I drafted several deposition transcripts, reports of federal agencies, and affidavits from which the students could find the necessary facts.

Persuasive Writing Assignment

To introduce the students to persuasive writing, I developed a problem based on the open memo. Instead of representing the plaintiffs, the students had to switch sides and represent the company. Using the research from the objective predictive open memo, the students drafted Pittston's argument challenging one of the elements of the IIED claim. This change of clients greatly challenged many students because they had become emotionally attached to the plaintiffs.

Gerald Stern's Visit

A grant enabled me to invite Gerald Stern to meet with my class. Prior to his visit, he agreed to read four or five of the best papers. He critiqued these papers and told the class how he would have responded to these arguments as the plaintiffs' attorney. He also met with the entire student body and faculty to discuss his career as a public interest attorney.

Why Use a Piece of Literature?

Unfortunately, legal writing classes are often perceived as dry and not as stimulating as the doctrinal classes. Students find learning about criminal law much more exciting than dissecting a paragraph. Although they realize research and writing skills are essential to the practice of law, it is difficult to develop writing problems that seem realistic. Problems can be designed that highlight particular legal issues, but usually they lack the necessary context to be anywhere close to real life. Legal writing professors have the constant challenge of narrowing the gap between the study of law and the practice of law. Using *The Buffalo Creek Disaster* or a similar work is an excellent way to address this challenge.

In addition, law schools aspire to training students to think like lawyers. However, this process often makes students detached and overly analytical. The academy excels at teaching students the rules of law. Yet it has been criticized in recent years for failing in its obligation to teach professionalism, ethics, and compassion. These concepts are mostly ignored in most courses, including Legal Writing. The only discussions of the human side of lawyering and the life of a lawyer occur, if at all, in students' Professional Responsibility classes. Most law schools are now encouraging all professors to incorporate these concepts in their courses. By using *The Buffalo Creek Disaster*, I was able to achieve those goals in addition to teaching the students all the necessary writing and analytical skills.

The following course objectives and goals were met by using *The Buffalo Creek Disaster*:

- It addressed the gap between the profession and the academy by integrating legal doctrine with a practical, realistic situation.
- It broadened the law students' reference base to include situations that they had yet to experience.
- It gave the social and historical context the students often miss when they read a judicial opinion.
- It humanized clients in a way more traditional legal writing problem cannot.
- It showed law students the complexities of a lawyer's work and a lawyer's life.
- It engaged the students more than traditional legal writing material.

Conclusion

Stories about lawyers, both fiction and nonfiction, are plentiful. Although stories will never replace course textbooks, nor should they, these narratives have a place in virtually every course. They can provide students with needed contexts relevant to their academic studies, and they have the added benefit of engaging students' interest and attention better than most materials.

Susan Hanley Duncan
University of Louisville, Louis D. Brandeis School of Law

Diagramming Crimes

In my Criminal Law class, I routinely "diagram" crimes to help students grasp the elements and master the skill of legal analysis. The technique is reminiscent of diagramming sentences, once a staple of grammar school English classes. A criminal offense diagram doesn't look like a sentence diagram, but each is useful in breaking down a criminal statute or a sentence to identify and understand its component parts.

A word of caution at the outset: diagramming is a tool to help extract from a statute or an opinion and clearly state the elements of an offense. It is not alchemy. It cannot, for example, transform an ambiguous statute into a clear one. But it can help students spot ambiguity in the definition of an offense and respond by developing and deploying statutory interpretation skills.

The instructor can construct offense diagrams prior to class using PowerPoint or drawing them by hand, photocopying them onto transparencies, and showing them on an overhead projector. I prefer, though, to recruit students to help create diagrams during class using a dry erase or chalk board. Collaborative construction gives students an active role and challenges them to discover the architecture underlying a criminal offense.

Diagramming Basics

Each offense element gets a box. The boxes are stacked in two adjacent columns with the nonmental elements on the right and the mental elements on the left. I start with the nonmental elements. I typically place the conduct element at the top and put other nonmental elements, such as a result or circumstance, directly below the conduct box. The nonmental column for a hypothetical statute penalizing the transportation of stolen archaeological artifacts would look like this:

NONMENTAL
transport
stolen
artifacts

The mental state boxes come next. I draw an empty box to the immediate left of each nonmental element box:

MENTAL	NONMENTAL
	transport
	stolen
	artifacts

Each empty box provides space for filling in any required mental state regarding the nonmental element to its immediate right.

Understanding Mental States

Mental state is a challenge for criminal law students and instructors. Simply drawing a column of empty mental state boxes helps students grasp several important points about mental state. First, it helps students distinguish mental from nonmental elements. Second, it demonstrates that criminal statutes may and often do require more than one mental state for conviction. The stolen artifacts statute, for example, might require *purpose* to transport, *knowledge* that the transported objects are stolen, but only *recklessness* that the objects are archaeological artifacts. Failure to distinguish clearly among mental states is a common problem in the criminal law's treatment of mental state.

Diagramming also reveals that mental state is relational. A person at any one time has many mental states regarding many different things. In order to speak and think clearly about mental state, it helps to clarify the reference point for the mental state in question. If one were to ask, for example, "What was the mental state of the defendant?" in a case arising under the stolen artifacts statute, it would be impossible to answer the question clearly without specifying the reference point for the mental state—the act of transporting the artifacts, their status as stolen, or their status as artifacts. Because a crime may require and a criminal may possess more than one mental state, it is critical to specify a reference point for mental state to avoid confusion.

Because mental state is relational, it helps to begin an offense diagram by constructing the nonmental element boxes *before* constructing the mental state boxes to clarify the reference points for the mental states. Having shown the students that a number of mental state boxes need to be filled in and that there are a number of ways a legislature or court could choose to fill them in, I next enlist the students to fill in the mental boxes based on the pertinent statute or case they have read.

If the class is familiar with Model Penal Code mental state terminology, one can use a "P" for purpose, "K" for knowledge, "R" for recklessness, and "N" for negligence. If a statute is written or interpreted as doing away with mental state regarding a particular nonmental element, I indicate that by putting "SL" for strict liability in the mental box next to that element. I sometimes emphasize the relational nature of mental state by adding an arrow to the mental state boxes as shown here:

MENTAL	NONMENTAL
P →	*transport*
K →	*stolen*
R →	*artifacts*

Some mental state boxes are easy to fill in. With negligent homicide, for example, negligence is the required mental state regarding the resulting death. Some statutes provide for alternative mental states. Pennsylvania, for example, includes both reckless and grossly negligent killings under manslaughter. (*See* 18 Pennsylvania Consolidated Statutes Section 2504.) Many jurisdictions provide that murder can be based on purpose, knowledge, or extreme recklessness regarding the death. Diagrams of such manslaughter and murder statutes look like this:

MENTAL	NONMENTAL
P →	*conduct*
R or N →	*death*

MENTAL	NONMENTAL
P →	*conduct*
P or K or ER →	*death*

Often, though, figuring out what mental states a statute requires for conviction is difficult. One routine ambiguity pertaining to mental state that diagramming helps illustrate is what I refer to as a mental state "carryover" problem. Sometimes, a statute sets out a mental state without clearly indicating the nonmental element or elements to which the mental state applies. Assume, for example, that the stolen artifacts statute made it a crime to "knowingly transport stolen archeological artifacts." What sort of knowledge is required for conviction? Knowledge that one is engaged in the act of transporting? Knowledge that the item transported is stolen? Knowledge that the item transported is an archaeological artifact? All of these?

Diagramming is a great way to illustrate this interpretive issue. I would put a "K" next to the nonmental element to which "knowingly" is closest in the statute and question marks in the mental state boxes next to the other nonmental elements.

The Model Penal Code has a rule to resolve this interpretation dilemma. Section 2.02 (4) states that a prescribed mental state applies to *all* material elements "unless a contrary purpose plainly appears." Diagramming helps demonstrate the usefulness of this MPC provision. In a MPC jurisdiction, I would replace each question mark with a "K" and use arrows to show that the mental state carries over from one nonmental element to the others.

Sometimes a statute requires proof of a mental state beyond those pertaining to its nonmental elements. Burglary statutes, for example, often require intent to commit a felony inside a building. The instructor can easily incorporate such an additional mental state by adding a mental state box at the bottom of the mental state column. There would be no nonmental element box to the right of such a mental state box, as in the following diagram.

MENTAL	NONMENTAL
P →	*enter*
K →	*dwelling*
K →	*at night*
P to commit a felony	

Statutory Interpretation

If a statute or a case found its way into a criminal law case book, there is a good chance that ambiguity will be found in the statutory language defining the crime at issue. Just as a map often facilitates following directions to an unfamiliar location, using a diagram to chart the extraction of elements from a statute aids students performing that extraction process. Diagramming represents and clarifies the process of analyzing a statute, something that can become quite murky when using language alone.

Diagramming allows the instructor to isolate and spotlight the ambiguity that gives rise to the need for interpretation. Statutes that are silent on mental state, for example, are regular sources of ambiguity. Should the silence be interpreted as legislative approval of strict liability? Or did the legislature intend to require some mental state without stating it in the text of the statute? If so, what mental state? Just putting a question mark in the mental state box next to a particular element can be a great way to illustrate the statutory interpretation question such a statute poses.

Kevin C. McMunigal
Case Western Reserve University School of Law

Integrating the Skill of Note-Taking into a Doctrinal Class

Without explicit and on-going guidance about why they're reading cases, some students will naturally construct an artificial wall between law and thought, assuming law is simply doctrine, rather than the product of reasoning and analysis. Consequently, what students choose to include in their notes may be significantly inconsistent with your expectations. For example, do you assume that your in-class examples and hypotheticals provide either doctrine or illustration and therefore should appear in their notes? What legal reasoning skill underlies the use of in-class hypotheticals? Do students understand the significance of hypotheticals? What about questions discussed in class? Consider for a moment this aspect of class as experienced by students. How do you respond to student responses? Do you routinely identify incorrect or incomplete responses, or do you respond with, "Anyone else?" We are not proposing that one approach is better than another, but that different approaches affect the choices that note-takers make.

This exercise provides one method for introducing, discussing, and monitoring the accuracy and completeness of note-taking. It is designed to encourage the instructor to consider the connection between what and how she teaches and what she expects the students to have written in their notes. We believe the small sacrifice in time required to do this exercise will go a long way toward helping students organize material, think about material on a deeper level, and identify areas of confusion. And, in the process of teaching note-taking, opportunities abound for reinforcing the doctrinal principles covered in that day's lecture.

Exercise in Basic Note-Taking: Using a Worksheet

At the beginning of class, hand out a worksheet and tell students to use it as the structural foundation for their class notes that day. In other words, they should complete the worksheet during the class discussion. Instruct them to use this as their notes for the day—they are not to do this in addition to taking notes in some other way. Accordingly, they should include where appropriate the information (e.g., analysis, strategy, doctrine, etc.) developed in class discussion.

Note-taking, especially in a law school classroom, is a difficult skill to teach. Obviously teachers have different teaching styles and expectations. Students, for their part, have different learning styles, and different levels of kinesthetic and information processing skills. This exercise tries to address those concerns, first, by encouraging the teacher to regard her class notes as not only the basis for her teaching, but also as the trigger for students' notes; and second, by providing students some guided practice in recognizing that structure and using it effectively.

The worksheet should provide students a structural outline of the day's class, requiring them to listen for the material and information that will complete the worksheet. The worksheet should set out the major headings and topics you expect to cover in class and include a place for students to fill in the details of the discussion, with cases and hypotheticals raised in class, and any rules, analysis, or policy put forward. At key points throughout the worksheet, you can also include headings for "student questions and comments," to remind students to consider what their classmates contribute and how and where those contributions fit in. Any section they leave blank indicates that they missed something that you think they should have caught.

We think it's a good idea to mix the level of detail you provide on the worksheet. For example, if you plan to cover three cases on the day you use the worksheet, you can make the structure for the first two cases more detailed than the structure for the third case. For the first two cases discussed in class, the worksheet might name the case, and then below, in outline form with just the headings included, prompt students to include for each case the "key facts," "holding," and "reasoning," with perhaps some direction in the reasoning section. You might also include a heading under each case labeled "Case illustrates...," to remind students to determine and note the key purposes for which the case was assigned. In contrast, the third case might simply list the case name, with no additional structural headings or direction under it. The more directive version is designed to remind students to include material (such as information from class discussions) that they might not otherwise. The less detailed version, which is more structural and less substantive, requires students to pay more attention to the choices they're making about what to write down.

The worksheet should derive directly from your teaching notes. In creating your worksheet, we suggest taking out some content but leaving enough to help students see the relationships among categories and to use those relationships to choose what details to include. The goal is to pay conscious attention to what you think should appear in students' notes. You may find, as we did, that creating the worksheet informs the content, organization, and delivery of the actual class. For an example of both a note-taking worksheet and how we would expect a student to complete it in the context of contract indefiniteness doctrine, please see our book, *Teaching to Every Student : Explicitly Integrating Skills and Theory into the Contracts Class* (forthcoming Carolina Academic Press).

The worksheet follows the order in which the material is taught, and therefore should not be used by students as their outline. After the class students still need to revise their notes, addressing any missing or unclear information, and then convert their notes into an outline.

Obviously, using the worksheet for the day's notes is based entirely on the professor's own concept of the class, (i.e., her goals and objectives) related to both doctrine and skills for the students for that day and as it fits into the course as a whole. That choice, we think, reflects two basic points about note-taking in law school. First, although there are, of course, common threads running through the skill of note-taking across all law school classes, each teacher comes to class with her own vision and expectation and that vision and those expectations render the task slightly different in each class. Therefore, if you choose to try this exercise in your class, you may find (as we hope you do) that in creating your worksheet, you go back and forth between it and your class notes, as you make connections between what and how you teach, and what you think the students should be "getting" and writing down in their notes. Second, the pedagogy of legal education makes note-taking in law school a mystery to many first-year students. While some students pick up rapidly what works, others take some time to figure it out. If we have confidence in our school's admissions office (or, better yet, wish to support an attempt to broaden the pool of admitted students), leveling the playing field early in the first semester, so that the less-prepared students don't lose the doctrine while they acquire the skills, is time and effort well spent.

David Nadvorney
City University of New York School of Law

Deborah Zalesne
City University of New York School of Law

Video Reenactments Make Simulations More Realistic

A staple teaching method in many clinical courses is the simulation. A problem is posed and the scenarios are handed out to the would-be witnesses, who are then interviewed or examined by the student lawyers. The trouble is that the witnesses have seen nothing, heard nothing, and experienced nothing. They are actors pure and simple, who have no true memory of the alleged incident. The result is that the simulated exercise lacks realism. It is a work of fiction that requires the witnesses to re-create the incident in their minds.

To make simulations more realistic, try using video reenactments. These are forms of "crime stopper" vignettes. The witnesses are given background information. They are told who they are, where they were, and what they saw. The witnesses then watch a video of the incident—only once. Following the viewing they write a witness statement, which ties them to what they have seen. The student witnesses can then be interviewed by counsel and examined upon what they actually saw.

Professor Michael Ahlen at the University of North Dakota first developed this technique. He used clips from "Cops." Typically, these clips show a police officer in pursuit of a stolen car or making an arrest. A problem is then posed surrounding the clip and students are instructed to prepare a direct and cross-examination.

An Example

One clip involves the pursuit of a stolen truck. The camera is in the police car. It follows the pursuit, which ends when the truck spins out of control, rolls, and lands in a field. The accused is charged with causing death by dangerous driving. The witnesses are told that they are law students who were in the police car as part of a "ride along" program offered by the local police department. The issue is whether the accused actually was the driver of the truck and, if so, was he driving in a dangerous manner. The witnesses watch the video, write their statements, and are interviewed by counsel, who prepare and present direct examination. The witnesses' statements are turned over to opposing counsel who conduct cross-examination.

I have added to the video vignette idea by creating trial problem re-enactments. Our students are required to prepare and conduct a full trial. They work in pairs and the problems are designed to have two witnesses per side so that each counsel conducts one direct and one cross-examination. The examinations are designed to be done in 15 to 20 minutes. For the trial re-enactments videos are prepared from the perspective of each witness. Therefore, instead of watching one scenario, each witness sees the event through his or her own eyes. Four witness perspectives are created.

A Sample Trial Problem

An action is brought against the local police department for assault and battery. The police shot a young woman as she was driving away from a liquor store. The police thought she was the driver of a getaway car. The officers received a dispatch call that a robbery was taking place at the liquor store. A description of the robber was given. When the officers arrived at the scene they saw a young man run from the store. He fit the description. They chased the suspect on foot until he got into the getaway car. As it was leaving the parking lot one of the officers fired twice. The young woman was shot. She survived. It was a mistake. The young man seen running actually was fleeing the real robber. The issue in the case is one of reasonable use of force by the police. The video is shorter than three minutes long.

The police officers view a video that starts with the dispatch call. The camera shows the man running from the scene. It then follows the two officers as they pursue.

The driver and the young man watch a video that begins with them arriving at the liquor store. The camera then follows the young man to the store and his return to the car. Another camera remains with the driver in the car.

The case is built on the witness statements supplemented with other material. I give counsel a map of the scene and a transcript of the dispatch call. I also provide a medical report so that counsel can prepare proper pleadings and conduct a meaningful settlement negotiation.

As a final exercise, we show the examining students the videos that their witnesses saw. This exposes two important realities: (1) The frailties of eyewitness testimony (it is amazing how differently witnesses will interpret and retain information regarding a given incident); and (2) the need for counsel to conduct a thorough and well-structured interview to uncover all the pertinent information from witnesses.

A Series of Reenactments

I have prepared five other video reenactments.

- Police Assault and Battery. The police pursued a speeding white van. They momentarily lost contact but saw a white van parked in the driveway of a home. The engine was still warm. The officers entered the home. The homeowner resisted arrest and was pepper sprayed.
- A Lawyer's Duty to Warn. A lawyer represented a man charged with the attempted murder of his wife. The man underwent a psychiatric evaluation and was released on bail. Family members came to the lawyer with concerns about the man. A rifle was missing and so was the husband. Later that day, the husband murdered his wife and killed himself.
- An Intoxicated University Student Brings an Action Against the University and Supplier of Alcohol. An underage student living at a university became intoxicated in his dorm room. He was provided with free samples of alcohol from a marketing representative of a rum distillery. The dorm floor supervisor allowed the representative to distribute the samples on the floor and was aware that the student was drinking. The student fell down a flight of stairs; the resulting injuries ended his football career.
- Acting in Defense of a Third Person. A couple were drinking in a bar. The husband engaged another patron in a pool game. The husband lost and was not happy. The couple left. Outside the bar, the couple argued over the car keys. The wife wanted to drive, and the husband refused to give her the car keys. They struggled and she fell to the ground. At this moment the bar patron who won the pool game came out. He saw the husband standing over the wife. The man reacted by hitting the husband.
- False Arrest. A young woman entered the university bookstore. She did not leave her bag in the lockers provided. Store security observed her put a book in her bag. As she left the store, the alarm went off. She claimed innocence. She also had a rental video with her. Such rental videos have, in the past, set off the alarm.

Readers can obtain copies of the re-enactments by contacting me.

Lee Stuesser
Bond University Faculty of Law

Using Graphs & Charts to Visually Represent Doctrine

Some legal doctrines lend themselves to visual representation. For a student struggling to understand a particular legal doctrine, or how two doctrines relate to one another, sometimes a drawing or chart can be a good supplement to words—or even communicate more clearly than words. Using Microsoft Word or just a pen, I have tried to reach visual learners in my Civil Rights class with:

- A chart of the umbrella legal standard for 8th Amendment claims, and the two subsidiary standards that govern such claims in the separate factual contexts of denial of medical treatment and putting down prison riots;
- A line showing a continuum from "something more than negligence" on the left all the way up to "shocks the conscience" on the right, illustrating the mental fault standard for substantive due process liability for executive action;
- A two-way arrow pointing to an example of quintessential private action to the left (off-duty cop, out of uniform, spanks his son for not doing the dishes) and pointing to an example of quintessential state action to the right (on-duty cop in marked police car, with lights and sirens, chases criminal suspect in response to 911 call), with a list in the middle of the factors weighed by courts in deciding whether a police officer has acted "under color of law";
- A stick figure drawing of a social worker balancing on a "constitutional tightrope"; below the drawing are two columns of parentheticals summarizing cases where social workers were sued for intervening in a family *too soon* (before sufficient evidence of child abuse) and where social workers were sued for intervening in a family *too late* (after the abuse has resulted in serious injury).

Students also respond well to the opportunity to create their own visual depictions of legal doctrines and share them with the class. One student illustrated the civil rights defense of "absolute immunity" as a brick wall, with different claims—each briefly summarized—ricocheting off the wall. Another student used a flow chart to illustrate the steps necessary for plaintiffs' counsel to qualify for attorneys' fees.

Sarah Ricks
Rutgers School of Law–Camden

Teaching a Legal Research "Laboratory Class"

Law students cannot get enough "hands on" experience in online legal research. Like many first-year law students, students at Rutgers–Camden, where I teach, receive comprehensive Lexis and Westlaw training at the beginning of the fall semester. However, in five years of teaching legal research and writing, I have consistently observed that students' search skills are weak. While there could be many explanations for this deficiency, I believe that part of the problem involves information overload and a lack of context.

Every year students tell me that it is difficult for them to assimilate basic search skills amid all of the other information that they are required to absorb as new law students. Moreover, because the initial Lexis and Westlaw training is not related to the problems that I teach, students lack the context necessary to help them assimilate new research skills. Below, I describe an in-class legal research exercise designed to help students self-assess their search skills and, ultimately, to become more effective legal researchers.

The Laboratory Class is a refined version of what I did in class one day—by accident. I had intended to go on Lexis and Westlaw using the classroom PC. When the projector failed to work, I wrote several legal questions on the board and had students formulate their own searches on their laptops. I then circulated around the room to see how the students were doing. What I observed was disturbing. Many of the students ran searches that were terribly overbroad or narrow. Many students seemed to have no idea of how to restrict a search. When I asked the students how they might get help with their searches, only one student mentioned the research assistance available through Lexis and Westlaw.

The Laboratory Class begins with a six-page handout that I distribute at the beginning of class. The handout is designed to familiarize students with : (1) researching cases electronically by subject; and (2) formulating Boolean word searches. I do not make the handout available prior to class because I do not want students practicing their searches. I want to see what they can, and cannot, do in class. I break up the class into groups of four to five students to work on the exercise. I then circulate around the room to see how students are doing and to answer questions. The entire exercise flows from one legal question, designed to give students context : if an airline negligently injures an animal that is a pet, can the pet owner recover damages for the loss of the pet's companionship? This particular question provides context for *my* students because all of my problems involve Animal Law.

The first half of the exercise focuses on Westlaw and is designed to familiarize students with topics, Key Numbers, and the KeySearch function. Students are given a relevant case to illustrate how a case can be a useful entry point into the digest system: *Soucek v. Banham*, 524 N.W.2d 478 (Minn. App. 1994).

The second half of the exercise focuses on Lexis and is designed to familiarize students with word searching and the Focus feature. The Lexis portion of the exercise concludes with a natural language search:

> Now run a natural language search in the same source (database). List the search you ran. Did you find relevant cases? Time permitting, run the same natural language search in Westlaw. Did you find relevant cases? Did you find some/all of the same cases [that you found using other search methods]?

Both portions of the exercise conclude by asking students to seek help from Lexis and Westlaw reference attorneys:

Westlaw:

> Now click on the Help tab at the top of the screen to begin a Live Help session. Describe the research process that the Reference Attorney suggests, including the names of the database and the specific search the attorney advised you to use.
>
> Now call Westlaw Customer Service: 1-800-REF-ATTY (1-800-733-2889). Describe the research process that the Reference Attorney suggests, including the name of the database and the specific search the attorney advised you to use.

Lexis:

> Now click on the Help tab at the top of the screen to begin a Live Research Help session. Describe the research process that the Reference Attorney suggests, including the name of the database and the specific search the attorney advised you to use.
>
> Now call LexisNexis® Law School Customer Support 1-800-45-LEXIS (1-800-455-3947) for assistance in researching this legal question. Describe the research process that the Reference Attorney suggests, including the name of the source and the specific search the attorney advised you to use.

At the end of the exercise, we discuss how the students' searches differed from the ones recommended by the reference attorneys. I caution students that professional researchers tend to generate highly specific searches and advise them to formulate their own searches before seeking assistance.

Self-assessment is critical to helping students become independent legal researchers. One of my teaching assistants, who performed this exercise when he was my student, described his self-assessment: "I hated doing the exercise because it made me realize how much I didn't know about legal research. I'm glad I did it though."

The Legal Research Laboratory Class is a classroom-tested method of helping students become more effective legal researchers. While students may not enjoy confronting what they do not know about legal research, most should be motivated to learn.

Sheila Rodriguez
Rutgers School of Law–Camden

The Use of TV Shows in the Classroom

Most professors complain that student attention spans are short and that students are not eager to read articles and books. A repeated complaint is that students are alienated by fast changing visual images in television shows, commercials, music clips, video games, and websites. But we all now live in a visually-oriented and technology-driven society, and our classroom teaching, rather than clinging to outmoded teaching methodologies, should adapt to the new realities of a fast-pace culture.

In my Criminal Law classes, where enrollment consistently numbers between 100 to 120 students, I implemented a teaching method that makes extensive use of the learning styles students demand, without compromising the objectives of achieving excellence in the discipline.

Although I constantly change the rhythm of the class and vary all classroom activities to avoid repeating the structure of my classes, my class sessions usually have a common pattern. I always start by posting on the blackboard, in a way that resembles interactive menus on cable TV, the objectives of the class, how this class fits with what we've done and what we will do, the topic of my talk, the class activities we will engage in, and what we will cover next class. My talk is usually short and goes straight to the points I want the students to discuss. Then we all embark on the class activities. One of the most successful is an analysis of video scenes from popular TV shows and commercial motion pictures depicting criminal events. It's amazing how many crimes are committed on TV every day! For example, when we discuss the concept of *mens rea*, I show a series of video scenes carefully selected from popular TV shows such as *Friends, Seinfeld, The Simpsons, The Sopranos*, or even *Beavis and Butthead*. Students have to identify the *mens rea* of the characters as in the show.

To illustrate: one of these clips shows the *Friends* character Rachel trying to move "Rosita," Joey's beloved chair. Joey makes it clear that Rosita can't be moved because she sits an exactly equal distance between the bathroom and the kitchen, and is at the perfect angle so there is no glare coming off "Stevie," the TV. When Joey heads into his room, Rachel tries pulling on the back of the chair until the hinge breaks and the back falls off. Students are asked to analyze whether Rachel acts with the required *mens rea* for mischief. This triggers a debate on *mens rea* itself and we relate to authors, such as Simmons and Fletcher, who propose alternative views on *mens rea*.

Another example is from a *Seinfeld* episode, during which Kramer sets fire to Susan's father's cabin. Students analyze whether the *mens rea* of arson is met. We examine what Kramer would have had to think in order to be guilty of reckless arson, as defined in the Canadian Criminal Code. We also analyze whether his conduct constitutes arson in other criminal jurisdictions, including common law, civil law, and even Islamic law.

Participation in crimes also lends itself to this kind of activity. For example, I show *Seinfeld's* "The Frogger" where Elaine and Jerry discuss the theft of a cake, which, because it comes from the 1937 wedding of King Edward VIII, turns out to be worth $29,000.

Seinfeld did not know this fact. Students engage in a very lively discussion of what requirements must be met in order to be considered a counselor to an offense or an accessory after the fact. We also discuss the doctrine of probable and natural consequences, and the differences between the requirements for an aider and an abettor.

Another scene I usually select is from the *Friends* episode "The One with All the Cheesecakes" where Chandler steals cheesecakes from his neighbor, and Rachel (despite knowing they're stolen) cannot resist eating the cheesecakes herself. This episode fosters active student participation in an examination of the requisites for being an accessory after the fact. Moreover the discussions lead to other aspects of criminal law, such as whether there is *actus reus*, or whether or not Rachel has a defense. Again, we try to extrapolate the debate to other criminal justice systems, not just the Canadian one.

These practices serve several purposes: pedagogical, criminological, and philosophical. From a pedagogical point of view, they relate to the way students look at the world without diluting the quality of learning. They cater to learners who are immersed in a visually- and technologically-oriented culture. These activities also motivate students to read the articles, cases, and books necessary for the analysis of the video segments. Additionally, they act as attention mechanisms (i.e., devices that foster synchronization of senses with the mind). Students are continually exposed to myriad external stimuli, which compete for their attention. The factors affecting the capability of stimuli to enter students' inner world are internal and external: some depend on the prior experiences of the students and some on the intrinsic qualities of stimuli. Resorting to popular TV and film characters helps the processing of attended information, which is conducive to learning.

Criminologically, it helps the student debunk the traditional image that crime occurs between strangers and on the streets and where the perpetrator is generally a marginalized, lower-class member of society. It helps them see that crimes take place in all social classes and milieus, and that, most of the time, victim and offender know each other very well. It also ruptures the unitary, doctrine-focused and homogeneous conception of the law which is invariably concerned with the dissection of appellate court decisions. At the same time, it proposes a more diversified, open, cooperative, and plural teaching and learning process.

Julian Hermida
Algoma University

The Dirty Dozen

Long ago law professors, seizing upon the name of a far better-organized philosopher than themselves, created the so-called Socratic system of instruction, an excellent technique when used properly. But like many good ideas, undesirable myths attached themselves, contaminating the main purpose. One such myth propelled by the all-knowing Professor Kingsfield in the Oscar-winning film, *Paper Chase*, suggests that: "In law there are no answers, only questions". This, in turn, implies that there is no reason to construct basic systems, axioms or classification schemes, such as those employed by virtually every other logic-based endeavor. Instead, the myth suggests that we should allow our students to wade through a Grand Canyon of cases and notes, as they pretend to construct their own sign posts along the way, attempting to find their own answers, which we tell them don't exist.

Imagine that you're a mathematician or scientist teaching a course with little uniformity and no standard axioms, structures or definitions. You might conclude that if science and mathematics were taught by law professors, perhaps we would all still be calculating with an abacas, debating which beads were being unfairly discriminated against. Thus, the *discipline* that the law demands appears to be lacking in the very educational structure responsible for its dissemination. And this lack of discipline shows. It shows in the shortcomings of our practitioners, the inefficiency of our judicial system and the poor development of our laws and statutes.

If the goal, therefore, is to confuse the students, especially the 1Ls, then why not do it right? Many casebooks already do it "right." But for those writers preparing to write a new casebook, here are the "Dirty Dozen" rules that must be followed:

1. Take the most important rules of law and bury them in the case notes. That way, the students who are worried only about being called upon in class (but don't have time to read the notes) will be thoroughly confused and mislead.
2. Present a long series of cases, all aiming toward one beautiful immaculate truth; then, at the tail end of some obscure case note, cite a statute that abrogates it.
3. In your bold-titled cases, present lengthy unedited opinions that present narrow exceptions based upon silly fact patterns; even better if the case involves a crooked pedophile attorney (such as John Mitchell of *Pennoyer v. Neff* fame).
4. Early in the book, be sure to present cases that utilize complex procedures and terminology that even lawyers have yet to understand. Be certain to provide some olde English cases from the 1700's.
5. Edit out that part of the case that tells who won. Or better yet, carefully cut bits and pieces so that only incoherent, discombobbled text remains.
6. Never include cases written by judges, who in plain English, tell us the outcomes. Make certain they contain language like this:

    > This court, therefore, modifies the lower court as to issues five and seventeen, which affirmed and at the same time reversed the trial court's ruling during the second re-hearing as to issues three and six, and is therefore, modified in accordance with the remainder of this incoherent opinion. Reversed on other grounds.

7. In your Teacher's Manual, instruct professors to tell the students that *Young v. Guy* and *Ferens v. John Deere* are "*easy*" cases that can be understood by any neophyte student; be sure to do this to the students during pre-finals week.
8. Before students have learned the significance of the Supreme Court or the New York Court of Appeals, give them some long winded slip opinions from a Mississippi trial court (with big bold titles, of course). If you can't find one, a Trent Lott speech will do.
9. Never present a cohesive, logically structured outline. Instead, scatter the topics hither, thither and yon, or do as most, and scatter them Curley, Moe and Shemp.
10. Always select cases that have several parties and entities with the same names. That way, the students won't be able to distinguish the plaintiffs from the defendants.
11. Always let the tail (minority positions) wag the dog when it comes to selecting cases for purposes of teaching precedents.
12. Never define a complex legal term; instead, refer the students to that "other" pillar of high priced, elegantly bound, confusion—*Black's Law Dictionary*.

Ashley S. Lipson
University of La Verne College of Law

Not Just a Study Break: Using *Body Heat*, Kanye West's "Gold Digger," and *South Park* to Teach (and Examine!) Wills & Trusts, Family Law, and Property

Consider the following activities:

- Settling in for a movie evening with the steamy 1981 noir thriller *Body Heat*.
- Singing along to Kanye West's 2005 chart-topping rap R&B hit "Gold Digger."
- Laughing out loud at a *South Park* cartoon episode about the boys' attempts to stop an Indian casino from taking over their town.

Three things that sound like fun indulgences for law students taking a little break from studying for their Wills & Trusts, Family Law, or Property exams? Maybe. But these pop culture gems (and many others) can also form the basis for challenging essay exam questions and lively review sessions—that is, if you are one of my students. Using Hollywood creations in the law school classroom is not just for Entertainment Law or Intellectual Property courses. It is also a highly effective way of fusing your students' pre-existing interest in TV, the movies, and popular music with their nascent understanding of law as a social and cultural production in its own right. Furthermore, as was pointed out quite trenchantly to me many years ago by classics professor Victoria Wohl (back when we were grad students at Berkeley), today's students' ability to "read" television and movies as "texts" is probably better-developed than their relationships with printed text. And, of course, it's fun!

Let's look at three of my recent favorites in turn.

Body Heat is a 1981 film, starring Kathleen Turner and William Hurt (and a pre-*Cheers* Ted Danson in a very funny supporting role). It is best remembered for making the sultry Turner an overnight sensation, and for its potent evocation of Hurt's borderline-incompetent lawyer in thrall to a modern femme fatale. But the film isn't just an exercise in professional [ir]responsibility (namely, why it's not a good idea to get caught up in a plot to murder your client's spouse). In fact, the plot turns on a rather intricate application of the Rule Against Perpetuities in the will-drafting context, and also of a subsidiary (and little-known) doctrine called "infectious invalidity." (Perhaps unsurprisingly, the screenwriter was a former law student of the late, great Jesse Dukeminier at UCLA!) The legal issues are intricate enough, in fact, that I have used a screening of the film as a portion of a Wills & Trusts exam, with great success.

The questions based on the film are simply two:

- Explain the plot of this film, from a Wills & Trusts point of view.
- Could such a plot be carried out in this state?

If You Have Not Seen the Film, Skip to the Star!

Answering Question (1) correctly requires recognizing that Turner's character deliberately induced the drafting of her husband's will in such a way that a RAP-violating provision is central to the overall plan; explaining how and why the provision violates RAP; explaining the consequences of the violation (that the provision is stricken); and finally, addressing her use of "infectious invalidity" to produce intestacy, followed by her inheritance of the entire estate as the surviving spouse of a testator leaving no issue.

Answering Question (2), whether such a plot could be carried out in the student's state, requires applying whatever Rule Against Perpetuities reform doctrine has been enacted by the jurisdiction. I have taught in Texas, New York, California, and now, Florida, each of which takes a different approach. Florida, where the film is set, has changed its perpetuities law twice since the film was made! Typically, because of widespread reform, as well as the fact that infectious invalidity is not the rule of most U.S. jurisdictions, the answer to this question is "no." Students are then asked to explain what would happen if the facts of the case occurred in their home state today. This issue ought also to include a brief discussion of the "slayer's statute," which does not allow someone who kills a testator to inherit from her victim (although in the film, she manages to get the lawyer convicted and escapes with the loot).

The questions themselves are quite simple and straightforward; this choice is intended to counteract the sometimes unbalanced reaction of students to such an unconventional exam. I have used this film as the in-class portion of a final exam, airing during the first two hours of a three-hour exam period and giving students one hour to answer the question. (I generally also bring popcorn for everyone.) I have also used it as a take-home exam question, reserving the in-class examination period for a more "conventional" exam. Either way, students find it unforgettable.

★ Kanye West's song "Gold Digger" (with Jamie Foxx) was ubiquitous in 2005; its second and most legally-dense verse is reproduced below:

> "18 years, 18 years
> She got one of yo' kids got you for 18 years
> I know somebody payin' child support for one of his kids
> His baby momma's car and crib is bigger than his
> You will see him on TV Any Given Sunday
> Win the Superbowl and drive off in a Hyundai
> She was s'pose' to buy ya shorty TYCO with ya money
> She went to the doctor, got lipo with ya money
> She walkin' around lookin' like Michael with ya money
> Should of got that insured, GEICO for ya moneeey
> If you ain't no punk, holla 'We Want Prenup!'
> 'WE WANT PRENUP!,' Yeaah
> It's something that you need to have
> Cause when she leave yo' ass she gon' leave with half
> 18 years, 18 years
> And on the 18th birthday, he found out it wasn't his!"

That we have reached a point in our history at which a traditional African-American musical device like call-and-response can be used to refer to this premarital planning device as a "prenup," on the assumption that the entire class of listeners will know what is referred to, is itself quite remarkable. But there's more here, much more. Some of the family law issues raised by the song include (1) the duration of the child support obligation; (2) the lifestyle standard used to calculate child support (can a pro football player be reduced to driving a Hyundai?); (3) the expenses to which child support can permissibly be applied ("car and crib," yes, "TYCO" (toys), yes, but "lipo"? no); (4) the relationship between child support and the division of community property during a divorce ("when she leave yo' ass she gon' leave with half"); (5) the scope of prenuptial agreements; (6) and the significance of a determination, at the termination of the child support obligation, that the man who paid child support is not the child's biological father. The song also raises theoretical and policy issues about race, gender and law, gender-based power (a theme running through the entire song which, after all, is called

"Gold Digger"), and financial responsibility for nonmarital children. It is a rare family law or community property essay question that can manage to do all this in fewer than 150 words. And, unlike any essay question I've ever written, my students already know all the words!

Finally, for those of us who teach first-year property out of the Dukeminier casebook, the *South Park* episode entitled "Red Man's Greed" seems almost tailor-made for the course. The casebook begins with *Johnson v. M'Intosh*, an 1823 U.S. Supreme Court case arising from competing pre-revolutionary claims to land between grantees claiming under a prior grant from the local Native American tribes, the Illinois and the Piankeshaw, and subsequent grantees claiming under the predecessor of the United States Government itself. No sooner are students introduced to one traditional maxim of Anglo-Saxon property law—"first in time is first in right"—then they encounter another, "might makes right," particularly as it played out on the North American continent. The very end of the Dukeminier casebook focuses on the constitutional doctrine of "takings," and *Kelo v. City of New London*, a headline-grabbing Supreme Court case from 2005, is the lead case in the section on the Fifth Amendment's "public use" requirement. The *South Park* episode entitled "Red Man's Greed," first aired April 30, 2003, brilliantly and hilariously fuses the two issues.

Matt Stone and Trey Parker create a funny and scathing send-up of the colonization and conquest of North America, by turning the (gaming) tables. This time, it is the casino-operating Native Americans whose greed stimulates a land-grab, even including the destruction of the town of South Park in order to build "a superhighway, built from Denver right to our casino!" To carry out this plan, according to Mayor McDaniels, "[t]he Native Americans have purchased the land out from under us," and even "bought the bank," although they offer the residents "retail values on your homes." The South Park residents attempt to parlay the $10,000 they receive in the forced sale into more than $300,000, the amount needed to buy back the town. But after winning once at roulette, they let the bet ride and lose it all. All that remains is to stand in front of the bulldozers (to the tune of Pat Benatar's "Love Is A Battlefield"). Much of the political humor of the episode derives from its historical quotations and reversals—the Native Americans maliciously provide the South Park residents with SARS-infected blankets (survival rate of SARS: 98%); Stan Marsh, one of the South Park kids says, "Just because you have a piece of paper saying you own it doesn't make it yours. We grew up here. Our parents grew up here. We shop at that Wal-Mart, and eat at that Chili's. We take fish from the streams and bread them and freeze them to make fish sticks. This is not just a town, it is our way of life."

As is typical of the show, the episode is dense with jokes, allusions, and historical references (as well as, of course, obscenity, profanity, and scatology), which implicate at least the following property law issues: (1) how is real estate used to secure a line of personal credit? (as Gerald does at the casino); (2) what happens if someone defaults on a loan secured by his family's home? (Gerald again); (3) do we have preferences among land uses, and how do we embody them in law? (casinos and highways, or homes, Wal-Marts, and Chili's restaurants?); (4) is the most profitable use of land always its highest and best use? (as Chief Runs With Premise puts it, "if we do not build a superhighway, our casino might stop seeing profits."); (5) under what circumstances, if any, can people be forced to sell their homes and take what is offered? (as Stan's father Randy says, "Stanley, we don't have a choice. The Native Americans own South Park now. We have to take what they'll give us for our homes."); (6) how is the price set in a forced sale of real property?; (7) what are the limits on the legitimacy of government action respecting property: is it ever proper to resist with force? (Mr. Mackey: "It's over, Stanley. What else can we do?" Stan: "We can stay. And fight.")

I can think of at least three different ways to use this cartoon: as an introduction to the course, as part of a year-end review, or as an in-class or take-home essay exam question. As an introduction, the episode might be aired (it runs approximately twenty-two minutes), and students asked to identify as many property law issues as they can. Presented at the end of the course, in a review session, during a timed in-class exam, or as part of a take-home examination, students could be asked essentially the same question, but obviously expected to identify more issues, and identify them more precisely, than they could have done months before. Property students at the end of the course can also be invited to comment on the accuracy and subtlety with which the legal issues are handled by the show (i.e., could the tribe "purchase the land out from under" the townspeople? Would eminent domain be available? And so on). If desired, students could be provided with a copy of the script.

All three of these popular entertainments—*Body Heat*, "Gold Digger," and "Red Man's Greed"—have the power to surprise, delight, and teach your students, and bring a little interdisciplinary flair to your classes. After all, there's no business like show business.

Diane J. Klein
University of La Verne College of Law

Nine Common Law Felonies and *Pirates of the Caribbean*

A fun way to focus the attention of our first-year law students is to show popular movies that relate to a part of their studies of the criminal law. While teaching the nine common law felonies, I required each student to make a chart of the crimes and their elements. After making the chart the students watched the big-screen version of *Pirates of the Caribbean: The Curse of the Black Pearl.* We are fortunate to have a digital wall and stereo sound so the screening of the movie is a small version of the movie theater. Showing this film on a regular television would dilute the impact significantly.

The students use their common law felonies chart to keep track of the events in the movie. I prime the thinking process by showing the opening sequence in which Elizabeth (Keira Knightley) takes a gold medallion from around the neck of the mostly unconscious Will (Orlando Bloom). The students decide whether this could be a larceny by listing the elements: a trespassory taking, a carrying away of the property of another, and the intent to permanently deprive. If the video clip shows all of the elements, they list this on their chart. If the action lacks one or more of the elements, they explain why this may not be a larceny according to the common law.

The visualization of the crimes makes understanding the differences between larceny and robbery, for example, more accessible to the wide range of students we instruct. The sequences themselves grab the students' attention in a way that would make Walt Disney himself proud. After the film work is completed, we solve a number of fact patterns based on scenes from the movie. Using the names of the characters seems to increase the interest factor somewhat. Having watched the video seems to increase the comprehension of many of the students and their performance on the subsequent hypotheticals is significantly improved.

A sample chart for the lesson appears on the next page. The nine felonies listed will provide ample learning opportunities.

NINE COMMON LAW FELONIES
PIRATES OF THE CARIBBEAN

Directions: Make this chart with two columns and ten rows. Auto fit to contents. While viewing the movie, chart each felony you see in the column on the right.

COMMON LAW FELONY	Description of the crime in the film:
Murder: the intentional, unlawful killing of a human being with malice aforethought	
Manslaughter: the unlawful killing of a human being without malice aforethought	
Larceny: the trespassory taking and carrying away of the property of another with the intent to permanently deprive.	Elizabeth takes gold medallion from Will on ship.
Arson: the intentional setting ablaze of the dwelling house of another at night.	Sinking ship is ablaze
Burglary: the breaking and entering of the dwelling of another at night, with the intent to commit a felony therein	Sparrow breaks into armory…
Robbery: the unlawful taking of the property of another from their presence by using force, threats, or fear	Pirates carry away the valuables of the townspeople. Pirates take silver from the governors' house.
Mayhem: the malicious wounding or disfiguring of the body of another human being with an intent to cause serious permanent injury.	Elizabeth pours hot coals on pirate's head.
Rape: unlawful sexual intercourse committed by a man with a woman not his wife through force and against her will	
Sodomy: oral or anal copulation between humans, especially the same sex.	

Tom Gear
The Academy of Irving

The ADR Toys and Tools Show: Using Props in the Law School Classroom

"To a man with a hammer, everything looks like a nail." Professors teaching Alternative Dispute Resolution (ADR) often use this quote, attributed to Mark Twain, to compare the litigation option to the numerous ADR processes available to attorneys, courts, and clients. We tell students that the course will give them additional "tools for their tool boxes."

Over time, scholars have organized ADR processes along two continua: (1) the degree to which the ADR process gives clients control over the process, procedures, and rules; and (2) the degree to which the ADR process gives clients control over the outcome of the process. Thus, litigation gives clients little control over the process and little control over the outcome. Unfacilitated negotiation, in contrast, gives parties complete control over the process and complete control over the outcome. A number of other processes fit between these two extremes: private judging, conventional arbitration, final-offer arbitration, high-low arbitration, nonbinding advisory arbitration, summary jury trial, mini-trial, judicial settlement conference, legal (or early) neutral evaluation, neutral fact-finding process, and several styles of mediation (evaluative, facilitative, and transformative).

The use of tools and toys has helped me explain these processes in a way that appeals to the students who absorb information visually and kinesthetically. They are freed from a boring lecture tied solely to a written description of each process. First, I display on a slide or overhead, an "ADR Spectrum" that visually makes associations between dispute resolution processes. Next, I frame each process on a placemat in the same order as they appear on the slide or overhead. Some of the placements correspond to more "courtroom-like" processes and so reflect the colors of a lawyer's traditional attire: navy blue suit, white shirt, and burgundy tie. These placemats serve as the frame for litigation, court appeals, arbitration, judicial settlement conferences, and legal neutral evaluation. For processes yielding an advisory nonbinding opinion—like nonbinding advisory arbitration, mini-trial, and summary jury trial—I use beige colored placements to signify neutrality. The props for the neutral fact-finding process "swim" among the fishes found in the waterscape of one placemat. The mediation processes are framed on green floral placemats, indicating a more placid and informal environment for this process. Taken together, the placemats, I hope, trigger associations among the processes based on color or pattern.

Next, I divide the binding processes—appeal, trial, and arbitration—from the nonbinding processes, using a line of duct tape. When I illustrate the final and binding nature of these processes, I wrap the toys representing the parties in duct tape.

I then represent each process with one or more toys and tools. Several types of toys serve as the neutrals, lawyers, and clients: Stuffed bears serve as judges and arbitrators, distinguished by the color of the child's clip-on tie I have attached around their necks. Bear-judges wear black ties (rather than black robes). Bear-arbitrators wear burgundy ties that match their burgundy arbitration placemats. The bears are white, tan, and brown, to represent diversity in the pool of neutrals. One wears a gray wig and a blue scarf to signify some gender diversity among this pool, as well. The three appeal-panel bears sit in doll chairs, including a red metal highchair made in the 1950s.

The retired judge serving in the tableaus for private judging, mini-trial, legal neutral evaluation, and evaluative mediation is a remarkably crafted china-head "grandpa" doll, complete with lounge chair, cardigan sweater, rug, and fuzzy slippers. A paper Mache penguin with glasses serves as my fact-finding neutral: in this case, a professor of environmental science who will help the lawyers determine whether a discharge of mine water waste into the local river will cause fish die-off. A Mr. Potato Head, clad in a yellow hard hat, serves as a fact-finding neutral in a hypothetical construction dispute, which is represented by a stack of brightly colored plastic blocks. Tazz, a plastic action figure from the Extreme Championship Wrestling series, who is clad in a black suit, serves as a mini-trial facilitator, a legal neutral evaluator, and an evaluative mediator. Six yellow rubber-duckies, wearing different colored straw sombreros, represent the mock jury in the summary jury trial tableau.

GI Joe dolls, dressed in camouflage uniforms, represent the "Rambo litigators," who, depending on the formality of the process, either stand or sit. The clients are represented by plastic figures of Dora the Explorer and a figure in an Asian costume. I chose these culturally diverse toys to allow me to explain how the need for cultural competency and sensitivity may affect a client's choice of neutral. For instance, the facilitative mediator is an Asian Barbie Doll.

Two action figures—Captain Boomerang and The Joker—also clad in suit-like attire, serve as the CEOs of disputing corporations in the mini-trial scenario. Finally, four smaller bears dressed in gingham fabric—mom, dad, girl, and boy—serve as the family in the midst of a divorce referred to facilitative mediation.

I use a stuffed blue car to represent nonbinding arbitration based on the Better Business Bureau's auto manufacturing program. A plastic figure of a crouching baseball player and a baseball, along with a book on Mark McGuire's record breaking home-run season, represent final-offer arbitration. For high-low arbitration, I cut the ends off toy dollar bills with a large pair of scissors.

Now for the tools, which I bring to class in a large, green, rusty tool box that my grandfather once owned. A metal hammer represents litigation. A rubber mallet (a little "softer" than the hammer, but not by much) represents arbitration. A cell phone, a credit card, a copy of the plastic box for tax preparation software, a TV remote control, and a disclosure brochure for a mutual fund all indicate typical situations in which consumers unknowingly enter arbitration agreements.

When describing the settlement conference scenario, I strike a house match to show how the judge "lights a fire" under the parties to get them moving towards settlement. Its sulfuric smell wafts through the classroom.

The legal neutral evaluation scene contains a trouble-light to indicate that the neutral will "shed light on the legal issues." It also includes a plumb bob that swings back and forth between the parties as the neutral evaluates which client is most likely to prevail on each legal issue at trial.

The neutral fact-finding tableau includes a magnifying glass and a folded wooden tape measure. These tools represent the objective analysis of factual data.

To represent facilitative mediation, I use gardening tools on the floral placemat. A small ceramic flower pot contains some soil. I add packages of flower seeds representing "hope," "doubt," and "agreement" that, with a little water from a small watering can and a little cultivation with a three-prong cultivator, yield a settlement, represented by a fabric flower.

To represent transformative mediation, I use a three-pound dumb bell and an old pair of wire-rimmed glasses. I do a bicep curl with the weight as I explain that mediators using this style of mediation hope that people experience "empowerment" by gaining greater self-respect, self-reliance, and self-confidence through the process. I peer through the pair of glasses while explaining that, by allowing each party the opportunity to acknowledge and to express concern for the other as a human being, this style of mediation meets its second goal of "recognition."

In solicited comments posted on the course TWEN site, students found the show "very helpful," "extremely beneficial," "quite effective," "fun and interesting," "a nice change," and "well-organized." More specifically, comments included the following:

- "It helped me visualize the scenarios, put them into action, and remember the roles of each toy."

- "The method made the material more exciting to learn rather than just showing the definitions on an overhead projector."
- "It seemed to hold the attention of the students throughout the entire class period."
- "[The consistent use of the same client figures and G.I. Joe attorneys throughout] helped me follow the illustrations."
- "I will always remember the match being lit."
- "When a large amount of material is being introduced that includes multiple sections, sub-sections, and to a degree, similar concepts, visual aids help me retain the information more quickly."

One student perceived a more subtle message I intended to convey: "Using the 'soldiers' to represent the attorneys [highlighted] their positions of strength in relation to the parties in binding processes. That coupled with the use of smaller toys to represent the parties showed the lack of process and outcome control of the parties in the binding processes."

Students with an aural learning style admitted that they found the props distracting, but adapted by focusing instead on the lecture. Some students thought the variety of props confused them, but these students did like my choice to post on the TWEN site photographs of each scenario with its description. Students who needed further review of the material then had easy access to it. Students with a verbal information absorption style liked the idea that I pass out a copy of this overview to supplement the class readings. In that way, they come to class with an orientation to the toys and tools. One student, a kinesthetic learner, wanted the opportunity to play with the tools and toys at the end of class.

One student reflected my own thinking in designing the prop-filled show: "We have lectures every day.... It's always a good thing to experience a new learning or presentation style."

Paula M. Young
Appalachian School of Law

Seeing Facts from More Than One Perspective: An In-Class Exercise

One difficulty law students and new lawyers face is seeing facts fully and using them creatively. Rather than recognizing potentially relevant facts and building their own narrative, they simply copy what we give them. Rather than seeing facts from more than one perspective, they appear to put blinders on.

A related problem we teachers have is helping our students "see" facts. One way that we do so is by increasing our expectations throughout the year. At the beginning of each year, for example, one might provide students with the facts in an assigning memorandum. Although one might provide more facts than the students need, or omit a few potentially relevant facts, the students find most of the facts they need to analyze in a single document. Later, perhaps, one provides fewer facts in the narrative description of an assignment but provides a handful of documents that contain facts material to the students' analysis. Finally, problems can be designed so that students must use "record" documents to derive the facts necessary for their analysis of the problem with very few of the facts summarized in the assigning memorandum.

Although these exercises build on one another to increase student autonomy in finding facts, many students still have difficulty approaching facts creatively. While students do possess excellent examples of how to use facts persuasively in their textbooks and in handouts, students often fail to recognize how limited their own perspective might be. To counter this problem, I recently engaged my second-semester legal writing students in an in-class exercise on seeing facts from more than one perspective.

Before class started, I created six virtually identical still lifes (various objects arranged as a set piece) from items I could easily obtain and placed them on desks around the room: One tennis ball, one pink and one blue highlighter, three small cedar balls, two clips, a drinking straw with accordion folds for bending, and a packet of gum. I positioned each still life on colored paper and arranged them so that the clips and small wooden balls were partially hidden by the tennis balls. I then divided the students into groups of two to four, with half of each group assigned to write a description of the still life in front of them with the other half assigned to observe and write a description of those students.

Before the exercise began, we discussed how lawyers must find facts and law and that it is the full and creative use of both that can make the difference in a case, whether that case is a transactional or litigation matter. I illustrated how surprise in the middle of negotiations or a deposition can be extremely unwelcome. We also discussed the use of intentional perspective in appellate briefs.

As I had expected, the descriptions of the still lifes varied enormously. Some of the descriptions consisted simply of lists: one yellow tennis ball; one blue highlighter; one pink highlighter; three brown wooden balls, and so on. Others went far deeper: one fuzzy yellow tennis ball, which has obviously been used; one flexible straw with narrow colored stripes, which has been bent so that part of it surrounds the ball; one pink highlighter with a metal clip; one packet of Dentyne Ice chewing gum, ADA approved, peppermint flavored, etc, all sitting on a green piece of construction paper

One student drew a picture of the still life, labeled each object, and wrote no other text; he just drew a question mark on the side. He explained that he was stumped by the relation of the objects to each other. He wanted to know why they were chosen, but did not go beyond identifying them.

Another student also looked for meaning in the choice of objects, although he also described their shapes and colors. Although I had chosen the objects more or less at random, he described them as being "collateral." He explained most of the objects were used in connection with work or recreation and had a utilitarian purpose; the tennis ball was used for play, the clips and highlighters were used for work, the straw for drinking. He was not sure about the cedar balls but thought that they were part of a game. The gum was used when "relaxing."

The descriptions of the students were similarly varied. Again, some students limited their descriptions to surface characteristics such as what the students were wearing, their hair color, whether they were tall or short, and other physical characteristics. Others described the students' expressions and body language and how they physically accomplished the task; whether they, for example, looked at the still life for a long time and then wrote notes or whether they quickly switched back and forth between looking at the still life and writing notes. Still others attempted to guess at what the students were thinking while they were observing the still lives.

The ensuing discussion demonstrated that the students recognized the differences in the individual approaches to the task. They recognized that some descriptions did not go beyond the surface, but that those that did were richer and more informative. They could "see" that seeing is a matter of perspective and that some perspectives were too limited to fully describe the facts. One student, perhaps reading my mind, said: "It seems that what people said depended on their perspective and their personality. There is more than one way to see something."

Exercise (adapted from VALERIE J. JANESICK, "STRETCHING" EXERCISES FOR QUALITATIVE RESEARCHERS, (2d ed. 2004)).

1. Concurrent Observations
   Five to eight Minutes
   - Observation of a Still Life

     Purpose: To observe and describe an assortment of objects on a table.

     Problem: To see these objects from your position at the table and room.

     Activity: In the time allotted, describe what you see on the table. Use descriptive terms and strive for accuracy.
   - Observation of a Person

     Purpose: To observe and describe a person sitting across from you. To note how individuals interact with each other and within their environment.

     Problem: To see someone as never before.

     Activity: In the time allotted, describe the person and describe the person's activities. How does the person you are observing approach the still-life observation?
2. Discussion and Self-Evaluation
   10 to 15 Minutes

   Discussion: What did you see?

   General Discussion: How did the individual descriptions of the objects differ? How did the individual descriptions of the people differ? How did the differences affect you as an observer?

   Self-evaluation: How did you approach this exercise? How is observing a person different from observing a thing? What did you learn about yourself as you described the person or objects you observed? What might you want to do differently? How did the discussion affect your self-evaluation of your observation skills?

Instructor: Link the discussion to the problem of "seeing" facts in cases and in building arguments.

Aïda Alaka
Washburn University School of Law

Teaching Persuasion and Critical Thinking Using the State of the Union Address

Like many law professors, I like to encourage my first-year students to be politically aware and engaged. I also want them to develop their critical thinking skills. In addition, as a legal writing professor, every spring it is my job to teach them the art of persuasive writing. I use the President's State of the Union Address as a teaching tool to do all three.

I tell my students that the State of the Union Address is an advocacy piece, and not simply an objective report on the state of the nation. The United States Constitution provides that the President "shall from time to time give to the Congress Information of the State of the Union, *and recommend to their Consideration such Measures as he shall judge necessary and expedient....*" In keeping with the nature of the speech, the President and his speechwriters use a multitude of persuasive writing techniques to convince Congress and the American people to support the President's agenda for the country.

For my first class assignment in the spring semester, I ask my students to watch the televised State of the Union Address. If they can't watch or record the speech, I ask them to read the transcript the next day in the newspaper or online. As they watch or read the speech, students must make a list of the persuasive writing techniques they recognize. These could be phrases intended to trigger certain emotions and historical comparisons (such as the "Axis of Evil"), rhythmic devices in speech (rhyme or repetition, short, staccato phrases, or other such devices affecting how the speech sounds), the order in which topics are discussed, or any other technique they think the President uses to make his case.

When we meet, I ask the students to list the persuasive techniques they found, and we review some of the examples on video. Then we evaluate whether each technique "worked." Did the President go too far or just far enough in his attempts at persuasion?

We discuss the use and effectiveness of persuasive writing techniques ranging from large-scale organization and sentence structure, metaphor and analogy, to rhythm and diction. The students recognize for themselves that there is room for creativity in persuasive writing, but that it is also possible to overdo it. They see that there are legitimate (and not so legitimate) ways to shade the facts in order to lead your audience to the conclusion you want. They get excited about learning and practicing the art of persuasive writing.

In addition, the exercise pushes students to think critically about the political issues of the day. First, they have to watch the State of the Union Address itself, which experience tells me many would not otherwise do. By analyzing the use of language in the speech, students begin to reflect on the political issues, objectives, strengths, and vulnerabilities the chosen language serves. More broadly, the students develop and exercise their ability to delve beyond sound bites, hyperlinks, and headlines in their thinking.

Claire C. Robinson May
Cleveland–Marshall College of Law

Chapter 3

Teaching with Technology

Depending on the speaker or author, technology is either the bane of law professors' existence or the savior of legal education. To some, technology is the only way to reach millennial learners; to others, the use of technology in teaching is another way law teachers kowtow to modern students' sense of entitlement.

We are more agnostic about teaching technology. To us, teaching technology is like any other teaching tool or idea. If a technology produces greater learning, if it better facilitates accomplishment of our learning objectives, it is good. Likewise, if an available alternative to technology would produce greater learning, that alternative is superior.

This short introduction addresses the factors law teachers should weigh in evaluating whether to adopt a technology and the best practices for using technology in teaching. The discussion concludes with an attempt at an alphabetical list of currently-available teaching technologies and their uses.

A. Factors to Weigh in Deciding Whether and How Much to Use Technology

The factors to weigh in deciding whether to integrate technology in teaching include: (1) the teacher's learning goals; (2) the potential benefits and trade-offs of using the technology; (3) other teaching and learning factors; and (4) practical considerations, such as ease of use, reliability, cost, and availability of technical support.

Learning Goals

As is true of making any other decision relating to teaching methods, good decision-making about the use of technology in teaching starts with the law teacher's learning goals. Higher education professors often make the mistake of starting with the technology (I want to use a video in my class) rather than starting with the goal (I want to engage my students or I want my students to understand the practical implications of this concept). Starting with the goal allows teachers to make focused choices about whether and to what extent technology can benefit their students; starting with the technology risks converting the exercise to show-and-tell.

Potential Benefits and Trade-offs of Using Technology

Using technology has many benefits, including engaging students in active learning; bringing authenticity, surprise, fun, and variety to the classroom experience; manifesting teachers' passion for students' learning; creating efficiencies, particularly in the area of formative assessment; and allowing teachers to reserve live classroom time for learning activities for which a live teacher's presence is necessary.

Generally speaking, teaching technologies engage students in active learning (e.g. analyzing, thinking, hypothesizing), facilitating greater learning than technologies that position students as passive recipients of information. For example, engaging students in creating their own Wiki for a course in which they create knowledge about the field involves active learning and sense-making. Similarly, creating a course discussion board on a course webpage and establishing expectations for student contributions can encourage students to ask and answer questions, share materials and ideas, pose and answer hypotheticals, question policy and theory, and otherwise actively engage the material. On the other hand, some law teachers use PowerPoint in the classroom merely to transmit large quantities of information, leaving their students to devote classroom time to copying bullet points from slides. Others show videos that do little more than illustrate concepts.

Teaching technologies also can facilitate student learning by bringing authenticity, surprise, variety, and fun to the classroom. A video of an interview or a video call with an attorney involved in a case the students have read or who has handled similar issues in practice can convert a staid, abstract discussion into an authentic, client-centered interaction. A hyperlink to materials from an ongoing dispute, such as the recent contract dispute between Conan O'Brien and NBC, can afford students insight into the practical implications of what they are learning and engage them in authentic problem-solving and analysis. Similarly, a video of a trial can be stopped and started to allow students to make objections and predict strategy. On the other hand, videos can provide little more than entertainment and may require the teacher to sacrifice other, more active and engaging classroom activities, such as cooperative problem-solving activities.

Another benefit of teaching technologies can be efficiency. Course webpage tools often include a capacity for making announcements about assignments, class session postponements, and additional learning resources, and almost all include resources that allow teachers to email one, some, or all their students. Most word-processing tools allow teachers to embed comments in student work-products, allowing teachers to pinpoint their feedback, speed their commenting process by using macros for commonly-made professorial feedback, and avoid student frustration with poor professor handwriting. Course webpage discussion boards allow teachers to identify and remediate student confusion about basic points and reserve classroom time for more optimal uses of a live professor. Similarly, podcasts and video recorded lectures allow teachers to move instruction focused on mere transmittal of information outside the classroom to reserve instructional time for higher-order learning goals. On the other hand, technical difficulties can waste classroom time.

A particularly significant use of technology is as a mechanism for providing students with formative assessment in ways that minimize the burden on the professor. Classroom responder units, also known as clickers, provide both students and the teacher with nearly instantaneous information about student learning. Online multiple-choice and short answer quizzes can help students identify gaps in their understanding and can be set up so that students receive guidance in their efforts to rectify those gaps. A particularly useful tool, developed by a UCLA undergraduate professor, allows teachers to implement a program of peer feedback with minimal teacher input; known as Calibrated Peer Review, this online tool initially guides each student through a process of evaluating a good paper, a mediocre paper, and a poor paper. When the student masters evaluating the sample papers, the software sends the student a peer's paper to evaluate. The students learn both through the process of learning how to evaluate the sample papers and from their peer's feedback. However, classroom responder units and multiple-choice tests, for example, can send unintended messages to students about what they should be learning. By focusing on "right" answers and not on arguments and articulating ideas, these tools may communicate to some students that they should focus on acquiring knowledge and not on developing skills.

In addition to the benefits of teaching technologies identified above, teaching technologies can have secondary benefits: their use can communicate to students that the professor cares passionately about their learning. The professor's evident effort in creating the learning tools communicates her commitment to the students.

Other Teaching and Learning Factors

Instructional designers would add another wrinkle to the analysis. Instructional designers, recognizing that live teachers are the single most expensive teaching resource available, emphasize the importance of using classroom time for the learning activities for which a live teacher is essential and relegating to outside the classroom those learning activities that can be accomplished without the teacher's physical presence. Technology can accomplish many learning goals outside the classroom. For example, CALI lessons are designed to adapt to students' progress in learning; students who demonstrate mastery move on to the next instructional unit whereas students who struggle continue to do practice problems in the area until they, too, demonstrate mastery. More generally, live teachers may not always be necessary to explain the analysis of multiple-choice questions or to transmit information; technology can accomplish both goals quite effectively. Of course, the flip side of this principle is that, in many instances, students would learn just as much from watching videos outside the classroom as they would from using up classroom time on videos.

Practical Considerations

Four practical considerations: reliability, cost, ease of use, and availability of technical support, are also worth weighing. While tools such as PowerPoint and course webpages have become almost ubiquitous such that it is probably safe to assume they will work nearly all the time, websites go down and projection units burn out. For other technologies, the risk may be greater and worth assessing. Cost is a relevant factor as each choice to purchase a technology precludes alternative purchases. Finally, ease of use and availability of technical support should be measured inversely; the easier a technology is to use, the less likely you are to need technical support so the availability becomes a less significant factor. Nevertheless, each of the editors of this book has used technology in our teaching, and each of us has had an otherwise reliable technology fail in a way we could not fix on our own. Without technical support, we would have been in trouble.

B. Best Practices for Use of Technology

The process of using technology in teaching is best done cyclically: identify a learning goal for which technology may help, consider the student experience of the possible technological option and set up and practice using the technology, implement the technology and have a back-up plan, and, perhaps most importantly, evaluate the effectiveness of the technology in accomplishing your goal and plan how to do even better the next time.

Identify a Learning Goal for Which Technology May Help

Optimal use of technology starts with a learning goal or set of goals. Start by completing the following sentence: By the end of this class session (lesson), my students will know ______________________, be able to ______________________, and/or value ______________________. Using the discussion of benefits and drawbacks above and the available technologies chart below, brainstorm technology possibilities that might help you accomplish your goal. For example, if your goal were to have your students apply and distinguish the line of Supreme Court personal jurisdiction cases, you might choose online multiple-choice questions to make sure your students accurately know and understand the basics of the doctrine and Calibrated Peer Review as a mechanism for providing meaningful practice and feedback in connection with a hypothetical.

Consider the Student Perspective and Set-up and Practice Using the Technology

For any technology, whether you are using a computer projection, a movie clip, a website, or even a black or white board, the key is whether all students can "read" the visual. For classroom visual technologies, check out the sight lines from all points in the room. Do students have to crane their necks to read a PowerPoint slide? Can students decipher your handwriting on a board? Is a screen large enough that students can accurately read and interpret the content? For videos with sound, make sure students can hear the video from any spot in the room. For webpages, make sure the navigation of the webpage is either self-evident or is explained clearly. If students need training to use the technology, determine how they will get that training and weigh whether the training time is worth the learning benefits.

Make sure you set-up the technology far in advance of the start of class and practice using it. Nothing is more frustrating, to both you and your students, than using class time to get the technology up and running. For example, if you are using a Classroom Responder Unit, make sure you sign in a few of the student devices and try out a few questions. It also is helpful to use a research assistant to test drive course webpage discussion boards, multiple-choice and short answer quizzes, and other tools.

Have a Back-up Plan

No matter how confident you are in the technology, always have a back-up plan. Technology sometimes fails. This possibility doesn't dissuade us from using technology; it just helps us make sure we have an alternative way to accomplish our learning goals. If you will be using PowerPoint slides, print them out so you can ad-lib on the spot if the projection unit goes down. If you have created a course webpage, make sure your students know whom to contact if they have trouble registering for or accessing the webpage. If you plan to use a Classroom Responder Unit, bring blank paper to class on which students can write their selections if a problem arises with the device.

Evaluate the Effectiveness of the Technology and Plan Future Uses

No matter how well you think things went, it is important to evaluate how things went—especially when you have used a new teaching technology—and plan how you can use the technology to even greater advantage the next time. You may want to even consider a second technology, such as SurveyMonkey, an online survey tool, to get your students' input into their experience of the technology you have adopted. In a short SurveyMonkey survey, you can ask students to rate their enjoyment of the experience and the degree to which the technology facilitated their learning, and you can ask them for input into how their experience might be improved. You might end up developing data you can use in an article such as one of the excellent essays on using technology in teaching that follow the chart below.

List of Possible Technologies and Their Potential Uses

Technology	Potential Uses
Blogs	Students create content during or after class
CALI	Provide practice and feedback
Calibrated Peer Review: http://cpr.molsci.ucla.edu/	Web software that trains students to provide meaningful peer feedback
Clickers or Classroom Response Units	Assessment
Course Webpages	
Cooperative learning group pages	Create group webpages to facilitate group communication and projects
Communication	Email and announcements
Content delivery webspace	Deliver handouts, tests, podcasts, PowerPoint slides, etc.
Discussions Boards	Facilitate peer teaching, share resources, expand discussion beyond classroom
Live Classroom	Online class session or supplement in-person class session
Testing Tools	Multiple-choice & short answer quizzes with ability to build in learning help
Survey Software	Implement student autonomy by providing students input into course design, teaching methods, and teacher evaluation
Document cameras	Share pleadings, contracts, statutes
Electronic casebooks	Build in links within book and to other resources and information
Electronic commenting	Speed commenting process by creating macros or by recording feedback
Games or Simulation software	Web-based or computer simulations
Internet	Find resources, background information
Podcasts	Deliver content
PowerPoint and Other Presentation Software	Communicate hypotheticals, visual aids, and content
Videos and Video Phone Calls	Illustrate concepts, bring authenticity, or create varied form of hypos
Wikis	Facilitate student creation of content

References

- Paul F. Caron & Rafael Gely, *Taking Back the Law School Classroom: Using Technology to Foster Active Student Learning*, 54 J. Legal Educ. 551 (2004).

- Steven Friedland & Gerald F. Hess, Teaching the Law School Curriculum (2004).
- Gerald F. Hess & Steven I. Friedland, Techniques for Teaching Law (1999).
- Michael Hunter Schwartz, Sophie Sparrow & Gerald F. Hess, Teaching Law By Design: Engaging Students From the Syllabus to the Final Exam (2009).
- Patricia L. Smith & Tillman J. Ragan, Instructional Design (3d ed. 2005).
- David I. C. Thomson, Law School 2.0: Legal Education for a Digital Age (2009).

The Novice's Guide to Teaching with Technology

The pervasiveness of computers and their related technologies makes it hard to avoid wondering if perhaps all professors should be using some technology in the classroom. For many, the mere thought of trying to understand the digital lexicon is enough to make them abandon the idea. Computer professionals and technology support staff frequently speak in a foreign language called "computerese." Terms such as RAM, firewall, adware, bugs, WAV, MP3, USB, among others, seem to be liberally sprinkled into conversations.

Nevertheless, neither a detailed understanding of such terms nor an understanding of how computers operate is necessary to utilize technology in the classroom. This article will provide a justification for incorporating technology into law teaching and suggest some uses of technology that can be adopted without a great degree of technological know-how or access to expensive hardware or software.

A. Why Use Technology?

The current generation of students appears to have been born with a cell phone in one hand, a laptop in the other, and an iPod attached to their ears. Additionally, an increasing number of law students use laptops in class. Consequently, students often expect their instructors to incorporate technology into the teaching environment. Because students are often viewed as "consumers" and customer satisfaction is the life-blood of any enterprise, it could be argued that technology utilization is expected and required to satisfy student expectations.

In addition, there is a strong temptation to use technology simply because it is there. Many law schools have installed computer ports at every seat (or have wireless access) and have the capacity to employ PowerPoint in classrooms. The very existence of this technology can create subtle pressure to use it.

While the ubiquitous nature of technology and student expectations might first draw us to explore its use, any new teaching methodology should be adopted only after evaluating how it will enhance the effectiveness of teaching.

There are numerous pedagogical reasons for teaching with technology. First, if properly used, technology can enhance the learning environment. Traditional law school classrooms are oriented toward auditory learning. Questions and hypotheticals are posed by the professor, and students must listen and then orally respond. Classmates must pay careful attention to exchanges between the professor and other students. However, many students learn primarily by nonauditory means such as visually or tactilely. Technology can level the playing field for these students and thereby enhance the learning environment.

Technology can also extend learning beyond the classroom and provide both faculty and students with more flexible communication. Though one-on-one interaction is still the best learning environment, both students and faculty are increasingly busy. Students often have work and other commitments competing with legal studies. Technology can be used to interact with students remotely. Even though such interaction is less than ideal, in many cases the alternative is minimal or no interaction. For faculty members, technology can improve efficiency, which is increasingly important in order to meet the numerous demands on time created by teaching, scholarship, and committee work.

Finally, law schools are professional schools that prepare their students to enter the legal profession. Today, that profession demands the use of computers for increased efficiency and productivity. Also, many clients utilize email for communicating with outside parties, including attorneys. Hence, student exposure to and use of technology in law school prepares them for the digital environment they will encounter in practice.

B. Equipment Needs — The Basics

The amount of technology available varies among law schools. However, despite disparities in installed technology, virtually all law schools provide faculty members with a computer on their desk, Internet access, and email. These simple tools are adequate to engage in substantial use of technology.

C. Email

Creating an email list of all class members is a quick way to contact the class regarding notices of class cancellations, changes in assignments, etc. It can also be used to inform the class about recent news items or cases relevant to material discussed in class. Such information has great educational value because it enables students to see that legal rules and issues discussed in class have real world, contemporary applications.

One pitfall I have discovered is that, in my zeal to provide students with additional material, I have sometimes overwhelmed them by sending too much. This choice can increase the stress already felt by law students, and is clearly counterproductive. An effective solution is to divide email messages sent to the class into two categories: messages they should read; and messages I call "enrichment" messages (which means students might find them interesting but it's not critical that they read them). All messages which fall into the second category, including newspaper articles, contain the letters "FYI" in the subject line. I tell students at the beginning of the semester that any email with "FYI" in the subject line is optional and can be deleted without reading it. I have not had any complaints about too much email since adopting this approach, and I know some students are reading the optional emails because I get questions about them.

D. Discussion Boards

Discussion boards can also provide a structured repository for questions, answers, and miscellaneous information posted during the semester. I have found it useful to create a different discussion board for each doctrinal topic covered. This approach makes it easy for students to review prior posts since they merely have to go to the appropriate discussion board rather than scroll through all the messages.

The student feedback discussion board allows students to air complaints about the class, law school, etc. It also provides a forum for making suggestions. Generally, I have found this board useful—it makes me aware of issues in the class that I might not otherwise know about. Additionally, students have, on occasion, made constructive suggestions that I have adopted. On several occasions, these posts allowed students to resolve perceived class problems without my intervention. Overall, the level of posts has been very professional.

E. PowerPoint: A Killer Application, or a Way to "Kill" Student Interaction?

Despite being a long-time technology user, I tried using PowerPoint in class only a few years ago. I have found PowerPoint to be an incredibly useful pedagogical tool if used correctly.

1. Reasons to Use PowerPoint

It is imperative that PowerPoint only be used if it has a clear pedagogical purpose. PowerPoint cannot be a substitute for teaching. Nor can the adoption of PowerPoint as a teaching tool enhance teaching unless careful thought goes into identifying the specific teaching goal you are trying to achieve.

I use PowerPoint to supplement classroom teaching. For example, when covering a problem in class I will state the problem to the class while it is projected on a PowerPoint slide. This approach makes it easier for students with various learning styles to participate. Students who are auditory learners simply listen to my statement of the problem. Students who are visual learners can read the problem on the slide. I also try to make the slides available prior to class for students who want to read and think carefully about the problem in advance (admittedly, this group usually represents a small proportion of the students in the class). I also leave the slide showing the problem up during the entire exchange, which allows students to refer to the problem during discussion, rather than working from memory.

Whenever possible, I provide a graphic or picture illustration of the problem. Other problems are more appropriately illustrated by a time-line which shows the relevant actions and accompanying dates. Such graphics or timelines allow students to work through the problem at a higher level because the relevant information can be seen throughout the entire classroom discussion. Such graphics, pictures, and time-lines can similarly be used as a backdrop when discussing an assigned case.

When I discuss a statute I will often project it on a PowerPoint slide rather than asking the students to look at the statute in their casebook or statutory supplement. I have found this to be a more efficient approach. It avoids typical student comments such as "I forgot to bring my statutory supplement," or "what was that statutory number again?" Additionally, it forces students to look up at the slide, which means they can't engage in the time-honored behavior of staring at the book and hoping they won't be called on. Instead, if they are looking up it is easier to make eye contact, which facilitates increased involvement.

2. Some General Rules for Using PowerPoint

When discussion deviates from what is being shown in a PowerPoint presentation, or if you want to draw student attention away from the slides, a great shortcut is to press the "B" key on the computer keyboard. This key instantly suspends projection of the slides, leaving a blank screen. Pressing the "B" key a second time instantly turns PowerPoint projection back on.

F. Using Audio Files

Audio files are the newest technology I use. On a limited basis, I make digital audio recordings of class for students who are absent due to illness or some other pressing reason. I also have made short digital audio files for specific topics including hints on how to study, how to brief cases, and how to take a law school exam. I have also recorded detailed answers or explanations for assigned problem sets and recorded optional review classes at the end of the semester. Using audio files can significantly improve efficiency for the teacher and for the students. For example, finding a time that works for both the teacher and all students to attend optional classes such as review classes is often difficult. Students have increasingly busy lives, often including work and family responsibilities. Hence, audio recorded once and reused for subsequent semesters frees up time for faculty members to engage in other activities.

The creation, use, distribution, and management of audio files can be done with minimal equipment. Some schools have built-in hardware and also have technical staff to make digital audio files available on demand in the classroom. CALI also has a service which will allow a professor to record a class via an ordinary telephone. CALI will then make that file available to students via a blog.

Once an audio file is created and transferred to your computer, two issues remain. First, how do you make it available to students; and second, what audio format should the file be in to minimize student problems downloading and listening to the files? If your school has unlimited technology funds you should have them purchase a streaming server which can be used to handle audio files. However, if your school is located in the real world of limited funds, you can upload the audio file to course management software (such as TWEN or Blackboard), discussed below. Once uploaded to TWEN or Blackboard, students have access to the audio file 24/7 from virtually any location in the world with Internet access. Audio files tend to be large so I usually recommend that students download the file and listen to it after it is downloaded. Students can also download the file in the school's computer lab onto a small keychain drive or burn it to a CD.

Numerous types of audio file formats exist. Some have no compression, resulting in extremely large files. Others have differing amounts of compression and varying sound quality. From a practical perspective, it is important to use an audio file format that is sufficiently common that most students will be able to handle it without having to worry about adequate hard drive space and file conversion issues. Currently I use the MP3 audio file format, which uses compression to reduce file size. This same format is commonly used for music downloaded from the Internet, and most computers purchased within the last few years include software that will automatically recognize and play an MP3 file.

G. Course Management Software

In the past, I have utilized my own website to provide the course management software function to my students. Building and using your own website allows you to customize the site to satisfy your own idiosyncrasies. However, it requires learning HTML among other things. Frankly, I do not believe it is worth the time and effort involved.

I have experimented with both TWEN and the Lexis-Nexis version of Blackboard. Despite advertising hype, both provide similar features and have good technical support. Both also allow you to set up a site for each course you teach. They each provide the ability to use class email lists, discussion boards, and upload all types of files for student use. Finally, and perhaps most importantly, both services assign each law school a representative who can answer questions and assist you in using either TWEN or Blackboard. Your law librarian can put you in touch with the appropriate representative.

Although each program is quite flexible and contains numerous options, I have a few suggestions which apply equally to both. If you aren't running a local program that is integrated with the registrar's computer system, I have found that allowing students to register themselves with either TWEN or Blackboard causes the least trouble. Additionally, both programs include a notification function which should be activated. This function automatically sends an email to students whenever something new is posted by the professor and when students post to a discussion board. Finally, although both systems allow you to upload files in virtually any format, you will have the fewest problems if you convert all files to PDF format and then upload them in that format. PDF is basically a graphic version of a document. Hence, it will look the same when viewed on any computer system.

Conclusion

Venturing into the world of teaching with technology can be accomplished in most schools without the purchase of expensive computer equipment and software. Properly used, technology can enhance student learning and make better use of both students' and faculty members' time. Additionally, technology has become ubiquitous in the modern practice of law so acclimating students to its use facilitates their preparation for entering the practice of law upon graduation.

Andrew Beckerman-Rodau
Suffolk University Law School

Using TWEN to Reach Evening Students

I have taught courses in the part-time evening divisions of St. John's University School of Law, Texas Wesleyan University School of Law, Brooklyn Law School, and Stetson University College of Law. Part-time students are a pleasure to teach in many respects. Most exhibit a tremendous dedication to their studies, particularly because many also work full-time jobs and have families. Yet teaching this group of students presents some unique challenges for the professor because the students' chaotic and busy schedules can impair communication. They often study at times—weekends or late at night, for example—when I am not available in my office to answer questions. Students may also live or work far from the physical law school building, so getting access to the library or to my office may be challenging. This article discusses my use of The West Education Network (TWEN), a free, electronic service of West and Westlaw, to better communicate with my part-time, evening students.

TWEN is an online meeting space where students and faculty in a course can exchange documents, engage in live chats, respond to one another's posts in discussion forums, take quizzes, and link to live research and news on Westlaw. A similar product is offered by LexisNexis and uses the Blackboard system. Other universities have a site license for Blackboard as a standalone product. Many of the features of TWEN that I will discuss here are also available on Blackboard.

When I create a course on TWEN, I typically begin by adding several discussion forums. These allow students or me to post messages, much like placing notes on a bulletin board. Participants can read and respond to these notes on their own time. This form of communication is "asynchronous" because the poster and the reader do not need to be online at the same time—an advantage for evening students given their hectic schedules. Unless deleted by the course administrator (me), posts are permanent. A user can go back and reference earlier announcements or posts without having to sort through his or her email. The discussion forums that I typically create are:

- Course Announcements. Here I post administrative announcements, such as class cancellations or changes to a reading assignment.
- Ask the Prof. This is a place for students to ask me or their classmates questions. TWEN has a feature that allows users to post anonymously to forums. I turn on this feature for this forum to allow students to ask the proverbial "dumb" question without fear of embarrassment. Often, I find that students will answer each other's questions before I get a chance to. Questions also lead to further debate or discussion about a topic.
- Additional Class Discussion. I teach Criminal Law, a hot-button topic that frequently generates lively class discussion. I encourage students to use this forum to continue the discussions we have in class. Because TWEN is seamlessly linked to Westlaw, users can link to judicial decisions or news articles. The forums are threaded, which means that all of the posts on a given topic can be grouped together for easy viewing.

The discussion forums are particularly suited for evening students because they allow students to communicate with me and with each other at any time or any place they have access to a computer and the Internet. They need not worry about catching me during office hours, because I can answer an online question at any time of the day or night. An advantage over regular email is that students can see questions their classmates have asked and what my responses were. (Obviously I also make myself available via phone, email, and office hours for students who prefer to talk privately.)

TWEN also has a synchronous communication feature that is similar to a "chat room." To use the chat room, all participants must be online at the same time. I have used this feature to meet with study groups during their lunch hours or on the weekends. Each user can log on from the convenience of their home or workplace.

I also create a number of "document pages." These are repositories or folders for files of any imaginable type—Word documents, PowerPoint presentations, Excel spreadsheets, or even audio or video. My part-time students have reacted favorably to receiving handouts in electronic form; this resource allows them to access the files during their lunch break, at home, or on the weekend. I likewise group these pages by category:

- Syllabus. This allows for easy downloading before the first day of class. I require students to register for TWEN by telling them that this is where they will find the syllabus, which in turn has the reading assignment for the first day of class.
- Class Handouts.
- PowerPoint Slides.
- Old Exams. I have my old exams scanned into PDF form. Students can view these at their leisure, without worrying about when the library is open.

The quiz feature can be educationally beneficial, although quizzes can be time-consuming to create. A professor can create a quiz that consists of multiple-choice questions. I typically post a quiz for each major subject we cover in class, although I do not count the results towards students' final grades. I do have the ability to see their results, although students cannot see how each other did. I can also track how the class as a whole has done on particular questions. The quizzes are time-consuming to create initially, although the interface is fairly easy to use. Once created, quizzes can be saved for use in future semesters by "copying" the entire course to a new semester.

The "Assignment Drop Box" feature has also been helpful to part-time students. In lieu of coming to the law school to submit a paper or other assignment, they can submit it online. I can grade the submissions (anonymously if I select that option) and submit written feedback, and students can retrieve the comments and grades, all online. This tool has an advantage over manual email submissions because TWEN keeps all of the submissions in one place. You do not have to wade in your inbox through listserv postings, blog updates, and spam to find a student's rough draft. TWEN can even calculate a student's final grade, if you tell it how much weight (e.g., 20%) to give to a particular assignment and grade. Alternatively, grades can be downloaded into a spreadsheet such as Excel.

Tied in with the Assignment Drop Box is the Calendar feature, which allows the administrator to post due dates, reading assignments, and set email reminders. If you would like to set up individual, in-person meeting times, the "Sign-up Sheet" function is particularly useful. You set the available dates and times, and students can sign-up for slots online. Once a slot is filled, other students cannot sign up for that time.

Instead of relying on the law school's listserv to send a mass email to students in a course, I use TWEN's email feature. It automatically generates a delivery receipt, a copy of which is delivered to the sender's (my) email box.

If you use any of the CALI lessons, you can link to relevant ones directly from TWEN. There is also a forum to add your own links to relevant sites. In my case, I typically provide links to criminal law-related blogs and agency websites.

Recent additions to TWEN include a wiki feature, which allows for online, collaborative writing; CiteStation exercises for Bluebook practice; and advanced features in anonymous grading and Honor Code certification management.

TWEN is fully customizable, easy-to-use, and supported by Westlaw's technical assistance department. I have used West's technical support several times and my questions were answered quickly. On the user end, students have told me that TWEN and Blackboard are all easy to use. While TWEN and services like it cannot be a complete substitute for face-to-face interaction, each can serve as a useful supplement, particularly when teaching a class with busy professionals who are going to school part-time.

For further information:

- http://lawschool.westlaw.com/twen/
- http://www.lexisnexis.com/lawschool/webcourses/
- http://www.blackboard.com/

Larry Cunningham
St. John's University School of Law

The "Live Write"—An Alternative Approach to the Scribe and PowerPoint Pit

Computers in the classroom scare me.

No matter how many experts extol the virtues of incorporating technology into the 21st century law school classroom, I confess that my mind tends to go in two directions when I think of computers in the classroom. And neither path is perfect.

On one hand I imagine students aimlessly pecking away on laptops, either working assiduously as the eternal scribe or, worse, taking breaks to ride the waves of cyberspace.

On the other hand I see the image of the PowerPoint Pit, where even those of us with the best intentions can inadvertently lull students into a state of passivity through the overuse of PowerPoint slides. This format is so efficient at conveying information that it essentially squeezes all of the "Soc" out of the Socratic Method.

With so many computers in so many hands, do the benefits of bringing computers into the learning environment truly offset the costs?

As a professor at a law school proud of its extensive use of computers in the classroom, I am constantly challenged to effectively integrate technology. My goal is to explore innovative methods to help students incorporate computers into the classroom and boost the analytical process.

One method I've employed with success is the use of what I dub the "live write." Utilizing a Smart Podium and projector, I have used technology to facilitate an active classroom environment. By using the "live write" process, I am able to take advantage of the technology available in my classroom while maintaining the involvement needed on both sides of the podium.

Before class, I turn on the Smart Podium, activate the screen, and open a word processing program. As the class progresses, I ask the students to formulate a sentence. In my doctrinal class, it may be the students' best effort at articulating a rule of law. In my writing class, it may be an attempt at a thesis sentence or part of a synthesized rule. Once the students are given time to write a near-perfect sentence on their own, I take the next step: I call on someone.

This student, usually a volunteer or a student "gently encouraged" by me, is prompted to read to the class what he or she has just written. As the student reads, I type the student's response into the computer on the podium, projecting the sentence onto the screen at the front of the room for all to see. Next, I ask other students whether the sentence can be improved. I then incorporate editing suggestions. Highlighting and other formatting changes allow me to make immediate improvements. Finally, I go back to the original student to ask what he or she thinks of the editing suggestions, and I incorporate those comments on to the screen as well. The result is usually a good sentence produced through group effort.

Although the risk of technical problems looms whenever a lesson relies on technology, this threat is easily addressed through the use of the whiteboard as back up. Further, the benefits of the "live write" method readily outweigh any risks.

The "live write" method encourages students to be risk-takers, and it contributes to the community of learners by allowing students to feed on the collaborative energy of their peers. Further, it serves as a formative assessment by allowing the instructor to get a quick snapshot of student progress and make immediate adjustments in material coverage. The "live write" method has clear advantages over the whiteboard or overhead: responses can be displayed all at once, or flipped back and forth, or juxtaposed in myriad combinations. Additionally, the results can be saved and distributed electronically for subsequent review. Finally, allowing students to see their work take shape on the screen encourages students to be active learners and discourages the instructor from falling into lecture mode. We are all involved, and we are all making good use of the computers in the classroom.

In the constant struggle to challenge and engage students, I believe my classes have benefited from the "live write." And I've learned that computers in the classroom don't have to be so scary after all.

Olympia Duhart
Nova Southeastern University, Shepard Broad Law Center

The Use of Clickers in the Law School Classroom

In the past several years, much has been written about the positive impact of integrating technology into teaching. The dilemma is how to incorporate technology in a way that is consistent with a law professor's teaching style and with his/her technological skills, and at the same time enhance student learning.

During the spring semester of 2007, one of the veteran professors at my law school, Daniel Moriarty, experimented with the use of "clickers" as part of teaching his 1L Criminal law class.

Professor Moriarty's teaching style is Socratic. Normally his students read the assigned material and respond to questions in class. Professor Moriarty explains difficult or complicated concepts and introduces new ideas.

One of the problems with Socratic teaching is that only a limited number of students can actively participate during a given class. A professor talks to a single student at a time. In principle, all the students should be trying to answer the professor's questions even when the questions are not addressed to them, but there is no way to know for sure that they are doing so without calling on them. Consequently, with a class of almost 70 students, a majority of the students (especially the shy ones) will remain unnoticed.

A laptop with wireless Internet access in front of each student poses an additional distraction. Even if the students are not checking their email or surfing the web and are actually using their computer to take class notes, they are not interacting with the professor or with each other.

The use of "clickers" has the ability to overcome these obstacles. It allows more students to actively participate during class and gives the professor the opportunity to evaluate all the students' comprehension of the material. The clickers also engage the students and focus their attention since they all must respond to each question.

Several of the professors at Albany Law School used *eInstruction*'s Classroom Performance System (referred to as "clickers" or CPS). At the end of the semester, the students in these classes responded to a survey and gave very favorable feedback regarding the use of the CPS system. One student commented: "It has enhanced my learning. The questions are used to guide us along and I think the professor does a great job of forming them, and making them work with our class. Since we started using them I really feel as though I'm learning a lot more." Another stated: "It encourages participation where one might otherwise be too shy or hesitant to stick their neck out in front of the entire class. By actually participating and committing to an answer I can see how well I actually know the material compared to how well I think I know it. Plus, it's a good gauge for me to see how well I understand the material compared to other people in the class." A third replied: "I hope that the school sticks with it and encourages more professors to use it."

Most of the professors who used the clicker system first semester also use PowerPoint on a regular basis as part of their teaching and are fairly comfortable with technology. Professor Moriarty, however, did not fit this description. He is adept at uploading documents to his TWEN (The Westlaw Education Network) website for his students. But in the classroom, his technology use was minimal. I am the Instructional Technologist at the law school and was confident that we could find a way to use the clicker system in Professor Moriarty's Criminal Law class.

We abandoned the idea of using *eInstruction*'s CPS with PowerPoint (which had worked for the other professors) and decided to have Professor Moriarty upload multiple-choice or True/False questions for each class to his TWEN site and assign them to students for homework. I set up his Criminal Law class in CPSOnline and on his laptop. Professor Moriarty only had to learn how to connect his laptop to the LCD projector and to start up the CPS system on his laptop at the beginning of each class.

To make sure that the students took the CPS experience seriously, Professor Moriarty announced to the Criminal Law class that the number of correct answers that each student recorded would be totaled and at the end of the semester, this score would count for 10% of each student's grade.

Professor Moriarty began most of his classes by having the students use the "clickers" to record their responses to the questions (on the TWEN site) that they had answered for homework. Professor Moriarty would then project on the screen a graphical representation of the class' responses and indicate the correct answer (See Figure 1 on the next page). A discussion ensued following each question and answer.

When Professor Moriarty started using the clickers, I was present in his classroom to make sure there were no technical glitches. My physical presence evolved into merely providing moral support. After several months, I didn't need to be in the classroom at all and was there often as a casual observer of the process.

The CPS system encouraged more class discussion, prodding even shy students to get involved as responses were debated. Another advantage of this technology is how it allows the professor to assess his own teaching. The report below shows that 88% of the students got question one correct, 73% question two, and 75% question three. Looking at this data, a professor is able to quickly correct any misconceptions that students may have (see Figure 2 on the next page).

The CPS reports also enable the professor to keep tabs on individual students' daily progress (see Figure 3 on the next page). A student who consistently receives low scores is either not doing the reading or is having difficulty with the material. The latter can then be corrected through remediation before the student fails an exam.

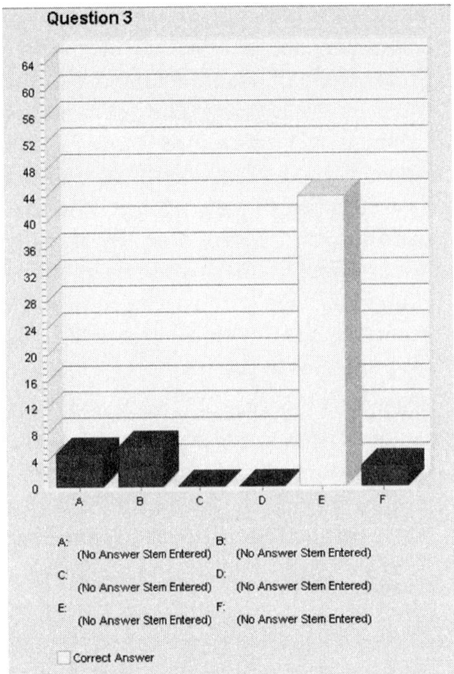

Figure 1

Class: Criminal Law

Class Points Avg: 2.36 out of 3.00 (78.53%)

(Includes only students who took assessment)

1	(No Question Stem Entered)	
☞ A	88%	(No Answer Stem Entered)
B	0%	(No Answer Stem Entered)
C	7%	(No Answer Stem Entered)
D	3%	(No Answer Stem Entered)

2	(No Question Stem Entered)	
A	0%	(No Answer Stem Entered)
☞ B	73%	(No Answer Stem Entered)
C	12%	(No Answer Stem Entered)
D	14%	(No Answer Stem Entered)

3	(No Question Stem Entered)	
A	8%	(No Answer Stem Entered)
B	10%	(No Answer Stem Entered)
C	0%	(No Answer Stem Entered)
D	0%	(No Answer Stem Entered)
☞ E	75%	(No Answer Stem Entered)
F	5%	(No Answer Stem Entered)

Figure 2

Grades															Totals		
HW 5 pts 1/29 Hour 6	HW 3 pts 2/5 Hour 9	HW 3 pts 2/8 Hour 11	HW 1 pts 2/13 Hour 13	HW 1 pts 2/15 Hour 14	HW 7 pts 2/20 Hour 15	HW 1 pts 2/22 Hour 16	HW 4 pts 2/26 Hour 17	HW 2 pts 2/27 Hour 18	HW 2 pts 3/5 Hour 20	HW 1 pts 3/27 Hour 25	HW 1 pts 4/2 Hour 27	HW 1 pts 4/3 Hour 28	HW 1 pts 4/5 Hour 29	HW 1 pts 4/9 Hour 30	Earned Points	Max Points	Avg
5.0	2.0	2.0	1.0		7.0	0.0	4.0	2.0	2.0	1.0		1.0	1.0	1.0	32.0	36.0	88.9
5.0	3.0	2.0	0.0	1.0	6.0	0.0	4.0	2.0	1.0	1.0		1.0	1.0	1.0	29.0	35.0	82.9
4.0	3.0	2.0	0.0		6.0	1.0	4.0	2.0	1.0	1.0		1.0	1.0	1.0	29.0	36.0	80.6
2.0	3.0	3.0	1.0		7.0	0.0	3.0	2.0	2.0	1.0		1.0	1.0	1.0	30.0	36.0	83.3
3.0	1.0	3.0	1.0	1.0	7.0	0.0		2.0	2.0			1.0	1.0	1.0	27.0	32.0	84.4
4.0	2.0	3.0	1.0		7.0	0.0	2.0	2.0	2.0	1.0		1.0	1.0		29.0	34.0	85.3
4.0	3.0	2.0	0.0	1.0	6.0	0.0	3.0	2.0	2.0	1.0		1.0	1.0	1.0	30.0	36.0	83.3
			0.0		7.0	0.0		1.0	1.0			1.0	1.0	1.0	16.0	20.0	80.0
4.0	2.0	3.0		1.0	7.0	0.0	4.0	2.0	1.0	1.0		1.0			29.0	34.0	85.3
4.0	3.0	3.0	1.0	1.0	7.0	0.0	2.0	2.0	2.0	1.0		1.0		1.0	32.0	36.0	88.9
	2.0	2.0					2.0	0.0		1.0		1.0	1.0	1.0	13.0	20.0	65.0
	1.0		0.0	1.0	5.0	0.0	2.0	2.0	2.0	1.0		1.0	1.0	1.0	18.0	27.0	66.7
	2.0	3.0	1.0	1.0	7.0	0.0	3.0	2.0	2.0	1.0		1.0	1.0	1.0	28.0	32.0	87.5
4.0	2.0	2.0	1.0	1.0	7.0	0.0	3.0	2.0	2.0	1.0		1.0	1.0	1.0	32.0	37.0	86.5
5.0	3.0	3.0	1.0	1.0	7.0	1.0	4.0	1.0	2.0	1.0		1.0	1.0	1.0	36.0	37.0	97.3
5.0	2.0	3.0	1.0	1.0	7.0	0.0	4.0	2.0	2.0	1.0		1.0	1.0	1.0	32.0	36.0	88.9
3.0	3.0	3.0	1.0	1.0	7.0	0.0	4.0	2.0	2.0	1.0			1.0		30.0	35.0	85.7
4.0	3.0	3.0	1.0	1.0	7.0	0.0	4.0	2.0	2.0	1.0		1.0	1.0	1.0	33.0	37.0	89.2
3.0	2.0	2.0	1.0		5.0	0.0	4.0	2.0	2.0	1.0		1.0	1.0	1.0	27.0	36.0	75.0
5.0		2.0	1.0		5.0	0.0	3.0	2.0	2.0	1.0		1.0	1.0	1.0	28.0	33.0	84.8
5.0	3.0	2.0	0.0		5.0	0.0	3.0	2.0	2.0	1.0		1.0	1.0	1.0	29.0	36.0	80.6
3.0	2.0	3.0	1.0	1.0	7.0	1.0	3.0	0.0	2.0	1.0		1.0	1.0	1.0	29.0	37.0	78.4
3.0	2.0	3.0	1.0	1.0	7.0	0.0	3.0		2.0	1.0		1.0	1.0	1.0	27.0	32.0	84.4

Figure 3

Surveys completed by Professor Moriarty's students posted positive reviews on the CPS system. When asked on how it enhanced their learning, one student said: "The professor is able to provide an alternate means of grading students by assessing understanding daily, and discuss certain issues more closely when there is misunderstanding." Another added: "It's much faster than a paper quiz. Less quiz time allows for more lecture time. We learn more."

Darlene Cardillo
Albany Law School

Adventures in PowerPoint

One day last semester, a student who had witnessed my struggle to get the PowerPoint projector, laptop computer, and remote control unit to work at the same time gently observed, "You're pretty new to computers, aren't you?" Yet, just a few moments earlier, I had been congratulating myself as a pathfinder forging hardily into a new technological frontier. These different perspectives illustrate the gap between the experience of many law students, who were born to the computer age, and that of their professors, who until recently found an electric typewriter to be an excellent example of technological wizardry. Using PowerPoint can be an adventure, especially if terms like "Java" turn your students' thoughts to computers, while you contemplate beverages.

Last semester, I decided to use PowerPoint slides in my three-credit Sales course. I decided to do so for several reasons. First, Sales is a course that requires constant in-class attention to statutory language. A visual aid, such as PowerPoint, enables the class to examine the statutory language on a common visual field, rather than look exclusively at individual Code books (a practice, by the way, that I had no intention of discouraging and indeed hoped to actively encourage). Second, I prefer to teach Sales through the detailed analysis of hypotheticals. I planned to project the basic elements of the hypotheticals on the PowerPoint screen in order to help my students (and me) remember the basic fact patterns I set out. In addition, the PowerPoint projector would enable me to highlight changes in the hypothetical fact patterns as the class progressed, something that I thought would be helpful. Finally, I hoped that PowerPoint would help me add a little pizzazz to what can be a hyper technical subject.

Now, a few months later and a semester wiser, I have emerged from my first adventure with PowerPoint with an increased enthusiasm for the medium. I also have a few words to share with those who might be considering the pros and cons of using this technology in the classroom.

PowerPoint and Class Participation

Many professors fear, with good reason, that the use of PowerPoint will dull class participation. Students who are equipped with PowerPoint printouts will simply gaze at the screen and forego note-taking, thinking, legal analysis, etc. This is a realistic concern, and professors who opt to use PowerPoint must consider both their expectations of class participation and the means they use to stimulate class discussion.

Class participation is a necessary component of any course that utilizes the problem method. The point, after all, is to get the students to do the problems. I found that the effect that PowerPoint had on class discussion depended on the way that I structured the slides. If I presented a slide that flashed the solution to a problem on the screen, students had little incentive to discuss the problem. On the other hand, if I used the slides to state the facts of a hypothetical or to project a portion of the statute, I found that I could continue to question the students in much the same manner that I would have employed had I been working without visual aids.

Using PowerPoint may indeed cause a professor to subordinate the desire for classroom spontaneity to the need for advance preparation of a slideshow that follows a particular lesson plan. My own approach to a class like Sales is very methodical, and I keep a tight rein on the class's progress in order to cover all of the necessary doctrinal material. This approach slotted in easily with the kind of preparation necessary for a successful PowerPoint class. In other classes, where I am interested in probing a subject in a more open-ended manner or in soliciting student input concerning the direction the class is taking, I would find it harder to prepare and use PowerPoint slides effectively. While it is possible to back up or go forward in the slide show to reach a slide that addresses a point raised unexpectedly, I have found that it was cumbersome to do so.

In the post-Langdellian world, it is perhaps a heresy to suggest that some professors may find that class participation is not of critical importance. In this case, PowerPoint slides will pose no threat. A class that is taught on a lecture basis can effectively use PowerPoint slides to break up the pace of the lecture and to emphasize key points. A word to the wise is pertinent here—*hatred* would not be too strong a word to describe the emotion inspired by someone who reads slides aloud. If you are going to use PowerPoint to supplement your lectures, it is best to use the slides to highlight rather than to replicate the spoken word.

PowerPoint and the Power Nap

"Don't do it!" "As soon as the lights go down and the PowerPoint slides go up, eyes start to droop." "You'll be sorry." PowerPoint skeptics were not shy about their misgivings. Forewarned is forearmed, so I went into my first PowerPoint session prepared to see the students drift off into the Land of Nod. As a mother who has never really succeeded in persuading her two-year-old that a nap is definitely a good thing, the task of actually having to prevent 100 students from napping during class seemed decidedly novel. After a few classes, I determined that there are two tricks to ensuring a nap-free PowerPoint class.

First, resist the temptation to turn the PowerPoint slides into the focus of the classroom. After hours of preparing and refining slides, I was often so enamored of my creation that I wanted to flash it on the screen and invite the students to admire my handiwork. The temptation was even greater when one of my colleagues showed me how to animate the slides. Even with the modest graphics and sound effects available in the standard PowerPoint software, I was entranced. As I cut and pasted my clip-arts and colored my fonts, I was having the best time I had had doing arts and crafts since kindergarten.

For better or worse, having fun with arts and crafts is not the way to run a successful PowerPoint class. PowerPoint is only a *tool.* The subject matter itself must remain the focus of the classroom experience, and the voices of the teacher and the students must remain the central focus of dialogue. PowerPoint should never become anything other than the means of delivering, communicating, and teaching a message. Through clip art and sound effects, PowerPoint can actually compete with the professor for the students' attention.

In order to counteract this tendency, teachers who use PowerPoint need to make sure that they take all steps necessary to overpower PowerPoint. I gradually learned to use PowerPoint as a prop to illustrate a point or to provide a way of focusing the students' attention on the statutory text. In some cases, I changed my own position in the classroom in order to draw the students' attention away from the slides in order to emphasize a new point. Ironically, PowerPoint itself gave me the means of walking away from the podium, where my carefully worded notes and drafts of hypotheticals rested in peace. Knowing that the PowerPoint slides would prompt me with the facts of the hypotheticals I had planned, I could walk around the classroom with confidence. In this way, I was able to help the students focus on my words and on my efforts to draw them into class discussion in a way that would have been impossible had I stayed with my notes at the podium.

Second, constant attention must be given to the students' visual experience. While it is tempting to transform your classroom into something akin to a darkened Cineplex, it simply is not necessary. I found (with no scientific analysis other than polling my students) that I could conduct a class with almost all of the classroom lights blazing if I colored my slides with a dark background (usually blue) and a light, bright lettering (usually white or yellow). The contrast was sufficient to ensure that the students could easily read the screens without sitting in a darkened room.

PowerPoint and Class Preparation

My own greatest reservation about PowerPoint was its capacity to print out the slides in a handout format. I initially resisted the students' request for me to do so, because I feared that they would substitute the handout for a deeply analytical approach to class. Yet I knew that some PowerPoint aficionados reported a successful integration of the handouts into their management of the classroom experience. After some time, I came to agree. Without handouts, students often struggle to transcribe the material on the slides into their notebooks, leaving little room for attention to class discussion. I am now teaching the course for the second time and have decided to post the PowerPoint slides on a password-protected website. Students who wish to have handouts may download them and print them. In general, I think this has enabled students to focus on class discussion and on taking notes of important analytical concepts, rather than copying down slides.

PowerPoint is not for everyone, nor is it for every class. I plan to continue using PowerPoint in Sales, because I have found the ability to project statutory provisions and hypotheticals to be helpful in my effort to encourage students to engage in a detailed reading of the statute. I do not plan to use PowerPoint on a regular basis, however, in my classes on health law, where I encourage students to engage in a lively discussion of policy concerns. As the saying goes, it takes the right tool to do the job right. Like most tools, PowerPoint does a great job when it is the right tool.

Sad to say, it doesn't add pizzazz. That's still up to you.

Alison Sulentic
Baker Botts L.L.P.

Stretching Toward the Future: A View of Laptop Computers from Both Sides of the Screen

I should begin this essay with a confession. I have surfed the net while in a law school class. I have even sent and received email and reviewed a transmitted document, all while the professor delivered the day's presentation. I do have some guilt about the confessed acts as I now spend most of my time on the standing side of the lectern. But last year I was again a law student, enrolled in thirteen hours a semester in an LLM program. I sat in classes, read for classes, got called on in classes, and took notes in classes. I will admit that, in the ten-plus years since my own law school experience, I forgot much of what I knew about being a student in the typical law school class. I had spent the previous five years teaching and becoming quite comfortable on my side of the equation. But, because we must stretch to grow, I went back to the throes of law school, on the streets as it were, and experienced a revelation on the issue of laptop computers in the classroom.

First of all, we should put to bed our worries about whether law students actually surf the net, instant message, play solitaire and computer games, and work on other projects while in class. They do. In fact, from my rear-row vantage point, I observed that almost all students were doing some form of mental multi-tasking on their computers during class. My spying uncovered undeniable incidences of complete and utter abandonment of anything even remotely connected to the class. In one class, a 15-student seminar on Law and Higher Education, the student sitting next to me spent the better part of the entire semester engaged in various sports websites, checking scores and sometimes actually placing bets in class. Because there is no stigma on this type of surfing during class, my fellow student made no attempt to hide these activities from me or from anyone. In the same small class, two students sitting next to each other engaged in an instant message conversation throughout the class, resulting at times in outbursts of audible laughter, sighs, and deep breaths of disgust. At times, I even mistook their grunts and groans as being related to class content and began to think more critically about the subject being discussed. Although some were more discreet, a simple walk around the table showed fifteen screens of content unrelated to the course.

What made this course exceptionally telling was the fact that it was a good course, well taught, on an interesting subject. In fact, the course was in demand and required an early or clever registration on the university's tedious web registration system. The classroom was small, perfectly suited to fifteen, with maybe one or two seats unoccupied. The reading was interesting and not overly demanding and the class engaged in long discussions of the relevant material. The professor was an expert in the field and managed to have a good sense of humor in the midst of substantive discussion.

And there was discussion, lots of discussion. In fact, almost all student contributions to the class were voluntary and it was quite apparent that most of the students had read the materials and were engaged in the class. The class was not an examination class, but required a paper, so the need for actual notes was minimal. However, the atmosphere was not one where you would want to be caught unaware or unprepared.

So, what happened? Were students engaged in the class? Did they enjoy the class? Yes. In fact, most students were attentively engaged at most times and only one student ever came to class without a laptop computer. My sports-betting friend would often, mid-bet, raise his hand and ask a question or make a comment on point. The chatting twosome would turn up their eyes and join in the conversation when the discussion hit certain points or certain course materials came up for discussion. No student was slack-jawed and bleary eyed; they were all willing participants in an interactive seminar on a chosen topic. In fact, I would love to teach to that level of attention and preparation.

My 40-something-self wonders at this result. How can they be betting, playing, and talking online while engaged in an active discussion? The answer, I think, lies in the inevitable differences in generations. I am of the typewriter generation. I got an IBM selectric as a high school graduation present and typed every college and graduate school paper on it, using correction tape and running out at night to get new ribbons. All my class notes were handwritten on notebook paper and I spent the first five years of my college education with a callous on my right-hand middle finger. When I left college for my first "real job," my secretary used carbon paper for all correspondence and a dubious system of color-coded filing which employed pink paper for file copies, yellow for external copies, and blue for internal copies. Sometime around 1988, the secretarial pool all got early-version word processors, a small step above the memory typewriter, and we felt a new energy in our work because mistakes could be corrected without a whole new piece of paper. By the time I left for law school in 1992, the office had come of age to the PC, and we had just started keeping files and forms on a database. However, many did not trust the technology and paper copies were still a mainstay. In law school, I took notes on legal ruled paper and finished my semester with handwritten outlines and hand-drawn diagrams and flow charts showing the analytical flow of contract offer and acceptance. A few were automated in their outline creation but no one took a computer to class. In fact, online legal research, such as Westlaw and Lexis, still required downloaded software. We were technology novices, grateful for every timesaving invention, but unable to comprehend the burgeoning world of the web and the laptop.

Because of this pure accident of birth, I am a different animal when it comes to computer use. First, I am still in the ancient world of "turn off the television while you do your homework." How can you watch one visual form of entertainment while your mind focuses on another thing? I certainly could not have done my algebra homework while The Brady Bunch was on, and watching MTV in the 80s never went hand-in-hand with studying college geometry. Not only did my peers and I lack the constitution for some mental multi-tasking, we were taught not to do it by our well-meaning parents. Concentration was the byword for academic success.

This is the prejudice I bring to bear in my own classroom. As a concerned teacher, I worry that students will not absorb the class while engaged in another world on the laptop. Part of this worry comes from the very nature of law teaching—it is about more than content. Good law teaching is a demonstration, at all times, of the analytical process. Students should be walking through the cases with the group, asking questions, working out the confusing parts collectively. I am not there merely to lecture, I am there to engage. This goal is an even greater priority now, as most in legal education seek a more interactive classroom. Law faculties define the interactive classroom as one where students are interactive with faculty, not one where students are interactive with the outside world delivered through the laptop.

But, is it possible that law students, professionals in their own right, can watch television and study? Can they email, surf and play on the laptop while remaining completely engaged in the class? My recent student experience leads me to conclude that they can. I saw it with my own eyes from an insider's perspective. The typical 20-something law student has an ability to multi-task her brain in a way I do not possess. She can sit in class with a split screen on her computer, taking notes on one side and transferring monies between bank accounts on the other. I cannot. I tried and found that while I was checking my bank balance or writing an email, the course discussion essentially melted into background noise and could have shifted to German without my knowing it. However, just because I can't manage this multi-faceted world, does not mean law students cannot. Therein lies the revelation.

In this regard, we are not like them and they are not like us. For most law faculty, the difference is age, where we fall in the modern technological progression of life. If we accept cultural differences defined by region, race, and religion, we should be ready to accept cultural differences defined by technology. The modern student culture includes a certain amount of, as one student called it, electronic doodling. Where you and I might have filled the margins of our notebook paper with Kilroy's, Star Wars characters, or the insignia from rock bands, these students fill their margins with sports scores and CNN. Where we might have passed a note to a friend in class, these students send emails. Of course passing notes and doodling are distractions regardless of format, but the modern culture has bred a greater ability to divide the mind's attention. One fellow student in a 60 person lecture class told me that he would go crazy if he couldn't keep something else going on his computer during class, alongside his note-taking. He said he just gets "restless" and needs the changing landscape of the screen to keep him engaged overall. He said that if he had to sit there for 75 minutes with just a piece of paper and a pen, he would not take notes well; in fact, he thinks he would just tune out and go to sleep. I would be more skeptical but I sat behind this student for twelve weeks and he took great notes. I even borrowed his notes once and they were not only thorough but also full of insights and questions he jotted down as the lecture progressed. He was thinking about the subject during class.

So what does this mean for law faculty? Many ban the use of laptops in the classroom. Banning laptops has been a topic of hot debate, and the conventional faculty wisdom always makes the same points in defense of the ban: students are not engaged in class, students do not pay attention to the presentation, and laptops interfere with the interactive learning process. My experience on the other side makes me doubt this wisdom and look at the reasoning in a different light. I know first-hand how hard it can be to teach to a room of down-turned faces. Sometimes, if the content is particularly important, as when I say, "this will be on the exam," my class view turns from a group of faces to a sea of tops of heads. It is disconcerting and the energy level in the room drops to almost nothing when every student's head is staring at the screen. However, when the student is taking notes, the computer is just an electronic notebook. If I mandated paper note-taking, I would still be facing a sea of heads, not faces. Note-taking is note-taking and we want it to happen. The argument against laptops in the classroom for note-taking is like the argument a senior lawyer makes for using the phone instead of email: it is faster and more personal. Well, only to one who has not grasped the alternative.

What we have to realize is that much of our apprehension about laptops in the classroom relates to us, not them. Ego is an essential ingredient in the talented scholar-teacher. We need to like the sound of our own voices, in print and in person. And we need others to like it too. When students are engaged with their computers instead of with us, we are slighted. In addition to an essential lack of energy in the classroom, we also lose that terrific side benefit of teaching, the rapt audience. Our egos suffer.

There are techniques to recapture the class from the web-based world. I sometimes only need the faces, not the heads, and I ask the class to close the computers for a minute or two and just listen and think. Most oblige and I get that needed boost of energy and ego. However, if every student in the class would rather be someplace else mentally, the class needs revision. We all do things in teaching that are great for us, but not so great for the students. I attended one class where the faculty member used a detailed PowerPoint presentation during every class period. He handed out an outline copy of the slides before class and posted the presentation online. There was essentially no need to take notes in the class—you had all the information. But, all good intentions aside, this technique served only to distance the students from learning. In that class, every open computer was engaged elsewhere, not screening other content while taking notes and listening but just looking at something else. In short, there wasn't enough distraction. For me, a member of the typewriter generation, the format was great. I did not have to open the computer and the notes were essentially ready-made, save for my margin comments. But for my 20-something peers, the PowerPoint and handouts simply took away their reason to be there and engage.

We cannot please everyone, but we should not make pleasing ourselves the goal. Accept the needs and differences of law students and bend accordingly. Banning laptops from the classroom is like holding back the river with a levee of sandbags—it's just a matter of time.

Catherine Ross Dunham
Elon University School of Law

Surfing for Contracts

Last year while teaching a first-year class on contract law, I used this fairly simple, technology-based assignment (Internet, Word documents, inserting pictures from files, using text boxes) to enhance student understanding of basic concepts that were entirely new to most of them. The extraordinarily diverse groups of students I work with share an interest in law, automobiles and the Internet. All the students have laptops and Internet access, but their computer skills vary widely. The difference in their technological ability does not seem a more significant bar to achievement than the use of legal pads and notebooks, and the attendant difference in writing skills that characterized the old school method. It appears that a lesson linking a widespread student interest (cars) to something of legal relevance (contract offers) is a good way to connect the study of law to life.

Students made a list of the required terms in an offer in a Word document. The next two steps required opening a new PowerPoint document, logging on to either www.cars.com or www.autotrader.com, and analyzing the vehicles for sale by private owner or merchant. In addition to a title slide, each student had to assemble ten offers they located at one of the sites. A slide containing space for both picture and text is necessary as a starting place for analyzing the number of terms present and their sufficiency or definitiveness (see below). All students were required to compose ten slides each, with two vehicles in the $10,000, $20,000, $30,000, $40,000 and $50,000 & up categories. Students would insert a text box at the side of the slide that addressed the required terms.

Subject: RX-8 in velocity red

Quality: 2004 model with 11,667 miles

Quantity: one car vin number JMIFE173740102421

Price: $26,988

In a group of nearly one hundred students, every one completed this assignment either on time or ahead of schedule. From their comments, and their willingness to share their work with each other and with me, I suspect they might even have enjoyed learning this way.

The slides sparked some rather lively discussions regarding the following questions:

- Are these terms sufficient to create a valid offer?
- Could this offer, as stated, create a power of acceptance in the offeree?

- Why or why not?

Shortly before writing this article I purchased a new car similar to the one shown above using the Internet only. The vehicle was delivered during a brief mock trial recess. The usual caveats apply.

Tom Gear
The Academy of Irving

Lessons Virtually Learned: The Evolution of an Online Course

I have offered a course on Law and the Internet, on the Internet, 15 times since the summer of 1995. The course has evolved over the years, and I've learned some lessons, not only about how to conduct an online course, but also about some ways to enhance my more typical offline courses. In this essay I describe those lessons briefly, with the disclaimer that both the course and this essay are always works in progress.

Rather than describe the course in any detail, I invite readers to visit the course website at http://ul451.gsu.edu/lawand/. Some screenshots representative of this course and the online components of a few others, and illustrative of some of these lessons, are available at http://ul451.gsu.edu/pwiseman/gallery/online.

Here, then, are the lessons, in no particular order (but for the last):

A. Simplify

Simpler is better, more often than not. In early versions of the course, I used every chat tool available for our synchronous meetings, from Internet Relay Chat (the most venerable of chat tools) to a Multi-User Dimension (an online "space" in which users can both converse and "build"). Although experimenting with different tools can be useful, it can confuse students. Now we use one tool for our relatively infrequent chat sessions.

But do not over-simplify. Some incarnations of the course home page have been so simple as to be cryptic. I now strike what I think is a happy balance between simplicity and instruction. Take care not to let the technology impede the pedagogy; both over-complication and over-simplification can do that.

B. Use the Right Tools

Different tools are suited to different tasks. In my experience, synchronous, "chat" tools are suitable for chatting, but not for doing much in the way of serious substantive work. While this may be a function of my teaching style, which tends to be more conversational than controlling, asynchronous tools (email discussion lists, online forums) seem to me to be much more suited to the serious work of delivering content, discussing issues, working on hypotheticals, and so forth. Chat tools, on the other hand, *are* well suited to brainstorming sessions and very small group work. They can also be very useful for "office hours," if a couple of students need to ask me for clarification on course requirements or procedures.

Avoid use of tools which rely on user discipline. In early versions of the course, the discussion took place on a single email discussion list, which was archived on a website. To keep the messages in subject-matter order, I asked students to choose the general subject category from a pre-determined list and to use it in the Subject: line of their emails. As you might imagine, this met with limited success. Now, each week's topic has its own, separate forum and email address, and it is much easier for students to post to the right forum than it is to remember specific subject categories.

Early on, I allowed the technology to drive the pedagogy; now, I try to make sure that the pedagogy is driving the technology.

C. Don't Teach

In a "constructivist" course such as mine (by which I mean a course in which students supply all the content), this is perhaps obvious advice: make students do all the substantive work. But I think the advice has application to more conventional courses as well, where, even if the teacher "knows more" than the students, the most effective way for students to learn the material is to help them teach themselves.

As important as not teaching is exercising professorial restraint and resisting the temptation to intervene when the lesson will be as well, and probably better, learned if you don't. Sometimes, with the right technology, the pedagogy seems to take care of itself.

D. Take Risks

I provide an anonymous online course evaluation site for my students to evaluate my courses as they proceed, risking hearing things I don't want to hear and providing an opportunity for inappropriate venting. I learn a lot from what students tell me on those pages; and, so far, nothing bad has happened. Unlike our usual course-concluding evaluations, which are of no help to the students currently in the course, continual evaluations, so long as I respond to them one way or another (which I do), give students a sense of ownership of the course.

Even (or maybe especially) risky use of technology can lead to pedagogical discovery.

E. Reinvent

Available online course tools certainly have their place, but I think many faculty, after using them for a little while, find them constraining. Most faculty, of course, are not programmers and so have to live with the constraints, but if you either are or have access to a programmer, I urge you to reinvent with abandon. Faculty are a creative lot and will come up with far more than anonymous online evaluations, dynamic syllabi, and course-based face books. Pedagogical innovation, if not necessity, can be the mother of technological invention.

F. Build Community

It is probably important in any course to foster a sense of shared enterprise, but it is especially important in an online course where students will not see each other while engaged in the course. Provide ways for students to get to know each other, perhaps by meeting face to face occasionally, by inviting students to introduce themselves in a class forum, or by providing an online "face book" of student pictures.

Hold students to some community standards (respect for each other's contributions to the community effort, a responsibility to contribute, etc.). I have rarely had to douse a flame war, but I do, early in each offering of the course, remind students that they are lawyers, not pundits, and that their contributions to our discussion should reflect that role. And be sure to always publicly credit students who make particularly good contributions.

These and other strategies can increase the students' sense of engagement with the course material and with each other, thus improving the sense of community in the course. If community is pedagogically important, technology can provide it.

G. Accommodate Diversity

I'm not speaking here of the obvious (and legally required) need to make all course webpages accessible to students with disabilities, but rather of the need to accommodate technological diversity. Unless you are fortunate enough to be in an environment where every student has state-of-the-art equipment, it is important to accommodate the lowest common technological denominator. So email from your course websites should be in plain text, not HTML. And you should minimize the unnecessary use of images and video and other bandwidth-demanding bells and whistles. Often, low technology suffices pedagogically.

H. Automate

I am able to do things online which I would not dream of doing otherwise, either because they would take up too much time done manually or because there is no offline equivalent. For example, providing students as a group with continual feedback on their forum performance (even if it's only quantitative) can be automated and is useful to them. Showing the passage of time on the class schedule or syllabus is not something which really has an offline equivalent, but it has proved a popular thing to do. Even more popular (with my students, if not with my colleagues and associate dean) is my practice of allowing students to retrieve their grades by email, something which I would not be especially happy to do manually for my 80-student first-year Property section. Also popular is my random selection of students for class participation, notice of which is automatically sent to the class forum at the beginning of each week. We also generate automatically, from our database of class rolls, email addresses, and student ID pictures, email distribution lists and online face books for every class.

But don't try to automate what cannot be automated. Giving individual, qualitative feedback probably cannot be automated. Grading nonobjective exams probably cannot be automated.

Not only does pedagogy sometimes spawn technological innovation, but technology enables pedagogical innovation.

I. Reflect

As I have experimented with the use of Internet technology in my teaching, I have reflected on what works and what doesn't. I continue to do what works and to try new things. I have probably, on occasion, persisted in doing something which didn't work, in the belief that I was just not doing it right. Experimentation with technology and reflection on its pedagogical usefulness are invigorating and, I hope, keep my teaching fresh.

Patrick Wiseman
Georgia State University College of Law

Using a Wiki to Increase Student Engagement in Administrative Law

Administrative Law is one of the courses students love to hate. This is particularly true in schools where Administrative Law is a required course, because many students in the class would not take it otherwise and gripe about being forced to. The problem with Administrative Law—for both the teacher and the student—is that it is such a vast topic that teaching it in a manner students can comprehend is difficult.

When I was asked to teach Administrative Law last year, I looked at this opportunity as a challenge, rather than a burden. Because I am fairly comfortable using technology in my teaching, I decided to use a wiki to involve the students in the course more than they would be if I spent all our class time lecturing.

Wiki software is designed to support collaborative writing. The best known wiki, of course, is Wikipedia, a collaboratively written encyclopedia. While Wikipedia has engendered some controversy, it remains a regularly updated encyclopedia of over ten million articles that has been written in less than six years.

Opportunities for collaborative writing abound in most law school courses. I am a supporter of collaborative learning in law school, at least generally so—like everything else, the devil is in the details. But as I approached teaching Administrative Law, I thought of ways that I might use a wiki environment to increase engagement in my class. I came up with two. First, I set up a wiki for the students to write the outline for the course collaboratively. Second, I set up small group wikis for research projects on particular agencies.

The wiki course outline was the toughest sell. I have always been concerned about the influence that the varied availability of outlines might have on student grades. Some students get good outlines and others do not, and it seems obvious that this, often random, factor might have an effect on the grade students ultimately receive for the course. So I had the students in this course prepare the outline together, and they all had access to the same product (the collaborative outline) for the final exam.

I found that several students welcomed this approach, several resisted it vehemently, and the rest were willing to go along with the experiment. I had a few students drop the course when I announced the wiki requirements. Most of the students in the course were 3Ls, and some were graduating at the end of the semester. I think the students resisting it were mostly students who felt they had their own process of getting A's figured out, and they didn't want anyone else to either (1) share it; or (2) interfere with it. I think the students who welcomed it (I received several encouraging emails) were students who typically struggle to prepare or receive outlines for courses, and often have to turn to commercial outlines (which can be particularly problematic for Administrative Law, because it is such a vast topic, and teachers teach it in substantially different ways).

Participation in the preparation of the outline amounted to 10% of each student's grade in the class, and nearly all students participated. A week before the final exam, at the final review class, I gave them printed copies of their work product. They were allowed to take this outline and the textbook (only) into the final exam. The final product was an excellent outline for the course, and exceeded 165 pages. It even included several tables and charts, some of which I had given the class as handouts, and others that were prepared from scratch by students.

The other use of wikis in the course was for group projects. One of the problems of teaching Administrative Law is that it often seems disconnected from the agencies involved in the cases. You can teach the principle from the case, but simultaneously teaching students how the relevant agency operates can be difficult. In addition, one of the critical skills of attorneys who practice administrative law is the ability to navigate and evaluate the operative aspects of the bureaucracy in which their client is entangled. So research skills also are important.

I assigned groups of 4 students to one of 11 Federal agencies. These were agencies that were involved in some of the seminal Administrative Law cases, and agencies that I thought would interest the students, such as EPA, the FCC, and OSHA. Students in each group used a group wiki to prepare a site of information about their agency. In the last 20 minutes of the second class per week, the group presented their wiki to the class. All the wikis were available for other students to access, but the small group members were the only ones who could build the site for their assigned agency. The group wikis—and the matching presentations—amounted to 20% of the grade for the course.

Students really seemed to enjoy the wiki projects. Most of the groups went above and beyond and created fantastic sites about their agency, with pictures, cartoons, logos and the like adorning them. Of course, they often included numerous links to sources outside the wiki—both within the agency, and sources that criticized or commented on the operation of the agency. At the end of the course, I gave the students "a gift you made yourselves" in the form of a CD-ROM of all the agency presentations. The CD included 88 MB of information.

Setting up the wikis was simple, because the facility to do so was built into the University of Denver's courseware system of choice: Blackboard. Our Blackboard sites include a wiki capability and also allow for group wikis to be configured. That process is simply (1) creating a new group wiki; (2) giving it a name; and (3) assigning the group members access to write to it.

Although not technically difficult, experimenting with a new technology and using it in two different ways was challenging. Most particularly, it was challenging for the students, because I was asking them to try something new to support their learning. By third year, students often have, as I like to say: "one foot out the door and the other on a banana peel." When you combine that reality with trying something new—in a course that is required and generally has a bad reputation—you are bound to get resistance. But I am glad I pushed through that resistance. At the end of the year, my student evaluations seemed to also indicate that the students were glad they hung in there with the course. Further, I was heartened by the fact that attendance in this class was very high (particularly for Administrative Law, with mostly 3L students). There were no students who missed more than four classes, and most students attended nearly all of the classes. I would recommend the use of wikis in other courses, particularly where the professor wants to encourage students to be more involved in their learning and believes that a collaborative writing approach might help to achieve that goal.

David Thomson
University of Denver College of Law

Chapter 4

Classroom Dynamics and Learning Culture

In Chapter 1, we explained seven core principles of effective teaching: expertise, respect, expectations, support, passion, preparation, variety, active learning, collaboration, clarity, and formative feedback. Many of these principles are crucial for creating an optimal classroom environment.

For example, by creating an atmosphere where the students know you respect them and where they understand your expectation that they manifest respect for each other, your students are more likely to respond respectfully in class and to feel better about the experience. Similarly, manifesting high expectations, both in terms of what students need to do for your class and what you communicate they are capable of doing, has a direct and powerful effect on the quality of student performance. Passion has a similar causal effect on students. Teachers who are passionate about their subjects produce students who are similarly excited. Finally, communicating and providing support for students in both the intellectual and the psychological realms has been correlated both with positive student attitudes about the learning process and the quality and quantity of their learning.

The four principles in the preceding paragraph and the concepts discussed below might seem, at first glance, less significant than the particular teaching techniques a teacher uses. They are, however, at least as important if not more important. The bottom line goal is to create a positive learning environment where students feel safe to take risks.

Below are some additional suggestions about what you can do to help build a positive classroom environment.

Know and Use Students' Names

If you have a hard time learning names, practice with flash cards. If learning students' names quickly is not feasible, we recommend that you use name tents so that you can regularly use students' names during the class. Practice remembering students' names outside of class a few minutes a day. Regular practice, a commitment to learning students' names, and using name cards enables most teachers to learn students' names within a few weeks, even in classes of over 100 students.

Be Conscious of the Messages You Send

Communication experts tell us that 75% of our message is delivered by body language. When in the classroom, be aware of what your body language may convey to students. Eye contact, nodding, listening attentively, moving closer to a student who is asking a question or who is speaking in class, and projecting a sense of confidence and openness are crucial to creating and open learning environment. When a student says something that appears to be way off track, look for the nugget of insight that underlies the student's error.

Your word choices also matter. The research on feedback counsels that students are much more receptive to feedback that emphasizes concretely what they need to do to get better than labels or characterizations. In other words, in dealing with poor student performance in class, it is best to describe the behavior and explain the consequence rather than accusing them of being unprepared, commanding them to work harder, or telling them their analysis is "too conclusory." (For example, you might say "Your argument did not include the facts in the second and third sentences of the first paragraph of the problem. By not addressing those facts at all, you undermined your cogent analysis of the first fact in that paragraph.")

More generally, you need to find a way to see students positively. You may find it helpful to think of your students as friends you have invited to a dinner party, as offspring, or as young relatives. For example, you might ask yourself "How would I respond if my favorite niece asked that question?" Consider your students future colleagues in practice or on the bench. Whatever you do, find something to be positive about.

Be Enthusiastic

Students greatly appreciate it when you project confidence and enthusiasm, and you can always find something to be enthusiastic about. Show enthusiasm with small gestures: start the class with a smile and "Good evening!" Students enjoy learning from teachers who clearly like students and enjoy teaching.

Model Taking Risks and Acknowledging Weaknesses

Students respect and appreciate teachers who are self-confident and acknowledge their weaknesses. It's ok to say, "Great question. I never thought of that. I'll have to think about it and get back to you." If you are trying something new, be candid about it: "I'm going out on a limb here. I am not sure if this exercise will work, but I am going to ask you to engage in a different kind of learning activity today. I believe it will work because ______________________."

When you make a mistake (we've all made tons), acknowledge it. "Last class I gave you some misinformation. Let me try to clarify." Let them know that you, too, have to work at writing complex prose, speaking in public, and teaching effectively. Apologize when you err. Admitting your errors and asking for students' pardon treats students with respect.

Be Transparent and Authentic

Explain to students what you are doing and why. Even if students want a concrete answer to an unresolved issue, explain why the answer is "it depends" and what it depends on. When you use different instructional activities, explain why, at least the first few times you use them. Be honest and direct. You may say that there is no right answer, but you likely mean there is no one single right answer. Instead there is a cluster of right answers and a group of wrong ones.

As the educator Parker Palmer says, "We teach who we are." If your style is to be self-deprecating and you are good at telling jokes, do so. Don't try to be someone you are not. It often takes several years of teaching to develop your teaching persona. Pay attention and be patient.

Attend to Context

Every class you teach occurs in a larger context, which includes important aspects of your students' lives and their other courses and your life and work as a teacher. Attending to context should not consume a lot of time. All you need to do is spend a few minutes before each class thinking about the context.

Student Context

Today's students face a wide variety of pressures, including maintaining relationships with spouses and significant others, family expectations, large loan burdens, and worries about finding jobs in a struggling economy, all of which are layered on top of the stressful and heavy law school workload.

In addition, our students' needs and motivations change as they progress through law school. Most first-semester, first-year students are interested in their courses and are eager to learn. Second- and third-year law students may display less interest in their courses but are eager to graduate, pass the bar exam, and begin their careers. They may respond well to a class with content and skills that are directly relevant to law practice, such as preparing a will. Similarly, students' previous exposure and their real world experience with the subject warrant consideration.

Teachers who explicitly acknowledge, consider, and weigh these issues create an atmosphere where students feel respected and valued.

Teacher Context

We all have strengths and weaknesses as teachers. We are more comfortable with some teaching methods, content, and skills than others. In designing classes, we should build on our strengths and address our weaknesses. In classes that address content and skills with which we are comfortable, we may experiment with new learning and feedback activities. On days when we are on shakier ground or are struggling with other matters, we may choose to stick with the tried and true.

We also all have personal and professional lives beyond the classroom; on occasion, family, personal and even professional issues can alter our normal preparation efforts and classroom performance. While we recommend against disclosing personal crises, we encourage you to be cognizant of your own, internal emotional context and work hard not to allow personal issues to spill over into the classroom.

References

- Susan B. Apel et al., *Seven Principles for Good Practice in Legal Education*, 49 J. Legal Educ. 367 (1999) (eight articles applying the seven principles to legal education).

- KEN BAIN, WHAT THE BEST COLLEGE TEACHERS DO (2004).
- STEVEN FRIEDLAND & GERALD F. HESS, TEACHING THE LAW SCHOOL CURRICULUM (2004).
- Gerald F. Hess, *Heads and Hearts: The Teaching and Learning Environment in Law School*, 52 J. LEGAL EDUC. 75 (2002).
- GERALD F. HESS & STEVEN I. FRIEDLAND, TECHNIQUES FOR TEACHING LAW (1999).
- James B. Levy, *As a Last Resort, Ask The Students: What They Say Makes Someone an Effective Teacher*, 58 ME. L. REV. 49 (2006).
- MICHAEL HUNTER SCHWARTZ, SOPHIE SPARROW & GERALD F. HESS, TEACHING LAW BY DESIGN: ENGAGING STUDENTS FROM THE SYLLABUS TO THE FINAL EXAM (2009).
- ROY STUCKEY ET AL., BEST PRACTICES FOR LEGAL EDUCATION: A VISION AND A ROAD MAP (2007).

It's What You Say *And* How You Say It

As the old saying goes: "It's not what you say, but how you say it" that matters. No place is that more true than the law school classroom where numerous studies show that students suffer acute stress due in large part to a competitive and sometimes hostile environment that pits them against both their teacher and each other. Educational psychologists have long recognized that the nature and quality of a teacher's classroom relationship with her students—the professor's so-called "emotional intelligence" skills—cannot be overstated in terms of their importance to student learning and academic success. Neuroscientists have recently begun finding scientific evidence to support what these psychologists have been saying all along; that socio-emotional considerations can have a significant impact on learning outcomes.

Indeed, there is an emerging consensus among both the "hard" and "soft" sciences that the teacher's emotional intelligence skills may play the biggest role in whether, and how much, our students learn. Countless studies in the field of educational psychology have demonstrated the indisputable power of self-fulfilling prophecies, the effect—for better or worse—of teacher expectations on student confidence, self-efficacy and motivation as well as the vital importance of social support networks. Now there are scientific studies that suggest that the quality of our relationships and our emotional mindset produce chemical changes in the brain that affect learning, retention, and cognitive efficiency. Thus, to maximize our effectiveness as teachers, we need to become more self-aware of the socio-emotional consequences of our classroom words and conduct.

Every time we interact with students—whether it is our classroom body language, the way we address our students or the feedback we provide on their assignments—those interactions are all imbued with emotional overtones that signal to students our true feelings about them, our perception of their abilities, and our expectations regarding their success. Neuroscientists tell us that our moods and emotions play a vital role in attention and memory, which are the building blocks of leaning. Research also tells us that teachers and students, as members of a classroom social group, tend to coordinate their moods and emotions as a result of the social-psychological phenomenon known as emotional contagion. Thus, there's a lot of truth to the conventional wisdom that to get an audience interested, one needs to be interested herself; we now know that's an empirically demonstrable fact. All of this tells us that, as teachers, we need to be thinking about not only the substantive content of our classroom lessons, but the emotional subtext as well.

While we are often conscious of the emotional overtones of our verbal exchanges with students, this essay argues that nearly everything we do in the classroom—which includes our body language, our lesson plans, and the feedback we give students on their assignments—telegraphs to students much about our true attitudes and perceptions of them. In a recent article in Volume 12 of the Journal of the Legal Writing Institute entitled "Building Credibility in the Margins: An Ethos-Based Perspective for Commenting on Student Papers," Professor Kristen Davis argues that students learn a great deal about their teachers' feelings toward them through the comments we write on their assignments and exams. Professor Davis argues that a teacher's classroom ethos is established, at least in part, through written feedback in addition to all of our other classroom verbal and nonverbal behaviors.

Research tells us we are most effective as teachers when we relate to our students in a way that connotes warmth, support and genuine care about their learning. That's not to suggest that we need to become Pollyanna's who are never critical of our students' work. To the contrary, honest feedback and constructive criticism are among the most important tools we employ. In fact, unjustified praise of students is counterproductive because they resent any perceived effort to manipulate them. Achieving a good socio-emotional classroom climate is more art than science, and a very difficult art at that. It requires the teacher to strike an appropriate balance between, on the one hand, being demanding, but, on the other hand, not so demanding as to create insurmountable goals for students to meet. We need to be warm and supportive but not cross the professional boundaries between teacher and student. And we should imbue the classroom with enough challenge to motivate students to stay on task, but not create so much stress that it interferes with our students' learning.

All of these insights mean that optimal teaching involves a holistic approach that nourishes both the intellectual and emotional needs of our students. Time devoted to crafting a substantively sound and intellectually interesting lesson plan may fall on deaf ears, or worse—may undermine learning if the teacher doesn't devote sufficient thought and attention to creating the appropriate emotional "mood lighting" for that class. Content and socio-emotional considerations have to work hand-in-hand for students to learn best.

Obviously, our job requires us to make demands of the students and critique them when they make mistakes. But we can, and should, learn to do it in a way that promotes the students' self-efficacy through warmth, support and a genuine belief that, in the end, they can succeed. When it comes to teaching, therefore, the most apt expression may well be that it's both "what you say" and "how you say it" that really count.

James B. Levy
Nova Southeastern University, Shepard Broad Law Center

Understanding Socratic Dialogue—Student Teaching Day

I have struggled to explain to many students what they ought to be getting out of a typical law classroom. We discuss why their professors ask the sorts of questions they do, as well as what students should be doing when they are not called on for a particular day. But no matter how I try to explain it or how many of the helpful texts explaining law school that they may have consulted, it nonetheless seems that those techniques which intuitively make sense to us as law teachers remain opaque and mystifying to most law students.

To try to counter this problem, and to create a better framework for an explicit conversation about what is happening in a traditional law classroom, I try to schedule a "student teaching day" about a month or six weeks into many of my classes. To make the class seem fun for everyone I tell the students that their colleagues will act as teachers while I will prepare for class as a student. I am eligible along with all other students to be called on. I then ask for two or three volunteer teachers, and have them submit their class preparation notes to me in advance so that I can make sure they are generally on-track in their planning. If I have questions or concerns I will meet with the student teachers before class to go over their preparation, as well as to give them practical tips about timing and so on.

When the student-led class begins I ask or dragoon several additional volunteers to serve as "critical observers." The observers' job is to consider and prepare to comment on what sorts of questions the student teachers asked the students about the assigned material. I ask them to try to unpack the teachers' reasons for asking those questions and to consider why the questions do (or do not) engage students in thinking more deeply about the material.

After about half of the class time has elapsed and much of the material has been covered, I stop the discussion of the material and start deconstructing the planning and teaching. I ask the observers to explain what they saw in the teaching, and I ask the student teachers to describe their planning and thinking as they prepared.

This debriefing usually results in the teachers and observers talking about trying to grasp not just what happened in the assigned cases, but how they related more broadly to the themes of the course, the underlying policies of the rules, etc. From there I can ask the whole class why they think law courses are constructed they way they are, and together we can brainstorm ways for students to get the most out of their preparation and class time, with a thoughtful eye toward their professors' overall goals.

I may sometimes conclude the class with a quick lecture on any points unclear or not covered from the student-led discussion, but I am usually very pleasantly surprised by what they can do and how well they do it.

Kris Franklin
New York Law School

"Academy" Awards for Law Students

As I'm sure is true for most law teachers, I want my courses to conclude in memorable and appealing ways. For example, I recall as a college student taking a survey course called Introduction to Archaeology. The young and dynamic professor ended the last class by showing a short documentary movie. (Other than cheesy film strips, a movie was about the only other visual medium then available.) When the film ended and the lights in the auditorium were turned back on, the professor was gone. His disappearance was dramatic, and many years later I can still recall the loud and extended applause that presumably the professor never heard.

While I've never come close to duplicating the archaeology professor's dramatic moment, many of my recent "last classes" in my Evidence course have included a brief awards "ceremony." The awards ceremony provides entertainment while recapturing some of the classroom highlights of the previous weeks. Many students have told me that the ceremony provided one of their fondest memories of law school. I describe it here for any who may want to adapt it for their own use.

Below are the awards I announced at the end of my final Evidence class for spring semester 2004. As you can see, a few of the categories are appropriate for every course.

Other categories grew out of student comments and behavior that was specific to this spring semester class. Up until this last semester, the awards were imagined only; I splurged big time in spring 2004 and distributed mint candies to the winners. While a few of the students had "heard something" about my giving awards, very few knew of the particulars and no one knew in advance that he or she had been selected for an award. I've protected the winners' privacy by providing only their initials.

1. The "Confrontation Award," to N. L. for supporting unlimited attacks on witnesses' credibility. (This award went to a student who argued that parties should be free to offer evidence contradicting anything said by an adverse witness, though the actual rule is not nearly that broad.)
2. The "Survivor UCLA" Award, to J.G., B.C., D.K., and R.C. for making it through two courses with me in the same semester.
3. The "Aerobics" Award to T.L. and S.M. for classroom arm waving. (This category went to two students who in my estimation asked the most questions during the semester, though in past years I've given the award to only one student. I did not actually keep track of how many questions students asked; the award reflected my impression at the end of the course. The reactions of the other students indicated that they agreed with my choices!)
4. The "Best Supporting Student" Award to C.G. for giving me the "doggy" article. (This award honored a student who'd found and downloaded an article on expert witness testimony relating to dog scent evidence that I incorporated into class discussions.)
5. The "Best Brown Noser" Award to B.S. for being the only student judge to rule in my favor after a foundational argument. (When I conduct role-playing foundational exercises, I typically appoint students to act as judges and advocates, but I occasionally play an advocate role.)
6. The "Best Achievement in Special Effects" Award to C.B. for her closing argument for the defense in the "Baby Ruth Murder Trial." (This award remembered a student's particularly stirring closing argument during one of the role plays.)
7. The "Lost in Cyberspace" Award to D.K. for sending me the most email questions. (While this category goes beyond the students' classroom experiences, the announcement of the award is always a source of great amusement. Again, I base it on an impression at the end of the semester rather than on empirical reality.)
8. The "Best Achievement in Sound" Award to P.G. for ensuring that nearby students could hear students' classroom comments and questions. (This award went to a student who sat on the side of the large classroom towards the back, who seemed to always be the one to raise her hand when another student spoke too quietly to be heard by her or the students sitting near her.)
9. The "Best Casting Director" Award to E.N. for adding two extras over the duration of the course. (This award went to a student whose wife gave birth to twins a few weeks into the semester, an event widely anticipated by his classmates.)
10. The "How Did You Ever Make It to Class after the Barristers Ball" Award to S.M. (This award went to a student who had described a wild night of third-year class partying in the law school newspaper.)
11. The "One More Office Visit and You'd Have to Pay Rent" Award to L.W. for most office hour visits. (This category too is beyond students' classroom experiences, but always a source of amusement.)

12. The "Gratitude" Award to all of you from me. (This "award" gives me a chance within the context of the ceremony to elaborate a bit on my feelings about the time we've spent together.)

Paul Bergman
UCLA School of Law

Making Cents of Intestate Distribution Concepts

When you teach the topic of intestacy, you will probably want your students to master the three alternative distribution schemes for intestate succession among descendants: per stirpes, per capita with representation, and per capita at each generation. I designed the following tactile learning exercise so students will experience how the differences between these schemes actually shift what property each heir receives.

To prepare for this exercise, create a family tree that shows one decedent at the oldest generational level, with three children (A, B, and C), with A having two children and B and C having one child each. (I use PowerPoint to create an organizational chart and use that.) Also, assemble several zip-lock bags, each holding four nickels and sixteen pennies (36¢). You should have one bag of coins and one copy of the family tree for each group of two to four students.

To lead the exercise, divide students into small groups and give each group a family tree and a bag of coins. Tell the students that a decedent has died leaving an estate of 36¢ (net of legal fees) and you will be administering the estate under several fact patterns and each of the three main varieties of intestate distribution statutes. Ask the students to place the coins on the decedent's square on the family tree to start.

You will next lead the students through applying each style of intestate distribution statute, varying who has survived the decedent each time. After you announce the descendants who have survived and the distribution scheme to apply, give the students a minute or so to move the coins to the squares on the family tree that represents the heirs who should receive the money. Then call on a group or volunteer to explain how they moved the coins. I also find it useful to show how the coins should end up, either by showing a PowerPoint slide or writing on the board.

First, tell students to consider the situation where the decedent has died leaving all three children living. Have them divide the coins to show how distribution would be allocated under per stirpes, then per capita with representation, then per capita at each generation. Because the distribution would be the same under these facts, in each case the students should move 12¢ to the squares for A, B and C.

Next, tell students to consider the situation where the decedent has died leaving two of three children living (A has died). Ask the students to move the coins to show how distribution would be allocated under each system of inheritance. Again, the three systems function the same way under these facts, so the students should move 12¢ to B, 12¢ to C, and 6¢ to each of A's two children.

Under the next fact pattern, tell students to consider the situation where the decedent has died leaving only one of three children living, where one deceased child has more children than another deceased child (A and B have died). Ask the students to move the coins to show how distribution would be allocated under each system of inheritance. Under these facts, the differences between the three distributive schemes do affect how the money descends. Under per stirpes and per capita with representation, A's two children each get

6¢, B's one child gets 12¢, and C gets 12¢. However, because the system of per capita at each generation uses a pooling concept and re-divides the assets that are not claimed at one generation equally among members of the lower generation who have lost a parent, under that system A's two children and B's one child each get 8¢, while C gets 12¢.

Finally, instruct students to consider the situation where the decedent has died leaving no living children (A, B and C have all died) with only grandchildren surviving. Ask the students to move the coins to show how distribution would be allocated under each system of inheritance. Again, under these facts the differences between the three distributive schemes do affect how the money descends. Under per stirpes, because the initial division is still made at the level of the children even though none of them have survived, each of A's children get 6¢ and B's one child and C's one child each get 12¢. However, under per capita with representation and per capita at each generation, the division is not made until the generational level where there are survivors, so all grandchildren share equally, with A's two children, B's one child, and C's one child each taking 9¢.

Students have told me that they enjoy this exercise and find it more useful than talking about the systems in the abstract or working through hypotheticals. I like that it drives home the point that varieties in intestate distribution statutes actually change who gets what, rather than just being a set of rules to memorize. Because I teach intestacy early in the semester (often the second or third class), it's a nice opportunity to set a more active and collaborative tone for the course. I hope you find it makes your class on death a bit livelier.

Alyssa A. DiRusso
Samford University, Cumberland School of Law

Learning by Magic—It's Not a Trick

"As I pass the cards from this shuffled deck past your eyes very quickly I want you to look at the cards and remember one card."

After I have showed all the cards in the deck, I close the deck and place one card face down on the table. I then ask the spectator to reveal the one card she remembered. Over 90% of the time it will be the card I placed face down on the table. If it is not that card, it will be either the top or bottom card on the deck in my hand.

To most people this simple card effect is amazing. The spectator is certain she had a free choice—and, in a sense, she did. But if she followed my directions, she was simply looking at the cards as they passed in front of her eyes until I said one word: "remember." When her brain processed the word "remember," it did what it was told without conscious effort. It went from "looking at" the cards to following my further direction to "remember" one card, and that card will almost always be the card that was in front of her eyes at that precise moment. A simple cut of the deck at that point after all the other cards have been shown allows me to place "the remembered card" on the table. (The cards that were just before and just after the remembered card will be on the top and the bottom of the deck just in case I am one card off the mark.) The rest is showmanship.

Why does this trick work? It works because, once one has a person's attention and willingness to comply, the brain will do what it is told. When a person is simply asked "to look at" something, the person will do no more than look. Because there is no stated need to retain any particular information, the brain doesn't. When the brain is told to "remember" something, the brain will follow the direction instantly.

The application of this simple magic effect to student learning in a classroom should be evident. Students will generally do what they are instructed to do. Watch what happens when you tell students, "This information is important;" or, "You need to know this for the bar exam;" or, "This will likely be on the final exam." What you are really saying is, "Remember this!" When you use these words, students' fingers are flying over their computer keys to be sure they get it right. They will also ask questions if there is something they don't understand. You have their full attention. More importantly, you have a direct connection to their brains.

When a teacher is merely lecturing or discussing a case, or even asking questions using the Socratic Method, the students' attention may not be focused. They may be taking notes, but note-taking can often be a somewhat passive exercise. The students' brains are not necessarily engaged. This difference between passive note-taking and active engagement helps explain why students learn best when they are given a task or an exercise to participate in. They have to use their brains to figure out what to do. By informing the students that they are to do something that requires the engagement of their brains, teachers engage their students in the learning process.

Most magic effects take advantage of the principle that, by diverting one's attention—called "misdirection"—a successful ending will be a magical surprise. The magical surprise of engaging the brain directly is that, by focusing students' attention on what is important, students will actually remember what they are taught. It is no trick. It will have truly magical results.

Stephen A. Gerst
Phoenix School of Law

Crumbling Myths and Dashed Expectations

Perhaps the greatest hurt comes from the dashed expectation. The canceled vacation. The rejection letter coming on the heels of a great interview. The other team's successful 60-foot desperation three-pointer when your team is up two with 0:01 on the clock. In law school, it's not just the unexpected non-A grade. It's the classroom experience so different and so unexpected that it triggers the same emotions as do the cancellations, the rejections, and the losses.

That law school education differs in terms of subject matter isn't the issue. It's the existence of a different educational objective: to help students acquire the habit of "thinking like a lawyer" and to internalize the experience of "practicing like a lawyer."

The second one may be easier. It can be fun. It's part of the motivation behind the explosion in available clinic experiences. It's the simulated trials, the appellate arguments in competitions and in practice preparations, the drafting courses with mock clients, the pro bono extracurricular activities, and probably some other things I have overlooked. Indeed, all of these things require diligence and effort. No problem. Hard work is always a lot easier when it's fun and when it feels good.

It's the first objective that is such a thorn in most students' sides, at least until they catch on to the reality. Most students are unfamiliar with the practice-oriented endeavors, so there's little risk of dashed expectations. But all students have been enrolled in classroom courses, and thus all students bring expectations of what should happen in the classroom. When those expectations are reinforced, it is even more difficult to break old habits and junk old approaches. Yet tossing out routines is easy. The challenge is developing and learning new ones. It's particularly disappointing when it comes as a surprise that "the way I was doing things doesn't work anymore." It's even worse when people pretend that there is some way to get by with the old outlook.

Creating expectations of what law school education will be by relying on previous classroom experiences creates a set of myths. Deconstruction of these myths is an unpleasant task, and the temptation is to avoid doing so. It's much easier to twist one's participation in legal education to fit the myths. The result? The dashed expectations appear during the first legal job because employers do not, and cannot, twist their clients' problems to fit the myths.

Myth #1. Law consists of rules, so the only thing faculty should do is just to tell us what the rules are.

Deconstruction: Law consists of the processing of rules in the context of facts. The rules alone are useless, and sometimes there are no applicable rules. In fact, the rules change, sometimes quite frequently, so just "knowing" the rules ultimately is useless. Thinking about the rules, how to use them, and how to change them brings perpetual value.

Myth #2. All we need are the answers, and if we don't get them, we're not being well taught.

Deconstruction: If law consisted simply of questions and definite answers, computers would replace lawyers. Clients generally pay for advice when the answer isn't clear, when there are two sides to the story, when there are conflicting appellate opinions, or when there is no authority whatsoever. Often there is more than one possible strategy, creating answers of "It depends" or "Who knows?" To think there always is a "clear answer" is an invitation to serious problems in practice.

Myth #3. The professor's job is to teach us by providing information.

Deconstruction: In graduate school, the responsibility for acquiring information is the student's. In theory, classroom discussion presupposes an equality of informational background among the participants. Sadly, it never quite works this way. The risk is that the professorial attempt to ensure that the informational background is not too dissimilar is translated into an "Oh, good, we get lectures and can take notes so we can regurgitate information on the examination just as we did in college" mindset. Yes, students are expected to have strong knowledge of the subject before entering class.

Myth #4. Anything not directly on point to the issue is a useless tangent.

Deconstruction: One of the most important skills of an efficiently thinking lawyer is the adept use of analogies. When there is no answer to the resolution of question seven, it helps to look at the analyses used for questions six, eight, and perhaps 43.j.2(a). Out on those tangents are the clues to resolving the problem confronting the lawyer or student that has no answer.

Myth #5. We are the ones who should ask questions, and good teachers do not ask questions in response to our questions or comments.

Deconstruction: Not only is the asking of a question in response to a student question often the hallmark of the quasi-Socratic Method, once and justifiably pervasive in legal education, it also is a genuine attempt to probe and develop a student's mind.

Myth #6. We don't need to attend school if we must teach ourselves, and thus law school courses should not be self-taught.

Deconstruction: Law school is all about learning how to teach oneself. There are good ways and bad ways to teach oneself. By attending law school, students learn how to identify and use the method of self-teaching that is most effective for them. Introducing students to a variety of self-teaching methods that seem strange (and intimidating) because they are new and different is part of that process. Helping people learn to teach themselves is called education. Students attend law school to acquire a legal education, not to be taught law.

Myth #7. Good teaching requires that all communication occur in the classroom.

Deconstruction: Does good lawyering demand that all communication occur in the courtroom or the partner's office? Intranets, email, digital bulletin boards, online filing, and electronic conferencing permeate 21st-century legal practice.

Myth #8. We can do well by cramming at the end of the semester because that approach worked in college.

Deconstruction: That approach doesn't work in the practice-oriented courses, and for the same reason it doesn't work in the other courses. Learning how to use rules in solving or preventing legal problems can no more easily be learned the night before an exam (or the night before a trial) than can an orchestra give a stellar performance of a new opus first encountered two hours before the house lights dim.

It's no fun finding out that class, practice, or life isn't tracking one's expectations. It's easy to translate that disappointment into "I hate law school," "I dislike this," "I resent that," or some other negative expression or to act out one's frustration in misbehavior of one kind or another. Rather than rebelling and griping, it's better to amend the expectation to comport with the realities of law and legal education and to abandon unrealistic standards. At that point, law school can become a fun experience that boosts self-esteem and enriches one's life. Far fewer cancellations, rejections, and losses.

James Maule
Villanova University School of Law

Motivating Students to Read for Class: A Practical Tool

As law professors, we know that a certain percentage of our students fail to complete the readings assigned for class. Some students complete all of the readings, but many—perhaps most—read only sporadically and some do not read at all, relying instead on the professor's lectures and commercial study guides as their only source of information about the subject matter.

In doctrinal or lecture courses, we hope that whether they read or not, students' knowledge, or lack thereof, will be roughly reflected by their course grade. Thus, we may not be overly concerned about students who fail to read for or participate in class, or whose attendance is a bit spotty. Some students can sufficiently master the material through sources and methods other than class sessions (study groups, study guides, etc.) and reading the casebook. Students know the risk they take and the price they will likely pay come grade time if they miss class or neglect reading assignments. Professors often allow students to make the choice—within reasonable limits.

But the problem is far more troublesome in seminar courses where grades, and the course itself, are structured around student research papers and class participation. Without a final examination, there is no mechanism to hold students accountable for mastering the information found in the course readings and class discussions. It is hard to know whether a student has mastered the subject matter other than that relating to the narrow topic of his or her research paper. Students may have little motivation to read the assigned materials. Usually, students get a good enough sense of the readings through the professor's lecture or general class discussion to enable them to make or respond to the occasional class comment or question, though often without much insight. This deficiency, in turn, degrades the quality of class discussion, which is so critical for effective seminars. Frequently, questions and comments betray the students' failure to read, consider, or think critically about the reading materials assigned for class.

The degree to which students neglect reading assignments undoubtedly varies widely across schools, courses, and professors. Apparently, there have been no studies of the problem in legal education. However, a recent longitudinal study documents a significant decline in undergraduate students' completion of course reading assignments over the last decade. These empirical results are consistent with a great deal of recent commentary in both the scholarly and the popular press reporting the decline of academic standards in higher education and the rise of the student-as-consumer culture, with attendant decline in the students' work ethic.

The Reading Certification

Although there are several pedagogical techniques available, it is difficult to motivate students to think critically, the way a scholar might, about topical readings. At a minimum, however, it should be possible to ensure that most students have read the course assignments. One pragmatic tool in the law professor's arsenal is the "Reading Certification," a technique that I have used in many of my seminar courses. This practical tool can be used alongside pedagogical techniques designed to foster critical thinking about course topics and readings. At the end of the semester, students are required to sign the following written statement:

> On my honor; I pledge that I have completed, in substantial part, the assigned readings for this course. My completion of the reading assignments is worth 7% of my final course grade.

Students may, of course, decide not to complete the assigned readings and thus not sign the pledge, thereby losing seven percentage points toward their final grade. The "substantial part" clause in the certification ensures that students who have fulfilled the spirit of the reading requirement are not unfairly penalized simply by virtue of having failed to read a few pages here and there.

At the beginning of the semester, I gently pitch the reading certification as a way for students to automatically earn seven "free points" toward their final grade simply by doing something that they otherwise would be expected to do for the course. I emphasize the purpose of the requirement—that students must read the assigned materials to get the most out of the course—and the specific ways in which completing it will improve their classroom experience. I also acknowledge that the reading certification is based on the honor system, and that while one cannot naively assume that all students are always honest, I trust that students will live up to their professional and ethical obligations. I point out that a student's failure to sign the reading certification at the end of the semester will not otherwise affect their grade (beyond the seven percentage points), or my regard for them as a student.

The results have been encouraging. The quality of class discussion has improved since I instituted the reading certification requirement, and I have the sense that most students are reading the assignments. In most courses, one or two students do not sign the certification, which may indicate student integrity under the honor system. Of course, some students "cheat." The extent of student cheating will likely vary according to the culture of the institution and the strength of its honor system; in addition, students may feel greater or lesser loyalty to particular professors. But some student cheating is a small price to pay in return for a seminar class where more students are prepared by virtue of having read the class assignment. It makes for a much richer learning experience.

Moreover, students have reacted favorably—or at least not unfavorably—to the reading certification requirement. One might be concerned that students would view it as too paternalistic, coercive, or patronizing, and perhaps they do, though I have not had a single student complain about the requirement. Indeed, some appear to appreciate it as a way to easily earn 7% of their final grade. Another concern is that the requirement acts as an extrinsic motivator for students, whereas we should be fostering and rewarding students' intrinsic motivation to read and learn. Reading certifications, however, are no different from a variety of other extrinsic motivators we routinely use in pedagogy. It is unlikely that reading certifications would reduce the intrinsic motivation of students who otherwise would have read the assignments, whereas it likely will motivate those students who require extrinsic motivation. In any case, recent psychological research has drawn into question the traditional assumption that intrinsic educational motivators are always preferable to extrinsic ones, or that extrinsic motivators decrease intrinsic motivation for learning.

Reading certifications provide an easy, pragmatic tool to help ensure that students complete the assigned readings in seminar courses. But getting students to think deeply and critically about what they read is, of course, the much more daunting challenge.

Richard E. Redding
Chapman University School of Law

My Faculty, My Students, Myself: Thoughts on Being New to Academic Support

As a new Academic Support Professor, the challenges I faced were myriad, but the sense of accomplishment and delight inherent in facing and conquering them was unparalleled. In looking back on the past year, I found that the challenges I faced could be attributed to one or more of three major groups, which I will term my faculty, my students, and myself.

But before I faced any of those issues, I had to first address a threshold question. I needed to define my purpose, to define my large scale objectives in the universe of my classroom.

After much thought, I decided that Academic Support, at least for me, would be a program, a set of classes and individual meetings, in which students would obtain necessary instruction and would benefit from a peer-supported learning environment. My classroom would be a forum where students could try on new, difficult, or otherwise missed ideas without fear of embarrassment, where students could tackle legal thinking and learning from a new angle, and where students would make understanding their own learning process part of addressing the larger questions that would ensure them improved classroom performance. I also wanted to create an environment in which students could rediscover the joy of learning that, more often than not, had carried them through their academic careers before the law school phase, but had been lost in law school, perhaps as a result of a forced curve, difficulty level, or other concerns.

I would address needed skills and try to impart a passion for thinking critically about legal issues. If there was any big picture idea I wanted my students to have, a relentless passion for new knowledge was it. This passion, I thought, would propel them through the remainder of their law school careers and do much to ensure that they became happy, healthy lawyers beyond the university halls.

My major goals were, then, twofold: to help students with practical and immediate learning-related issues, and to ensure that the process of addressing those issues resulted in students who were able to carry those skills beyond the Academic Support Program (ASP) classroom. These goals seemed reasonable tacks for a new educator and, as I grappled with these and other ideas throughout the course of my first year, I found that these were indeed workable goals for my teaching experience.

But after settling these larger questions, I still found a need to address the other, less theoretical challenges that would face me as a new Academic Support Instructor. I broke these challenges into three categories: dealing with the academy environment as an Academic Support instructor, reaching difficult students, and managing my expectations with respect to both myself and my charges. In other words, they broke into three clear categories, my faculty, my students, and myself.

Dealing with the academy was the first challenge that I faced outside of the classroom. I found that it was my duty to dispel what I call the Magic Wand Theory of ASP—the idea that, with the help of a few key texts and exercises, absolutely anyone could turn a struggling student into a strong one, and that, as a result, ASP was not entitled to a legitimate, important status within the legal academy.

Fortunately for me, I work with a wonderfully open-minded faculty, all of whom love to talk, listen, and debate. They dialogued with me as I explained teaching methods I had just learned about or described conference presentations by which I had been enlightened. They listened when I told them the stories of brilliant students who had struggled initially and, after a semester in ASP, had demonstrated their capability beyond all doubt. Slowly, conversation by conversation, a task that had at first had seemed daunting, began to be pleasant as I discovered that what I had thought was a complex problem could be solved by the simplest of actions; just talking with our faculty has proven the most effective and straightforward means of clarifying the importance and efficacy of ASP. Today there are few, if any, adherents of the Magic Wand Theory remaining and the result of all this talking is that I enjoy a wonderful working relationship with many of the people who I once worried would never embrace ASP.

The challenge that has proved far greater, and the one that, after years of preparation for the job I thought I was most prepared to face, has been dealing with difficult student situations. Student troubles vary tremendously, often presenting me with a classroom of people who each have unique strengths and weaknesses, backgrounds and behaviors. I have been at this job for less than three semesters and already I have seen issues that run the gamut.

Ranging from extreme PTSD to deep-seated family troubles, from an alarming lack of boundaries to simple anger at not having performed as expected, these individualized problems have presented my greatest challenges. Dealing with each has been very much an exercise in working case-by-case. In tackling these problems, I have found that identifying a student's problem is often half the battle. And in the identification game, I have found nothing more valuable than the students' trust. The rapport building needed to establish this trust takes time, and I have learned to allow the students to open up to me on their own schedules, to give them whatever space they need before we take on their troubles together.

Building rapport with students, convincing faculty that ASP is something to be embraced, and facilitating a classroom environment that stands in line with my specific, daily and long-term, global teaching goals has sometimes felt daunting, but has also proven exhilarating. And in the course of addressing these goals, my third challenge emerged. Learning to pace myself and allowing things to take time, instead of trying to do everything for everyone all at once, has been more difficult than I ever imagined. When I began at ASU, I wanted to do so many things. I wanted to maintain the spectacular program my predecessor had put into place. I wanted to both emulate her and develop my own style both in and out of the classroom. I wanted to expand our program and add an upper level ASP class. I wanted to give a presentation to the faculty. I wanted to meet everyone in our national ASP community. And I wanted to solve every student problem, whether academic or personal, with precision, perfection, and compassion. Needless to say, I learned very quickly that all of these things, together with preparing for a new slate of classes and establishing roots in a new city, were impossible to do all at once and, after months of sixteen-hour days, the law of diminishing returns found me at last and forced me to acknowledge that I had become one of my own professional challenges.

Today, I allow things to evolve more naturally. Like building rapport with my students and my faculty, developing my program takes time. I am delighted now to look back on the past year and recognize how far I've come. I spent my first two semesters doing the essential, getting to know the material in my classes, the seminal literature in the field, the culture of my institution, and the needs and personalities of the individual students. This semester, I have inaugurated a program for upper-level students. Next, I will begin writing an article that I am researching. The semester after that, who knows? I have learned to trust that, with continued hard work and commitment to helping my students succeed, new goals, and the means by which to meet them, will arise in their own time. For now, I am delighted to work every day toward helping my students through the law school learning experience, guiding and supporting them as they seek out their own goals and truths, to become stronger people, more effective law students, and, I hope, in the end, lifelong legal learners.

Corie Lynn Rosen
Arizona State University, Sandra Day O'Connor College of Law

Class Participation Preference Survey—Silent Students

In a questionnaire (below), I elicit student preferences for how to participate in class discussion from the following:

1. Being called on without warning;
2. Being called on with advance warning;
3. Being called on as part of a group;
4. Being called on to respond to questions provided in advance;
5. Participating when you've been assigned a particular role to play; or
6. Silent class participation—short in-class writing.

Almost no one likes option 1, cold calling. Most prefer options 2, 3, 4, or 5. Some students prefer option 6. Most students appreciate being asked. Most also appreciate that, in response to the questionnaire, I have eliminated cold calling from my classroom.

To honor some students' preferences for "silent class participation"—and to ensure everyone is keeping up with reading—I've added several short in-class writing exercises to a class for which there is no exam (Civil Rights Litigation).

One example is an in-class short essay. Students have 20 minutes to read the scenario, draft, and upload a short essay response. We then spend about ten minutes discussing the key points as a class. While it would be a useful self-assessment even if it ended there, after class, I skim the student essays and post four of the best ones on the course webpage, for an additional opportunity for students to assess their understanding. The essay could count as a small part of the student grade or could instead be subsumed into class participation (what I do).

Another example of "silent class participation" is a multiple-choice or True/False quiz. Students have 15 minutes in class to read and upload answers. The class as a whole then spends ten minutes discussing the quiz. Students appreciate the immediate feedback on their absorption of class material. (I have students send answers as the subject line of an email so I can quickly scan my inbox to gauge correct and incorrect answers for each question—but this likely could be accomplished more efficiently with clickers, a technology I currently do not have.)

Sarah Ricks
Rutgers School of Law–Camden

Questionnaire for Civil Rights: Current Issues in Constitutional Litigation

Name:

Brief description of 1L and 2L summer jobs:

Brief description of all law jobs held during any law school semester, if any:

Career plans—short and long term goals:

Previous experience with civil rights litigation, if any:

Why you're taking this class (fine to say "time slot") & some things you hope to get from the experience:

Generally, are you comfortable speaking in class?

Do you have any preferences among the following:

1. Being called on without warning;
2. Being called on with advance warning;
3. Being called on as part of a group;
4. Being called on to respond to questions provided in advance;
5. Participating when you've been assigned a particular role to play; or
6. Silent class participation—short in-class writing.

What can I do to help make you more comfortable speaking in class, if anything?

Motivating Students to Learn

Motivation is the fulcrum that moves student learning. Indeed, no learning can take place unless students are motivated by the subject matter. At bottom, motivating students is about capturing their interest and attention. All the time we spend as teachers developing a syllabus, preparing lectures and creating classroom materials will mean little if we do not also have an appreciation for the critical importance of stimulating our students' interest in the subject matter.

Motivating students to learn is a complex skill involving aspects of psychology, rapport between teacher and students, and students' innate interest in the material presented. With respect to the latter, there is general agreement that students have to assume some responsibility for their own learning. More specifically, to get anything meaningful out of the experience, students need to show up to class wanting to learn. Even the best teacher cannot force a group of students to learn about a subject they do not care about. Nevertheless, teachers can develop the ability to positively influence students' internal motivating mechanisms through an understanding and application of motivational theory. While numerous theories exist to explain human motivation (one commentator catalogues at least 32 of them), most of them share several elements in common that have direct application to the classroom.

Law students, like the rest of us, are more likely to engage in a subject if they see a good reason for doing so. In the parlance of motivational theory, this notion is referred to as the "value" component to student motivation. This component consists of both an intrinsic and extrinsic element. The intrinsic element refers to the extent to which the subject matter appeals to a student's personal, academic or professional goals. Teachers, therefore, generally do not have much difficulty motivating students to learn in electives or other courses they self-select. The challenge for most teachers is to motivate students in the required courses, and especially the unpopular ones like legal writing, which I teach.

Obviously, the more we can do to make the material as interesting as possible, the better motivated students will be to learn it. Beyond that, we can do as much as possible to relate the classroom material to our students' professional goals of becoming lawyers. When discussing material in class, illustrate key points with examples from practice. Try to relate the material to the kinds of problems students will face. One technique I use when teaching them analytical skills is to use role-playing. For example, I will present students with a hypothetical legal problem based on the cases we have read for class and then place them in the role of attorneys who have to advise a client on an appropriate course of action based on their analysis of those cases. The more I can do to make the classroom mirror what students can expect to happen in practice, the more success I have getting them to learn the material.

The extrinsic value component of motivational theory refers to the external rewards the teacher connects to the material. Grades, and the desire for approval from the teacher or peers, are the most common examples. This aspect of motivational theory tells us that we can boost student motivation by adding graded components to the semester, such as occasional quizzes or take home assignments or by making class participation count towards the final grade. I have experimented with using class participation as a course component, and motivational theory confirms my own experience that the quality of class discussion improves when I tell students it will count toward their final grade.

Research tells us that intrinsic factors tend to be more powerful motivators than the extrinsic ones. This same research tells us, however, that student motivation is optimized when the teacher relies on a combination of intrinsic and extrinsic factors. Thus, we need to both make the material interesting, important and relevant to our students as well as create the proper academic incentives to encourage them to take it seriously.

There is also an "expectancy" component to student motivation. This concept refers to the idea that students who believe they can succeed at a new skill or task are more likely to engage in it. Thus, we can affect student learning positively by creating a supportive atmosphere in the classroom. This task must be done with integrity, however, because falsely praising students can undermine their motivation. If a student perceives praise as insincere or facile, they can become less, rather than more, motivated. No expert has ever suggested that merely heaping praise upon students will help them do good work. On the contrary, studies show that teachers who set high standards for their students and then establish a supportive atmosphere in the classroom that encourages them to do their best work are the most effective at motivating students to learn.

The next aspect of motivational theory is the "affective" component which refers to the students' emotional response to the task at hand. A classroom that engenders feelings of excitement, enjoyment and interest will enhance motivation to learn while classrooms that produce anxiety, stress or boredom have a deleterious effect on student motivation. A practical example can be found in the emotional milieu we create in connection with our Socratic dialogue with students during class. If we question students in a way that increases their fear of failure or provokes shame or embarrassment, then we negatively impact their learning. On the other hand, if we proffer questions to them in a way that is designed to engender excitement in discovering their ability to find the "correct" answer, we can positively influence their learning. It is vitally important that we be aware of the way in which the emotional atmosphere we create in our classrooms affects student learning. This point has particular application in the law school setting where studies show that students suffer more stress and anxiety than those enrolled in any other post-graduate course of study.

Connected to the affective component of motivational theory is the fact that our own attitudes about the material we teach can have a great impact on student motivation. Social psychologists have documented the phenomenon known as "emotional contagion." The emotions and attitudes of the speaker have a great impact on those of the audience. In short, if we are demonstrably enthusiastic about what we are teaching, we will tend to make our students enthusiastic about it as well. Conversely, if we project disinterest, boredom, or worse, denigrate the material we teach, we tend to infect our students with those kinds of attitudes as well. For this reason, researchers studying effective classroom behaviors of college professors have found that a teacher's passion for the material being taught is directly related to student motivation to learn. Indeed, this research shows that passionate teachers tend to not only better motivate students to take their own courses more seriously, but also inspire students to explore the subject matter further outside of class. In the end, that is the goal of all good teachers.

James B. Levy
Nova Southeastern University, Shepard Broad Law Center

Teaching Outside the Box: A Focus on Learning

We all desire to be the best we can be at our teaching. But, is *desiring* to be the best the same as *preparing* to be the best? Will our best shot at teaching bring about the students' best learning? Maybe it's time to take a step back, outside our role as teachers, and focus instead on learning and the connection between learning and teaching.

Parker Palmer may have said it best in *The Courage to Teach* (1998),

> [T]eachers possess the power to create conditions that can help students learn a great deal—or keep them from learning much at all. Teaching is the intentional act of creating those conditions, and good teaching requires that we understand the inner sources of both the intent and the act.

To be an effective teacher we need to be clear about *why* we teach what we teach and what we hope to accomplish in the process. Many of us derive *what* we teach from our textbook—14 weeks of assignments, 14 weeks of instruction—simple! However, simply adopting a textbook as the focus of *what we hope to accomplish* places the emphasis of instruction squarely on imparting rules from instructor to student, on covering a pre-determined outline of information. Glaringly absent from this focus is the student. Moreover, when what we hope to accomplish is limited to simply imparting information, we often experience less than satisfactory results from our students and little if any teaching satisfaction for ourselves.

It's time to toss aside that well-worn textbook and take up pen and paper. Of course we need to teach our students the rules. But, what else can we teach them in the process?

- In what ways does your knowledge go beyond the black letter law?
- What experience do you have to share?
- What skills can you impart that would be useful to students?
- How could you teach those skills?

This is where the pen and paper come in. Begin by making a list of what, besides substantive content, you could be teaching your students. This list can be the foundation for a new set of learning goals.

A learning goal (versus a learning objective) is a broad statement of what the learners will be expected to know and be able to do once they have completed a specified course of instruction. As you read through the following three broad goals, notice how they generally can provide the answer to the question: what do you hope to accomplish? You just need to fill in the details, gleaned from your answers to the questions listed above.

- Teach the students the black letter law.
- Teach the students how to analyze a problem by applying the law to a particular factual situation.
- Further the students' ability to be critical thinkers by providing a set of processes and concepts that will allow the students to think through any subject or discipline, through any problem or issue.

Traditionally, law school courses focused on teaching black letter law, with the Socratic Method employed to assess a student's ability to glean rules from case law. The goal was to teach the substantive content of an area of the law.

With the publication of *The MacCrate Report*, law schools began pushing towards more application-oriented teaching, reflected primarily in the creation of new clinical programs. In some classrooms, problem-solving skills were added to substantive learning. Without a doubt, this approach takes us a step beyond merely imparting a substantive area of the law to the students.

Can we go further? *The Carnegie Report* and *Best Practices for Legal Education* urge us to teach students how to approach the practice of law. Can we teach our students to be critical thinkers? And, if critical thinking skills are our goal, what does that look like in our classrooms?

First, we must be willing to step outside the box of traditional law school teaching methodologies and into a new paradigm of legal education. This change requires moving the focus of attention away from the professor standing at the front of the classroom (teaching) and onto the students (learning). If we truly believe that the purpose of law schools is to foster and develop students who demonstrate higher-order thinking skills and the ability to skillfully evaluate the application of the law, we must get out their way and give them the opportunity to learn these skills.

In turn, the students must leave their role as scribes, faithfully and passively recording our words of wisdom with minimal thought or understanding. It's time to wake them up and give them a reason to think about what they are hearing. We must engage them and provide opportunities in the classroom for them to explore, apply, and puzzle-out answers for themselves. We must ask them to analyze and assess their understanding and reasoning, identify strengths and weaknesses in their analysis, and develop strategies that will enable them to apply critical thinking to any possible problem or issue. With a critical thinking approach, the students have opportunity to think rather than memorize, argue effectively rather than recite, think of possible implications of the law rather than prepare an outline.

For those still squeamish about embracing a focus on students and critical thinking, we pose three questions.

1. Is there anything in the content of what you teach that isn't adequately addressed in case law, a hornbook, or other secondary source?
2. Could a well-trained attorney locate and understand such information?
3. What characteristics come to mind when you read "well-trained attorney"?

Learning through critical thinking will look different with each teacher and in each classroom. We can, however, point out some common denominators. First, critical thinking skills grow best in a nonthreatening, as well as supportive, learning environment. As professors, we must respect the students as decision makers; we must nurture their willingness to explore the state of law and the ramifications of how it has developed or could be developed. *The MacCrate Report* says, "Learning is dependent on thought, produced by thought, analyzed by thought, comprehended, organized, maintained, and transformed by thought." We must enable learning by focusing more on that thought process, and less on the conclusion reached.

Second, designing a classroom around student engagement and critical thinking comes with a cost—significant use of class time. There is tension between the need to get through the designated course content and spending time on critical thinking skills. How to resolve that tension lies in the question needing to be answered: What do we hope to accomplish? Is our goal to teach the students all the intricate rules of every subject matter? Or is our goal to teach the students how to figure out an intricate rule on their own, if and when the need arises?

Yes, this approach is very different from traditional law school teaching. To be done effectively, it requires effort and change. It can be unsettling. We must leave behind our safe and secure role as the sole source of correct information, dolling it out in a manner that is eerily similar to that of *The Wizard of Oz*. We must leave behind our almost childlike hand-hold on the students as we insist on leading them through the maze of rules. What we get in return is a classroom where students are engaged in the learning process.

Enthusiastic participation replaces bleary-eyed passiveness. Learning sparks the moment and life-long skills are developed. We, as professors, may be left well outside our comfort zones, but may soon discover that this new place, in fact, is the perfect place to be.

What thoughts does the approach invoke for you? Have you tried it? What successes and/or challenges have you had? Have you rejected it? Why? We would love to hear from you. Nothing better than a spirited debate to get us all thinking!

Vickie Eggers
Thomas M. Cooley Law School

Joni Larson
Thomas M. Cooley Law School

Chapter 5

Questioning and Discussion Techniques

> "Discussion is one of the most effective ways to make students aware of the range of interpretations that are possible in an area of intellectual inquiry."
>
> —Brookfield

A. Why Use Questions and Discussion in Your Course?

Engaging students in discussion helps their learning. By discussing a topic, students engage in it at a deeper level than when they read or listen, and, through questions, they can discover that a topic is more complex and contextual than they first might have assumed. For those students who crave black letter rules and definite answers, questions and discussion help them learn to navigate legal ambiguities.

In addition, engaging students in discussion allows for more diverse views and a wider variety of responses. Effective discussions involve more than the teacher and a handful of students who are eager and ready to speak in front of their colleagues; even in a large enrollment course, all students have the chance to speak with others through responding to questions and discussing their responses with the whole class or a group of classmates. Including a variety of participants in the discussion values and respects the students' differences and engages more of the students than when only a few people participate.

Students also benefit from discussion by hearing how their classmates approach a question. Often a law teacher, years away from being a law student, may struggle to understand a student's question or comment; another law student, however, may readily understand and do a better job clearing up the confusion. The peer's newness to the discipline affords insights into student thinking that are unavailable to the expert. Teaching and learning scholars note that no matter how well teachers explain material, students learn more from talking to each other than they do from hearing us speak.

By posing questions, we also teach students the important process of asking questions. For example, in asking students to name and then apply a test for what constitutes a hostile work environment, we model and walk them through the kind of internal questioning process they should take when encountering that issue. We also teach them the importance of not just reading texts, but engaging with the texts, questioning the material and trying to build extensions and hypotheticals to develop their understanding of doctrine.

In conducting classroom discussions, we also help students develop analytical skills and fluency. As lawyers, students will need to have the verbal skills to respond to questions that challenge their assumptions and demand evidence for their reasons. They will need to be articulate, flexible and mentally agile when discussing legal issues with clients, colleagues, decision-makers, and other audiences. By responding to and asking questions, students practice these skills and also learn to apply their thinking to new scenarios. By giving them feedback on their responses and questions, we also help them learn how to participate as professionals in legal discourse.

B. Creating Effective Classroom Discussions

Depending how we use them, questioning techniques can be one of the most effective ways to engage students in achieving all levels of critical thinking. Creating effective discussions works well when you:

- Provide clear expectations for student participation;
- Create a positive classroom learning environment;
- Teach students effective discussion techniques;
- Prepare students in advance;
- Ask clear questions;
- Ask one question at a time;
- Ask a range of questions;
- Elicit different levels of thinking;
- Allow sufficient wait-time (three seconds or more);
- Encourage and promote effective responses;
- Respond appropriately to ineffective answers;
- Address controversial topics and behaviors.

Provide Clear Expectations for Student Participation

At the beginning of the course, and in your syllabus, explain how you expect students to participate. Set parameters for the discussion. Will you rely on volunteers? Will you call on people randomly? What happens if students "pass"? Some teachers choose to count the quality—not quantity—of students' class participation as part of their grade. Other professors name the participation requirement "professional engagement" to stress that listening and respecting others is as important as speaking.

Especially for first-year students, explain why you use discussion as a teaching tool: discussion promotes in-depth learning and problem solving. Many new law students are unfamiliar with assessment instruments that require students to apply learning to new situations. It is helpful to show students examples of how they will be assessed in order to aid them in understanding the value of discussion. For example, giving them a short quiz early in the course quickly helps them realize that "learning the law" alone is not enough.

Create a Positive Learning Environment

To help students participate effectively in class, first create a positive learning environment where students feel safe taking risks. Build a positive classroom by showing your enthusiasm for student learning, appreciating their contributions to class discussion, calling students by name, modeling risk-taking, acknowledging your weaknesses, and being authentic.

If you do not know the answer to a question, admit it. If you make a mistake, acknowledge and correct it immediately or in the next class.

Teach Students Effective Discussion Techniques

Teachers can help students participate effectively by explaining the attributes of effective discussion, or, even better, by inviting students to help develop a list of effective discussion techniques. Most students, when asked, can quickly identify important features of effective discussion. They typically note that all participants should:

- Treat each other with respect;
- Listen and not dominate;
- Be prepared;
- Contribute occasionally in the discussion;
- Stay on task and be concise;
- Focus on the topic, not the speaker;
- Disagree civilly and avoid personal attacks;
- Speak loudly enough for everyone to hear.

Teachers can reinforce these principles by publicly acknowledging students when they are using these techniques.

Prepare Students in Advance

From handouts, webpages, syllabi, or other formats, give students enough information in advance so that they are prepared to discuss the questions. Particularly for more complex thinking skills, giving students advance notice of the problems the class will be discussing or, at least, the kind of thinking you want them to engage in will help them target their out-of-class studying. Not all questions have to or should be given in advance, but giving students core questions before class will help focus and deepen the level of discussion in class.

Model the kinds of responses you are looking for. For example, if you want first-year students to analyze and evaluate a defendant's response to a negligence claim, first show them how you would do so. For example, you can present students with a problem and then model the steps you would take in solving the problem, talking through each step, and admitting where you are stumped in the process. Pause as you go, allowing students to catch up with you and take notes.

Ask Clear Questions

Asking good questions is harder than we think. When we ask questions, we know what we are looking for. The students, some terrified of "getting it wrong" in front of their peers, may stumble and have little clue what we are asking. Writing down the questions ahead of time and being sure that they align with your class learning objectives will help improve the clarity of the questions you ask, and allow you to determine what type of thinking you are looking for. For students who are not auditory learners, or who are non-native English speakers, projecting your questions electronically or writing them on the board will allow the students to more readily process the question and focus on answering it. Avoid questions that suggest you are asking, "What am I thinking?" If you have a definite point you want a student to make, you may be effective in stating a proposition and asking students whether and why they agree or disagree.

We are more likely to ask clear questions if we know *why* we are asking them. For example, if we want to ascertain whether students understood material from the reading, we could ask them generally about the authorities they read. But we could make it easier for students to engage in the dialogue by naming what we are seeking to learn, such as, "The court used a number of factors in rejecting the claim for punitive damages. I'm wondering if you all identified the same factors, or interpreted this opinion differently. Phil, please start us off by identifying one of the factors that the court seems to use?" If you don't wish to call on a particular student, you could invite any student to respond, "Could someone start ... ?"

Ask One Question at a Time

Discipline yourself to staying with one question at a time. It is tempting to ask a question, and, then, if no one volunteers, rephrase the question or add to it. While it is ok to repeat a question if it is long or complex, adding questions compounds student confusion. Having written the questions out in advance is particularly helpful for avoiding such problems altogether.

Ask a Range of Questions

Open-ended questions are more likely to generate discussion than yes or no questions. Vary the kind of question and the length of time it takes students to respond. Some questions are effectively posed in a quick and ongoing repartee—think of a lively dinner table conversation—rather than a long question followed by a longer answer.

Elicit Different Levels of Thinking

Ask students questions along the range of thinking hierarchy. Depending where you are in the course and the context of the class, develop questions from lower and higher levels of thinking. For basic knowledge and comprehension, you could ask students to name a rule or give examples of how it might apply. For more sophisticated levels of thinking such as application and analysis, you could ask students to apply a rule to a new set of facts, analyze which test would apply to which set of circumstances, or discriminate between different issues. For the highest levels of thinking—synthesis and evaluation—ask students to contrast and combine different analytical approaches or tests, compare theories, or evaluate decisions.

As you progress through the course, ask students questions at increasingly more complex levels. Embed material about a concept studied earlier in a question about the current class topic, for example: "Let's review the tests administrative agencies use to ... [name tests briefly]. Let's apply those factors to ..." This allows students to integrate earlier concepts with more recent material, and helps them develop connections among different aspects of the course.

Allow Sufficient Wait-Time After You Ask a Question

The research shows that we usually wait only a second or two before we fill the silence with our own voices by making a comment or rephrasing the question. One second is not enough time for most students to generate a meaningful response. Giving yourselves and students three to five seconds to process the question usually results in more students being able to respond. You can explain this fact to students to address the awkwardness of the quiet. "I see that Becky's, Juan's, and Cole's hands are up. How about some others—people who haven't yet spoken this week—I'll wait."

Another way to give students time to think is to ask them to write a response in 30 to 60 seconds or to briefly discuss their response with a neighbor or two. These processes allow students a chance to reflect and work through their thinking.

Encourage and Promote Effective Responses

Actively listen to students' responses. Look at them, lean toward them, and avoid fiddling or interrupting. Acknowledge students' effective responses, both when they respond and later, (e.g. "Rafael made an excellent point. Remember how ..."). Be encouraging and coach students to develop their responses. "Great start! Now can you help me out by explaining how you arrived at that answer?" Smiling, nodding, being quiet, and making eye contact encourages students to elaborate. Leaning forward, writing students' responses on the board, and inviting others to help their classmates can all help build student confidence in responding to questions. Show delight when your students develop particularly insightful points and be sure to acknowledge insights that are new to you; your students will remember those moments, both as a sign of your respect for them and as a reflection of your own self-confidence in your expertise.

If the discussion needs to end, and students still have their hands up, you can end it with "last point goes to Nan" and invite others to talk to you after class.

Respond Appropriately to Ineffective Answers

When students give a "wrong" answer, help guide them to a better response, if at all possible. Focus on the answer, not on the student, and acknowledge any positive aspect of the response. Using a gentle sense of humor can help diffuse a potentially uncomfortable moment for the student, "Yes, that is so-o-o close! Take a look at the point on page 679 where it says ..." Give hints and cues (e.g. "Why didn't the attorney appeal the administrative decision?"; " What rules might you use as support in making your argument?") You can also invite the student to ask for "co-counsel" to assist, and then return to the student to have the student end the discussion with a positive contribution.

Address Controversial Topics and Behaviors

Sensitive issues or challenging behaviors arise in almost every course. Reading a court opinion with offensive language, addressing inappropriate behavior such as students rolling their eyes when a classmate speaks, and raising polarizing issues can be springboards to deep learning. According to students, one of the worst things we can do as teachers is to ignore these sensitive issues of race, class, politics, religion, gender, and sexual preference. Instead of ignoring the issues, we need to acknowledge the challenge and invite students to engage in a respectful discussion about the topic.

When a controversial issue arises in class, focus on providing a safe, respectful environment in which students can learn, and learn from their discomfort. Students want to see us model calm and constructive leadership. Take a minute to stop, pause, and then name the challenge, use silence, or ask students to reflect on what just happened in the classroom. "I see that many of you are uncomfortable with the opinion just stated, that there is no longer a need for affirmative action. Before we continue, let's pause for a minute to think about why some of us might hold that view." We want students to learn how to listen to controversial views and to try to understand the perspectives of others.

With any controversial topic, or when a student becomes very upset, talk to the student involved after class. It is difficult for most students to discuss controversial issues with acquaintances; having an audience of 20 to 100 is even more difficult. If the student is unavailable right after class, email the student noting that you were aware that the student was involved in a controversial discussion and encouraging the student to talk to you about it in person.

C. Promoting Student Participation

The techniques above all help engage students in classroom discussion. This section offers tools for helping students who are terrified to speak in class or for students who for some reason do not want to participate in class discussions. For these students you can provide safe ways for them to practice participating in class discussions. You can also give them alternatives to participating in whole in-class discussions.

Allowing Students to Practice in Advance

Some teachers want all students to verbally participate in whole class discussions. For students who find that expectation extremely challenging, you can invite them to tell you about their fears, and work with them to find a time when they are willing to contribute. For example, you can notify them before class that you will be calling on them that day, or you can ask them to pick the class where they will be ready and willing to be called on. Students can also practice answering questions during office hours or with classmates before they try to "solo" in the large class.

Provide Alternative Ways to Contribute to the Discussion

If speaking in front of the whole class is not essential to the course learning goals, but all students are required to participate, students can participate by posting questions and responses to online discussion forums, such as on Lexis and Westlaw. You can either allow the students to post and respond to questions, or you can post questions or problems for students. This approach is effective for students who would prefer to contribute in writing, and allows other students' to learn from their quieter classmates.

Give All Students a Chance to Talk Through Their Response

Also known as *think-write-pair-share*, this technique is one of the quickest, easiest, and most versatile in-class activities. Pose a question verbally or in writing. Ask students to think about the question for a minute and then jot down a response. Once they have completed their responses (one to three minutes depending on the complexity of the question) ask students to exchange their ideas with a neighbor. Ask them to discuss their answers and the reasons for them (one to three minutes).

Call on a few students to provide responses or ask one or two students to volunteer his or her neighbor's response. Note responses on the board, enter and project the responses on a screen, or verbally reinforce responses. After students have talked with a neighbor, who has either confirmed the difficulty of the question, acknowledged confusion with the issue, or affirmed the student's response, a much greater range of students volunteer and are comfortable with being called on.

References

• John C. Bean, Engaging Ideas: The Professor's Guide to Integrating Writing, Critical Thinking, and Active Learning in the Classroom 169–181 (2001).

- Stephen D. Brookfield & Stephen Preskill, Discussion as a Way of Teaching: Tools and Techniques for Democratic Classrooms (1999).
- Barbara Gross Davis, Tools for Teaching 97–132, 168–173 (2d ed. 2009).
- L. Dee Fink, Creating Significant Learning Experiences: An Integrated Approach to Designing College Courses (2003).
- McKeachie's Teaching Tips: Strategies, Research, and Theory for College and University Teachers 36–54 (Marilla Svinivki & Wilbert J. McKeachie eds., 13th ed. 2010).
- Linda B. Nilson, Teaching at Its Best: A Research-Based Resource for College Instructors 105–118 (2d ed. 2003).

An Experiment in Participation

Several months ago, I ran into a student in my Family Law class at a law school event. "Professor Goodmark," she said, "I love your class. I just wish I felt more comfortable speaking up." We discussed her reticence about participating, which she attributed to general discomfort with public speaking. The more we talked, though, the more it seemed that the real issue was with the quick processing required to answer the hypotheticals and policy questions I frequently threw out in class. By the time she had thought through what she wanted to say and felt comfortable with what her answer would be, I had already moved on to another topic.

Together, we brainstormed ways to help her feel more comfortable speaking in class, and finally came upon a proposed solution. What if, prior to each class, I sent her a question that I knew I would be asking in class the next day? The question would call for opinion, rather than a demonstrably "right" answer, so that there would be no pressure around being "wrong." And giving her the question ahead of time would provide her with an opportunity well before class to think through her answer, so that she would feel comfortable raising her hand at the moment the question was asked. I told her that I would look to her first to answer the question I sent her. If she raised her hand, I would call on her; if not, I would move on, without calling attention to her in any way. She agreed that this approach might help, and our experiment began.

During the next class meeting, as arranged, I asked the question that I had provided the student with the previous evening: "Should fault be considered in the distribution of marital property?" To my delight, her hand immediately went up, and this student, who previously had never volunteered an answer in class, gave her perspective on the issue at hand—a perspective, incidentally, that was different than the views expressed by many of her classmates. After class, I emailed her to see how she had felt about our experiment. Her reply was very positive, ending with "Expect to hear a lot more from me." I asked her whether she thought it would be beneficial to provide the same opportunity to other students who were hesitant, for whatever reason, about participating in class. Again, the student was extremely enthusiastic, particularly because she believed that it might encourage the expression of a diversity of views in class discussions and allow the class to move away from hearing from the same individuals with no reservations about participating in any of their classes.

I sent an email to the entire class that read, "If you are hesitant about speaking in class and would like to work on feeling more comfortable doing so, please email me privately—

I have an experiment that we could try." A few students, believing that the email had targeted them specifically, replied with confusion or sarcasm. But about a half dozen students (in a class of 51) affirmed that they were hesitant about participating in class and would very much appreciate trying something new. As students expressed interest, I sent them the following email:

> During each class, I tend to ask a couple of opinion questions. Because those questions ask for your opinion, there aren't "right" and "wrong" answers—just what you think, and why. If you choose to participate in our experiment, I will send you one or more opinion questions for the next class the night before. Having the question(s) ahead of time will allow you to think about what you think and why you think it and to formulate your answer. Then, when I ask the question during class, I will look to those of you participating in this experiment first for an answer, before I call on anyone else. If you raise your hands, I'll call on you; if not, not a problem. But I'm hoping this will lessen the pressure around participation somewhat and give you the ability to practice participating in class a little more. Let me know what you think, and if you'd like to try it out.

The night before each class session, I came up with a thought question for my group. The questions included, "Should a court be able to consider race in an adoption proceeding?" and "Should a court be able to order a parent to find more lucrative work?" I sent the question out to the group under a blind copy, so that their identities would not be disclosed. Frequently, one of my participating students kicked off the discussion of the question. Most, but not all, of them answered at least one question over the course of the rest of the semester, and some of them began to volunteer to answer questions not previously provided to them.

At the end of the semester, I asked the participating students what they thought of the experiment, and how they might improve the process. All who responded agreed that for them, the experiment had been a success—even those who had not volunteered answers. One student wrote that, although he remained silent, the experiment had given him the opportunity to think more deeply about the issues and feel better prepared for class. Others suggested changes that I plan to implement the next time I teach the class: asking the question toward the beginning of class, which might encourage students to participate more frequently throughout class that day, and waiting longer for an answer after the question is asked, to allow participating students to process for a moment before volunteering.

The student who originally kicked off the experiment later enrolled in our Family Law Clinic, which required her to perform regularly before other students—and she did a wonderful job. For me, her growth is proof enough that our experiment was a success.

Leigh Goodmark
University of Baltimore School of Law

Everybody Weighs In

"I'd like everyone to weigh in on this." I use that prompt several times each semester to ask every student to respond orally to a question I pose in class. Below is a brief description of the "why," "when," and "how," of this discussion technique, along with an example.

Why Ask Every Student to Weigh In

When students respond to questions in class they are actively engaged in thinking about the question, formulating a reply, and delivering a response. When we ask every student to respond to a question, we get active engagement from all of our students.

Further, asking every student to contribute also conveys our expectation that all students will contribute to class and demonstrates our confidence that every student has something valuable to offer. This technique ensures that we hear from our quiet students, not just those who are most comfortable talking in class. Finally, as each student responds, the class gets a broad range of perspectives on the question.

When to Ask Every Student to Weigh In

Although I use the "everybody weighs in" technique in every course, I limit my use of the technique to one, two, or three times during each course. This technique works best for open-ended questions that give rise to diverse responses. It takes a significant amount of class time for every student to respond; for example, thirty-second responses from twenty students consumes ten minutes of class time. Consequently, ask every student to respond only to the most significant issues in the course. For example, I use this technique to have each student evaluate a statutory scheme at the end of a unit: "Identify a major strength, weakness, or appropriate amendment for the National Environmental Policy Act."

How to Ask Every Student to Weigh In

Several practices help maximize the benefits of asking every student to respond.

- Pose the question in writing on a slide, handout, or the board so that all students know the prompt.
- Give students a suggested time for their responses: "I'm looking for a 20 to 40 second response from each of you."
- Tell students who will speak first and how you will proceed around the room.
- Play the role of facilitator. Model careful listening to each student response. Summarize students' contributions on the board or the screen, if appropriate. Resist the temptation to comment on each student's response.
- Adapt the technique to fit class size. In a small class, each student can respond to the question. In a large class, each student could respond to the question in a small group and then each small group could share one response with the large group.

An Example of Each Student Weighing In

In my Civil Procedure course, students read *A Civil Action*, Jonathon Harr's gripping nonfiction account of children who die of leukemia in Woburn Massachusetts and the subsequent litigation. The book raises significant issues about civil litigation and the role of a lawyer. I ask each student to respond to a prompt such as "What implications does *A Civil Action* have for you as a future lawyer?" Several years ago, while going around the room, I came to a very reserved student. She had spoken only once previously in class and that was because I called on her. She paused a couple seconds and then began with "I'm from Woburn." The students and I were captivated by her somber insights into life in Woburn and her opinion that the role of a lawyer is to help people during times of severe distress. I doubt she would have spoken if I hadn't asked every student to weigh in.

Gerry Hess
Gonzaga University School of Law

Responding to Wrong Answers

Law teachers struggle with ways to respond to incorrect student answers. It is important to let the other students in the class know that the responding student is off track, but how do you do so without embarrassing the student?

Six experienced law teachers offer ideas on how to effectively and gracefully respond when a student gives a wrong or misdirected answer.

The number one thing is to not make the student feel stupid. As the teacher, if you say or do anything that makes the student feel foolish, you've not only lost the trust of that student, but of much of the rest of the class. If you make it clear that you understand why the student might have committed the error before steering the student and the class on the right course, the student will feel that you are on the student's side and will continue to work hard in your class.

Daniel Keating
Washington University School of Law at St. Louis

Sometimes the error results from an ambiguous or unclear question. When teacher error in phrasing the question is a plausible explanation of why the responding student is on the wrong track, then the teacher can take responsibility for the problem by saying something like: "Interesting point, but I am sorry, I must not have been clear in what I was asking. Let me rephrase." This technique takes the heat off the student and simultaneously humanizes the instructor. However, the approach will not work—and will seem disingenuous—if the question was clear and the student was just plain wrong.

Stephen L. Sepinuck
Gonzaga University School of Law

Often (usually!) the misdirected student is not the only one in the classroom who doesn't understand a particular point. I sometimes ask for a show of hands as to (1) how many students agree with the initial answer; (2) how many students disagree with the students' response; and (3) how many students aren't sure. Assuming that there are significant groups of students in all of the above categories, the professor then can engender a dialogue between the different groups ("Why do you disagree?" "Are you still sure about your original answer?"). This effort often helps the student with the incorrect answer feel less isolated and also may encourage the students to continue this discussion among themselves outside of class. The technique only works, though, if the student is not really off base all by himself, although even then the professor might be able to honestly note the fact that this is an answer that has been given before (or that some judges have gotten wrong as well).

R. Lawrence Dessem
University of Missouri School of Law–Columbia

We can put confused student minds at ease by admitting that we suffered from the same confusion ourselves when encountering a case or issue the first time around: "You know, that's how I interpreted this language when I first read it. The court is not making its point as clearly as it could. But other parts of the reasoning suggest a much narrower holding. Why do I say that?" After all, if the professor took a few wrong turns when he or she first encountered the case, the student has nothing to be ashamed of, but the professor has made it clear that further analysis will take the class in a different direction.

Sometimes I even prepare the students ahead of time for some predictable miscues on their part by revealing that I was capable of the same thing: "How many of you had to read this case about six times to make any sense of it? When I started teaching this case, I realized that it was perhaps the most difficult page and a half in the casebook, so I looked back at my student notes to see how I briefed this case for class back in law school—and it turns out that my brief was hopelessly confused. But I overcame my confusion during class discussion and outlining, and I hope we can start to make sense of it together today, even if we have to struggle a little and take a few wrong turns along the way."

Of course, if I can't honestly admit to such initial difficulties myself, I might aim for a more generalized means of assuring the student that he is in good company in his confusion: "Because of the emphasis we all naturally place on the second sentence, it is very easy indeed to conclude that the entire subsection applies only to transactions between merchants. Most people seem to read it that way initially. However, take a moment to read it aloud, and tell me if part of the subsection might apply more broadly."

Charles Calleros
Arizona State University, Sandra Day O'Connor College of Law

One solution is to respond to the student by saying "So you think ..." and then repeat what they said followed by a silence to let them think. Often, they will realize there is a problem with what they have said and may think out loud to correct it. If not, say "Let's examine that" and use the Socratic Method to guide them through the shoals. It is never necessary to say the student is wrong. However, if what the student said is wrong and you suspect the class buys into the erroneous information, a good option is to say "I'll bet most of the class would agree with you, and [with humor] you are all wrong." That assertion will draw a laugh and create anticipation of the correct information which you can provide.

Greg Munro
University of Montana School of Law

---

1. In body language and response, make it no big deal.
2. Say, "That is not quite right, but let's examine why ..."
3. Tell the student that the answer is incorrect, but then explain why, with the same student's help.
4. Say, "That is not correct." Then ask the same student follow-up questions, giving the student an opportunity to offer a correct answer and save face (if applicable).
5. If there are repeated incorrect responses, follow up through a subsequent email message to the student, inviting the student to discuss why he or she seems to be having some difficulty.

Steven I. Friedland
Elon University School of Law

Using Multiple-Choice Questions to Spark Discussion

Two challenging tasks for many law teachers are (1) to help students identify legal arguments that run contrary to their initial reactions to legal problems; and (2) to spark genuine discussion among students. As novices, law students struggle to see beyond their own perspective, and a significant number of students mentally discard their own ideas once another student has asserted a contrary view during a class discussion. I have found that multiple-choice questions can help teachers train their students to look for counter-arguments and empower their students to disagree with each other. By formulating multiple-choice questions for which there are two equally plausible "right answers," teachers can open up and encourage robust discussion of even the most challenging hypothetical questions. This discussion addresses how, when, and how often I have used this technique.

How

I often use classroom responder units for these questions. But I have had equal success giving students cards on which they write their selections, (i.e., a, b, c or d). In fact, sometimes I put students in groups of two or more and ask them to come up with a single group answer using the cards.

I create two types of such questions. For the first type of question, I pose the hypothetical (either on a PowerPoint slide or in a handout), and offer only two answers:

1. Plaintiff will win;
2. Defendant will win.

The advantage of this approach is that students must take a stand and then supply the reasoning during the class discussion.

For the second type of question, I provide the standard, bar-exam-like four choices. This approach occasionally produces great spread among the answers, but it is helpful for students who are really struggling to see if the answers they have chosen are far off the mark. Even with these questions, I try not to supply the reasoning so that I can use the class discussion to allow the students to articulate the arguments on both sides.

When and How Often

I use this technique in three contexts: (1) when I sense my students are struggling to learn how to see beyond their own perspectives; (2) when I suspect insightful voices in the class are being silenced or are silencing themselves; and (3) when I know students will struggle with a particular hypothetical I am planning to pose.

I generally delay using this technique until I have asked Socratic-style questions for which there were good arguments on both sides and have also used at least a half dozen multiple-choice questions for each of which there was one correct answer. I do so because the surprise is part of the technique. Part of what empowers students to fully articulate their arguments is the exciting and surprising discovery that half the class agreed with them and half the class disagreed with them. I therefore start by allowing a student on one side or the other of the issue to fully articulate the argument. I then point out the percentage of students who disagreed and wait quietly for someone to offer the counter-argument. If I am patient and quiet, the discussion unfolds beautifully.

Later in the semester or whenever I am concerned that students will hesitate to trust their own beliefs, I tell the students explicitly that the question has two, equally plausible answers.

Like any other technique, I use this idea sparingly, maybe five or six times over the course of the semester. It is particularly useful after students have received their first set of grades because the students who did well benefit from realizing their lower-scoring peers have valuable insights to offer, and the students who did not do as well benefit from knowing they have valuable insights to offer.

Michael Hunter Schwartz
Washburn University School of Law

Strategic Classroom Interaction: Questioning with Intentionality

It is easy to quickly fall into habitual teaching behaviors, including questioning techniques. Before we know it, we are starting a discussion of cases with the same question (i.e., "What are the facts of the next case?") and a standard ordering (i.e., case discussion, important point, then hypothetical). There might be a certain type of questions we ask repetitively, certain students who get asked to participate all of the time, or certain areas in the room that are on the receiving end of the most questions and others we are ignoring. Sometimes this ritualistic sensibility is effective, but sometimes the techniques employed might simply lie within the teacher's comfort zone and could stand to be refined or improved.

To avoid a rut and promote effective questioning, a teacher can be more intentional about the nature of the questions asked, the students to whom the questions are addressed, and the geographical administration of questioning within a classroom—in which quadrant of a room are the discussions and questions being propounded? This idea of self-assessment is like a 60,000-mile car check-up.

Nature of the Questions

Consider shaking up the content and order of your questions. The shake-up or reordering depends on the outcome sought (e.g., basic knowledge of a case, how to use the case in answering a hypothetical, or a larger policy or skills goal). Some different question objectives follow, as well as different orderings.

Question Objectives

1. Knowledge. Whether students know the content. Generally in a nonleading form: what, when, where, how or why.
2. Advocacy. Whether students can argue about points of contention in the case.
3. Issue-Spotting. Whether students can identify major and minor issues in the case.
4. Meta-Cognition. Whether students understand their mental processes in learning the skills and knowledge.
5. Engagement. Whether students are involved in the discussion.

Question Ordering

1. Case first, then problem.
2. Problem first, identify issue, then review case. Problems often serve as a hook to student involvement.
3. Background discussion about doctrine, then case, then problem.

Student Participants

It is all too easy to call on students who are familiar or provide an obviously prepared response. It is important to teach to the whole class; that goal means eliciting some form of participation from even those students who are typically quiet. Participation does not have to mean involuntary cold-calling on students to speak. It could involve asking students to state their opinion on an issue, play the role of a judge in a hypothetical situation, or identify questions they have. The premise is that students who speak are likely more invested in the class and will not simply treat the class as a note-taking experience, but one with active thinking practice as well. Thus, teachers should call on students with difficult names and make sure a comity principal applies.

Location

With respect to geographic location, trial attorneys learn quickly that where you stand can matter a lot—especially if your back is to the jury or the judge. Also, using the four corners of the room, making sure eye-contact and questioning occurs within each quadrant, can promote overall attention and participation. (The quickest way to turn students—and jurors—off is to ignore them.)

Of course, it is not just thinking about the questions and choosing words with care that matters. The energy underpinning the words and the way the questions are delivered are also extremely important.

Steven I. Friedland
Elon University School of Law

Developing Core Questions

"How does breaking the law affect whether the defendant breached the duty of care?" This is a core question in my first-year Torts class on negligence per se, one I repeat many times during that class session. Having these kinds of core questions helps me and my students engage in a productive class discussion. For me, constructing a core question is like preparing an effective issue for a brief, oral argument, or presentation—the process guides me in having and returning to essential themes. In addition, as a central theme helps the audience focus on an important issue, so does having a core question help students concentrate on essential learning objectives.

What Are Core Questions?

A core question identifies an important class learning objective. In Torts, one of my objectives is: "Given a scenario with a person violating a statute, students can accurately identify and analyze when that violation shows evidence of or conclusive proof of breach." The core question above comes directly from that objective. I focus on one to three core questions for each class. While the class session addresses many sub-issues, such as the test to determine whether a statute is relevant and the different ways jurisdictions treat statutory violations, the core question serves as an organizing principle for the class discussion. The amount of time spent on a core question during the class varies with the complexity of the question and the students' difficulty learning the material.

How to Design Core Questions

Preparing core questions requires you to think about the knowledge and skills you want students to practice. A core question will require students to use the legal authorities they have read (knowledge) and to engage in higher level thinking activities (application, analysis, synthesis, evaluation) with that knowledge. As with writing exam questions, when constructing a core question, consider how a student might answer it and whether the phrasing might be misleading. The goal is to build upon the reading to stimulate student engagement.

Using Core Questions During Class

Writing on the board or projecting them on a slide, I pose the core questions at the beginning of class, telling students that these questions are the focus of the day's session. I don't ask a student to answer a core question at the beginning of class. Instead, I'll start with a basic question, such as, "If a defendant has violated a statute, does that always show the defendant has breached the duty of care?" "What is an example of when the violation of a statute clearly shows breach?" "What is an example of when a defendant's statutory violation clearly does not show a breach?" "How do the cases illustrate the analysis of negligence per se?"

During the discussion that follows, I repeat the core question multiple times, reminding students what we are trying to find out. A colleague who does this extremely well repeats the core question as frequently as every two minutes, especially if he is teaching first-year students a difficult topic. To remind myself to repeat the question, I write the question in my class notes in large print. As the class continues, the core question resurfaces as students identify law, facts, and policy that help answer the core question. The core question comes up again as students practice applying their learning to different fact patterns. At the end of class I return to the core question, summarizing key points and "take-aways" students should have in their notes and outlines.

Sophie Sparrow
University of New Hampshire School of Law

Dialogue in a Video, Dialogue in the Classroom

Veni

Coming to my Civil Procedure class on the day dedicated to pleading standards, students are primed for a substantive debate about race, religion, and law enforcement. After all, they have read *Ashcroft v. Iqbal* (2009), the blockbuster U.S. Supreme Court opinion ordering the dismissal of a discrimination suit brought by a war-on-terror detainee against the attorney general and the director of the FBI. But my charge is to teach them a superficially less provocative lesson about how *Iqbal*'s focus on the plaintiff's failure to plead "plausible" facts upended the long-standing interpretation of Rules 8 and 12. To guide that potentially tedious discussion, I cue up the renowned pedagogue Larry Thomas, otherwise known as the "Soup Nazi."

Video

Why Nazi videos in the classroom? Videos are a sure-fire way to grab the attention of students, whose standards for entertainment in a classroom are not high: any scene from any movie or television show is more riveting than its quotidian law school alternative. But a video can backfire. Unless it both focuses and permeates the discussion that follows, it risks becoming, at best, a mere break from classroom drudgery, or at worst, a pandering attempt to gain fleeting approval. Having gotten the students' attention, a professor should capitalize by ensuring that the dialogue in the video translates into dialogue in the classroom. When the popular culture piece seamlessly integrates with the substantive material, the results can be eye-opening.

Seinfeld's well known (even to today's students, thanks to reruns) "Soup Nazi" episode brims with parallels to pleading. A four-minute clip from it can trigger an energetic 40-minute debate about *Iqbal*'s impact. If customers fail to obey the authoritarian ordering procedure decreed by the chef (Mr. Thomas's character), they leave empty-handed after a sharp rebuke: "No soup for you!" The comedic tension raises deep procedural questions. Should our system allow plaintiffs' cases to survive until we are sure they lack merit? (Considered individually, each paying customer would seem to deserve soup.) Or for the sake of efficiency, should we dismiss cases that do not seem as strong as others? (People who have not even considered what kind of soup they want surely should not be allowed to hold up the line indefinitely.)

As the students and I analyze the import of the pleading scheme sketched by *Iqbal*, we repeatedly refer to the video. On the one hand, the "Soup Nazi" regime evokes the formulaic steps of baroque common law pleading: "Just follow the ordering procedure, and you'll be fine. As you walk in the place, move immediately to your right.... Step to the left and receive your soup." On the other hand, echoes of the simpler, notice-based system of the federal rules abound. Reminiscent of Rule 8(a)'s requirement of "a short and plain statement of the claim," for example, is the instruction to "hold out your money and speak your soup in a loud, clear voice." Likewise, the admonition that "it's very important not to embellish on your order—no extraneous comments, no questions, no compliments" mirrors that of Rule 12(f), which allows a judge to strike "any redundant, immaterial, impertinent, or scandalous matter." Students rush to point out that although the "Soup Nazi" abides by Rule 1's call for the "determination of every action" to be "speedy," he may fare less well under the companion criterion that it be "just."

Vici

When students come to school and see a video that pays dividends in ensuing classroom dialogue, they can conquer an otherwise daunting doctrinal foe. As to pleading standards, students taught via *Seinfeld* understand that any system comes with tradeoffs. They recognize that justice, like soup, costs money, and if there is only so much to go around, triage among plaintiffs may be appropriate. Conversely, they see that defendants may have more information, such as about the makeup of mulligatawny, and that it might thus be unfair to cut off cases at the pleading stage, before discovery. A skilled classroom professor could impart that nuanced perspective through traditional pedagogy, but I believe that my students benefit from the time I cede to Mr. Thomas. My only fear is that when they practice law, they may add a catchphrase to their motions to dismiss: "No suit for you!"

Alex Glashausser
Washburn University School of Law

Deposition Techniques & the Socratic Method

Although the Socratic Method remains a favored way to teach law students, this method is difficult to use effectively. Professors often employ the Socratic Method to demonstrate the complexity of the law without giving students a basic framework for understanding it. Those teaching the law could likely learn a lesson from those practicing it. This essay explores the application of generally-accepted deposition techniques to the Socratic Method.

Deposition techniques can be applied to the Socratic Method because both have similar purposes (i.e., eliciting information and presenting theories through questioning). When taking depositions, practicing attorneys seek to discover facts while asking questions that present their legal theories. Similarly, in the classroom, professors employ the Socratic Method to compel students to relate the facts of a case through questions that seek to illuminate legal concepts.

Effective deposition-taking and effective Socratic teaching both begin with extensive preparation. Prior to taking a deposition, lawyers often spend a substantial amount of time reviewing relevant documents and preparing lengthy outlines, so that their questions are succinct, focused, and maximize the use of available time. A professor using the Socratic Method must be equally diligent. To guide students through a case, statute, or other material, professors must understand every aspect of it.

When teaching a case, statute, or other topic, a professor using the Socratic Method should employ the funnel technique that is commonly used in depositions. The funnel technique is an information-gathering method in which examiners begin with broad, open-ended questions and refine their understanding of an issue through increasingly focused queries. For example, one could begin discussing a case by asking questions like:

- What can you tell me about this opinion?
- Can you describe the facts of this case?
- Can you take the class through the court's analysis?

Beginning with broad, open-ended questions gives students the freedom to show their understanding of the law and develops their ability to teach the law to others.

As the deposition or Socratic discussion moves forward, the funnel technique allows a progressively more focused discussion about what the person being examined knows. By asking narrower follow-up questions, a professor can help introduce omitted facts and remedy logical leaps made by a student. A professor can also help to explore aspects of a case, statute, or other topic that a student may have overlooked. The ultimate goal of the funnel technique is to exhaust and fully explore, in an orderly and logical manner, what the person being questioned knows.

In addition to the information gathering aspect of depositions and the Socratic Method, both seek to present legal theories through questioning. Discussion in the classroom will usually be less adversarial and entail a more explicit examination of the law, but the goal is ultimately the same (i.e., to demonstrate how the law applies to facts through questioning). Examiners in both contexts seek to guide others to their views while adapting to new facts and ideas discovered in the course of the discussion.

To achieve this goal, generally-accepted deposition techniques once again prove useful. After information gathering occurs through the funnel technique, the examiner should engage in theory-testing to reinforce important legal concepts and clarify the importance of the topic being discussed. Theory-testing is a technique commonly used in depositions when a questioner attempts to get a person being examined to say or agree to the questioner's theory of the facts or the law. To some, theory-testing might seem disingenuous in the classroom because it could cloister independent thought. However, the goal in the classroom is to instruct, and an unbounded discussion often does very little to deepen a student's appreciation of the law.

Theory-testing in the classroom generally takes two forms. First, a professor may seek to clarify and reinforce important concepts in a discussion by using leading questions. For example, a professor could ask questions such as:

- Mens Rea is the mental state required for a crime, correct?
- The rule in this case is that an agent is liable if a principal is undisclosed or partially disclosed, correct?

Second, a professor could also engage in theory-testing by asking open-ended questions that are designed to highlight major concepts. In fact, open-ended questions may produce more desirable results than leading questions because they force students to state concepts in their own words and synthesize them. In discussing an opinion, a professor might ask:

- What is the rule that we should take from this case?
- How would you incorporate this case into your outline for the class?

These two approaches can of course be combined as needed to refine the classroom discussion.

Ultimately, the goal of both depositions and the Socratic Method is to provide a defined framework for thinking about a case or other matter. In depositions, good lawyers are always conscious of what a judge or jury might think when they hear the testimony collected. Professors should be equally conscious of what students might think while hearing a Socratic discussion. Professors must provide a balance between showing students the complexity and the frequent ambiguity of the law while introducing students to defined legal concepts and constructs. The use of deposition techniques when employing the Socratic Method helps professors better guide classroom discussion.

Eric Chaffee
University of Dayton School of Law

Teaching Issue-Spotting — A "Questions Only" Game

Students cannot effectively analyze fact patterns or spot issues on law school exams, or in practice, if they cannot identify discrete and well-formulated factual and legal questions about the material. Indeed, most law professors strive to convince students that the hard work in legal thinking comes not from coming up with "right" answers, but with thinking critically about the law and facts. To some degree, Socratic dialogue is designed to model and draw out "good" questions about legal doctrine. But, when they sit down to take exams, many students struggle to apply what they learn from that methodology to new facts, and many law classes do not spend much time explicitly teaching or practicing this skill.

One way to teach the critical mindset needed for effective issue-spotting is to spend time in class doing and discussing exactly that. Pitched as a competitive exercise, the experience is even more lively and engaging. Telling my students "let's play a game," I ask them to form small groups of three to five students and hand them a fact pattern based on material they have studied (a classic homicide case in a Criminal Law class). Groups are given a set amount of time (usually seven to eight minutes) to write down *as many questions as possible* that a thoughtful attorney should ask about the fact pattern. Groups do not have to answer their own questions, instead they simply brainstorm to come up with the greatest number of good questions possible. When the time elapses, each group (or selected or volunteer groups in a very large class) displays its list publicly, either by writing it on flip charts, projecting electronic files, or posting to a class website.

Led by the professor, the whole class then "scores" the displayed lists, giving one point for each distinct question that, as a class, we agree ought to be considered in order to effectively analyze the fact pattern. We discard any questions that seem to be too off-point, repetitive, vague or incomprehensibly crafted, etc. We award one point for each remaining question. The group with the largest list will win some unnamed *fabulous prize* such a bag of M&Ms or a study aid for the class's subject matter.

Though the brainstorming sessions to draft the questions are themselves helpful practice, the real value of the exercise tends to come from the scoring and the conversation it elicits. We necessarily argue about which follow-up questions seem reasonable based on the facts and which seem to be unnecessarily making up or fishing for new facts. We disallow questions calling solely for conclusory responses (e.g., "was there proximate cause?" as opposed to "how foreseeable was this particular sequence of events?"). We point out any opportunities that each group might have missed to expand its score, such as breaking down a larger compound question into multiple more specific questions. Groups frequently disallow questions that are vaguely formulated even when similar inquiries by other teams are counted, because some versions of the questions are more specifically formulated and consequently more likely to be effectively analyzed.

Students tend to get quite excited about good-naturedly challenging one another's questions, but they also can be quite generous in developing reasons why some questions ought to be worth credit. Over time, groups usually derive some common law rules about what questions they will allow and which ones they won't, so the scoring becomes faster and easier. But the value of the debates, and the fun students have with them, continues. Usually, as I point out when I wrap up the exercise, the hardest and most creative thinking that lawyers do comes not in *answering* specific questions, but in deciding which ones to ask. And good questions in law must be built both on a thorough understanding of the underlying legal doctrine and a thorough and critical examination of the specific facts. Moreover, the very structure of the game shows that more thoughtful and well-framed questions we generate, the more critically and successfully we will analyze the issues before us.

Kris Franklin
New York Law School

Using the Socratic Method in Legal Writing Classes

The Socratic Method isn't just for casebook classes; it can enrich all of the components of a legal writing class. Further, because legal writing classes are generally smaller and more tightly-knit than other first-year classes, students are more comfortable speaking and less afraid of making mistakes, and thus can derive more benefit from the questioning process that is at the heart of the method.

It is important, however, to use the Socratic Method effectively. Many professors are reluctant to use it because they remember fear-filled experiences in their encounters with the method as law students. However, these experiences are not the result of the Socratic Method, but rather its misuse. Used correctly, the heart of the Socratic Method lies in professor–student interaction. In its most traditional application, the professor calls upon a student and engages that student in a colloquy. As the student answers, the professor poses another question to get the student to delve into the problem in more detail. The students who are not actively answering the question are expected to be following along and considering the questions and answers so that they can contribute if called on.

Using the Socratic Method effectively requires preparation. The professor must not only prepare as if he or she was giving a lecture on the subject, but also determine what questions to ask, and what questions will follow, that will lead students to what the professor hopes is the correct result. The questions must be clear, and not so complex that they cannot be answered effectively. Then, the professor must skillfully guide the discussion to keep the class on track. Most importantly, the professor needs to maintain an environment of respect for the students, and demand that they respect each other as well. Used properly, the Socratic Method promotes active learning and teaches cognitive skills; it also encourages students to "find their voice" in the classroom and to communicate effectively.

The Socratic Method can help students learn analytical skills in the legal writing classroom in several different ways. One of my most effective case synthesis classes was inspired by an exercise in Linda Edwards's text, *Legal Writing and Analysis*. The original exercise introduced four short case briefs from an imaginary jurisdiction addressing attractive nuisance, and asked students to synthesize a rule. I expanded the briefs into short written opinions (one to two pages) and then introduced a problem for the students to solve involving the young grandchild of one of their law firm's major clients who was injured in a neighbor's koi pond. We went through the cases Socratically one-by-one. With each case, I questioned the students on the rule of the case, what it added to our understanding of attractive nuisance, and how it affected the result in our koi pond case. I also questioned the students at each juncture regarding what additional facts we would need to discover to predict the result, and what effect those facts would have on the result. The students were very enthusiastic throughout the process, and indicated that they enjoyed the opportunity to apply the rules to a concrete problem.

I also use the koi pond problem, combined with the Socratic Method and a helping dose of technology, to teach research. Legal research is best learned by doing. However, students can easily become frustrated if they have to undertake the initial attempt without sufficient guidance. I use the Socratic Method to bridge the gap between simply presenting the students the materials and turning them loose to research. Once they have been introduced to the idea of research strategy, I ask them how they would go about taking the first step to research the problem in a particular jurisdiction. Once I've elicited that they need to figure out what the governing rule regarding attractive nuisance is in that jurisdiction, we discuss the best research path to follow, and how to do it. I use .pdf files of individual pages of treatises, legal encyclopedias, ALR articles, case digests and cases to show them the results of their research as they suggest each stage. At each juncture, we Socratically discuss where to go next, what to look for, and how to get there. Through the process, they learn to use the legal materials in a holistic manner to drill down to the answer they are looking for, and to become aware of some of the problems that they might encounter along the way. We also then walk through the problem using electronic resources so that they can see how those resources can help or hinder the process, depending on how they are used.

Using the Socratic Method in this manner requires advance preparation. The professor needs to anticipate the students' "right" answers and prepare the result, and to anticipate the most likely "wrong" answers and show where those will lead and how the students can get back on the right track. The "wrong" answers are as helpful as the "right" answers to this learning experience. In my koi pond example, one of the initial resources leads the students to an ALR article concerning animals as attractive nuisances (koi are animals, after all). Although the title is initially promising, it soon becomes apparent within the first few paragraphs that the article deals only with situations where the animal involved was the cause of the injury. This error helps teach the students to make sure that they check to see not only what the article includes, but what it doesn't, and to look for guidance as to how to get back on track. I should note that, while the technology here may seem complicated, it doesn't have to be. The first year I tried this I didn't have a lot of time to prepare the technology, so I resorted to using paper copies and a document projector to work through the exercise. Teachers even more technologically advanced can add increasingly more sophisticated bells and whistles.

While this type of exercise is not a substitute for research exercises requiring students to find answers on their own, it is effective in demonstrating the uses of the different forms of legal information, and giving students a guided first experience at research. This approach helps to minimize student frustration when they do their own research, and introduces them to some of the pitfalls they can expect to encounter along the way. The Socratic Method allows all of the students to participate in the process and contribute to the research strategy.

Further, the Socratic Method is not limited to time in class. In their article *Teaching Students to Think Like Lawyers*, Mary Kate Kearney and Mary Beth Beazley report success with using the Socratic Method to comment on students' writing. Under this approach, the professor responds to the student's writing with Socratic questions rather than concrete suggestions for revision. These questions help the student to comprehend the problems a reader has in understanding the student's writing, and force the student to take responsibility for revising it.

While these examples are by no means exclusive, they counteract the perception that the Socratic Method has little value in legal writing classes. Rather, the Socratic Method provides benefits in learning legal analysis that extend throughout the curriculum. Used effectively, the Socratic Method can be a helpful tool in the toolbox of teaching methods for legal writing.

Jeffrey D. Jackson
Washburn University School of Law

Reversing the Norm: Promoting Student Questioning Proficiency

In most law school classes, students develop skills in legal analysis through one particular delivery mechanism—the professor questions the students. Professors' questioning methods often draw from a variant of the Socratic Method.

The functional importance of questioning is well-established. Questioning can elicit useful information, trigger analytical thought, create a dialogue between people, and further a relationship between the speakers. Moreover, questioning signifies engagement in the subject matter and is emblematic of a broader intellectual curiosity. Thus, questioning is a signifier of learning, symbolic of cognitive thinking.

Yet, interestingly, with questioning such an important part of learning, it is generally only the professor who practices questioning techniques in class, not students. If questioning is so important, why not have students learn to improve their own questioning skills in a controlled setting where they can get feedback?

While students ask questions in moot court experiences and Trial Advocacy or deposition training, students are generally the receivers, not the proponents of questions in the classroom—unless the students act as independent intervenors. We can intentionally teach students to ask questions by dedicating class-time to practicing the art and skill of questioning. This short component of a class would be designed to assist students in improving their own proficiency in asking on-point, communicative and analytically beneficial questions.

One Method for Teaching Students Effective Questioning Techniques

- First, have all students in the class write out their questions for approximately four to five minutes. (This "all write" concept promotes participation and allows students time to reflect and deliberate on their approaches.)
- Then, select students from different parts of the room to ask three or four questions each. The questions should be wrapped around a particular role-play. The more specific the directions, the better, such as having students do a direct examination of a defendant in a torts negligence trial in which the plaintiff has testified in a particular manner.
- The professor should make some nonjudgmental observations about the questions, as well as highlight one area for improvement. At the end of all of the questioning, the professor can make some general comments about the questioning that occurred and how questioning can be relevant for the students.
- Note that the questioning generally works better when directed within a particular context.

Examples of Questioning Exercises:

1. Students Question a "Witness"

   Many students have seen lawyers' questioning witnesses in popular culture, some have seen them in actual court cases. Thus, questioning witnesses is within the comfort zone of most students and serves to transform students into lawyers. Questioning a witness can engage students even in large classes. Questioning a witness is ideal for a practice-oriented course, like Evidence, but is useful in any course where distilling and organizing facts matters. For example, a student can be briefed on his or her role before class and called up in front of the class to answer three types of questions: background; setting the scene; and the action in question. A plaintiff in a negligence action involving an auto accident in a shopping center parking lot can be asked about her background, the parking lot, and how the accident happened. The important facts depend on whether this is a Torts, Evidence, or Civil Procedure class, for example, and how the facts are being used. Students again can be asked to write down questions. A variant on the "all write" approach is to have small groups of three or four students develop group questions, with everyone assigned a role: questioner, scribe, "devil's advocate," and co-questioner.

2. Students Question a "Client"

   Such questions again place the students in the role of a lawyer and allow students to sift through facts as well as engage in a variety of lawyering skills. This framework can be used in all classes as well.

3. Students Question a Judge about the Judge's Opinion

   This questioning can show students that a judge's rationale or statement of a rule is subject to questioning and alternative formulations. This activity can be useful for newer students learning about issues, rules and analysis, as well as more experienced students focusing on a nuanced point of law. Students also can be assigned to play the role of the judge, leading those students to a larger (or smaller) appreciation of how a judge constructed the opinion.

4. Students Propound Interrogatories on a Party

   While this mechanism is especially appropriate to Civil Procedure, it also applies to any course in which the professor wants a different vehicle for approaching a hypothetical problem. Student questions have to identify the critical issue and begin to create the analytical structure for resolving it. For example, in Civil Procedure, students can be asked to propound three or four interrogatories to a plaintiff who claims a federal court has jurisdiction based on diversity of citizenship. In Constitutional Law, students can be given a hypothetical problem about segregation in a school district and told they represent the plaintiffs in a lawsuit. Students can then be asked to create three to four interrogatories to the defendant school district about unknown or ambiguous facts that will assist them in showing intentional discrimination.

5. Students Ask About the Components of an Opinion

   This structure can be used as a means of directed homework for a case assigned to 1Ls. Instead of just asking students to read a case, students can be asked to come up with two questions each about the issue in the case, the pertinent legal rule or principle, the holding, and the rationale used to resolve the case by the judge.

By expressly promoting student questioning in class using these or other methods, the technique of questioning is given legitimacy. In addition, the technique encourages students to cultivate good questioning practices on their own, and, perhaps most importantly, advances the learning process through a different road than the one most taken.

Steven I. Friedland
Elon University School of Law

Responding to Cynicism

Two experienced law teachers offer ideas on how to respond to cynical comments, such as saying that to be an effective lawyer you must be dishonest or half-truthful.

I usually try to treat any student comment as a serious matter. I first tell them that, if such a question is being asked in class, that attitude is certainly reflected in society as a whole. I then ask them several things: (1) If someone filmed all of your conduct for a reality show, would you feel proud of the way you acted as an attorney? (2) If you saw a $20 bill sticking out of an ATM would you take it? Why or why not? Then, I say that the real ethical issues often arise when no one else is looking. As the discussion winds down, I tell them that being effective means being prepared and proud of the way you handled the matter—not simply whether you won or lost. The means do not justify the ends. Some good lawyers will lose despite their efforts and some bad lawyers will win despite their efforts.

Steven I. Friedland
Elon University School of Law

In her song, "The Last Time I Saw Richard," Joni Mitchell makes the claim that cynics are romantics at heart, romanticizing pain. When I hear a student make a cynical remark, I remember that song. It seems to me that cynicism is a protective device, a defense against distress and deep disappointment, a way of saying "this can't hurt me because I don't care." A student making a cynical remark is a student in distress, contemplating a dark and depressing future. I see and respond to the distressed human being. Because I teach in the clinic and work one-on-one with students, I have the opportunity to gauge what each student needs in the moment. Usually the student needs compassion and acknowledgment of his or her worth and distress. By listening, I find a way to shift the focus, to help the student see that pain and distress are not the only facets of the law school experience. I never try to make the student feel foolish for making the cynical remark. They already do feel foolish, or they wouldn't be saying cynical things.

Gail Hammer
Gonzaga University School of Law

Chapter 6

Collaborative, Cooperative, Group, and Team Learning Techniques

> "Researchers report that, regardless of the subject matter, students working in small groups tend to learn more and demonstrate better retention than students taught in other instructional formats." — Davis

A. Why Use Collaborative, Cooperative, Group, or Team Learning?

Research shows that peer learning and teaching help all students learn across a variety of disciplines, learning preferences, and course goals. In addition to helping students learn course content and skills at a deeper level, working with others helps law students learn how to collaborate as professionals, essential skills for practicing law. Researchers also have found that those who know how to work well with others are more successful and effective in their chosen profession.

In this chapter, group learning refers to collaborative, cooperative, group and team learning techniques. Group learning works for many reasons. It actively engages all students in the class, not just those who are engaged in a one-on-one Socratic-style dialogue with the teacher. When students interact with their classmates in informal groups or semester-long assigned teams, they are more likely to talk, as the group environment is less intimidating than talking in front of the whole class. The research shows that when students are engaged in active learning, they deepen their understanding and retention.

Group learning helps students at all levels. Students who are confused or lack confidence find it much easier to voice concerns and questions when they are among their peers. Students who understand the material benefit from organizing and articulating their thinking so that their classmates can understand. The research shows that even students who do not think they benefit from group learning do perform better than when they work in isolation.

Students receive valuable feedback from participating in groups. As one expert notes, this eliminates the "illusion of understanding." When students have to apply or discuss material in a group setting, they often realize what they know and what they do not know. They may think that they fully understand the material when they read the text or hear the teacher, but when they have to explain it or defend their positions to others, their awareness of their own learning is considerably increased.

Students also benefit from having a group of peers with which they discuss their learning. Law school is stressful, and many students work alone, contributing to their stress level. When students work in groups, they become part of learning communities. Experts in teaching and learning note that students learn more effectively when they are in a "community-centered" environment.

Groups of students also perform better than students do individually. Much as two heads are better than one, three or seven heads are better than two. With their different experiences, skills, approaches, and values, students each contribute value to solving different kinds of problems. One student may be a creative "out of the box" thinker, another excellent at reading and analyzing legal rules, a third at organizing material, and a fourth at making factual inferences and seeing the big picture. When students work together in groups, they learn others' skills and perspectives.

Working with others also teaches students to avoid "early closure" where they latch onto an answer before thinking through the nuances in a problem. Striving to get the "right" answer to a question, they may avoid looking at the question from different angles, considering counter-arguments, or generating alternatives. When they talk to classmates about the question, they realize that there are other ways to solve a problem and learn about weaknesses and ambiguities. "Oh. I didn't see it that way," is a comment students often make when participating in groups.

Students also learn how to work well with others even when they are under stress. "Playing well with others" is much harder when students are tired, overwhelmed, and irritable. But law practice is stressful, and students benefit from practicing how to work together with professionalism and civility when they face deadlines, receive less than "A" grades, and work harder than in the past just to keep up with course assignments.

B. Promoting Effective Group Work

Many students today have had bad experiences with working in groups. They have been in groups where they have done all the work, where other members of the group have coasted while contributing nothing of their own, where working in a group has taken more time than working alone, and members of the group have acted disrespectfully. They may resent having to listen to a group member who insists on dominating a group discussion, or feel frustrated that others do not participate. They may also have had bad experiences from trying to coordinate schedules with group members who are uncommunicative.

This is understandable. Humans are complex, and working in groups often presents the possibility of conflict, particularly if the group has to produce a product or is graded on group efforts. There are, however, techniques to help groups work together productively and efficiently. A number of these techniques are described below.

Help Students Understand the Value of Group Work

Given that many students have had bad experiences working in groups, it helps to explain why you are using this technique. Briefly explaining some of the research about group learning may encourage students to keep an open mind and approach group work with a more positive attitude. The value of group work can be reinforced by giving student groups a complex task to work on in class early in the semester. Giving students a complex and challenging task, one that will benefit from a number of diverse perspectives, enables them to see that collectively they produce more sophisticated results than any one of them does alone.

Ask Students to Generate the Principles of Effective Group Work

Because of their previous experiences working in groups, most students can quickly and easily identify what makes groups work effectively. Without any guidance from the teacher, students usually identify the following:

- Be prepared;
- Arrive in class on time;
- Treat everyone with respect;
- Don't monopolize or dominate;
- Contribute to group work;
- Communicate problems or issues;
- Have a sense of humor—don't take disagreements personally.

Having students identify these principles at the beginning of class, reinforcing them by writing their ideas on the board and posting them to the course website keeps these principles in students' awareness. It also empowers the students because they, not the teacher, have named the principles for effective class group work. When the students design the parameters of student group work, they are more likely to feel accountable for group discussion and projects.

Create Diverse Groups

Students can work effectively in groups of two to seven, with the group composition varying depending on the nature of the course, the comfort level of the teacher, and the amount of time students work in groups. Experts in group learning suggest a number of approaches, including having students work with one or two neighbors, assigning different small groups each week or class, or, in team-based learning, assigning permanent diverse groups of five to seven for the entire semester. Regardless of how students are assigned to groups, the least effective way is for students to self-select.

Some experts in group work suggest that members of student groups have assigned roles, such as facilitating discussion, recording the discussion, reporting results of group deliberations, and keeping the group on task. Students may be assigned different roles for each class, rotating among all members of the group. Other experts have found that designing effective group assignments and incorporating group accountability eliminates the need for specific group roles.

Give Groups Clear Tasks and Directions

Student groups benefit from having clear directions. Many groups get off task when they are unclear what they are supposed to be doing, and they waste valuable time when they struggle to figure out the group task. It helps to keep groups focused by keeping the description of a group task short, if the task is given verbally. For any complex task it helps to put it in writing, by putting it on a handout, projecting it electronically, or writing on the board.

Specify an amount of time for students to work in groups. Groups tend to be more focused if they feel that they have to work quickly to solve a problem. Allow less time than you think students will need, and add time if students are still focused and more time would help them attain the learning goals. Part of the way through the allotted time, and shortly before the group time ends, prompt students by calling out the time remaining. You can gauge how things are going by asking the class as a whole or circulating and asking different groups whether they would like another couple of minutes. Similarly, if students appear to have concluded their discussions, you can cut the time short and reconvene the class as a whole.

Be clear about the outcome of group work. If each group has to identify an issue, solve a problem, name a rule, or prioritize strategies, be explicit about what they will be expected to do once the time is up. You may tell students that you will call on different groups to provide responses, or have them post their responses on a sheet of paper taped to the classroom walls. Groups may be required to synthesize their varied responses into a paragraph or work with other groups to identify the best solution to a problem.

If all the groups are working on the same problem, avoid having groups do a "reporting back" where each group gives a presentation on the same topic. The reporting back group responses get tiresome and most students disengage after a few minutes. A more effective approach is to ask students to simultaneously vote on the best response, with all groups showing a written response on a sheet of paper or holding up the letter corresponding to what they determined was the correct answer to a multiple-choice question.

Design Effective Problems and Questions for Groups

The best group problems involve students in higher level thinking, asking them to apply, analyze, synthesize, and evaluate. Pose a question or problem that would be difficult for a student to solve alone. Students can collectively discuss and answer questions at different levels of thinking, (e.g., "Which element is at issue in this client's case? How would you describe federal preemption to a layperson? Contrast the courts' different tests for issuing preliminary injunctions.")

Provide Students with Time to Check-in with Their Groups During Class

While students can easily identify the important principles of effective group interaction, they may disagree about what those principles mean. For example, almost all students will note that "treating others with respect" is essential for effective group work, but they may differ on what respect looks like. What one student sees as respectful behavior is another student's version of failure to participate. Similarly, while one student feels oppressed by having to always lead the discussion, members in that students' group may be irritated with the student and perceive her as dominating. Giving students time periodically to check-in and discuss what is working well and where they can improve provides them with a space to discuss these issues. You can facilitate the discussion about group dynamics by providing an example of your own challenges with group work, modeling language that can be used to name conflict, and inviting students to brainstorm ways to resolve group conflicts.

Restrict Group Work to In-class Assignments

Group work is often ineffective when it requires students to get together outside of class. Students are busy, have competing demands on their schedules, may have long commutes, and have diverse preferences about when to meet. Requiring students to be prepared for class, and then engaging students in group work during class is more effective than requiring students to work together out of class.

Facilitate Group Work by Acting as Coach and Guide

As groups work together in class, you may want to circulate among them, offering to be a resource for students to call upon, sit in and listen to a few groups, or allow them to work on their own. There are trade-offs with each choice. If you circulate, you can identify and address any common areas of confusion and get a sense of how the groups are functioning. If you allow the groups to work on their own, at least some of your students may be more likely to take risks. Once groups have discussed their responses, call on a couple of different students—ideally those who have previously not contributed to the large group discussion—to talk about the group's responses. Once you have a response, invite students who had a different response to contribute.

Provide Closure to Group Discussions

Students learn a lot from each other, but one of the things they learn is the way their knowledge is limited. After groups have worked together, it helps if the teacher provides "take-aways," summarizing key points groups generated, correcting misunderstandings and responding to lingering questions.

If the teacher has listened in on group discussions, the teacher can honor groups by identifying their insights, congratulating them on their collaborations, and noting what they have done well in their interactions as well as in their substantive results. For example, the teacher might note the process a group used to solve a problem, and the precision with which another group analyzed legal principles. At the end of a group discussion, the teacher also could comment on effective group behaviors, stating, "Some of you huddled together when you were working on the hypothetical—that is great! It allows everyone to hear and see each other, and I noticed a lot of eye contact while you were brainstorming." Other groups will adopt effective behaviors and seek to have their work acknowledged in future classes.

C. Addressing Barriers to Using Student Groups

Some barriers to using groups come from teachers, other barriers from students. Teachers may feel that they are "not teaching" when students are working in groups. They may feel guilty that they are not controlling the discussion from the front of the room, and may worry that the chaotic nature of the classroom reflects disorder and incoherence. They may worry that they appear to be slacking by having the students doing the talking. The fact is that learning involves a delicate balance of challenge and support, and students come closer to finding this balance when they are actively engaged. If teachers can believe that "teaching is creating a space in which students learn," they can see students' loud group discussions as learning space rather than as a lack of learning.

Having students work in groups does mean that teachers release some control of the classroom. Posing a question for students to solve in groups causes the class to erupt with energy and animated discussion. Getting students to wrap up their group discussions and reconvene as a whole class can be a challenge. Blinking the lights, giving students a one-minute warning, and calling on a group for a response can quickly return students to whole-class discussion.

Resistance from students takes many forms. Some students will refuse to participate, and others may show annoyance or irritation when asked to work with their classmates. Talking to the students individually, outside of class, may help some realize the effects of their actions. Others students may benefit from talking to you about ways to work effectively with recalcitrant classmates. If at all possible, provide students with guidance and suggestions about ways to work together, but avoid intervening in the group dynamics. If one of the benefits of group work is preparing students for practice, one of the things students need to learn is how to self-manage. Teachers can supply knowledge and strategies, but the goal is for students to figure out how to work together effectively.

References

- John C. Bean, Engaging Ideas: The Professor's Guide to Integrating Writing, Critical Thinking, and Active Learning in the Classroom 169–181 (2001).
- Barbara Gross Davis, Tools for Teaching 190–221 (2d ed. 2009).

- L. Dee Fink, Creating Significant Learning Experiences: An Integrated Approach to Designing College Courses (2003).
- Linda B. Nilson, Teaching at Its Best: A Research-Based Resource for College Instructors 127–136(2d ed. 2003).
- McKeachie's Teaching Tips: Strategies, Research, and Theory for College and University Teachers 190—201(Marilla Svinivki & Wilbert J. McKeachie eds., 13th ed. 2010).
- Team-Based Learning: A Transformative Use of Small Groups in College Teaching (Larry K. Michaelsen, Arletta Bauman Knight & L. Dee Fink eds., 2004).
- Team-Based Learning: Small-Group Learning's Next Big Step (Larry K. Michaelsen, Michael Sweet & Dean X. Parmelee eds. 2009).

Creating More Intimacy in Large Classes

Five experienced law teachers offer ideas on how to provide a more intimate, meaningful class for large enrollment classes.

Pair and share is one easy tool of a larger arsenal. If I ask a question to a class of 100 students and am met with silence, I ask them to take a minute to discuss it among themselves. The classroom is immediately bursting with 50 conversations (sometimes not directed at the problem, but I influence that by walking among the students and listening to their conversations). Having rehearsed and shared their ideas in friendly, intimate small groups, they emerge energized and a little more confident about sharing an idea with the larger group.

Charles Calleros
Arizona State University, Sandra Day O'Connor College of Law

---

1. Divide up the class into judge and advocate groups. Give the students a moot court exercise and, especially if guest professors or attorneys are available, supervise smaller segments of the class concerning their potential arguments. Then have the class engage in the exercise, promoting participation.
2. Ask a question and have everyone attending the class write down a response. Then have the students either discuss or read the responses to a neighbor in a "pair/share."
3. In classes that are longer than one hour, stop halfway through the class and give the students a "note-taking break"—an opportunity to catch up on and to organize their notes in small groups. Facilitate by asking what the important points of the class have been up to that time, or how the students would address a problem arising from the first part of the class.
4. Hold periodic "extra optional" review sessions of 15 to 20 minutes in length for smaller groups during the semester. Divide up the class based on a random, objective method (e.g., in alphabetical order). Go to a classroom where everyone can sit in a circle, if possible. Emphasize that the classes are entirely optional and will consist of problems and questions from the students. (If helpful, record the sessions so everyone in the class can have access to the information.)

Steven I. Friedland
Elon University School of Law

Even in a big class with fixed seating one can occasionally use small groups as a learning device. Prepare an exercise that would involve small group brainstorming and outlining some particular area of law. Have them turn their chairs and face each other in groups of six or eight. Each group appoints a member as the reporter for the group. When they have completed their short exercise, have the reporters report and get the material on the board in the form of an outline of what would have been the subject of your lecture. This is an active and participatory learning method that can be used to develop most anything that is normally the subject of lecture. Another solution is for faculty to quit teaching students in classes of 100. Our faculty developed teaching load standards that allow credit for teaching a second section of a class in the amount of 50% of that for teaching the first section. The same standard also allows a teaching load bonus if a faculty member uses substantial assessment and feedback in the class as opposed to a single exam at the end of the semester. Consequently, faculty members have real incentives to teach in smaller classes allowing more assessed exercises.

Greg Munro
University of Montana School of Law

Master the names and faces of everyone in the class. Then make frequent cross-references to important points made earlier by other students in the class, and include the name of the student who made the point. Try to call on more than just a few students each class, and make sure that you are calling on students from all different parts of the classroom. Consider creating "law firms" consisting of three or four students who are sitting next to each other, and let them handle your questions as a team.

Daniel Keating
Washington University School of Law at St. Louis

We all know the challenges presented by the large lecture class, particularly if we want to keep students lively, interested, and learning more deeply through application of the concepts presented. Although new technologies, such as 'clickers,' have developed to address these concerns, I like to use a low-tech, "tried and true" approach that also engages the social and interpersonal side of students. I first heard this technique described, using the moniker "think, pair, share", at an Institute for Law Teaching and Learning conference many years ago. I have used it many, many times, in groups of students, lawyers attending a CLE program, and law teachers at conferences, and it seems to reliably produce the results mentioned above.

Fundamentally, the teacher takes a break from presenting information for a few minutes, and poses a question or topic of discussion for students to reflect on. I usually encourage people to write notes for themselves as they reflect ; this seems to help them stay focused. After one to two minutes of quiet reflection (usually a minute is enough, in my experience), I ask them to form pairs or groups of three, convenient to where they are already sitting, to share their thoughts.

It is good to state a specific time (perhaps two minutes) for each person to share, and emphasize that the other(s) should just listen during that time. As an option, and one I also find effective to keep the process focused during these breakouts, tell the class that each pair or group should choose a recorder to take notes of the main ideas that come out within the small group discussion. Then have everyone begin. At the end of the allotted time for the first person to share, announce the time and advise everyone to switch roles, so that one of the listeners now takes the same time to share her thoughts while the others listen.

Call time again after the allotted minute or two, and when all have had the chance to speak out their thoughts within the pair or small group, direct everyone's attention to the front. Have each group (through the recorders, if you asked them to choose one) share with the class the main ideas that came up during their discussion. The students will be most interested in what the other groups focused on or decided. For increased emphasis, and to affirm the value of their ideas, I like to visually list the ideas on the board or a flip chart as they are stated. At some point you may want to comment on the points the students are raising, or you may choose to defer and allow the student comments to stand "on their own". Try it both ways and notice the apparent effect on the group.

You will find that several benefits accrue from this practice: (1) the students become very animated and actively discuss and apply aspects of the principles you have been raising that are of most interest to them; (2) you learn how much they understood and what those aspects of greatest interest are (you will usually be impressed with the depth of the discussions, brief though they were, and the insights that develop from them); (3) students experience autonomy support, which is known to enhance learning, competence, and positive sense of self; (4) students enjoy their classmates, experience relatedness to each other, and increase the sense of community within the class; and (5) you get a welcome break while the learning goes on!

I particularly like to use this technique in the last few minutes of a class. The greatest effect I notice in any application of this technique is the exponential increase in energy within the room, as passive listeners transform into active teachers and discussants within their pair or group. As a result, and regardless of how effective I may have been in my teaching up to that point, students leave the room upbeat, energetic, and focused on the material. As a side benefit, they will also leave appreciating you as a teacher!

Larry Krieger
Florida State University College of Law

The Play's the Thing: Learning Civil Procedure by Breaking the Routine

It's late mid-semester. The newness of law school has worn off for most first-year students, but most of them do not yet feel completely comfortable with the case method. In addition, in Civil Procedure they have been learning rule after rule delineating who can and who must be part of a lawsuit and what claims and defenses those parties can or must present. Only a few students, however, have begun to move facilely from rule to rule, from issue to issue, with any general sense of how lawsuits come together overall. It's time to break the routine and play a game of hot potato.

Yes, play. As educational experts recognize, play is one of the best ways of learning. The first year of law school need not be any different. Properly organized and presented, play allows students to grapple with the complexities of law in a nonthreatening and non-stressful environment; to discover loopholes, gaps, contradictions, and other puzzlements in the law itself; and to grapple with that infamous bugaboo of first-year law-exam-taking skills: the relationship of facts to law.

In teaching Civil Procedure, I schedule a day to review the Federal Rules of Civil Procedure governing joinder of claims and parties right after my students finish interpleader (FRCP 22) and intervention (FRCP 24). Because I teach the Federal Rules of Civil Procedure more or less in order, by that point my students have also covered notice pleading and Rule 8; special pleading rules and Rule 9; Rule 12 motions; counterclaims and cross-claims under Rule 13; third-party practice under Rule 14; amended pleadings under Rule 15; joinder of claims and remedies under Rule 18; mandatory joinder under Rule 19; permissive joinder of parties under Rule 20; and misjoinder and nonjoinder of parties under Rule 21. Half of Review Day we play hot potato.

Hot Potato

Equipment needed: one "potato" (a real potato, a small bean bag, a toy, etc.) and one timer.

The method:

1. The professor starts by giving a *basic* scenario, such as a car accident, out of which a simple (one plaintiff, one defendant) lawsuit arises. The game works best if the facts are minimal.
2. The class's goal: to "use up" a list of available Rules before the time is up. My list: FRCP 8(a), 8(c), 9(b), 12(a), 12(b), 12(c), 13(a), 13(b), 13(g), 13(h), 14(a), 14(b), 15, 18, 19, 20, 21, 22 (or statutory interpleader), and 24. Students have 30 to 40 minutes for the exercise; the timer prevents guessing about when the time is "up."
3. The goal of the student holding the hot potato is to get rid of it. To get rid of the hot potato, the student must: (1) tell which party; (2) is doing what action; (3) under which Rule; (4) making up appropriate facts as necessary to explain the new claim or the new party. The student cannot get rid of the hot potato until he or she has legitimately expanded the lawsuit.
4. Once the student has accurately used one or more Rules, the student walks the hot potato to another student.
5. Other students can volunteer to take the hot potato, but the student with the hot potato decides to whom to pass it.
6. Students can work in groups.
7. If the class uses up all of the listed Rules within the available time, they earn a "prize." (I have allowed class to end at the same time the game does—generally five to ten minutes early, and made participation in the next class entirely voluntary instead of calling on students.)
8. If the timer goes off before the class finishes the list, the student left with the hot potato is "it" for the next class (i.e., the first person to answer questions).
9. During the game, the professor keeps track of how the lawsuit has expanded and what Rules the students have used. Writing an initial list of Rules on the blackboard and crossing them off as students use them, works well. The professor ensures that each student meets all aspects of the Rule, including checking for jurisdiction problems.

Benefits of Playing Hot Potato

- Students closely read the Rules and identify fact patterns that will allow them to apply specific Rules, an exercise that helps them apply the law to facts throughout the course.
- Students get a sense of how the Rules work together. When a student figures out how to use two or three Rules in conjunction, the rest of the class cheers.
- Students discover which Rules are "easy" to use up (because they apply in several situations or have requirements that are easy to meet, like permissive counterclaims), and which are "hard," (because they only apply to particular types of claims and/or particular types of parties). In an auto accident scenario, for example, students dream up many people to join as parties but struggle to create an indispensable party under FRCP 19.
- Students welcome a change in the class at a point in the semester when their energy is beginning to wane.
- Students learn how to create their own practice problems, a helpful study device.
- Because students can collaborate, they experience a sense of community effort toward a common goal.
- When the class "wins," as it usually does, students have shown themselves that they can, in fact, master Civil Procedure.
- Finally, perhaps most importantly, the facts students create inevitably get us all laughing—something that everyone in law school can use!

Robin Kundis Craig
Florida State University College of Law

The Value of Teaching with Small Groups

When student-peers interact in learning, they are more likely to view themselves as engaged in a cooperative process in which both participants are actively learning. Unlike a teacher-centered classroom, each peer is also teaching—teaching in a way that is cognitively different from that of a faculty member. Since the peer has only recently learned (or is currently learning) the material, the peer teacher is more likely to think through the steps of the learning process consciously than one who has greater expertise. Thus, the learning that occurs in peer groups is a cooperative, active process of constructing knowledge.

The affective dimension of the small-group process also influences student learning. Peers working in small groups are less exposed to the risk of public error and competitive pressures than when called upon individually to recite before the full class. Unlike the one-on-one dialogue with the professor in the larger class, students working in small groups are more likely to explore possibilities, ask questions, take risks, and learn from their mistakes.

An easy way to structure cooperative learning in the classroom is to invite students to work in pairs or teams to discuss questions or problems posed in class. For faculty first beginning to use this technique, some basic guidelines can help avoid problems.

Plan your small-group assignments carefully. Tasks requiring mere recall of information will rarely sustain discussion and may convey an unintended message that individualized preparation of materials is unnecessary. Conversely, if you are asking for a very carefully phrased response (e.g., draft the legislation) rather than ideas, solutions, or arguments, in-class cooperative groups are less likely to work effectively. Writing is essentially an individual activity, and cooperative work with written assignments is better left to cooperative critique and editing, rather than drafting.

Brainstorming might appear to be a useful activity for small groups. However, research indicates that, in fact, groups do not produce more or more creative ideas when brainstorming than do individuals working on their own. This is likely because brainstorming requires creative thinking and creativity requires taking risks. Risk-taking while in a group setting requires trust. Few groups in a law school classroom are so well-established as to have the level of trust necessary to nurture good brainstorming. However, if students are directed to first brainstorm on their own and then share their ideas and have the group elaborate on those ideas, brainstorming can be an effective group activity.

Cooperative learning is most effective for tasks requiring critical analysis. Questions that work very well in small-group settings include those requiring the students to generate or choose among solutions to a problem presented by the case or problems assigned for class. Good candidates for group work include questions like: "Which rule/approach is better and why?" "How might the attorneys have avoided this problem?" "How is this rule likely to affect people's actions in the future?" "What is the best argument for and against this approach?" If a problem or question would require students to absorb any significant additional facts before discussion, these problems should ordinarily be provided to students ahead of class.

Prepare students for cooperative tasks. Unless you are asking students to share personal experiences or observations, provide them with sufficient background to address the in-class work effectively. In-class group work can become an exercise in pooled ignorance if students have not mastered the basic materials for the class (either because the assigned materials were not sufficient or because the students have not prepared). Students may also need some preparation for the cooperative work itself. Providing students with some basic guidelines for brainstorming techniques, active listening, and allocating responsibilities in the group can enhance groups' effectiveness. This is especially important when students are not kept within the same group throughout the entire semester or when you use group work only occasionally.

Preface group tasks with individual tasks. Unless you have asked students to prepare a problem or question ahead of time, when you pose a question for group discussion, provide students with time to think before beginning discussion. Giving students time allows those who are more introverted to work within their preferred learning mode, and reinforces a more general message that glib responses are not necessarily preferable to thoughtful ones. One minute is ordinarily sufficient. At least occasionally, preface group work with techniques to ensure individual accountability (short quizzes, random questioning on basic materials, or written assignments). Combining group work with audience response systems can be especially powerful. Ask the students to respond to a question individually, display the data, and then ask the students to convince their fellow students that their choice is correct. When the students re-answer the question, the rate of correct responses will increase significantly. One can replicate this in a low tech way through scratch-off answer sheets or even through asking students to hold up cards displaying their preferred answer. Students understand well that group work presents free-rider risks and will quickly come to resent regular group work if the instructor does not design the classes to minimize this risk.

Listen and learn. As the students begin discussion, walk around the classroom and listen. Work with students who seem stuck or reluctant to engage in this type of work. For professors who feel like this technique is too much out of control ("How do I know they are learning it right?" "How can I be sure they aren't just socializing?"), walking around and listening to the discussion will demonstrate fairly quickly that this technique is effective teaching. At a minimum, group work provides an excellent assessment device for you to discover how and what students are learning.

Diversify group tasks. Students can work on different questions. Divide the class in half; have groups generate opposing arguments or different aspects of the problem. Or divide the students into groups to come up with questions, hypotheticals, or problems, rather than arguments, answers, or solutions.

Bring them back together. When the discussion begins to wane, or the time allotted for discussion ends, students need and deserve some feedback on their discussion. A brief comment on their discussions may be sufficient (e.g., "All the groups came up with some good solutions ..."). If students have been asked to record their ideas, you can collect their reports and provide written feedback. Another closure device would be to take a poll of groups ("How many groups decided this was the correct approach?"). You may also want to use the small-group discussions as the starting point for further exploration. Small groups can be asked to report back on their work. This is more effective if students are asked to engage in different tasks or the range of responses is very broad. Otherwise, to avoid repetition, you may combine group reporting with polling ("How many other groups agreed with this position?").

Barbara Glesner Fines
University of Missouri–Kansas City School of Law

Group Review Sessions: Proceed Productively

Near the end of every semester, my Property students ask me if I plan to conduct a review session. I think they want me to deliver a performance beyond my ability. However, by thinking about teaching methodology, I have come upon a way to meet their needs.

First, it is helpful to review traditional review formats. Consider the method often used in liberal arts courses. If I were teaching such a course, perhaps my students would be satisfied if I touched on the main themes I covered and "pulled it all together." However, while highlighting the themes of a course is certainly valuable, it is not enough. The students also need to understand the sophisticated technical and policy analysis that goes to the heart of a substantive legal course such as Property.

The alternative method is to focus only on the specific questions that are troubling the students. The difficulty here lies in determining which questions the students want me to answer. I could simply make an educated guess. I could ask students to submit questions in advance. I also could respond to questions that students raise during the session. Yet, in none of these scenarios could I be sure that I was addressing the topics that were bedeviling the majority of students.

These traditional formats are terribly inefficient for students. In each format, the student listens to the instructor discuss themes or respond to questions. If the student already understands the theme or knows the answer to a question under discussion, the student is wasting time. Even if the instructor answers a question that puzzles a student, the answer is designed for the entire class and not particularly tailored to the student's individual needs. If the instructor fails to reach questions on which the student needs help, the student loses a significant amount of valuable study time.

My alternative format seems to work better. It is more interactive than the traditional method and more tailored to the needs of the individual student. However, success depends on two requirements. First, students must engage in some review and bring questions to class. Second, students must be willing to help their colleagues.

This is how I describe the format to my students:

> Here is how it works. You come to class. I break you up into groups of about six. You take turns answering one another's questions. When you run into insurmountable disagreements, you ask me to come over to your group. I come over and do my best to straighten you out. Then, I move over to another group seeking my assistance. Of course, you are always more than welcome to talk with me outside of class.

This format has proven successful. About two-thirds of the students come. Presumably, the remaining students either are insufficiently prepared to take part or do not believe that the session will benefit them. During the session, I am quite busy moving from one group to the next. The groups seem willing to wait until I can get to them. When a group addresses all the questions before it, its members quietly depart. The session usually takes one hour.

This format has four benefits. First, the participating students get all of their questions answered. Second, a student's questions get particularized attention either from other students or from me. Third, students help one another in groups. The experience may open them up to the possibility of engaging in team work and joining or revitalizing study groups. Fourth, because participating requires preparation, the format may motivate students to begin serious study of notes and outlines at an earlier stage.

This format satisfies the realistic goals of a review session. To condense the entire course into a one-hour lecture is an unrealistic goal. To conduct a session in which I intentionally drop hints about the contents of the forthcoming exam would be inappropriate. The only realistic, appropriate goal is to address the questions that students have at their specific stage of exam preparation. This review format deals with those questions in a way that is responsive and interactive.

Louis J. Sirico, Jr.
Villanova University School of Law

Six Collaborative Learning Techniques

Human Continuum

A Human Continuum is a social learning activity that requires students to form, communicate, negotiate, and defend their positions. Students receive index cards on which the professor has written a concept, topic, or other item of information. Students then negotiate the cards' order based on criteria specified by the professor and place themselves in a continuum that reflects the negotiated order. The Human Continuum can be done with the whole class, a group of students in front of the class, or multiple groups of students simultaneously.

For example, in Basic Federal Income Tax, Professor Holcomb uses this instructional strategy to illustrate the distinction between business expenses (which are deductible) and personal expenses (which are not). On ten index cards she writes ten different expenses that might be deductible as business expenses (for example, "$500 for office supplies," "$350 for a new suit," etc.). She then distributes the cards, and students place themselves in a continuum that spans from "most likely to be deductible" to "least likely to be deductible."

Method

1. Create up to 10 to 12 index cards, each with a different concept or phrase. If you have more than 10 to 12 students, you can create multiple sets of the cards and have multiple groups or have one group do the exercise in the front of the room.
2. Give each student an index card.
3. Give the students the opportunity to line themselves up by negotiating their placements based on the criteria you specify. The time allowed for this activity can vary. For the Income Tax example above, Professor Holcomb allows the students up to five minutes to agree on their placements. Other times, like in the variation below, you can require the students to line up in 30 seconds.
4. Once the students have formed their Human Continuum, have the students explain why they have placed themselves in that particular order. You can facilitate this discussion for as long as is useful, anywhere from one to five minutes is typical.

As a variation, students do not need to be given cards; instead, they can form a continuum based on their own opinions. For example, you can ask the students to form a line from most supportive of the Supreme Court's willingness to uphold restrictions on obscenity to least supportive. Once that continuum is formed and discussed you can ask the students to form a continuum based on another criterion related to the topic.

This exercise is a great way to get students moving while they learn. Remember, we have kinesthetic learners in our classes, too!

Carousel

Carousel is a social learning activity that can be used for brainstorming or review. Students are assigned to small groups that rotate through stations around the classroom, much like a carousel. At each station, students generate ideas or answer questions.

Method

1. Determine the number of stations (topics or questions) you will have.
2. Write a different topic or question on the top of large sheets of chart paper.
3. Hang the chart paper around the room at well-spaced intervals, creating stations.
4. Divide the class into groups of two to five students and give each group a different colored marker.
5. Assign one group to each station.
6. Instruct the groups to discuss their station's topic or question and to record their ideas or responses on the chart paper.
7. When you call time (time will vary depending on the objective), each group stops writing, takes its marker, and rotates to the next station.
8. At each new station, the groups read the chart papers and add new responses and/or make notes or comments on other groups' responses.

   a. New groups may not write something that a previous group has written. This ensures that each group reads the other groups' responses and generates new ideas.
   b. By the third or fourth rotation, you might need to extend the time groups spend at each station so groups can read and discuss what previous groups have added to the papers.
9. Repeat the process until each group has been at every station.
10. Suggested reflective/processing activities: Once groups have returned to their original station:
    a. Ask each group to highlight the three most important ideas listed on its chart paper and then share those with the larger group; or
    b. Ask each group to categorize/summarize the information on its chart paper and share it with the larger group; or
    c. Have students return to their seats and facilitate a discussion based on the ideas and comments written at each station.

You do not always need to keep time when doing this activity. Instead, you can tell the groups that they have a set amount of time to visit all the stations. You also can have more groups than you have stations. Some groups can stand back and discuss the topic or question and then step up to the chart paper when it becomes available.

Professor Byrn uses this activity often in her Seminar on Assisted Reproductive Technology. Examples of questions at the stations are: "Do you think society should do anything about the large and increasing number of frozen embryos in storage in the United States?" and "Should legislatures regulate the disposition of frozen embryos?" Each group is required to answer "yes" or "no" and then support its answer. She typically allows three to five minutes at each station and 10 to 20 minutes for class discussion at the end.

Defining Features Matrix

A Defining Features Matrix is a social learning activity that requires students to explore how concepts relate to one another. Working with a chart or grid, students use their reasoning skills to compare and contrast concepts. This is a great activity for visual learners and helps all students organize information.

Method

1. Create a grid.
   a. Across the top, list the key concepts, cases, or themes.
   b. Down the left side, write the features or characteristics that these concepts might share.
   c. You can leave some cells across the top and down the left column blank for the students to fill in.
2. Assign the students to pairs or small groups.
3. If the concept is associated with the feature or characteristic, the students record a (+) in the cell. If the feature is not associated with the feature or characteristic, the students record a (-) in the cell.
4. Encourage students to explain the rationale behind their choices.

5. Encourage students to add additional features or characteristics that occur to them as they work through the grid.
6. When the grid is completed have the students analyze the information by:
   a. Discussing the similarities and differences among the concepts;
   b. Discussing any new information discovered about the concepts; or
   c. Noting which cells are still blank and considering what information is needed to complete those cells.
7. Depending on the degree of difficulty and detail in the chart, this activity can take 5 to 20 minutes.

For example, you can use this activity in Constitutional Law to discuss suspect classes under equal protection:

Classification → Characteristic ↓	**Race**	**Alienage**	**Women**	**Legitimacy ...**
14th Amendment				
Immutability				
History of Discrimination ...				
(May leave some lines blank for students to add add'l characteristics)				

Structured Controversy

A Structured Controversy is a social learning activity that allows students to discuss a controversial issue from divergent viewpoints. Structured Controversies require students to identify the arguments supporting both sides of an issue, identify the strongest arguments for each side, and present and advocate both positions. Structured Controversy promotes critical thinking and develops students' ability to re-conceptualize their positions. This is a great way to maintain a high level of discussion on politically charged or sensitive topics.

Method

1. Select a topic about which students can have differing viewpoints, for example abortion rights.
2. Assign students to groups of four and divide each group into two pairs.
3. Assign each pair one side of the controversy.
4. Instruct the pairs to identify the arguments in support of their position and to prepare a short presentation (two to five minutes).
5. Have the pairs take turns presenting their position to each other (4 to 10 minutes).

6. Instruct students that they may take notes and ask questions during the opposing pair's presentation, but may not debate or disagree.
7. After the students in each pair present their position, have the pairs switch sides of the controversy and repeat the process. This requires students to advocate for the side of the controversy with which they personally agree, as well as the side with which they personally disagree.
8. If you choose, you can allow time for each group, or the entire class, to discuss the issue freely.

Jigsaw

Jigsaw is a social learning strategy that uses two stages of small-group work to help students learn a subject comprehensively. Jigsaw allows students to share expertise and gain a more complete understanding of a topic by learning from and teaching each other. Because this activity requires two separate groups to meet, it can take significant class time. In fact, Professors Byrn and Holcomb typically take an entire 50-minute class period to do a Jigsaw. They agree, however, that Jigsaw is one of the most effective instructional strategies they use. It requires planning to set up, but then the professor can stand back and watch every student on task and learning with little input from the professor. To shorten the time necessary for the expert groups to discuss their topic and ensure that all students come to class prepared, Professors Byrn and Holcomb typically assign the topic before class.

Method

1. Assign students to groups of three to four. This group is their expert group.
   a. Jigsaw works best when dealing with a subject that can be cleanly divided into discrete topics. Professor Byrn uses Jigsaw to review intentional torts and Professor Holcomb uses it to review partnership taxation.
   b. You may assign the topic during class; however, Professors Byrn and Holcomb typically assign the discrete topic before class and have each student come to class prepared to discuss his or her topic. This shortens the time necessary for the expert group to discuss and ensures all students come prepared.
2. Assign each expert group a discrete topic of the larger subject.
   a. For example, Professor Byrn assigns battery to one expert group, assault to another expert group, and so on.
   b. If you have a large class, you can have more than one expert group for each discrete topic. We have used Jigsaw in classes ranging from 16 to 60 students. For large classes, consider reserving a second classroom to give the groups space to work.
3. Allow students to meet in their expert groups to discuss their topic. The students should compare information on their topic and ensure that each member of their group is an expert on that topic.
4. Assign each student to a teaching group. Teaching groups consist of at least one expert on each topic.
   a. For example, a teaching group on intentional torts would include an expert on battery, an expert on assault, and so on.

   b. You can have the teaching groups form on their own, but it saves time if you assign the groups ahead of time and post the groups on an overhead in the classroom.

5. Each member of the teaching group then teaches the other members of the group about his or her assigned topic.
6. While the expert groups and teaching groups are meeting, you can move around the room to assist groups and address any questions or confusion that arises within a group.

As another example, Professor Zusman uses Jigsaw to deepen students' understanding of case briefing. Professor Zusman distributes a short case and a partially completed brief of the case to the class. She then assigns one component of the case brief to each expert group. The experts deliberate, rewrite the portion of the sample brief assigned to them, and return to their teaching group. If the case and case brief are distributed ahead of time, this activity could take 15 to 20 minutes.

Cooperative Quizzes

Cooperative quizzes are a two-part assessment. In the first part every student takes a quiz individually. In the second part, students are assigned to groups to re-take the same quiz during the same class. The individual part of the assessment creates an incentive for each student to prepare for the quiz and gives students the opportunity to get feedback on their own learning. The cooperative part of the assessment provides students the opportunity to review the quiz and their answers during the same class, giving them immediate feedback as to their understanding of that topic. It also allows students to learn from and teach each other. As a result, students are able to both self-assess and receive peer assessment.

Method

1. During class, the students first take the quiz individually.
   a. This exercise works well with quizzes that consist of objective questions such as, true/false, short-answer, and multiple-choice questions.
   b. Professor Byrn uses this instructional strategy in Constitutional Law, giving a cooperative quiz after each unit. Her quizzes usually consist of 7 to 10 true/false, two to three short-answer, and three to four multiple-choice questions.
2. Collect the quizzes.
3. Assign the students to groups of three to four students and give each group one copy of the same quiz.
4. The students then complete the quiz together.
5. Each student's final grade is based 50% on the student's individual score and 50% on the cooperative group's score. The percentages, of course, can vary.
6. Professor Byrn allows about 20 minutes for the individual quiz and about 25 minutes for the cooperative quiz.

Using criterion-based grading for the quizzes (i.e., not grading on a curve) prevents the students from worrying about which students are assigned to their group or whether other groups can hear what they are saying. This allows all the students to view the quiz as a learning tool and not as a competition.

In addition to serving as a self-assessment tool for students, cooperative quizzes provide professors an opportunity to assess students' learning and, thereby, their own teaching. Cooperative quizzes also reveal patterns of errors that allow professors to identify and address the concepts causing confusion for the students.

Mary Patricia Byrn
William Mitchell College of Law

Morgan Holcomb
Hamline University School of Law

Sally Zusman
William Mitchell College of Law

Risking Collaborative Learning in Core Courses

Acknowledging Students' Fears

Although collaborative skills are important to law practice, because working well with others is rarely emphasized in legal education, students are generally reluctant and fearful of having final grades determined by group effort. Keenly aware of these fears (and that student disapproval would likely hurt my course evaluations), I incorporated collaborative learning in core classes. I did so with confidence, assisted by being recently tenured and by trying collaborative learning while visiting at a couple of other law schools.

Collaborating on Collaborative Design

Teaching a small Civil Rights class, the students and I enjoyed many spirited discussions on how the civil rights statute should be redrafted or reinterpreted. Around midterm, I suggested that the class, working in small groups, redraft Section 1983. I asked the class to consider having this exercise count as their final grade, rather than a traditional final examination.

Students had strong, mixed reactions. Some were enthusiastic, sharing articles on collaborative learning, and urging the benefits of varied teaching and evaluative methods in legal education. Others argued that trusting a group final exam and grade was risky. Since I had not raised collaborative grading in the syllabus, we did not go forward. Yet, building on the students' reactions, I solicited their help in designing a collaborative, graded assignment for the next semester. Through many out-of-class discussions, we debated the benefits, costs, and parameters of such a graded component. With their help, I started to structure a collaborative graded exercise.

Creating a Collaborative Focus Throughout the Semester

The next semester I taught Constitutional Law to a class of over 100 first-year students. From the beginning, the course emphasized collaborative learning: the syllabus stated that 40% of each student's grade was a mid-semester, collaborative, out-of-class, open-book examination. In setting the grade weight, I followed my former students' suggestions that collaborative work should count less than 100% because students needed significant individual control over their grade in a four-credit course, and more than 10% of the final grade to encourage fuller participation.

Before mid-semester, I discussed the benefits of collaborative legal work and administered three 30-minute collaborative in-class group exercises:

1. Students worked together in small, self-selected groups on a written hypothetical, followed by a whole class discussion.
2. After completing the power of judicial review, students were randomly assigned to groups to evaluate *Bush v. Gore*.
3. I assigned students to groups to discuss congressional power issues. I did not tell the students that I intentionally assembled them in diverse groups, based on my perceptions of race, gender, nationality, personality, and political differences.

Students' Learning Goals for In-class Collaborative Exercises

At the beginning of the semester, I formulated and shared with the students the following learning goals for the in-class collaborative exercises:

- Learn Constitutional Law. Students could learn alone in self-study and then with me in traditional Socratic-style classes. The group exercises gave students the opportunity to learn from each other.
- Work with classmates with whom they did not usually associate. I hoped they would learn that people outside their usual circles were equally intelligent and interesting, and could help them grow as lawyers.
- In low-risk situations (in-class exercises were ungraded, though class participation counted for 10% of the final grade), learn about the fun, stresses, and successes of collaboration.

Structuring and Administering the Graded Collaborative Exercise

In the graded exercise, students worked in self-selected groups of three to seven members to prepare one typed ten-page response to an exam question. Students could not receive any assistance from any other person, and had from Thursday morning until Monday morning to complete the assignment. I was unavailable to mediate any group disputes. I graded the group papers anonymously.

Not all students were happy with the structure. Some students, primarily those who were quieter and less social, taking the class as second- or third-year students, or international students, wanted me to select the groups. One international student explained that some international students were not confident with their English language skills, and were afraid other students would not invite them to join a group. They feared being in a group of all international students would disadvantage them because of poorer English skills and less understanding of American history. I shared how I had coped as a black female when I was in all-white classes. In class I suggested that more diverse groups would likely produce a richer response. The Registrar's and the Student Affairs' offices also worked with international students to determine how the school could best meet their needs.

Evaluating Results

Overall, students indicated they learned a great deal. Some even enjoyed the process. I learned the most from the many individuals and groups who voluntarily came by my office to share and evaluate themselves and the collaborative process. Some of their comments were:

- "We really learned Constitutional Law. As we went over the fine points in our group, we finally understood the concepts we discussed in class."
- "Our societal focus on majority rule should be reexamined. The majority can drown out a lone voice of dissent ... that voice is often pointing the majority to something needing attention."
- "Working with others is a drain on your time, but is well worth it." (The exercise would have taken one student three or four hours to do alone; groups took 30 to 40 hours.)
- "Diversity is essential." (This comment was from a group of six white males. They had intentionally sought to avoid dealing with any gender or racial working dynamics. They said that a more diverse group would have been more productive.)
- "In my group we all drank, smoked, and ate a lot. Those who didn't smoke, started smoking. We have a lot to learn about managing stress before we become lawyers."
- "I learned to be careful who I plan to practice law with. Intellect and ability to work with others do not necessarily go hand in hand."

Angela Mae Kupenda
Mississippi College School of Law

Enlist Students as Peer Teachers

Sometimes a teacher cannot get an idea across to his or her students. And sometimes a teacher cannot understand what is preventing students from catching on.

Thinking back to my law school days, I remember instances when a teacher tried to explain some legal rule or application of a doctrine and then faced a sea of perplexed faces. The students might ask questions, hear the teacher's answers, but remain confused. Sometimes one student would understand what the other students were missing and come to the rescue. I wish I could say that, as a teacher, I have never faced this problem. However, I suspect every teacher has.

The problem seems to arise most acutely when a course is reaching a particularly difficult concept. Every course seems to have certain "hard knots." For Torts students, the hard knot may be proximate cause; for Evidence students, it may be the hearsay rule. My Property students, however, face a number of these knots, principally estates and future interests, covenants running with the land, and land recording acts—in other words, nearly one-quarter of the course. Over the years I have improved my methods for teaching these topics; nonetheless, I inevitably fail to reach some students.

At the same time, students often help one another understand difficult material in settings outside the classroom, perhaps in a study group. However, students who do not study together miss out on this opportunity. Why not, I thought, enable students to teach one another in the classroom? In that setting, I am available to clarify and steer students away from misunderstandings.

Many of us already employ peer review exercises and small-group exercises. We can build on these methods by encouraging students to help one another via peer teaching in class.

Here is my procedure for enlisting students in peer teaching. After I work through some difficult material and take questions, I say, "Now, I'm going to give you a few minutes to talk with one another and explain to one another the material that we just covered." The students always comply readily. I think these moments also provide a welcome break from the intensity of the standard classroom routine.

Once the students start their conversations, some of them inevitably call me over to answer a question. Their questions give me some insight into what is troubling the class and, in turn, teach me how to improve the way I present the material. When the class discussion seems to be getting too relaxed and students are clearly talking about other things, I reconvene the class. I then try to clarify the material, based on the conversations I have just had, take more questions, and move forward with the course.

Because we have become professional teachers and have delved deeply into our subjects, we sometimes find it difficult to place ourselves in the position of novices first grappling with difficult concepts for the first time. To reach novices, we sometimes must invite the novices to become teachers as well as students.

Louis J. Sirico, Jr.
Villanova University School of Law

Show and Tell for Law School — Collaborating with Students in Generating Course Material

Adult learning theory tells us that students learn more and remember it better when they can see how they will use what they are learning. The problem for many law teachers is that the cases are often old (*Hadley v. Baxendale* was decided in 1854), involve fact scenarios to which many students would be unlikely to relate (the hunter in *Pierson v. Post* was chasing a fox), and are from jurisdictions in which the students have no intention of practicing (unless you teach at a law school in the state of Washington, only a small percentage of your students would ever be likely to cite *Garrett v. Dailey*).

Many of us also worry that our students use the Internet, in or out of class, for play rather than learning.

In Contracts, I solve these problems by rewarding students who bring to class current applications of the doctrine they are learning, contracts they have signed, advertisements that might be deemed offers, and cases or statutes from a state in which they would like to practice law. The Internet is a rich source of information about current events and disputes that have legal ramifications.

The result is a win-win-win. The student who brings the case, the newspaper story, contract, or statute to class benefits from the mental effort involved in finding the current materials or the statutes and cases; he or she will forever better remember the material. The entire class benefits from the authenticity that the student's efforts have given the class materials. Even you, the professor, benefit because you get great ideas for future exam questions or class discussion problems.

The rest of this entry details how I implement this idea.

Rewards for Students

All of the following rewards have been successful in getting students to bring the desired materials to class. In some semesters, I have offered one-day immunity from being called on to the student who brings the best "show and tell" item to class that day. In other semesters, I have allowed students to meet their "professional development obligation" (see my entry in Chapter 9) by bringing a specified number of such items to class throughout the semester. In still other semesters, I have put my students into teams and created group competitions; I promise to take the winning team out to lunch or dinner or to bring donuts or bagels to class for the winning team.

What Students Must Submit

Occasionally, I have had students submit cases, contracts, newspaper stories, or statutes that reflect little effort or thought. Consequently, I now ask students to submit a one-paragraph explanation of how their submission fits with the course material.

What Submissions "Count"

I have chosen to be as generous as possible in giving credit for submissions. As long as students' submissions reflect genuine effort to apply or relate what we are studying, I give the students credit.

Michael Hunter Schwartz
Washburn University School of Law

Teaching a Collaborative Seminar

Until three years ago, I had never taught a seminar. In fact, I had avoided seminars. I viewed the typical seminar as a collection of students, each writing a paper independently of the other students. In the closing weeks of the course, the professor might attempt to introduce some interaction, perhaps by assigning a few students to critique another student's paper. Thus, I saw the seminar as one of Kurt Vonnegut's "granfalloons," that is, an organized group of people who think they have something meaningful in common, but don't. I would rather teach what Vonnegut would call a "true karass," a group of people whose lives are bound together in profound ways. (See his book, CAT'S CRADLE.)

When it came my time to teach a legislative drafting seminar, I drew upon the pedagogy that I had practiced in teaching legal writing. I decided to reject the individually oriented seminar in favor of a collaborative seminar, one in which students would genuinely help one another turn out excellent products.

At the beginning of the course, I told the students what I had in mind. Students would choose problems that concerned them. Each student would draft a statute, ordinance, or regulation that addressed the problem and write a detailed commentary explaining and advocating the legislation. The commentary would resemble a legislative committee report. In almost every class meeting, each student would explain at what stage of the process he or she stood and what problems the student was facing. Then, the rest of the students would offer their assistance. Each student would also hold several individual meetings with me where I would review their efforts and make suggestions. In short, we would help one another.

In fact, we adhered to this plan and really did help one another. I was often pleasantly surprised at the information and suggestions that students offered their colleagues. Some students could offer factual information about the issue. Others could suggest alternative ways to deal with it. Still others could offer advice to insure that people or organizations would not find ways to circumvent the proposed legislation. (Offering this advice and helping students in learning to use precise language were my primary contributions.) As a group, the students had far more to offer than I as an individual could have offered.

For example, a student seeking to permit beer sales on Sunday learned that the issue was entangled with Pennsylvania's system of state liquor stores and licensed beer distributors. He learned that the present system exists not because of moral concerns, but because it raises substantial revenues for the state. A student wanting to preserve open lands realized that any new program requiring state funding faces a serious obstacle. He responded to critiques by developing a free market system to achieve his goal. Another student was concerned that powerful groups avoid financial disclosure laws by making contributions to issue advertising instead of political candidates. He realized that he would have to settle for a statute that still permitted some contributors to avoid the requirements of any statute that he could devise.

In the closing weeks of the course, I decided not to hold a mock legislative hearing, with each student facing a "legislative committee" composed of other students. Although other colleagues had found that format to be effective, I decided to continue the collaborative process. Students would make their presentations and expect other students to offer constructive suggestions. Students would not turn in their final products until after the presentations. With this format, the presentations would serve as the final collaborative effort.

The seminar worked splendidly. The students helped one another significantly and perhaps learned more about the value of working with others.

Louis J. Sirico, Jr.
Villanova University School of Law

Constructing Visual Tools: Group Graphic Analysis Project

We know that many students, especially those with visual learning preferences, benefit from graphic representations of complex ideas. Many law professors are good at creating effective maps or diagrams for concepts that they teach, but I prefer to have my students experiment with constructing these for themselves.

To push students to think about how the elements of negligence relate to each other in Torts I ask students to work in groups to create graphic representations outlining their responses to a complex fact pattern. I use a specific fact pattern for this exercise so that students can ground their thinking, but I encourage them to create graphic illustrations that are as generic as possible, so that they can use them for almost any negligence problem they encounter. I try to make sure that the fact pattern I have given them has ambiguous facts to raise just about every negligence sub-issue we have studied, so that their final products will be thorough.

In some years, I have asked the groups to tackle the whole problem; other times I have assigned half of the groups to work on the alleged breach of duty while others consider causation. I give the students access to a range of mind-mapping software, flowcharting and diagramming programs, and video or audio recorders; I do not require them to use any specific technology, or even to complete the project electronically. They may use simple markers and paper. Student groups have chosen a variety of ways to present their analysis, including theater, flowcharts, Venn diagrams, animation, video, and interactive games.

In small classes, groups of students present their work and explain why they chose their particular form of visual representation. If the class is too large, my teaching assistant and I will choose "semi-finalist" groups to present their work in class. I then allow the class as a whole to vote on which tools they find most helpful in evaluating the fact pattern and as a template for new fact patterns. I usually take the winners out for a meal, but the goal of impressing their classmates seems to be the greatest motivator for this project.

This sort of project should work equally well for comprehending complex relationships among topics and subtopics in many courses, such as hearsay exceptions in Evidence, personal jurisdiction in Civil Procedure, and substantive due process standards in Constitutional Law.

Kris Franklin
New York Law School

Team-Based Learning — An Overview

Imagine teaching a course where students spend 75% of the time in class actively discussing complex problems, arguing with each other about nuanced rules, reading closely for relevant facts, and choosing to consult readings to support their positions. These are fun classes to teach. If you want your students to take responsibility for their learning, engage in applying their critical thinking skills to complex material, and learn course material at deeper levels, try using team-based learning. I have been using team-based learning in required and elective courses for three years. I am still learning how to use teams more effectively, but am more convinced of this teaching strategy's ability to transform learning than any other I have seen or tried.

What Is Team-Based Learning?

Team-based learning is a learner-centered teaching strategy designed to promote active engagement and deep learning. Educators have applied the principles of team-based learning for over 30 years, using it in 23 countries in a range of disciplines, including medicine, business, sciences, and the humanities. They have used team-based learning effectively in classes of nine to more than 199. Teachers using team-based learning have found students' performance improves when compared to traditional teaching. In addition to improving their ability to apply important concepts, students also learn skills essential to succeeding in a job: working well with others. And all this happens without sacrificing course coverage.

What Are the Core Principles of Team-Based Learning?

Larry Michaelsen, who first designed and developed team-based learning in the 1970's, identifies the essential principles as follows:

1. Groups must be properly formed and managed;
2. Students must be made accountable for their individual and group work;
3. Group assignments must promote both learning and team development;
4. Students must receive frequent and timely performance feedback.

The principles are straightforward; the challenge is in applying them effectively. As with any new teaching method, start small and learn from your mistakes.

What Is the Role of the Teacher in Team-Based Learning?

Because team-based learning's focus is on what the students are learning—all of them spending almost all the class time applying concepts—the teacher's role is to plan the course and the individual classes, then coach students through the learning process. To the outside observer of a team-based learning class, the teacher may appear not to be really "teaching." This is deliberate; the focus of the class is on what the students are doing, not what the teacher is saying. The teacher, however, has done significant preparation to harness the power of student learning teams.

What Is the Role of the Students?

In a team-based learning course, students spend the vast majority of class time engaging in team discussions and solving problems in their groups. Working in permanent diverse teams of five to seven students, they collectively draw on their perspectives and understanding to solve more complex problems than they would individually. Think of this as "five brains" are better than one, or as a group of lawyers working together to solve clients' problems.

Having students work together is only effective when all students are prepared; one of the biggest complaints about group work concerns "social loafers." Social loafers are those students who poach on teammates' work without contributing any work of their own. In team-based learning, students assess their teammates' contributions to the team (usually 5 to 15% of the grade). When students are not prepared or contributing, their grades suffer. They are thus accountable for being prepared and participating in their teams for every class.

How Do You Plan a Team-Based Learning Course?

At the most fundamental level, you need to take four steps:

1. Identify core learning objectives: what students should be able to DO as a result of taking the course?
2. Break the course into four to seven learning units;
3. Determine how to create diverse student groups; and
4. Design a series of formative and summative assessments over the semester to engage students at increasingly higher levels of thinking.

For most teachers, the hardest and most time-consuming aspect of using team-based learning is designing the series of quizzes—one per learning unit—and problems that are appropriately challenging for a group of students to solve. There is no question that using this teaching strategy involves a steep learning curve and a ton of work at the beginning, but the value is well worth it.

Fortunately, many helpful resources are available. Websites, videos, books, and listservs can be accessed at http://teambasedlearning.apsc.ubc.ca/ and www.TBLCollaborative.org.

Sophie Sparrow
University of New Hampshire School of Law

Chapter 7

Experiential and Service Education — Relating Law School to Practice

"Education is not a preparation for life; education is life itself." — John Dewey

Experiential and service-oriented teaching methodologies are well-entrenched in many educational domains. These types of educational experiences feature direct involvement with the things being studied. Because these experiences engage students in interacting with an unpredictable world, they involve some uncertainty. However, the experiences are never entirely open-ended; rather, these opportunities are directed and channeled by the teacher to promote particular results. The use of this learning modality has met with generally favorable results when administered and executed properly.

A. Recent History

Historically, American legal education has included little experiential or service learning. Instead, traditional American legal education primarily utilized the study of appellate cases to promote cognitive legal analysis, with the objective of teaching students to "think like lawyers." This educational process occurred mostly within a linear structure — teachers conducted class and dispensed information as experts, students received and organized that information in notes, and then prepared on their own for the next class. The process was then repeated.

In the 21st Century, the rapid transformation of business, including the way the legal profession operates, coupled with advances in technology and globalization, have created pressures for law schools to prepare more "practice-ready" graduates. With recent highly publicized critiques of traditional legal education in *Best Practices for Legal Education* and *The Carnegie Report*, there is pressure from within the law school community to produce competent students who are better able to engage in the legal profession as skilled practitioners.

One consequence of these external and internal pressures appears to be a greater willingness to try new approaches, such as experiential and service learning. Experiential and service learning serve as professional bridges, connecting law school with law practice. These experiential and service learning modalities integrate theory and practice by using active learning methods. Instead of tasking students primarily with listening and taking notes, often considered a passive experience, students are instead asked to participate in the educational process in differing ways. Instead of the traditional linear conception, where the teacher/expert delivers information to the students, the framework is instead dynamic and interactive.

B. Experiential Education: Direct Encounters of the First Kind

1. Theory

Oscar Wilde once said, "Education is an admirable thing, but it is well to remember from time to time that nothing that is worth knowing can be taught." Perhaps what he meant was that actual experience is one of the best ways to promote learning in a directed manner. As noted above, experiential learning is not simply experience without design. Rather, it refers to direct encounters with the thing being studied, coupled with the reflection and effort to glean structured insights from the process. As one commentator has noted: "Learning is not education, and experiential learning differs from experiential education. Learning happens with or without teachers and institutions.... Education, in contrast to a learning opportunity, consists of a designed, managed and guided experience." (James Moliterno, *Experiential Education, Legal Education and Professional Responsibility*, 38 Wm. & Mary L. Rev. 71, 78 (1996)).

Learning theorists have argued that knowledge obtained from experience, and not just "thinking about it or contemplating the possibility of an encounter," (Field Study: A Sourcebook for Experiential Learning 9 (Lenore Borzak ed., 1981)), is one of, if not the most, useful form of learning for prospective professionals. Such learning can have broad implications, such as promoting diversity and a greater appreciation for other cultures.

David Kolb's seminal work on experiential learning advanced a cyclical model, in which learning is not about the accumulation of facts and data, but rather constitutes a process of forming and reforming ideas through experience.

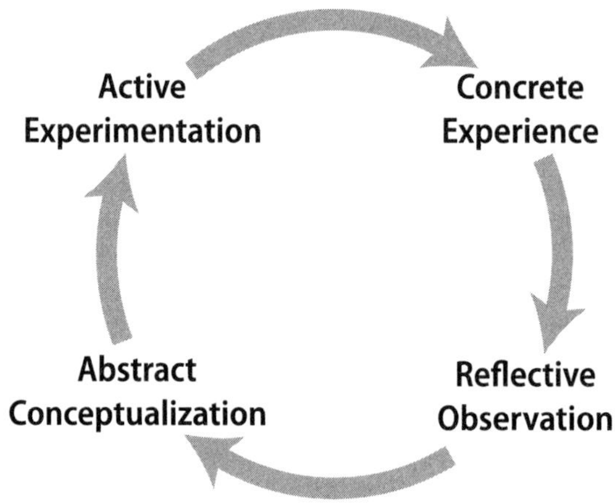

Kolb's Model

Kolb built on the work of John Dewey, who said, "There is an intimate and necessary relation between actual experience and education" (John Dewey, Experience and Education (1938)). Kolb asserted that learning is not just construction, but a continuing process of reconstruction and remodeling, with experience as the base. According to Kolb, "knowledge results from the combination of grasping and transforming experience" (*Kolb 41*). The cyclical model of experiential learning goes from concrete experience to reflective observation, to abstract conceptualization, to active experimentation, to concrete experience, and repeats. The cycle can start at any point and is a continuous upward spiral (*Kolb 41*). This idea mediates theory and practice, where practice is a used to interact with and continually improve pertinent theories.

Donald Schon's work is corroborative of Kolb's thesis and takes Kolb's ideas into the professional domain. Schon contends that, for professionals, a "technical reality" model is how most learning generally occurs. Schon asserts that professionals develop a predictive and standardized body of knowledge in order to resolve recurring professional issues. Schon suggests, however, that a better way of learning for professionals is "reflection-in-action," where knowledge grows out of a combination of experience and reflection.

Significantly, experiential learning is not educational simply because it offers real world experience, but rather because it engages students in concrete experience coupled with guided, critical reflection on that experience. The experiential learning combines pedagogical strategies, from the use of pragmatic real world knowledge, to the use of meta-cognition, exposing the blueprint of the learning process.

2. *Practice*

The most common illustrations of experiential learning in legal education continue to exist in the form of clinics and externships. These practical applications offer differing experiences for students and are directed and designed by faculty members or practitioners acting as supervisors and mentors. The American Bar Association's accreditation standards require some form of reflection-in-action as part of clinical and externship experiences.

Clinics

Clinics are opportunities for law students to represent clients and participate in actual cases. Most states allow third-year students (and, in some states, second-year, second-semester students) to practice under the supervision of a qualified attorney, and many schools take advantage of this blending of education and practice. Clinical experiences generally are in-house, where the clinic operates out of the law school, or through an existing independent organization (which then becomes an externship). A clinical program operates like a law office, with a staff and supervision by members of a law school's faculty. The faculty members use the experience as teaching opportunities to advance the skill sets needed to practice in the particular clinical area in which the students are working.

Externships

Externships are programs where students primarily learn from placements at existing legal organizations, such as agencies, courts, prosecutors, public defenders, law firms, public advocacy groups, and nonprofit organizations. Students often spend significant time either representing clients or providing some component of the work lawyers regularly perform. Members of the external organization, not the law school, directly supervise the students. The law school, however, does have a faculty member who facilitates the learning process through meetings at the school or online and other directed learning, such as journaling and other reflective practices.

Objectives for externships ought to be clearly delineated to promote the best outcomes. This expression can be difficult, particularly the development of specific criteria. As noted in *Best Practices for Legal Education*, "Law teachers have had a surprisingly difficult time articulating the educational goals of externship courses ..." (*Best Practices* 198). Some objectives include a deeper appreciation and understanding of the legal system and its processes, enhanced problem-solving competency, and ethical and professional enrichment.

One issue that arises in externships involves the quality of the interaction with the extern's supervisor. Sometimes, the supervisor can consist of a chain of command, including the person with ultimate authority over the extern and the person with direct contact with and day-to-day oversight of the extern. Often, the supervisor is a practicing lawyer who has numerous other responsibilities. To ensure the highest quality of educational experience, the faculty member needs to maintain oversight of the supervisor, open lines of communication, and develop procedures for dealing with issues that recur in such a process. Especially because feedback is an important part of the experience, it helps if the supervisor is trained in and understands the goals and structures of effective feedback.

Field Components

Field components are usually associated with externships. On rare occasions, traditional courses have field components as well. These field components can be informal, such as a single field trip, or more formal, such as a series of visits to law offices. An informal field trip might include a trip to the jail in a Criminal Law class or a trip to court to view witness examination at a trial in an Evidence course. The learning component of the field trip is not simply the experience, but rather a directed experience. Students can be asked to observe certain things or to participate in the field component, perhaps by interviewing someone associated with the trip or journaling about it afterwards, which Gerry Hess discusses in an article in this chapter.

Real-Life Experiences

Further, real-life experiences can occur within the typical class structure and not just on a field trip. This idea involves bringing the experiences into the class, including videos, guest speakers and case documents, or other lawyering artifacts. For example, a fingerprint expert can describe fingerprinting in an Evidence or Criminal Law course, and then students can take their own fingerprints at the direction of the visitor.

3. *Promoting Efficacy in Experiential Education*

To promote efficacy in the experiential learning process, several parameters should guide design of the experiences. These parameters are:

- Learning ought to be the primary object of the experience. Experiential learning is not an end in itself but, rather, a means to an end, and the professor should spell out the specific learning objectives with precision and specificity.
- To promote learning, the student role within the experience must be explicit and transparent. Rubrics should describe what successful performance looks like. In addition and as much as possible, the faculty role should be transparent as well.
- A key component of any experiential learning is an associated critical reflection component. The reflection on the experience, including journals, small-group discussions, and other forms of formal interactions serve to enhance and facilitate understanding about the relationship of the experience(s) to the targeted objectives.

C. Service Education

Today's younger generation has some strong inclinations toward service. Organizations promoting service for young adults include a variety of programs: *Teach For America*, in which college graduates agree to teach for at least two years in under-resourced schools; *AmeriCorps*, a government-affiliated program on the state and national levels that attempts to address educational, environmental, health, safety and other community needs; and *Atlas Corps.*, a program through which young adults volunteer abroad for two-years while people from other countries reciprocate and volunteer within the United States.

1. Defining and Distinguishing Service Education in the Law

Service education within the legal education context means systematic community involvement through a law-related activity. A duality of goals exists, including both short-term education and longer-term self-sufficiency and success. Essentially, the school provides an environment in which students can "take responsibility for their own learning and behavior so they may develop the skills and habits needed to be successful in school and life." (N. Susan Emeagwali, Lisa Berkey, Martha Guempel, *Celebrating Service and Learning*, TECHNIQUES, Apr. 2010, at 22, http://www.acteonline.org/tech_april10.aspx).

Service learning has a different orientation than experiential education. Service learning intersects with work that is *pro bono publico*, for the public good, a narrower subset than the platform for experiential learning and its objective is to combine educational advancement with a service to the broader community. A prime illustration of this type of learning is Street Law, a course offered at many law schools for credit in which law students teach high school and middle school students about the law. The interfaces with the high and middles school students occur in the mock trial and constitutional law areas. Law students must create lesson plans and implement them in the high and middle school classrooms. If mock trial is the subject, it invariably culminates in a mock trial competition, either between groups of students attending the same school or between schools. The Street Law program, started by Georgetown Law School and now in almost 100 law schools, has been an unqualified success in bridge-building within communities as well as for the law student participants.

Service learning focuses on affective learning as well as cognitive advancement. Service learning emphasizes qualities such as accountability and self-management. In Street Law, for example, the law students must not only be able to communicate difficult concepts with clarity to middle or high school students, but the law students also have to prepare a lesson and execute it.

The inclusion of a reflection component maximizes the service learning. This reflection includes small-group discussion, round-table discussions among the law students, journals, and essay writing. The engagement in the community has been found to promote ethical and professional identity development as well, particularly if the professor emphasizes these aspects of the experience by asking students to reflect on these potential lessons.

Service learning also can occur through individualized projects, designed and implemented by students as well as teachers. The student input and accountability promotes student ownership of the project and its outcome. Students can align with nonprofit organizations or work on their own.

2. Outcomes

Service learning can achieve a variety of desirable outcomes. The education can foster enthusiasm for a subject, provide needed texture to deepen understanding, create accountability, and improve other skills, such as client communication, and collaborative interaction. Just as importantly, the focus on human relations promotes self-esteem and a sense of self-worth, reaching across the aisle from the cognitive to the affective domain.

References

- JEFFREY CANTOR, EXPERIENTIAL LEARNING IN HIGHER EDUCATION: LINKING CLASSROOM AND COMMUNITY (1997).
- BARBARA GROSS DAVIS, TOOLS FOR TEACHING 166–172 (1993).
- DONALD L. FINKEL, TEACHING WITH YOUR MOUTH SHUT (2000).
- Michael F. Follo, *Field Trip as a Teaching Method, in* HANDBOOK OF COLLEGE TEACHING: THEORY AND APPLICATIONS 189-195 (Keith W. Prichard & R. McLaren Sawyer eds., 1994).
- Stan Friedland, *Developing Hearts and Minds,* PRINCIPAL LEADERSHIP, Apr. 2003, at 70.
- GERALD F. HESS & STEVEN I. FRIEDLAND, TECHNIQUES FOR TEACHING LAW (1999).
- Gerald F. Hess, *Heads and Hearts: The Teaching and Learning Environment in Law School,* 52 J. LEGAL EDUC. 75 (2002).
- Gerald F. Hess, *Principle 3: Good Practice Encourages Active Learning,* 49 J. LEGAL EDUC. 401 (1999).
- DAVID KOLB, EXPERIENTIAL LEARNING: EXPERIENCE AS THE SOURCE OF LEARNING AND DEVELOPMENT (1984).
- David Kolb & Roger Fry, *Toward an Applied Theory of Experiential Learning, in* THEORIES OF GROUP PROCESS(Cary Cooper ed., 1975).
- LARRY KRIEGER, THE HIDDEN SOURCES OF LAW SCHOOL STRESS: AVOIDING MISTAKES THAT CREATE UNHAPPY AND UNPROFESSIONAL LAWYERS (2005).
- DONALD A. SCHON, THE REFLECTIVE PRACTITIONER: HOW PROFESSIONALS THINK IN ACTION 3–69 (1983).
- Jayson Seaman, Jesse Beightol, Paul Shirilla, & Bart Crawford, *Contact Theory as a framework for Experiential Activities as Diversity Education: An Exploratory Study,* 32 J. OF EXPERIENTIAL EDUC. 207 (2009).
- ROY STUCKEY ET AL., BEST PRACTICES FOR LEGAL EDUCATION: A VISION AND A ROAD MAP (2007).
- WILLIAM M. SULLIVAN ET AL., EDUCATING LAWYERS: PREPARATION FOR THE PROFESSION OF LAW (2007).
- Symposium, *Humanizing Legal Education,* 47 WASHBURN L. J. 235 (2008).

Self-Guided Field Trips and Interviews

In every course I teach, an important goal is for students to apply the content and skills from the course to real life, not merely to learn the material in the abstract. Consequently, experiential learning plays a role in my required first-year courses (Civil Procedure, Litigation Skills and Professionalism Lab) and upper-level electives (Environmental Law, International Environmental Law).

Field trips and interviews are experiential techniques that promote student learning outside of the classroom. These techniques can be structured to facilitate students' application of course skills and content to real-life law practice. Field trip and interview exercises can be carefully arranged by the teacher. For example, the teacher can set up a court field trip and meeting with a judge or lawyer. On the other hand, the teacher can assign students to arrange their own field trips and interviews.

Self-guided field trips and student-arranged interviews can result in significant student learning with a minimal amount of teacher time to manage the experience. These assignments work best if students receive clear instructions and if student reflection follows their real-life experience.

Below is an example of a field trip/interview assignment in Environmental Law. This format can be adapted easily to many other courses.

Field Trip/Interview Assignment

By the 12th week of the course, complete a self-guided field trip *or* an interview related to Environmental Law. After your field trip or interview, produce a one-page, single spaced paper about your experience. Your paper is due at the beginning of class on ...

Interview. The purpose is to report on an interview with a person involved with some portion of the environmental law covered in this course. For example, the interview could feature an environmental lawyer, a regulator, or a person subject to regulation. The paper should describe the person's views of environmental law in practice and include your reflections on what you learned from the interview.

Field trip. The purpose is to see an industry, business, governmental facility, or site affected by the environmental law covered in this course; for example, a wastewater treatment facility, industrial facility, or a farm. The paper should describe how the site or facility is governed by some aspect of the law we covered in this course and your reflection of what you learned from the trip.

Early in the course and again in the middle of the course, I spend a couple of minutes of class time reminding students of the field trip/interview assignment and answering their questions. I encourage students to work in pairs or small groups to set up interviews or trips. The day that the papers are due, I devote 30 minutes or so of class time to this assignment. I have students trade papers so that they can read about one-another's experience and reflections. Then, sometimes, I have students discuss their experiences in small groups or I may have each student summarize what they learned from the experience in a 30-second presentation to the class. After class, I read and make brief comments on the students' reflection papers. That feedback process takes me about five minutes per paper.

The self-guided field trip or student-arranged interview assignment provides tremendous "bang for the buck." Students have a personal experience with the course skills or content applied to real life. They interact with professionals in the field. Students reflect on the insights they gained from the experience. My investment is 30 minutes of class time and five minutes per student paper. I'll take that deal every time.

Gerry Hess
Gonzaga University School of Law

Legislative Simulation as a Teaching Tool

I have run this legislative simulation since 2002 as a seminar with an enrollment limited to 20 students. While I previously used Popkins, *Materials on Legislation: Political Language and the Political Process,* because I thought its focus would interest students, I now use my own book, Brown & Brown, *Statutory Interpretation: The Search for Legislative Intent (NITA 2002)* (new edition forthcoming). Of course, studying statutory interpretation inevitably leads into the study of the legislative process. I was, however, concerned that students might find the readings too abstract and dry. My solution was to plan a legislative simulation. Consistent with the approach of the book, students would experience both roles: law making and law interpreting. Thus, I planned first to place them in a legislative setting where they would enact a statute, and later place them in the roles of advocate or judge involved in statutory interpretation. My plan was to have them engage in interpreting the very statute they had enacted so they could see the relationship, or lack thereof, between the legislative and the interpretation process.

Years ago, I had attended an AALS workshop in which Phil Schrag explained the extensive legislative simulation that he was then running at Georgetown. He gave an inspiring talk, but I wondered if the simulation would work if run on a much smaller scale. Before I could deal with that question, I agreed to cede the course to another professor. When I recovered the course a few years after ceding it, I needed an answer. It was clear to me that I did not have the time or resources to simulate the Congress, or even a state legislature, in a credible manner. I also realized that an even bigger obstacle was subject matter. If the legislature were going to adopt a statute, what would it concern? Topics that I suggested, primarily in the real estate area, got collective groans from the class. I was amazed that they did not want to fix the rule against perpetuities, but forcing my interests on them would have undermined the simulation. I solicited their ideas, but every student's suggestion got a similar negative response. Even in areas in which they admitted having an interest, most students (primarily 2Ls) felt they lacked sufficient background and could not possibly fix what they did not understand. Shifting the focus to the substantive law underlying a legislative proposal would have been time-consuming and distracting.

Then, it occurred to me that our one common area of interest and expertise was the law school itself. I asked them what they would change if they were the law school's legislature (i.e., the faculty). They certainly had some ideas about that! Moreover, they liked taking over the law school, even if only in a simulation. After a hot debate, they decided to reform the grading and examination process. Like a real legislature, there was time pressure. The session would end in the eighth week of the semester. I warned them that if they failed to adopt a statute, I would have to pick or write one for them to use in the second half of the simulation; no one wanted that to happen.

They attacked the task with gusto. With only a few organizational suggestions from me, they divided up into committees (and subcommittees) and went off to do research. Over the next four weeks, I allocated part of each two-hour class to legislative meetings. The committees exchanged reports and drafts. People lobbied for particular positions. We had a final legislative session in class. The presence of laptop computers greatly simplified keeping track of amendments and the production of a final act. Finally, they adopted a statute. I acted as the clerk of the legislature. They gave me the reports and the adopted statute so I could make copies for everyone and provide each student with a complete "legislative history." The next step was for me to examine the statute and devise the problems, i.e., fact patterns in which the application was uncertain. That task was less difficult than I anticipated. Over the last three weeks of the semester, we devoted part of each class period to one of these problems. Students were assigned the roles of advocates and judges. In these roles they used the tools they had learned to interpret the very statute they had enacted. Drafting and enactment proved to be lighter work than the application and interpretation process that forced them to look critically at their own earlier work.

This exercise was very effective at sensitizing them to how difficult it can be for a legislature to foresee problems, even when it is well informed about the subject matter; how difficult it can be to draft a statute; and just how uncertain language can be. Because they had participated in both the enactment and interpretation phases, they could see how the traditional methods might, or might not, lead a judge to uncover what the legislature had actually intended.

This simulation does not introduce students to the ins and outs of Congress or a particular state legislature. It involves a unicameral legislature without established rules or procedures. It does not deal with the threat of an executive veto. But it is not unlike many local legislatures such as city councils or county commissions. Moreover, it was an effective way to introduce students to the nature of the enactment and interpretation processes in a limited time and with minimal obstacles. My experience, including comments on student evaluations and conversations with students, convinced me to repeat the simulation, although the class chose an entirely different project: reforming the processes of registering for and adding/dropping courses.

Ronald Benton Brown
Nova Southeastern University, Shepard Broad Law Center

The First-Year Trial Practicum

Legendary Harvard Law Dean Roscoe Pound believed that the application of law has a decidedly human dimension. Dean Pound, who made a distinction between "law in action" and "law in the books," fully appreciated the legal knowledge that every lawyer must possess to succeed. (Roscoe Pound, *Law in Books and Law in Action*, 44 Am. L. Rev. 12 (1910)). But he also knew professional success required a synergy of knowledge with advocacy, counseling, and problem-solving skills. Drake's First-Year Trial Practicum not only implements Dean Pound's insight, it represents Drake's response to the indictment, popularized in the movie *Patch Adams*, that the first year of professional school education often is too detached from the patients or clients whom the students hope to eventually serve.

Drake Law School's "Lawyering from Day One" mission is reflected in an experiential education pyramid, from the bottom up: observation-simulation-participation. Experiential learning begins with Drake's First-Year Trial Practicum, in which every student observes an actual jury trial in the spring semester of the first year. From jury selection through jury verdict, students are placed in an educational setting that includes small group discussions led by clinical faculty, seasoned judges, and veteran attorneys. Lectures and practice panels focus on the key legal and procedural issues and on the litigation strategies and techniques of the lawyers trying the case. The Trial Practicum is not a moot court or mock trial experience. The case observed is an *actual* jury trial. Conceptually, it may be helpful to think of it as the laboratory component to the classroom.

The Trial Practicum is a week-long, five-day experience. The one-week time commitment enables us to include complex cases and enables students to observe the entire process from jury selection to closing arguments to verdict. The Trial Practicum not only brings to life the subject matter of several of the first-year courses, but it also creates a shared foundation for Evidence and other upper-level litigation-related courses, as well. The evaluations by students, faculty, attorneys and court personnel have uniformly praised both the fairness with which each trial has been conducted and the dynamic learning experience each Practicum has afforded.

For many students, the highlights of each Practicum have been the debriefing sessions conducted after the conclusion of the trial. The first is held with the lawyers who actually tried the case, the second with the jurors who decided the case. These sessions have enabled students and faculty to question the lawyers as to their strategies and to ask the jurors about both the rationale for their verdict and the effectiveness of the lawyer's presentations. Over the course of the trial week, the presiding judge meets daily for an informal brown-bag luncheon with groups of 20 to 25 students.

Each year, 20 to 25 lawyers, judges, and faculty have volunteered a week of their time to serve as small-group discussion leaders and practice panelists. The central and collaborative role the Trial Practicum design affords judges and lawyers in the educational experience contributes significantly to the program's success. This very substantial commitment serves as a testimonial to the program's educational integrity—former justices of the Iowa Supreme Court, retired district court judges, senior partners in Des Moines' largest law firms, and busy public interest lawyers do not donate a week's time, year after year, unless they believe they are making a difference. They bring a "real world" perspective to the small group discussions that follow the conclusion of the trial proceedings each day and often can provide instant commentary during the trial when they are observing it via closed circuit TV in adjoining seminar rooms. Their volunteerism has also meant the Trial Practicum has been incredibly low budget, making it a feasible curricular innovation at every law school.

The Trial Practicum would be just another law professor's idea gathering dust without the judiciary's embrace, and the cooperation of court and security personnel and prosecution and defense counsel. A felony criminal jury trial in your on-campus courtroom is not something you order from West Publishing Company. It happened only because the judiciary and counsel are confident that the integrity of the trial, and its security, would be preserved. In 2002, when this article was originally published in *The Law Teacher*, four Trial Practicum experiences had been completed, and a brief sketch of the four cases was included. Thirteen Trial Practicums have now been completed, and readers can read summaries of all cases on the Drake Law School website: http://www.law.drake.edu/academics/?pageID=trialPracticum.

In 1998 and 1999, the first two Trial Practicums involved burglary (*State of Iowa v. Stephen Blumberg*) and murder trials (*State of Iowa v. John Molloy*) tried by 12-person juries, with district judges Arthur Gamble and Larry Eisenhauer presiding. Both trials resulted in convictions that have been subsequently affirmed by the Iowa Court of Appeals. The third Practicum featured a civil trial, *Ken Downing v. City of West Des Moines*, involving allegations of constitutional tort and defamation. It was tried by an eight-person jury which awarded the plaintiff $10,000 in damages. District Judge Rob Blink presided. Prior to Judge Blink's ruling on court-awarded attorneys' fees, the case was settled for $40,000.

The 2001 Trial Practicum involved the trial of an armed robbery, *State of Iowa v. Clarence Willis*, presided over by Judge Robert Wilson. The three-and-a-half day trial resulted in an acquittal. As criminal trials are high drama, the students fully appreciated that a man's liberty was at stake. Armed robbery under Iowa sentencing laws carries a mandatory prison time of at least 22 years. The case centered on the reliability of eyewitness testimony in a cross-racial identification. The educational value of the small group discussions and jury debriefing was readily evident. The students' discussions in the small group settings, and undoubtedly the juror deliberations, centered on inconsistent testimony, credibility of witnesses, and the reliability of eyewitness testimony. The case also involved a successful *Batson* challenge by defense counsel of the prosecution's strike of an African American juror, and this action was the source of considerable small group discussion. The juror debriefing confirmed the initial vote was 9 to 3 for acquittal, and it was fascinating to listen to jurors explain their thoughts about the conflicting evidence that eventually brought consensus for acquittal. The depth of our students' understanding and appreciation of the crucial difference between the "beyond a reasonable doubt" and the "preponderance of evidence" standards of proof gained from the Trial Practicum is not something that can be replicated through case analysis in a classroom. They learned from the juror debriefing that the jurors felt it was likely the defendant had committed the crime, but the jurors concluded defense counsel had succeeded in raising sufficient doubt about the prosecution's case so that they could not convict the defendant.

The activity occurring during the week of the trial, and all of its accompanying programming, represent only the tip of the iceberg in terms of the preparation and planning that goes into each Trial Practicum. The greatest challenge is to identify cases that will actually go to trial, which can be tried within one week's time, that can be tried at the Law School's on-campus courtroom with the consent of the litigants and counsel, and that are educationally valuable. Since more than 95% of cases settle, often on the court house steps, court personnel and law school support staff screen approximately 200 criminal and civil cases each year to select an appropriate case and several backup cases.

Since the beginning in 1998, Chief Judge Arthur Gamble has issued a series of Administrative Orders designating the Smith Law Center courtroom as a place to hold court under the Iowa Code. This order provides an important safety net for the Trial Practicum, as it permits the court to assign trials from the Polk County Court House in Des Moines to the Drake campus even when the consent of the parties has not be obtained. In 2007, the only time the consent of the parties was not obtained, the Iowa Supreme Court rejected an interlocutory appeal challenging assignment of *State v. Bobby Stouffer* to the Smith Law Center for observation in the Trial Practicum.

In *Patch Adams*, actor Robin Williams plays an irreverent medical student who is critical of a curriculum that provided no patient contact during the students' first two years of medical school. The movie demonstrated that effective medicine requires a holistic approach that includes learning compassion and communication skills so physicians can accurately diagnose and heal. The lessons of *Patch Adams* readily transfer to the study of law in general and the practicum experience in particular. First-Year Trial Practicum teaches students about the trial as a story, about the judicial process and the responsibility of jurors in the decision-making process, about lawyers and effective advocacy, and much more. It introduces students to law in action in a way that no textbook can ever capture, to lawyers and lawyering, and to fundamental values of civility, professionalism and public service. In 2008 Drake Law School received the E. Smythe Gambrell Professionalism Award from the American Bar Association at the ABA's annual meeting in New York City, "In recognition of outstanding achievement in the design and implementation of [Drake Law School's] model professionalism program." The Trial Practicum was one of the four Drake programs specifically praised by the ABA in making the award to Drake. http://www.law.drake.edu/newsEvents/details.aspx?eventID=gambrellAccept.

Russell E. Lovell II
Drake University Law School

Go Forth and Prosper: The Ten Commandments of Externships

The externship teaching method has tremendous potential for developing student skills and critical thinking. This approach to education also requires particular attention because of the possible variability in supervisory skill and other factors at the field placement. The following are concepts that can be helpful in developing a strong externship program.

I. Thou shalt love the externship, thy Program, with all thy heart, with all thy soul, and with all thy might.

Create a program you can passionately believe in, and support/defend it without hesitation. Articulate and address directly any concerns that you have, including consultation with adult learning specialists if necessary. If you doubt your program, who won't?

II. Thou shalt bear no false gods before thee, but shall prosper in the Truth in all thy ways.

Be alert to recognize and address directly any biases and assumptions that suggest externships are not responsible programs generally. Common assumptions include, for example, that externship is an irresponsible teaching method; that a good externship will mimic, as closely as possible, an in-house clinic; and that, as the "bottom line," students learn more and learn better in an in-house clinic. If your program is designed and administered well, you will not have (long-term) problems. Avoid accepting negative stereotypes, and don't fall into the trap of defending apparent imperfections in externships. The best scholars and teachers have students daydreaming, texting, and surfing the web in class, and no in-house clinic is perfect either. Why apply the (impossible) standard of perfection only to field placements?

III. Yea, though thou walkest through the valley of the shadow of uncertainty, thou shall fear no evil, for thy Program is with thee.

It is crucial to create a clear and descriptive set of educational objectives and methods, and to have them approved by your curriculum committee or overall faculty. Live by them, and amend them as necessary to reflect the *reality* of your program. The inevitable uncertainty of some field placements (and supervisors) is a reflection of the reality of law practice and real lawyers, and will not undermine the program if you have considered these realistic imperfections in your program design.

IV. Thou shalt humbly render the regulators their due, but thou shalt not bow down before them. And through thy steadfast righteousness it shall come to pass that they also shall believe upon thee and upon thy program.

Develop camaraderie with the faculty and work against any "we-they" attitudes. Generate an educationally responsible program that complies, at least in substance, with the accreditation standards. Be consistent and confident in the administration of the program, and avoid reacting to, or generating, negativity.

V. Let there be no wailing or gnashing of teeth over thy status or thy rewards, for verily I say unto thee that thence shall be planted many dark seeds in thy heart; and they shall be as a blight upon thy Countenance and upon the Countenance of thy children.

Complaining can make you miserable, and is likely to affect your home life as well as your job satisfaction. Avoid constantly comparing your pay or perks with those of others—you'll always come out "better" or "worse" than someone else. Work for salary and status parity, but don't forget to appreciate the great job you have and your chance to shape skilled and decent lawyers. If these considerations are not enough, try remembering how happy you were to leave the old job for this one; and if recalling why you became a law professor doesn't restore a positive attitude, consider going back.

VI. Neither shalt thou bow down before the God of the In-house Clinic, for She is a True God, but She is not the One True God, nor is She thy God.

One of the particular assumptions that creates a defensive posture for externships is that the in-house clinic is the superior (or, perhaps, only legitimate) approach to clinical training of good and decent lawyers. It is clearly the more established and accepted approach, but look out for the unspoken standard that a good externship must necessarily model a good in-house clinic. That assumption is a setup for guaranteed stress, as you try to ignore, deny, or cover up the obvious differences between the two. The legitimacy of your program will depend only on its own design, objectives, and whether it is conducted to responsibly meet its objectives.

VII. Thou shalt teach Goodness, Self-Reflection, and all these Truths to thy students, so that they may go forth and prosper in the whimsical Land of Externship.

Look realistically at the goals of your program, and the general level of reliability and expertise of your field supervisors; then, decide how much preparation and relative autonomy your students will need to learn successfully at each placement. Prepare them fully with these factors in mind. If this approach is not feasible, change placement offices, or amend the goals or structure of the program.

VIII. In thy dark moments quaver not before the plight of thy students, nor the fancy of their supervisors, but in all ways be true to thy Scriptures.

Inevitably, some students will have problems with their supervisors. This type of problem, of course, is also true of classroom students and their professors, or any other set of mentor-mentee relationships. Students may learn well from the experience if you have prepared them properly, and/or they may need to be transferred to a new supervisor or even a new office. Work to amend the supervisor's approach (if errant), by reference to your published objectives, methods, and supplementary materials. If that approach fails, make the necessary changes to maximize the student's semester, and consider suspending the placement or amending the relevant objectives and credit award in future terms.

IX. Suffer not the little accreditors to come before thee, for theirs is the Kingdom of Power and Glory. Neither tremble nor prostrate thyself in fear before them, though their ways be vexatious and strange. For I tell you, verily shall they lift thee up in thy time of travail, and shall anoint thee in righteousness before thy dean and thy faculty.

Accreditation visitors are, indeed, in a position of relative power and, unfortunately, different teams will have different approaches and attitudes. Try to learn the identities of the members early, and hope for someone with externship experience, or at least a minimum of biases. But remember a few things: If your program makes sense and you are convinced and passionate about its worth, the team is likely to be persuaded by your thinking and passion. And if you need resources, the team is likely to note that fact in the report, thereby encouraging the administration to give more support to your program. Few programs have been closed as the result of accreditation visits. Approach the visit openly as a learning (and teaching) opportunity, in your own thinking and when interacting with the team. Communicate with the assigned visitors well before they arrive, to arrange for a cooperative and time-effective visit.

X. Go forth in Light, and joyfully sow the seeds of thy placements upon the fields. For though thou dwellest in toil with the doubtful and the weak of understanding, thou shalt be

delivered mightily by the Light of thy Program, and shalt prosper in the Fields of Externship forever.

This result should be the natural result of creating an educationally responsible program, standing confidently behind it, and avoiding negative reactions to possible biases. The worth of your program will be well articulated and supported for you by your students, alumni, and at least some of your faculty. Additionally, quality clinical programs are increasingly demanded from outside the college both by hiring attorneys and more skills-oriented regulatory standards. Stand clear and firm, approach difficulties honestly, care about your students, appreciate your work, stay positive ... and thrive.

Larry Krieger
Florida State University College of Law

Public Comment and Eclass

In any course that involves administrative rule making, an engaging and practical assignment is for students to submit a public comment to an agency. The example below arises out of an Environmental Law course, but the public comment assignment would work well in Administrative Law or in any course in which a federal or state agency plays a significant role. Likewise, this example is structured to be completed online, but could be modified easily to be done in or out of class without online components. The students were given the following information and instructions about the exercise.

Our January 25 eclass deals with public comments.

The Syllabus describes the Public Comment assignment: The purpose is to make a public comment in a proceeding relating to a portion of environmental law covered in this course; for example, a proposed rule, a permit application, or an Environmental Impact Statement. Include the text of your written or oral comment and your reflection on what you learned from the comment process.

This assignment and eclass involves five steps.

1. Locate and read about a proposed federal agency action dealing with the environment. The action could be a proposed rule or any other proposed agency action. I'd start with www.regulations.gov, which is a site designed to facilitate public comments on proposed agency actions. Or you can find proposed agency actions on the websites of various federal agencies.
2. Submit your public comment to the agency.
3. Post your comment on TWEN. Go to the TWEN page for our course. Click Forums. Click Public Comments. Click Add Topic. In the subject line, put your name. In the message box, cut and paste the text of your public comment and a paragraph with your reflection on what you learned from the public comment process. Click Post the Topic. Complete this step by 11:00 a.m. on January 25.
4. Read a couple of your classmates' public comments. In class on Wednesday, I'll ask for your thoughts on your classmates' public comments. Complete this step any time before class on January 27.
5. Read my reply to your TWEN posting. I'll reply to each of your public comment postings. Go to the TWEN page for our course. Click Forums. Click Public Comments. Click on the

topic you posted. My reply will appear below the text of your posting. Complete this step any time before class on January 27.

Most students find the public comment exercise to be challenging. Although it is easy to find agency proposals open for public comment, it is difficult to learn enough about the issue to submit a meaningful comment. Students take the assignment seriously because they are submitting a real, not hypothetical, comment to an agency, with their name on the comment. This assignment helps students understand both the value and the limitations of the public comment process in administrative practice. In addition, each student gets feedback from me about their comment and their understanding of administrative environmental law. It takes me five to ten minutes to read and remark on each student's comment.

Gerry Hess
Gonzaga University School of Law

The Activity-Based Seminar

Seminars are challenging to design. As advanced level courses that deeply explore doctrine, policy, theory, or interdisciplinary approaches, they are more interactive than other classes, relying on a high degree of student engagement and participation. Different models for the course prevail: the end-of-semester presentation that culminates in a long paper; the colloquium, where students read essays and interact with guest scholars; the reaction paper that asks students to write regular short responses to assigned readings; student-led discussions where students both select readings and facilitate the class; small group projects that culminate in papers, class presentations, or both; or the workshop that blends doctrine and skills. After choosing goals and the general format to achieve them, the instructor has to carefully select materials, determine the best method for assuring student participation, and decide how to assess performance. Assuming that enrollment in a seminar is open to all students, or at least all students who have completed prerequisites, the instructor has to expect a range of commitment to the course. Some students will be stars; others will be along for the ride. Thus, a plan to raise the level of student commitment is critical.

In spring 2009, I designed a seminar with an enrollment of 20 students called Advanced Topics in Immigration Law, focusing on issues "ripped from the headlines." For the 14-week semester of two-hour class sessions, I chose three broad issues: detention, adjudication, and enforcement. For each four-week unit, I added an experiential learning project to complement a wide range of types of readings: statutes, regulations, cases, law review and newspaper articles, government and nongovernmental reports, litigation documents, and opinion pieces.

My goal was to provide students with opportunities to understand the law and its impact in context through a range of activities supported by readings and class discussion. These opportunities would facilitate students becoming well-informed investigators, observers, commentators and participants in the immigration system, at a time in history when reform is imminent.

Immigration Detention: A Client Letter

After a blitz orientation reading relevant statutes and several Supreme Court cases, articles about the conditions of confinement, and published government standards, students participated in the New York Legal Aid Society sponsored local detention center project. Armed with a comprehensive questionnaire, some materials about possible immigration remedies, but no particular skills training, the students paired up to interview two clients. I debriefed them twice, once at the detention center and once at back at school. The assignment was for each student to draft a client letter. Because our class would not be representing the clients, we actually did not send the letters, but many of the students performed some follow-up tasks for the detainees, such as contacting relatives or arranging for medical attention. In one instance, the students referred a detainee to the Immigrant Rights Clinic at NYU Law School, whose students were able to secure his release. At the last class on this topic, students presented the circumstances of their particular interviews, describing how the individual came to be in custody, which allowed them to see in action the detention statutes and cases they had read, what possible relief existed, and to witness some of the extraordinary hardships imposed by detention. The detention center activity provided a summative writing exercise, "client" contact, and an eye-opening exposure to the effects of harsh detention and deportation laws.

Immigration Adjudication: Visits to Immigration Court and a Second Circuit Opinion

This unit began with an in-depth, in-class exploration of the immigration adjudication system. Then students went on a research-based treasure hunt for circuit court cases critical of immigration judges, observed a hearing at the New York Immigration Court about which they had to submit a short essay describing their impressions, and attended one of five possible oral arguments of an immigration case at the Second Circuit Court of Appeals for which they had been given the briefs and record on appeal. Their assignment was to write the decision (no more than ten pages) and a reaction essay about the oral argument. This activity involved a substantial writing exercise, exposure to an appellate record, observation of the potential impact of oral argument, and a chance to evaluate for themselves the quality of immigration court judging on the ground and from appellate heights.

Immigration Enforcement: Op-Ed

In another research hunt, students located examples of local laws aimed at immigrant communities, and then read cases involving legal challenges to them. They also read court documents relating to prosecutions resulting from recent workplace raids including plea agreements, watched news accounts of raids, and read GAO and NGO reports. In the midst of this unit, the Supreme Court decided a case directly affecting the prosecutions stemming from the raids. By the end of the semester, immigration reform was in the air as President Obama's new administration had begun to pay attention to raids and detention, and as his appointees began to unravel some of the initiatives of the prior administration and develop new policies. News articles were full of stories about these changes. The students were ready to join this policy conversation. Their last writing project of the semester was an op-ed. With some guidance on how to write an op-ed, gleaned from online sources, students picked a topic, researched it, and wrote an op-ed that they delivered in class. A selection of their titles reveals the variety of issues addressed: *DREAM Act Makes Cents; Failing Haiti;* and *Immigration Reform—More Assimilation, Less Deportation.* This exercise required factual and legal research and learning a new advocacy voice. Many of the op-eds were quite moving and made a big impact on the rest of the class.

Last Class: Book Critique

By the fourth class, students had to select one from a list of four recently-published books that presented historical, theoretical and topical perspectives, and then spend the rest of the semester reading the entire book. The book choices were:

- Kevin R. Johnson, Opening the Floodgates: Why America Needs to Rethink Its Borders and Immigration Laws (NYU Press 2007);
- Dan Kanstroom, Deportation Nation: Outsiders in American History (Harvard University Press 2007);
- Mark Krikorian, The New Case Against Immigration: Both Legal and Illegal (Sentinel HC 2008); and
- Hiroshi Motomura, Americans in Waiting: The Lost Story of Immigration and Citizenship in the United States (Oxford University Press 2008).

Two weeks before the end of the semester, they met in small groups to plan a collaborative class presentation. For the most part, their presentations were purely descriptive; they recapitulated the themes of the books and identified some of the books' highlights. Probably, the rush at the end of the semester accounted for their lack of focus. Nevertheless, the ability to read at this level throughout the semester was valuable, as was the opportunity to collaborate.

Conclusion

This course was a lot of work! In addition to planning readings, class assignments, and a two-hour weekly class session, I had to arrange for and go on the students' detention center visits, meet outside of class with ten pairs of students, locate and procure the Circuit Court records, and read and grade three assignments. I was extremely lucky that the course attracted curious, enthusiastic, and some well-informed students. They worked as hard as I did, enjoying the variety and novelty of the classes and assignments. The course also allowed me the satisfaction of drilling down into selected topics that I often have to cover superficially in the survey immigration course.

Stacy Caplow
Brooklyn Law School

Integrating Public Service Legal Work into Nonclinical Courses

At New England School of Law (NESL) in Boston, faculty members have begun to experiment with incorporating public service legal work into the classroom experience. In each instance, nonclinical faculty members have collaborated with practicing lawyers engaged in public service legal work. The faculty and lawyers have identified research and writing issues within the subject area of the course. Instructors have then assigned students to complete projects related to those issues.

Some of the projects that have been undertaken by my colleagues are described below. Although we are early in our experimentation with this model, a number of benefits are already evident. First, the projects provide interesting topics that have helped our students understand the subject matter of the course and develop their research and writing skills.

Second, we have provided our students with an opportunity to perform public service legal work. Third, the structure has allowed us to engage in collaborative projects with lawyers outside the academy. Fourth, the endeavors have made our teaching more fulfilling. Our classes are engaged in exciting projects, and collaboration among faculty members has increased as we have shared common challenges emerging from our efforts to integrate theory and practice.

A number of factors contributed to the advent of this teaching model at New England at this time. First, the faculty recently established our Center for Law and Social Responsibility (CLSR), designed in part to support faculty teaching, scholarship, pro bono projects, and other activities that focus on unequal access to, or treatment under, the law. Second, the faculty members teaching seminars have engaged in pro bono legal work while at New England. Each faculty member remains dedicated not only to teaching, scholarship, and participation in law school governance, but also to performing work that benefits the profession and the public (see ABA Standard 404). Third, New England has worked to break down barriers between classroom and clinical work, integrating both nonclinical faculty into clinical courses and clinical faculty into classroom settings. The New England program involves full-time and part-time faculty, clinical and nonclinical faculty, in a co-teaching model. The program even blends the in-house clinics and externship placements into hybrid clinical courses. Fourth, New England is attempting to increase public service work performed by its students. The new CLSR includes a Public Service Project, created to identify, support, and increase public service work among New England faculty, students, and alumni. Through the seminar courses described in this article, an additional 40 to 50 students are performing public service legal work, a figure that will grow as more faculty experiment with the model.

Description of Projects

Peter Manus has experimented with this model twice in his Environmental Justice seminar. Manus and his students took on various projects on behalf of several federal, state, and public interest law offices working in the environmental justice area. For example, the class produced one memorandum evaluating various state environmental justice policies and bills, offering a detailed analysis of how elements of such policies and bills might function in relation to existing Massachusetts environmental regulations. The memorandum culminated with sample language for an environmental justice statute or its implementing regulations.

David Siegel has incorporated legal projects into his seminar on Mental Health Issues in Criminal Proceedings, offered for the first time in the spring 2001 semester. In his seminar, Siegel identified projects involving unsettled areas of law. Students ranked their top three preferences and sorted themselves into groups of two to five persons. Two groups worked with a senior lawyer in the local public defender's office, who oversees the office's mental health-related litigation. One group researched competency issues in probation surrender hearings, a form of garden-variety litigation for public defenders, for which there is very little "law." Another group explored procedural issues that could arise in the implementation of a new sex-offender commitment statute. A third group worked with a professor of law in psychiatry at a medical school's postgraduate program in law and psychiatry, conducting a nationwide study of the use of actuarial instruments to predict dangerousness. A fourth group worked with a retired state court judge to study programs that teach police officers to recognize and divert mentally ill persons from the criminal justice system. This group conducted factual research on the existence of such programs and legal research on the degree to which they could be implemented locally. The group then prepared a grant application to create such programs.

Judi Greenberg also experimented with the model in the spring 2001 semester in her Domestic Violence course. Greenberg collaborated with two Boston lawyers, one of whom is a New England graduate, to develop projects for her course. One project related to the interface between protective orders and schools while another dealt with batterers' misuse of the courts.

Conclusion

The new model contributes to our school's efforts to break down the traditional dichotomies between theory and practice and classroom and clinic, while providing our students with public service legal work that enhances their understanding of their course work. This assertion is not to suggest that all experiments with the new model have met with complete success. Manus concluded that the legal work had taken over one course to the point where students learned less of the theoretical underpinnings of the law than he considered optimal. In another class, the outside attorney was unable to commit the minimal amount of thought and time necessary to maintain a presence in the course, rendering the legal work little more than a "real-life simulation." In both those instances, however, the failure to achieve the desired balance in the course did not render the course an overall failure. Students learned at least as much as they would have in a seminar involving guest speakers using issues from current cases. Even with its problems, the model offers the potential of giving students a vision of being lawyers who think beyond their cases to better serve their clients and community.

Russell Engler
New England School of Law

Experiential Learning — Law Practice in Class

"Law schools cannot prepare students for practice unless they teach doctrine, theory, and practice as part of a unified, coordinated program of instruction." (*Best Practices* 99). *The Carnegie Report* similarly recommends integrating theory and practice so that "[t]he teaching of legal doctrine ... become[s] part of learning to 'think like a lawyer' in practice settings." (*The Carnegie Report* 9)

In addition to the recommendations of experts, another good reason to bring law practice into the classroom is positive student response. My student evaluations tell me students appreciate the opportunity to hear from and ask questions of practicing lawyers. ("The guest lecturers were very informative and a great way to expose students to the real world of law.") Students enjoy developing legal skills while learning doctrine and connecting what happens in the classroom with real world legal practice. ("The law practice simulations and the guest panels were really helpful to understanding what we were learning" and, "This class more than any other law school class taught me the real-life implications of the law.... I loved the simulations.") Students also enjoy variation in teaching methods. ("[Simulations and guest speakers were helpful in] breaking up the monotony of being lectured to all the time in other classes").

Below are four ideas for bringing law practice into the classroom. These ideas are supported by several rationales: to vary teaching methods, to connect the classroom to legal practice, and to integrate the teaching of doctrine and skills.

1. Maximizing Learning from Guest Speakers

Before class, in this case, Civil Rights Litigation, I ask students to read the guest speakers' bios, skim their law offices' websites, and perhaps Google them to generate excitement about what students might learn from the guest speaker. Students also are asked prior to the presentations to upload three questions for the speakers to ensure the students engage the speaker during the event. During the guest panel, all students must close laptops. During the Q & A that follows all guest presentations, students must try to ask a question. After the presentation and in later classes, I encourage reflection about what the guest panelists said, how the presentations connect to topics covered later in the course, and how the presentations might influence student views of the class subject.

2. Law Practice Simulations

My Civil Rights Litigation class is structured around ten law practice simulations. These realistic simulations allow students to creatively explore attorney roles in shaping and applying legal doctrine. Some simulations involve doctrines that have split or are likely to split the federal circuits. Simulations include interoffice debates among attorneys deciding whether to appeal or seek certiorari; meetings with clients to decide the next steps in the litigation following an adverse district court ruling; settlement conferences with in-house counsel alone or before a mediator; testimony before a legislative body; and appellate oral arguments. No research is needed for any simulation—the materials necessary to craft arguments are the assigned readings for the course.

For each simulation, I provide a short description and logistical guide. There are five or six students in the simulation: two advocating for one side, two for the other, and one or two students in a neutral questioning role. All other students must upload two to three questions in advance to ensure they consider the differing views. Students must close laptops during the simulation. After the five to six students have engaged in the simulation for about 18 to 20 minutes, I open up questioning to all students in the class. Students must try to ask at least one question. The entire simulation is about 35 to 40 minutes but could easily be shorter or longer.

3. Realistic In-Class Drafting Exercises

We do several in-class writing assignments as the examples below illustrate. At the end of the course, students turn in a portfolio including all in-class and other writing they have done. In-class writing can be a useful learning experience, as well as a useful self-assessment tool, even if it is not collected.

Examples

- To reinforce understanding of action "under color of law," in class we watch a short YouTube video of a bar security video involving a drunk off-duty police officer assaulting a bartender, and I cast the students as the lawyer for the plaintiff bartender. In class, students spend ten minutes drafting questions to ask the client—focused solely on differentiating private action from action under color of law—and then compare with the person next to them. During class, we go around the room sharing the questions each student pair drafted, without repeating questions.
- To reinforce what types of documentary evidence are necessary to prove a municipal liability claim, I ask students in class to watch the same YouTube bar

security video above, and then spend ten minutes drafting document requests likely to produce relevant evidence. We then discuss the document requests as a class.

- To reinforce understanding of when procedural due process protects an employee's interest in a government job and what procedures must be followed to fire an employee with a protected property interest in the job, I ask students to imagine they represent a city and the Mayor is on the phone, telling them he has just fired an employee. What information does the attorney need from the client to determine whether the firing complied with procedural due process? What specific questions does the attorney need to ask the Mayor? After five or so minutes, I ask students to upload a short list of questions to ask the client, and we discuss the exercise as a class.

4. Headline Handout

To remind students that Civil Rights Litigation is not an esoteric area but daily fare for many lawyers, I often take recent headlines and ask students what course materials would be relevant to analyze the legal problems presented.

Conclusion

Using exercises based on real-life legal practice to reinforce concepts is a good way to vary the rhythm of a class, to hold student interest, to give students a taste of legal practice, and to help students appreciate the intellectual challenge of translating abstract legal doctrine into law practice contexts. As one student evaluation of my Civil Rights class stated: "You get a great grounding in the doctrinal aspects of the law, but you also have the practice simulations, the guest speakers, and the writing assignments which complement the course so well. There's no other course I've had that was anything like this one, and I really enjoyed the variety in terms of structure and class participation opportunities. I feel like I've learned a ton in this class."

Sarah Ricks
Rutgers School of Law–Camden

Truth in Labeling: Identifying Experiential and Special Engaged Learning Course Components in Syllabi and Course Catalogues

Following *The Carnegie Report* on legal education, there was considerable buzz about transforming the traditional Langdellian core of legal education, a case-oriented, legal-analysis-based educational process, especially by broadening its focus on cognitive legal analysis to incorporate a variety of skills. While schools have begun to heed the call to integrate varying professional skills and experiences into the core curriculum, the transformation has not been an easy one. Instead, wholesale change, even when favored, has been slow. With one or two highly publicized exceptions, it appears that the majority of change has occurred on the periphery of the educational process. A by-product of this greater illumination, however, has been an information gap about whether skills and experiential learning already are occurring within traditional course structures on an individual basis.

To better track how law teachers are delivering the education within a particular course, and to publicize what faculty members are doing individually, it might be useful to voluntarily label experiential or special engaged learning class segments in syllabi, course catalogues and school websites. (Special engaged learning is used here to mean skills training and directed participatory techniques as illustrated below.) Such labeling also serves to promote the integration of experiential and engaged learning in core courses by expressly recognizing these approaches, provide notice to students and teachers alike that this recognition is occurring, albeit within the traditional shells of basic courses, and provide more transparency overall about the ingredients of the educational process.

Examples of experiential or special engaged learning components in some courses follow.

1. Evidence: Conducting mock trials as part of the course with students acting as the attorneys, applying and synthesizing their evidence knowledge. These trials should definitely be discussed in the syllabus, including what percentage of the course grade, if any, is allocated to the trial performance. (In assigning such trials for many years, I did not count the trials as part of the final grade, but noted how such participation is terrific evidence practice, particularly in synthesizing the rules. Students grumbled about the extra work and then, after they had participated, almost uniformly found the exercise to be beneficial.)
2. Criminal Law: Visiting the local jail, especially as part of a discussion of theories of punishment, as well as a special unit dedicated to CSI (Crime Scene Investigation). The jail visits are often powerful and provocative, generating many opportunities to link various units in the course and to create controlled reaction papers. The CSI component provides a bridge to evidence law and experts in general, with invited experts from a local crime lab or police department talking about related subjects, such as fingerprint analysis, blood spatter, and general crime scene investigation. See the CSI article later in the chapter.
3. Contracts: Negotiation exercises, illustrating an alternate remedy to a lawsuit involving a breach of contract. Planting different types of competitive competencies in the first year, and not just the adversarial trial process, is often more representative and realistic.
4. Civil Procedure: Writing and arguing a motion to dismiss or for summary judgment. These writing exercises often provide a bridge and comparison to the writing exercises students are doing in their legal writing courses.
5. Criminal Procedure: Writing and arguing a motion to suppress evidence under the Fourth Amendment or statements under the Fifth Amendment. Writing and advocacy exercises promote learning by having students use the cases and synthesize doctrine.
6. Property: A mock hearing over disputed property. (e.g., the lawsuit concerning ownership of the baseball hit by Barry Bonds for his record-setting 73rd homerun, *Popov v. Hayashi*, 2002 WL 31833731 (Ca. Sup. Ct. 2002)).
7. Constitutional Law: Simulating or listening to oral arguments in a Supreme Court case covered in the class. The professor or students can get transcripts of the oral arguments and students can be assigned to play different people involved in the arguments. Having an actual argument reenacted offers an opportunity to see some of the raw materials from which the judicial opinions will be crafted, much like watching a cooking show with an expert chef.

Steven I. Friedland
Elon University School of Law

Maximizing Student Learning from Guest Speakers

As a student, I sometimes viewed guest speakers as opportunities to zone out. As a professor, I try to maximize student benefit from guest speakers in my own classes by getting students to engage the subject of the speaker's talk in advance. Some useful techniques are:

- Providing students with biographical background on the guest speaker (such as job title, description of current position, significant professional accomplishments or awards, etc.);
- Assigning students to visit the website for the guest speaker's organization (such as websites for law firms, government offices, agency that hears civilian complaints of police misconduct, feminist legal organization, etc.);
- Requiring students to turn in three questions for the speaker in advance of the talk. Student questions run the gambit from attempts to understand the practical considerations of representing clients (How do you decide which clients to represent? How do you decide the settlement value of a case?); to eliciting war stories (Have any of your clients ever been ordered to simply apologize?); to questions that prompt reflection on the moral and ethical challenges of the guest speaker's legal practice (Do you think the potential to be sued or held liable for civil rights violations influences police behavior? What do you say to people who think that criminal defense is "helping the bad guy"?); to questions about specific cases or initiatives by the guest lawyer (Your organization's report on domestic violence recommends that court personnel be trained on the cultural, ethnic, and religious issues surrounding domestic violence. Have these issues affected police response to domestic violence calls? Your organization's website states that the largest number of complaints against police are for abuse of authority. Please explain what types of claims this category includes.)

To maximize student engagement during the presentation itself, I require students to close their laptops. During the time I always reserve for Q & A, I encourage students to ask questions by reminding them (before the guest speaker arrives) that asking questions will count toward their class participation grade. If the guest speaker is a judge, I require students to dress appropriately and to stand and ask their questions, addressing the judge as "Your Honor" or "Judge." After the guest speaker leaves or in a later class, I encourage a few minutes of reflection on what the speaker said. In subsequent classes, I try to weave in references to points the guest speaker made.

Sarah Ricks
Rutgers School of Law–Camden

CSI, Criminal Law and Procedure

Certain experiential exercises fit nicely with particular courses. A crime scene investigation (CSI) unit for Criminal Law or Criminal Procedure meshes quite well and generates excitement and interest that carries over into the rest of the course.

This unit can occur in a single class or an extended class, depending on how many components are included in the segment. The conceptualization of CSI includes a variety of exercises. Students actually can observe a mock crime scene, looking for clues and evidence. They can see slides of actual bloody crime scenes and how those scenes are interpreted by experts. Also, students can participate in taking latent fingerprints—namely their own.

I have seen one teacher, Carol Henderson, a professor at the Stetson University School of Law and the Director of the National Clearinghouse for Science, Technology and the Law, use a crime scene to great advantage in her Scientific Evidence course and I have adapted her approach to my basic first-year Criminal Law course.

Rationale for Using Class Time

The actual observation and participation in a realistic criminal law exercise adds texture and a three-dimensional frame to Criminal Law, a course where sanitized cases often belie the gritty nature of the subject matter. The experiential focus is appreciated by the students, who also begin to understand that the scientific depth of the CSI subject areas is formidable, although linked closely to numerous criminal law rules and principles, such as those relating to expert witnesses and evidence. On a cognitive level, students are disabused of the notion that a superficial familiarity with the popular culture CSI genre creates real understanding of the field. This class also places the students in the shoes of a different and important group of people in the criminal justice system; crime investigators. Finally, for those students who are considering a career in criminal law, the experiential application of the law can facilitate interest in (or disinterest in) a career as a criminal lawyer.

Nuts and Bolts

I provide notice about the CSI component in the course syllabus and expressly discuss the reasoning behind the inclusion of this subject matter in advance. Students are sometimes assigned special readings for that class session.

I have three experiential components: the crime scene developed and staffed by experts from the state crime lab or professors from a local criminal justice program; a blood spatter expert from the state bureau of investigation; and a fingerprint expert. All three groups operate simultaneously, so I divide my class of approximately 60 first-year students into thirds. Each group rotates at the end of the session, so that the students get to experience each rotation in a relatively small group. The group observing the mock crime scene is led through the protocols of an examination by the trained criminologists. The fingerprinting group observes slides on the science of fingerprinting, discusses where, when and how fingerprinting occurs, and then gets to take their own prints, using bags of potato chips to facilitate the quality of the prints. (Students get to keep whatever results they have for posterity.) The third group hears about the science of blood spattering and then observes actual spatters and discusses the slides with the special agent from the bureau of investigation.

Students stay in each rotation for 30 to 40 minutes, yielding a total class time of 90 to 120 minutes, not counting transition time. This class is conducted early in the last week of school or late in the second to last week of school so that it can be debriefed and connected to the substantive material students have been learning in the surrounding weeks.

Conclusion

This exercise has had a positive impact on the overall course. Students appreciate the visitors' expertise, the opportunity to participate in a "hands-on" experience, and the chance to connect to the real world in a topical way.

Steven I. Friedland
Elon University School of Law

Chapter 8

Writing Across the Curriculum

> "The most intensive and demanding tool for eliciting sustained critical thought is a well-designed writing assignment on a subject matter problem."
>
> —John C. Bean

A. Why Use Writing Exercises in Your Course?

The research from those who study writing and developing complex thinking shows that all students benefit from having to put their thoughts into coherent prose. Writing improves thinking. We know that writing is critical to law practice. In fact, most law professors, when talking about teaching students "to think like a lawyer" also mean "to think like a lawyer *in writing*." Most law students have the advantage of being taught how to put complex legal analysis in writing in dedicated legal writing courses. But students benefit from having additional writing exercises in other courses.

When students write about an area of law, or use legal rules to draft documents, they increase their understanding of that doctrine. For example, students who apply the principles of preliminary injunctions realize how the test applies when they have to draft a court order denying an injunction. Similarly, students preparing an affidavit supporting a divorced parent's request to relocate will learn to use the legal standards in identifying and structuring the facts. These kinds of assignments require that students transfer their knowledge of rules to new domains, allowing them to engage in deeper learning. In short, they are learning how to be lawyers by *doing* the things lawyers do.

Similarly, writing is like other forms of mental exercise, in that regular practice builds confidence, efficiency, and effectiveness. The more students practice applying legal principles in prose, the better writers they become. Even the best law students, the ones who excel academically and hold leadership positions on law journals, benefit from the practice. Lawyers who are good writers note that they continually find areas to improve; we help our students develop that continued engagement and commitment to improve when we provide them with multiple opportunities to write in and out of class.

Writing also provides us with information about what students have learned. We may believe that everyone understands the material because of their verbal responses, lack of questions, and nodding heads. But when we read what they have written about a topic we more accurately see what they know and where they need more guidance. Having this information during the semester gives us valuable data about areas we need to reinforce during the course and how we might revise our course design next time.

In addition, students develop important metacognitive skills by writing about their learning, values, and perspectives. Asking students to reflect on what they have learned by completing a project, observing an administrative hearing, interviewing a lawyer, or exchanging views with their classmates provides them with a chance to pause and reflect. This helps them develop a greater understanding and appreciation for their own learning process and captures their evolving views of their chosen profession. Writing, as experts have long noted, develops thinking.

Writing exercises are appropriate in every course. Proponents and experts of Writing Across the Curriculum have discovered that when students write about such diverse subjects as math and music, their learning improves, because writing requires students to develop their thinking. Similarly, students can benefit from having writing exercises in any law course.

The key is to make writing exercises effective and manageable. Not every writing assignment needs to be read and commented upon. Nor does every writing assignment need to be more than one page or follow a specific format. The teacher does not need to be an expert in teaching writing to develop effective writing exercises. Incorporating writing does not need to reduce the content students learn in the course. Students benefit from writing in and out of class, and having a variety of kinds of writing exercises. Start small, pay attention to what works, and gradually you can add a whole host of writing exercises to your courses.

Writing plays an important role in students' academic performance. Most students' law school grades are based on their ability to apply legal principles in writing, such as on formal writing assignments and essay exams. Using writing to assess students' learning is addressed in Chapter 12, Summative Assessment—Evaluating and Grading Students.

B. What Kinds of Writing Exercises Can You Use in Your Course?

Because writing is primarily an individual process, the actual writing is best done alone, either in or out of class. It helps students to brainstorm with the teacher and classmates before, during, and after the assignment, but most people do not write efficiently by working with others. Below are some examples of the kinds of writing exercises students could do in and out of class.

Out-of-Class Writing Exercises

- Litigation-based legal documents. These can include partial or complete pleadings, motions, discovery requests, trial memos, exhibits, affidavits, appellate briefs, court orders and opinions, and bench memos.
- Nonlitigation-based legal documents. These can include partial or complete contracts, wills, engagement and demand letters, leases, settlement proposals, by-laws, articles of incorporation, trusts, internal memos, comments on regulations, environmental impact statements, policy manuals.
- Preparation for class documents. These can include case briefs, topical outlines, answers to study guide questions, flow charts, annotated concept maps, case matrices, annotated summaries of legal authorities, drafts of answers to practice exam essays, multiple-choice questions, and hypotheticals.
- Reflective documents. These can include reflective papers, journals, observations, responses to questions about student learning, self-assessments, peer assessments, descriptions of future jobs, course learning goals, descriptions of interviews with lawyers, and letters of advice to future students in the course.
- Other writing to learn exercises. These are limited only by your imagination. Students could write scripts for a skit; dialogues among lawyers, jurists or law students; book reviews and letters to authors; descriptions of legal concepts to

nonlawyer friends; legal advice columns; short stories; letters to the editor on controversial topics; blogs; online postings, cartoon captions; poems; speeches; and song lyrics.

In-Class Writing Exercises

- Micro papers. These can include asking students to spend a few minutes to write a paragraph or two explaining a concept, answering a question, summarizing points made in the class, identifying the main point of a text or authority, or analyzing a hypothetical. These can be done at the beginning and end of class and anytime in the middle.
- Free-writes. Particularly when students may be preoccupied or stressed, giving them five to ten minutes to just write without editing or censoring can help reduce stress and focus on class. When free writing, students are asked to write whatever they think (even if they write "I hate writing" over and over), keeping their pen or fingers moving for the whole time. These are for the students' eyes only.
- Shorter versions or small parts of out-of-class writing assignments. For example, students could draft a few definitions for a new statute, the introduction of a client letter, or a question presented for a trial memo.

C. How Do You Design Writing Exercises?

Before you design a writing exercise, identify what you want students to learn from it. You may want them to practice organizing the analysis by factors or elements, incorporating facts and factual inferences, applying rules and exceptions, identifying issues, following directions, developing self-awareness, or drafting with precision. You may have many goals, or only a few, depending on the students' level of expertise, the amount of time and effort you expect them to put into the writing exercise, whether the exercise will be graded, and how students will get feedback. Ideally, you want to design a writing assignment that requires students to engage in a lot of thinking before they complete a writing assignment.

Consult the Experts

There is a currently a wealth of scholarship and resources about teaching legal writing and analysis. (For example, go to: http://www.lwionline.org/) Every law school has legal writing teachers who are experts in teaching students how to convey complex analysis in writing or teachers who care passionately about student writing. Those who teach legal writing also teach other courses, and have written about ways to incorporate writing and collaborate with colleagues on improving students' writing. Enlist their help in brainstorming ways to design writing assignments. Chances are they will enjoy helping you talk through your goals, generate ideas about the kinds of assignments you might incorporate in your course, and may be willing to review a draft of your assignment.

Additional resources are available from teaching and learning centers at most universities. Writing is an important focus for all undergraduate programs, and the experts who staff these centers usually have lots of ideas and information about incorporating writing assignments in courses and teaching students to write for a specific discipline.

Getting Started

If using writing exercises is new to you, try starting with a short assignment and focus on a few goals. The goal can be as simple as having students practice putting their analysis in writing. Or it can be more elaborate, asking students to draft a one-page client letter briefly explaining or advising the client about a course topic, such as getting a declaratory judgment, making a claim for private nuisance, or preparing a simple will. The goals for a client letter could be to (1) accurately identify the relevant law; (2) apply the law to the client's facts; and (3) organize the material coherently. As your students engage in more writing, you can add more goals, such as focusing on legal nuances, factual inferences, creative solutions, writing style, and tone.

Preparing the Assignment

Once you have a sense of what you want students to learn from the writing exercise, draft it. If students will be writing their responses to a short hypothetical in class, prepare a handout or text you can project in class so that all students can see it. Students benefit from having even very simple hypotheticals put in writing; they can focus on writing their responses rather than having to memorize the facts and question.

If the students are completing the assignment out of class, provide written directions. At the very least, these directions should include:

- Task. What are the students expected to do?
- Learning goal(s). Why are students doing this?
- Role of the author and the audience of the writing. Who is the student writing to and in what role?
- Expectations about the process. What resources should students use? How long should they take? How might they approach the assignment? Can they work with others? Can they ask you questions as they prepare?
- Format. What are the assignment's page, word, and character limits? How will the assignment be completed? When is it due?
- Grading criteria or rubric, if applicable. If students are going to earn a grade, how will their writing will be evaluated? What aspect of the assignment carries the most weight? What are the essential elements of the assignment?

Task

At the beginning of a course, particularly a first-year course, it helps to provide concrete guidance and very focused questions. Identifying the task as "discuss proximate cause" provides insufficient guidance. A more appropriate task is "identify the best arguments the defendant can make to show that the defendant did not proximately cause the plaintiff's harm."

For an upper-level course, where students are closer to entering law practice, it may be more appropriate to provide a question and ask them to figure out the format, structure, and resources, much as they would have to do on the job. For example, students could be given this assignment: "Your supervisor has just asked you to figure out whether a state employer can look at a state employee's email. She needs your response in an hour, and wants no more than one page."

Expectations About the Process

If at all possible, do the writing assignment yourself before you assign it to students. Time yourself. If students are new to the substantive area, they may take twice as long to complete the assignment (or they may take less time if they skip important parts). Either way, help them understand about how long you expect them to take on the assignment.

Depending on the nature of the course, you may also help students by explaining what you understand the hardest parts to be. Is it figuring out rules and exceptions? Reconciling conflicting authorities? Synthesizing a line of cases? Organizing a complex solution? Explaining that you expect the writing process to be messy, and that students' revisions will be where they convert mess and confusion to coherent prose will help them understand the nature of complex writing within a discipline. If students can understand that they are expected to struggle with preparing first drafts, and that the hard part of writing is thinking, they will learn to navigate through uncertainty rather than jumping to conclusions too quickly. As experts have noted, "students' skill in writing varies according to the cognitive complexity of the writing task." (Bean 63).

You may want to include a sample of the assignment, particularly at the beginning of the course. While some professors dislike providing samples as they find that students want to slavishly adhere to them, most of us in practice benefit from seeing how others have tackled similar problems, and our students are no different. Even if the sample is a rough outline with parts missing, students will appreciate having some guidance about what they are expected to do.

Assignment Content

Because writing deepens students' learning, it helps to assign students to write about topics that typically challenge them or where they often develop misunderstanding. If you have taught the course before, you likely know where students struggle, based on how they perform on final exams and papers. Those content areas are excellent sources for writing assignments. Sample practice forms and factual scenarios from cases provide abundant resources for a wide range of writing assignments.

D. How Do You Provide Feedback on Writing Exercises?

This is likely the biggest reason more writing exercises are not incorporated in class. In a large class, asking 80 students to write even one page makes most teachers groan in dismay as they envision a stack of papers, each of which must be read and commented upon. Even if this only takes five minutes per paper, teachers are looking at more than six hours of hard work. For many teachers, given the other demands on their time and attention, this is an insurmountable challenge, or one which they are only willing to attempt once or twice during the semester.

For formal writing assignments that carry a significant part of students' grades in the course, students deserve individual comments, scores, and feedback about what worked well and where their writing can improve. This will help them develop better skills they can use in the future. This takes considerable time and may be one of the hardest parts of teaching. Legal writing experts have developed a wealth of expertise on grading and commenting upon student work, including providing feedback on early drafts or outlines, providing students with feedback during individual conferences, and using a range of approaches to help students learn from their feedback. If you are using formal writing assignments, consult these experts and learn from their collective decades of experience and wisdom.

For less formal and less heavily weighted or ungraded writing assignments, there are plenty of alternatives that take less time and still provide students with important and valuable feedback. Because writing is such a powerful tool for developing thinking, it is crucial to find efficient ways to help students learn from the process. Below are some approaches that can work in large and small classes, and can be combined with each other.

Provide an Answer Sheet or Sample and Invite Follow-up Questions

After students individually prepare a writing assignment, give them an answer sheet or drafted answer (yours or a previous student's) in class or post it online. Walk them through the answer sheet or give students time to read the answer sheet or samples. Ask students to compare it to the assignment they wrote. Another approach is to show students three samples, one very strong, one average, and one poor. Ask the students to read and note the differences and invite them to rank them. Following any of these approaches, invite students to ask questions. If students want to have you look at their writing individually, invite them to come to your office hours, where you provide verbal feedback. (Our experience is that many students find the feedback from the sample or answer sheet is sufficient, and that it generally takes about ten minutes to provide additional in person feedback to those students who seek it.)

"Live Grade" in Class or Online

Invite students to volunteer or pick a student's work to be "live graded." During class, project the student's assignment and comment on areas where it is effective, and where it could be improved. Depending on the class, the student's work may be identified or anonymous. Ask other students to review their assignment in light of the comments you provide through "live grading."

For online "live grading" post the student's work and your comments, rubric and margin notes for the class. Allow students to follow up online or in person with questions about the feedback or their work.

Peer Feedback

Students learn a great deal from reading and commenting upon classmates' work. Students can be assigned peer editors to review their assignments or work in small groups to comment on one or two of their classmates' work. Students can either provide "reader-based feedback" where they respond to the assignment in terms of what makes sense, what seemed confusing, and where they had questions, or "criterion-based feedback" where they use a answer sheet, rubric, scoring guide, or sample answer as a basis for providing feedback to their classmates.

Self-Assessment Directed Feedback

For teacher or peer feedback, students can identify up to three areas on which they want feedback on their writing. This approach usually works better when students are familiar with writing about legal topics and have an accurate sense of what they do well and where they struggle. By identifying a few areas for feedback, classmates and the teacher can more quickly review students' writing assignments and provide feedback on a few specific areas.

Competency Feedback

For shorter assignments that require students to show that they have engaged in fundamental course skills, you can limit responses to a check or check minus (competent or incompetent). Part of the course requirements can be that all students satisfactorily complete a number of writing assignments. Using a check or check minus competency standard, along with a scoring sheet or rubric, you can quickly go through many assignments verifying students' basic mastery of the assignment goals. Students who receive check minuses may be asked to redo the assignment or offset it by doing competent work on all other assignments or completing an additional assignment.

Group Feedback

After students complete a writing assignment, in small groups (four to seven) they collectively decide which students' writing is the most effective, or they use parts of their individual work to arrive at a composite group assignment. The teacher provides feedback to the group assignment.

Selected Feedback

Randomly select a sample of writing assignments on which to comment. For example, in a class of 80 students, pick ten students' work to comment upon for the first assignment, a different ten for the second assignment, and so forth. Each student will have multiple opportunities to write, and each student will receive some individual feedback.

There is no one right way to integrate writing into a course. Giving students even a few small opportunities to put their analysis in writing will help them develop the skills they need as lawyers.

References

- John C. Bean, Engaging Ideas: The Professor's Guide to Integrating Writing, Critical Thinking, and Active Learning in the Classroom 1–132, 183–265 (2001).
- Barbara Gross Davis, Tools for Teaching 305–341 (2d ed. 2009).
- Peter Elbow, Writing with Power: Techniques for Mastering the Writing Process 240–263 (2d ed. 1998).
- Peter Elbow & Mary Deane Sorcinelli, *Using High-Stakes and Law-Stakes Writing to Enhance Learning, in* McKeachie's Teaching Tips: Strategies, Research, and Theory for College and University Teachers 213–234 (Marilla Svinivki & Wilbert J. McKeachie eds., 13th ed. 2010).
- L. Dee Fink, Creating Significant Learning Experiences: An Integrated Approach to Designing College Courses 116–119 (2003).
- Linda B. Nilson, Teaching at Its Best: A Research-Based Resource for College Instructors 141–152 (2d ed. 2003).

Teaching Upper-Level Legal Research and Writing in a Hybrid Clinic/Writing Course

Since 2003, my colleague Eve Biskind Klothen and I have run a Pro Bono Research Project that matches upper level students with real legal research requests from nonprofits, government agencies, or private attorneys working pro bono.

Up to 20 students annually have researched issues for nonprofits such as the Education Law Center, Volunteer Lawyers for the Arts, the Regional Housing Alliance, and government agencies such as the Environmental Protection Agency. Students are co-supervised by the outside lawyer and a Rutgers faculty member. Students learn more sophisticated research and writing techniques as they produce real legal work.

I recently used the model of the Pro Bono Research Project to create a hybrid clinical/writing course, Public Interest Research and Writing. Students peer reviewed each other's research plans, outlines, and drafts. To avoid client confidentiality concerns, all students did research for a single entity. One semester I taught it entirely online—the course is well suited for distance learning. Whether online or live, the course culminated in oral presentations to the outside lawyer who requested the research. In Spring 2010, my colleague Jason Cohen taught the course live with a focus on research for an LGBT organization.

Benefits of a Hybrid Clinical/Writing Course

- Students are motivated when they realize that a practicing lawyer will use their work. Research and writing is usually taught via simulations—students write memos or briefs for a fictional but realistic client—students appreciate that their work will benefit a real client.
- In this economy, not all students can expect to find jobs that will assign them sophisticated legal work. Some students may not find 1L (or even 2L) summer jobs. A hybrid clinical/writing course can expose students to challenging legal research and writing assignments and give them practice orally presenting the results of their research.
- Students fill a research need in the public interest community. The outside organizations do not have to be local. Students can communicate with the outside lawyers via email, phone, or Skype.

Sarah Ricks
Rutgers School of Law–Camden

Writing Across the Curriculum: Practice Documents, Affective Professionalism, and Good English

I incorporate practical writing skills into the learning objectives of every law school course I teach, from Property, to Legal Methods, to Alternative Dispute Resolution. I believe that these writing-across-the-curriculum assignments are important because communicating like a lawyer is a necessary practice-ready step to thinking like a lawyer. Additionally, writing hones thinking skills, so I can reinforce what thinking like a lawyer is through writing assignments. Finally, these assignments allow me to reinforce what professionalism means both in terms of lawyer-client interactions and quality of work product.

I have three goals with my assignments. First, I want to expose students to writing assignments that they would be unlikely to see in any other law school classroom, but would be likely to occur in a legal job. Second, I want students to consider audience, purpose, and tone in their legal writing to build the emotional intelligence or *affective* professionalism that is critical to the practice of law. Third, I want to reinforce principles of good English writing. I have designed many writing assignments that reach these objectives from different starting points. In this piece, I have chosen four examples: a client letter; a demand letter; an informal memo; and a custody agreement or will. These types of writing assignments could be adapted for almost any casebook course.

With the client letter, my purpose is to reinforce that typical legal discourse is often both confusing and harsh for lay clients. While it is important to communicate with the client about the legal situation, students need to learn how to communicate in a way that clients understand. Additionally, students need to consider client letters' unintended audiences. For example, in a custody dispute, I encourage students to consider the spouse as a current or future unintended audience. I suggest that, as lawyers, students write their letters in a way that would respect the interest of the client and not cause problems between the client and unintended audiences.

With the demand letter, I encourage students to juxtapose the client as audience to the other party as the intended audience. (My inspiration for this assignment came from Carrie Sperling's 2008 presentation on Demand Letters at Rocky Mountain Legal Writing Conference in Salt Lake City, Utah.) First, I encourage students to consider the demand letter as one of the first types of communication that they would have with the opposing party. I encourage students to set the tone for likely future negotiations, since most legal disputes end in some form of negotiation. I also encourage students to consider carefully whether to use broad or narrow language in their demand letter. We discuss how language that is too generic allows the other parties to interpret the request to their benefit. However, language that is too specific might unintentionally exclude key evidence from discovery. Through this discussion, I reinforce that the intended audiences would be not only the other party, but also the other party's attorney and perhaps senior partners within the student's firm, for which the student would want to demonstrate competence.

With the custody agreement or will, I encourage students to consider both intended and unintended audiences. (My inspiration for this assignment came from Denise Riebe's 2003 class on Family Mediation at University of North Carolina School of Law.) For intended audiences, I encourage students to focus on how the document could be a source of healing for the couple or survivors. We discuss how the tone of the document could set the tone for their future disagreements and resolutions. With respect to unintended audiences, I encourage students to consider the children or survivors, either presently or in the future, as a potential unintended audience. We discuss using language that makes the document's purpose explicit, and using a tone that shows that the clients deeply care about their children or survivors.

With the informal memo, I again ask students to juxtapose audience, purpose, and tone with the standards for more formal research memos. In my assignments, I ask students to update their senior partner about the developments of an ongoing negotiation, addressing what the parties agreed to, any additional communication with the client, and analyzing possible strategies for further negotiations. We discuss that although the memo serves as an update, the senior partner has many cases to supervise, so my students should provide a full recitation of key facts while emphasizing recent developments. We also discuss the similarities and differences between predicting legal interpretations and predicting people's behavior in a negotiation. This last exercise encourages students to see how the fundamental principles they learned in Legal Writing can be adapted to numerous situations.

Each of these assignments exposes students to writing that lawyers routinely do, but often aren't exposed to until they begin their first internship or job. Through my assignment descriptions and feedback, I provide guidance on the expectations senior partners would have of incoming associates. By providing guidance with assignment descriptions and feedback, I avoid taking class time to teach these simple, but often overlooked, principles of legal analysis through communication, of client-centered practice, and of professionalism.

By juxtaposing audiences, I encourage students to consider how purpose and tone changes for different intended audiences. I also encourage students to think of the unintended audiences who might read the documents. Finally, I encourage students to contemplate instances where purpose and tone do not need to change even when the audience changes. These early lessons help students build their affective values necessary for the ethical and professional practice of law.

With all writing assignments, we discuss how the basic elements of standard English help lawyers communicate with lay people and other lawyers more clearly. To encourage students to engage in revising their work, I provide them with the "Diagnosis to Revision" strategies Joe Williams provided in *Style: The Basics of Clarity and Grace.*

Hillary Burgess
Charlotte School of Law

Focus Writing for Doctrinal Classes

To give students practice writing about course topics, every few weeks I start the class by engaging students in focused writing. I used to try to fit writing exercises in at the end of class, but would often allow insufficient time for the exercise or its discussion. Having writing exercises at the beginning of class provides a starting point for the class discussion and allows me to provide the class with feedback during the session.

Focus Writing

As with every class, I post a written agenda for the class on a slide or on the board. On writing days, the topic and "writing" will be first on the agenda. After briefly taking care of any administrative details, I tell the students to get their pens or keyboards ready. When everyone is present, I reveal the question, tell the students they have eight minutes to write without reference to notes and texts, and start the timer. When they start, I start, answering the same question. For example, in a Remedies class on specific performance, the focus question might be, "When is a client entitled to the remedy of specific performance?" Depending on the topic, I might add, "Provide at least one clear example and one ambiguous example."

Students start writing from what they remember. This shows them what they have retained of the material so far. If they have run out of ideas before the time has expired, they can consult their notes and course materials. If everyone is fully engaged in writing, when one minute remains, I ask students if they want more time. If they do, I add a three or four minutes to the exercise. If students are done early, I cut the time short, usually providing them with a 60 second warning that they should complete their thought and then turn their attention to the rest of the class.

Debriefing the Focus Writing

When everyone has finished writing, we discuss what students have written. Students each contribute one point, starting with the topic's general legal rules, then moving to sub-rules and exceptions. I capture the points on the board. Going around the room, they explain how their contribution relates to other points already on the board. We continue until no one has added new material. If all the important points are included, we have an outline of the topic. If points are missing, I ask questions or pose hypotheticals to trigger additional contributions.

Once we have a thorough outline of the topic, we move on to clear examples, testing them against the outline. When we get to the ambiguous examples, students make arguments for different results, referring to the topic outline on the board. As we work through the analysis, students usually realize they have questions and gaps in their understanding about how to apply the analysis. As we discuss their questions and make arguments, I point out where we are in the class agenda and draw their attention to areas that tend to be the most problematic in practice and on exams. Depending on the topic's complexity and the kinds of examples students generate, the discussion will take most of the class.

Variations

In large classes, after they have finished writing, students will first create the collective outline in groups, and I'll call on groups to individually contribute material to get the outline on the board. In working through examples, students will pick the best ambiguous example in the group, and offer that one for class discussion. Groups will be assigned to prepare and argue for different answers to ambiguous examples, using law, facts, and policy.

Benefits of Having Students Write at the Beginning of Class

- The class starts with a quiet calm as we all write in near silence.
- All students are immediately engaged in learning and rehearsing what they have learned.
- Students are motivated to learn because they realize where they have questions.
- Students get excited when they realize how much more they know about the topic than they did before the course.
- Students practice writing about the topic.
- Students experience variety, which generates energy.
- I learn about students' misunderstandings and can correct them immediately.
- Discussion is enriched as students have collaborated in building an outline and generating examples.
- Students contribute a wider range of examples than I tend to produce alone.
- Students can solve more sophisticated problems later in the class as they have already engaged in four different kinds of learning activities on the topic: writing, talking, seeing an outline, and listening.

Sophie Sparrow
University of New Hampshire School of Law

A Will-Drafting Exercise

At my institution Wills and Trusts is a four-unit, second-year course. At other institutions where I have taught, the course has been required. Many students come in expecting the course to be dry, boring and a course "for rich people." To stimulate student interest and share *my* excitement and enthusiasm for the subject, I have looked for ways to liven things up.

My first step is selecting texts. Although I had the great fortune to be taught by Jesse Dukeminier, and use his casebook, my primary "text" is the Annotated Texas Probate Code. My students are best served by an in-depth study of the probate code and leading cases applicable in the jurisdiction where most of them are likely to take the bar and practice. By the end of the semester, each student's edition of the Code is well-thumbed, and students can confidently maneuver through it. I supplement the casebook and Code with Mark Reutlinger's excellent *Wills, Trusts & Estates: Essential Terms and Concepts* (now in its second edition).

These materials ensure that students feel that they are learning the "real" law of Texas, rather than the "law of nowhere" of so many casebooks. Students' sense that this "bar course" will really prepare them for the Texas bar ensures a higher level of participation than might otherwise be expected. My next goal is to get the students thinking like estate-planning lawyers.

The appropriate practical exercise in a Wills and Trusts class is having the students draft an actual will. In my Wills and Trusts class, the midterm assignment consists of a will-drafting exercise together with a family tree, for intestate succession purposes. I use a role-playing approach and have students pair up to draft one another's wills. Each student serves as both client and lawyer. As clients, students must provide lists of assets and bequests. Lawyers and clients meet to discuss the plan and review draft documents. Although the project does not count for more than 15% of the grade, most students spend a significant amount of time and effort on it.

The will-drafting assignment requires students to draft and execute the will. Most students include self-proving affidavits, whose precise language is provided by Texas statute. Drafting, and especially executing, an actual will, an instrument that could take legal effect in the unlikely event that a student dies, rivets students' attention in a way that an abstract discussion of notions like animus testandi never does. Those students who wanted to be sure that the will drafted for the assignment never took effect quickly learned the ins and outs of holographic revocation. The students' first impulse, simply scrawling "no animus testandi" or "sample will" across the bottom of a formally executed and attested will, doesn't work, however obvious it might seem.

The comments I provide on the wills also puts them in an unusual position for law students—imagining answering or explaining their drafting to a lawyer or dissatisfied heir of a client, rather than sitting as a would-be appellate judge, evaluating the work of others. It is much easier to critique some nameless lawyer's bad drafting than to explain your own unclear language.

The will-drafting exercise and follow-up comments open students' eyes to the dramatically forward-looking nature of will-drafting and the imagination required of a first-rate estate planner. Instead of analyzing only the imaginary-seeming estates of long-dead testators in books, students actually have to consider what will happen—and what the testator *wants* to have happen—if she has another baby, if his brother the executor predeceases him, or if the family home is sold ten years before the testator dies. Students must wrestle with the actual issues facing will-drafters—how many highly specific bequests to leave, how much to dispose of through a residuary clause, how best to anticipate after-acquired property, and when changes in the estate are so significant as to warrant the drafting of a new will or codicil.

The role-playing component of the assignment also vividly brings to life a point Wills and Trusts and Estate Planning professors often make—that the legally or financially best plan is not necessarily *what the client wants*. For example, I advise my students that it is often desirable to have a non-natural person (a church, an educational institution, a charity, etc.) as a contingent residuary legatee. In their role as lawyer, most students urged this upon their partners—but as clients, they suddenly realized that they simply might not want to do this, whatever its purported advantages. Students learned that educating and persuading clients—up to a point—is a crucial part of estate planning.

Most of all, actually drafting a will and participating in setting up even a rudimentary estate plan is *fun*. Because of the many rules, it has the feel of a game, while also giving students a taste of the intimacy and gravity of this legal area. Each year, a number of students go all out on this assignment, using proper paper and backing, and staging elaborate execution ceremonies with real notaries, part of the self-proving affidavit process under Texas law. On their own initiative, many choose to review and adapt various form wills available online and elsewhere. While many students may never enter this area of practice, I like to think that those who do will remember, probably with a mixture of pride and embarrassment, the first will they ever drafted.

Diane J. Klein
University of La Verne College of Law

A Contracts Drafting Challenge

Several years ago, I was looking for a hook to get the students interested in Contracts on the first day of class. How could I show new 1Ls that Contracts really was as interesting as Criminal Law or Torts? The only thing that might interest them more than the blood and guts was, of course, themselves and surviving law school. So the very first thing I did was to write on the board in very big letters, "If you do exactly what I say, then you will get an 'A' in Contracts." After introducing myself and briefly reviewing the syllabus, I asked them to read what was on the board. Then I asked them, "Will you be able to force me to give you an 'A' in Contracts based on what is on the board?" What followed, after a little prodding, was a spirited discussion that revealed their preconceptions about contracts. It was helpful and interesting information for me.

Then I told them that the rest of the semester would be devoted to answering that question; that question was what contracts was all about. That stimulated more questions. A quick trip through the casebook's table of contents revealed that the subject covered the creation of obligations and the remedies available to enforce them. I brought up the problem a few times during the semester as we completed sections of the book. Each time, they seemed interested in the possibility that a valid contract might guarantee them an "A."

More recently, I decided to incorporate a drafting exercise into the Contracts course. I wanted the exercise to be something they would want to do. Of course, they would want a contract that would get them an "A." So I built on the first-day hypo to create a challenge they would find irresistible. I decided to make it an extra-credit opportunity, rather than an assignment, in hopes that would stimulate a more positive attitude. Since it was irresistible, they would all do it anyway. So, during the second class I presented them with the following:

> Professor X wrote on the board, "If you do exactly what I say, you will get an 'A' in this course." He hoped that would motivate students to approach the course in a way that would maximize their learning experience. Unfortunately, he has learned that the students don't take what he's written seriously. Your task is to write an educational contract that Professor X can use with his students. You must produce a valid and enforceable contract. The contract is to be written in plain language, not "legalese." You are also to write a memo to accompany your contract. In that memo, explain your contract and address the relevant issues raised by each chapter in the casebook. This is not a research project; you need not go beyond the casebook and hornbook. You may discuss the issues in general with classmates and the professor, but you are on your honor to do all the writing without consultation of any kind with any other person. You may not have any person review what you have written. Your project must be turned in to Student Services, identified only by your exam number, no later than the beginning of the final exam in this course. A successful project may earn you enough extra credit to raise your grade to the next grade level (e.g., from a "C+" to a "B").

I specified that the memo should consider the issues raised by each chapter in the casebook to promote a thorough examination of contracts doctrine in a practical setting. The setting is one they can all easily understand; they are not distracted by and do not waste time trying to figure out the transaction or the parties' expectations as might occur if I used a real estate sales contract or a construction contract. I pointed out that working on the project should improve their understanding of the doctrine on which they would be tested at the end of the semester, so doing the project would provide them with a triple benefit: (1) a drafting experience; (2) extra credit; and (3) the likelihood of a higher grade on the exam. How could anyone resist?

One obstacle, of course, would be time. Students might worry that the project would take too much time in a semester, their first in law school, when time seemed in very short supply. To address this, I encouraged the students to work on the project over the course of the term rather than leave it for the end. Approached in this way, the time required each week would not be too great. To encourage them during the term, I make it a point to discuss the drafting issues raised by the cases whenever possible.

I have now used this project in my last two Contracts classes. I must admit that a significant number of students were, somehow, able to resist its allure. However, a more significant number did take part. Based on anecdotal evidence, it appears that it did provide students with the benefits promised because they did well on the exam and felt the experience was highly beneficial.

Ronald Benton Brown
Nova Southeastern University, Shepard Broad Law Center

Writing with Word Banks

Short writing assignments provide active learning opportunities. However, it can be difficult to incorporate writing exercises in a classroom filled with 110 smiling students. A grade school exercise can be adapted to the law school classroom: the word bank. The word bank exercises provide each student with a defined universe of words or phrases. Using all the words or phrases, the students, individually or in groups, write the excerpt. Having a defined set of words that must be used establishes parameters for the assignment while permitting students to think creatively about how to string the words together. The class discussion can then explore the multiple ways to combine the words and the different consequences to each combination. Below are two example word bank writing assignments.

Word Bank

Using the designated word bank, write the specific bequest. You must use all the words in the word bank. Insert the appropriate punctuation.

to	antique	Maria	survives	brooch	my	favorite	me	niece
if	give	diamond	my	she	I	sapphire	Sanchez	and

Possible Answer: I give my favorite antique diamond and sapphire brooch to my niece, Maria Sanchez, if she survives me.

Phrase Bank

Sometimes creating a bank of individual words will be too overwhelming for the students. In that case, a phrase bank could be used. This exercise could be made more tactile by actually cutting the phrases into separate strips and having the students physically manipulate the strips into an excerpt.

Using the designated word bank, write a Perpetuities Savings Clause. You must use all the phrases in the word bank. (This provision is based on the Perpetuities Savings Clause found in Mary F. Radford, 2 Redfearn: Wills and Administration in Georgia § 17: 40 (7th ed. 2008).

all property of every trust created under this Will	who was in life at the date of my death unless sooner vested as provided herein.	to prevent any possible violation of the Rule against Perpetuities
and this provision should be so construed.	at the expiration of twenty-one (21) years	The purpose of this provision is
after the death of the last surviving beneficiary of this Will	Anything in this Will to the contrary notwithstanding,	shall vest in and be distributed to the persons then entitled to the income from such property

Possible Answer: Anything in this Will to the contrary notwithstanding, all property of every trust created by this Will shall vest in and be distributed to the persons then entitled to the income from such property at the expiration of twenty-one (21) years after the death of the last surviving beneficiary of this Will who was in life at the date of my death unless sooner vested as provided herein. The purpose of this provision is to prevent any possible violation of the rule against perpetuities and this provision should be so construed.

Karen J. Sneddon
Mercer University School of Law

Using "Forensic IRAC" to Teach Students to Write

As a law teacher, my job is to develop students' writing and analytical skills in the shortest possible time to improve law school performance and bar passage. I have found the shortest distance to improved writing skills is improved reading skills and the use of what I have termed "forensic IRAC."

Since students are far more willing to read than to write, shifting their focus to reading helps motivate them. However, since most students are not trained to be careful, thoughtful readers who question the content and meaning of what they read, I show them how to do so by modeling my own reading strategies. In class, I think aloud about a case and share my questions and thought processes. Similarly, I point out the structure of the court's analysis and how it follows the IRAC structure. Students can begin to see cases as examples of IRAC that they can use as models for their writing. After we've worked on reading skills, we move on to writing.

During the semester, students complete four writing assignments, each based on a hypothetical. The first assignment is for diagnostic purposes only, the next three are graded. For each question, I provide several sample answers, usually two I have written and one of the top student responses. This way students can see a variety of approaches to the same question and that there is room for variation within the basic IRAC structure. In addition to providing sample answers, students receive a grading sheet which shows the precise point allocation. The grading sheet is as detailed as possible in showing the breakdown of the rule and the facts that should have been used in the analysis. I also provide individual feedback on papers, evaluating students' essays for substance and structure, and focus on the precise use of language, especially in writing issues, rules, and fact analysis. When students review their work they can see exactly where they gained or lost points.

Even with extensive feedback, it is difficult to improve students' written analysis. Teaching writing requires finding a way into students' thought processes because the problems they have in writing about the law mirror the problems they have in thinking about the law. Teaching writing also requires a way to "objectify" the process so that students and teacher can identify what students are thinking and correct flaws in the process without stigma. Using "forensic IRAC" allows me to do both.

"Forensic IRAC" uses the familiar "Issue, Rule, Application, Conclusion" structure of legal analysis to work with a student's written product to see the internal thought process. Forensic IRAC works by examining each sentence the student has written in terms of its place in the IRAC structure. I call the process forensic IRAC because the techniques I use are similar to those that crime scene investigators and forensic experts use to determine how bits of evidence lead to a particular result. While such experts rely on fingerprints, ledger books, and DNA, I use IRAC to work with the student's written essay to figure out what the student was thinking that led to that particular response. By applying the mechanics of legal analysis to what the student has written, I can see where the student's thinking has gone astray. And if I can see it, the student can learn to see it.

Part of forensic IRAC involves sentence diagramming—mapping sentences to show how the parts of a legal argument are structured. Each sentence in an essay is labeled appropriately: a sentence is either an issue; rule (rule can break down to general statement, element, factor, definition of element or factor); fact analysis (fact analysis can break down into argument pro or con); or conclusion. This approach works particularly well when multiple issues are tested on an exam and the student has an almost impossible time learning to organize a response. Diagramming allows me to show the student how and where the issues have been mixed together. Forensic IRAC also objectifies the process, and the sting of writing a poor answer is somewhat ameliorated. It is very hard for anyone to go back over what they have written and be critical of it. But it is essential in any endeavor, especially law school exams, and this process allows it to be a lot less painful and a lot more practical.

Example

"Ben" and I are reviewing his answers to my Contracts midterm. We review each sentence and identify whether it was a statement of the issue, one discussing the applicable rule of law, or a sentence applying the rules to the facts of the particular case. We label each sentence with an "I," an "R" or an "A." The sentence must "fit" somewhere.

This is useful for several reasons. First, it "physically" identifies organization problems. If Ben has discussed the "facts" of the particular problem before he has recited the relevant "rule," then we find "A" sentences before there are any "R" sentences. Second, when we work sentence by sentence, we see what function each sentence serves in the IRAC equation. Ben can see whether a sentence is repetitive, for which he will lose time and not gain any points, whether a statement analyzes the facts because it connects law to relevant facts by means of such language as "because," or whether it merely recites the facts contained in the hypothetical, serving no purpose. By labeling the sentences, Ben can "see" what he has written. But even more important, by examining exactly what Ben has written we can begin to see whether he understands the rules and how to use them. By examining each sentence in the essay, problems can be identified at the appropriate step in the student's thought process. And once identified, problems can be corrected.

Results

I have been using this approach for several years with much success in preparing students for the bar exam and in improving law school grades. While the approach requires considerable work, it is well worth the effort when students relate their excitement in finally connecting with the process of learning the law and share news of improved grades.

Suzanne Darrow-Kleinhaus
Touro College Jacob D. Fuchsberg Law Center

The Writing Tip of the Day

In Saskatchewan, second-year students must take one legal theory course. Each course has 20 students and meets twice a week. Since one purpose of these courses is to develop writing skills, students must submit two papers, one midterm and one on the last day of class. I help students' legal reasoning and writing skills by spending the first five minutes of class giving students a "Writing Tip of the Day." Before I begin, I stress students' need to become the best writers they can be. Words are the only tools that lawyers possess, and the more adeptly students handle words, the better lawyers they will become. To set the stage for the Writing Tip of the Day, in the first week I devote an entire class to matters of style, grammar, and revision.

The Writing Tips fall into several thematic groups. The first cluster, classified under the Delphic maxim of "Know Thyself," includes general points about becoming professional wordsmiths. These points include: recognize your most creative time during the day, and use it, if possible; identify your personal style of writing; and acquire the tools of the trade, such as dictionaries, thesauruses, and grammar books. I bring into class excellent dictionaries and other reference material, and recommend books such as Joseph M. Williams' classic, *Style: Toward Clarity and Grace* (1990).

The second group of Writing Tips focuses on errors students make repeatedly. I call these common problems "yuk-yuks"—basic grammatical mistakes or stylistic infelicities that cause readers to dismiss the writer. I begin with simple ones, such as the difference between "it's" and "its." Other yuk-yuks are overuse of passive voice, nominalizations and incorrect comma placement. For these Tips, I typically distribute a handout describing the problem and suggesting methods of fixing it. The handouts are exercises I have devised or pertinent pages from a grammar text.

I scatter a third group of Tips among the others. These offer ways of recognizing and constructing solid arguments. I stress to students that their purpose in writing as lawyers is to present cogent arguments. If they can distinguish good and bad arguments, they will become better writers. These Tips support the substantive content of the course, which contains a large section on judicial reasoning. I use examples of different types of arguments and fallacies from the course readings, distribute handouts highlighting argument components, and suggest books, such as, *Attacking Faulty Reasoning* by T. Edward Damer (4th ed., 2000).

These Tips enhance class discussion because students learn to identify fallacies and develop ways of strengthening arguments made by authors excerpted in the course materials. Moreover, as the weeks progress, students become increasingly frustrated with vague, confusing, or convoluted arguments, and complain about some authors' writing styles. Hence, the Tips also show students the virtue of writing clearly, accurately and precisely. Several students later told me that they found these Tips especially illuminating.

Midterm, students submit their first paper. In assessing each paper, I note particular problems, referring the student to the relevant Tip or attaching new handouts. Assessing papers this way augments my knowledge of writing because I have to identify precisely a student's weakness and cannot rely on general criticism about writing style, such as ubiquitous comments of "this paragraph is awkward," or "your writing style could be improved."

The fourth group of Writing Tips comes after the first assignments. These Tips use anonymous examples from students' papers to focus on more structural issues, such as how to build smooth and cogent paragraphs. They reinforce comments on students' papers and integrate earlier Tips about legal reasoning, using examples from course readings and students' papers. These Tips, which may take between 15 to 20 minutes, include how to write topic sentences, counter-arguments, compelling factual narratives and segues.

Many students' final papers show considerable improvement. They begin with a thesis paragraph, flow more coherently, and contain concise conclusions. All of them have fewer grammatical and stylistic glitches. Some students report that they invest more time in second papers, incorporating comments from their first papers and the Tips. One student told me that when he wrote his second paper, he revised his first draft for the first time in his six years of university education, and that he now understands the tremendous benefit of revisions!

Overall, students react positively to the Writing Tip of the Day. Anonymous student evaluations, conducted mid- and end-of-semester, have contained many positive comments about Writing Tips. Students have told me, during office visits and after the end of term, that they greatly appreciated this course feature. For example, one month after the end of term, a student said that she thought that the Tips and feedback on her first paper had increased her marks in other courses by at least a full grade. Several students suggested adding Writing Tips of the Day to every seminar and theory course.

Benefits of Including a Writing Tip of the Day

- It is inexpensive and requires no fancy equipment.
- It is relatively quick for long-time teachers, who can draw upon their experiences in finding examples and devising tips.
- It motivates students to work hard on their assignments. When students prepare their first paper, they already know the common errors I have mentioned in the Tips, and can avoid them.
- It increases attendance. Students do not want to miss the day's Writing Tip, if only to know what not to do in their papers.

I think this technique succeeds because Writing Tips go beyond grammar and punctuation. They encompass the essential subjects of constructing flowing paragraphs, developing convincing arguments, setting appropriate tones for particular audiences and other substantive matters. Each one is not merely a Writing Tip—it is a thinking tip.

Donna Greschner
University of Victoria, Faculty of Law

Mad Libs Legal Writing: More Writing with Less Grading

A pen floating over a crisp white page. Fingers hovering expectantly over a keyboard. These are actions that lawyers do every day. While the form and function of the writing varies, lawyers are writers. In the crunch of syllabus time, it can be difficult to incorporate writing assignments into a course. Professors can draw inspiration from their childhood completion of Mad Libs to add another active learning technique to their arsenal. Starting in the 1950s, teachers have used the Mad Libs fill-in-the-blank system to help students learn the parts of speech and enrich vocabulary. For example, a Mad Lib could contain the following sentence within a story:

Johnnie was	_______	_______	to the	_______	with his	_______	_______.
Insert:	*verb*	*adverb*		*noun*		*number*	*nouns*

This fill-in-the-blank format can be adapted to the law school classroom to integrate short writing assignments that provide a structure for class discussion and a technique for immediate feedback or diagnostic analysis. Students can complete variations of these assignments individually or in groups, in or outside of class, and within as little as five minutes.

A. Legal Writing Courses

To ease students' frustration when approaching writing their first memo or brief, the fill-in-the-blank format can focus the students on choices made in each sentence. For example:

Example sentence from Rule Section of an Office Memo:

An individual	_______	disabled under the Americans with Disabilities Act if he or she
	is/was	

(1) ________ a physical or mental impairment (2) that substantially ____________
has/had *limits/had limited*

(3) a major life activity. 42 U.S.C. § 12102(1)(A).

Example sentence from Rule Explanation of an Appellate Brief:

The court ______________________________________ that seasonal uses of a
argued/determined/found/held/looked/noted/stated/wished

property may fail to satisfy the "open and notorious" requirement.

The class discussion about these sentences can focus on the students' decision-making process and the ultimate impact of the different choices. As the students' skills develop, the excerpts can transform from discrete sentences to an entire paragraph, with prompts becoming increasingly abstract. For example:

____________ a nonparent who has established a child-parent relationship has the right
insert transition

to ________________ ________________. The statute __________ a child-parent
insert procedural posture *insert short cite* *defines/defined*

relationship as ____
insert paraphrase of statutory definition

________________ ________________ *O'Donnell–Lamont* ________________
insert short cite *insert signal* *insert case short cite*

____
insert explanatory parenthetical that states

____
why the threshold was satisfied in O'Donnell–Lamont

B. Beyond Legal Writing Courses

When faced with 87 students, including a writing assignment can seem impossible. The fill-in-the-blank format integrates practice-related documents with substantive discussions.

For example, the following assignment could be used in a Trusts and Estates class:

All the ____
definition of the residue

I give to ____________________________, if ____________________________
initial taker/s (by name or by class) *survivorship*

If ____________________________ does not survive me, then I give the property to
initial taker/s (by name or by class)

____________________________________, if ____________________________
alternate taker/s (by name or by class) *survivorship*

This excerpt provides a structure to discuss the function and purpose of a residuary clause in a will. In a slightly different version of this assignment, a professor could provide an excerpt of an actual will. Then the professor could provide another excerpt with critical information removed. By comparing the two excerpts, students could contemplate the practical drafting implications behind the cases, while focusing on discreet learning objectives with each blank.

These techniques are adaptable to any course such as Criminal Law (jury instructions), Civil Procedure (pleadings), Business Organizations (articles of incorporation), and Evidence (motions).

C. Exam Preparation

Applied to exam writing, the fill-in-the-blank format helps professors teach exam writing generally, and their preferences specifically.

To teach students the basic elements of writing an exam and organizing its content, a professor could provide a sample fact pattern and a model answer, being sure to follow IRAC and FIL (fact, inference, link to rule). Then, depending on which element of the analysis the professor wants to highlight, the professor could remove those elements and instruct the student to fill in a sentence that meets the purpose. For example, if the lesson focused on understanding the role of explicitly identifying inferences, the professor could remove several of the inferences from the model answer and label the blank space with "inference." Students would then have to provide the inferences. Here's a sample paragraph:

An offer must communicate the offeror's willingness to enter into a bargain in a way that justifies the other person believing that assent concludes the bargaining (Elemental Rule). In this case (signal), the facts do not indicate that Stephen made an explicit offer to Kevin (Fact). However, the facts suggest that Stephen implied an offer when Stephen explained his problem and reminded Kevin about Stephen's past help on Kevin's project (Implication of fact), because a reasonable person ______________________ (Link). Therefore, Stephen's explanation could be considered an offer (Conclusion). (This example is based on a fact pattern from *Bridging the Gap*, p. 98.)

By working with multiple samples over the semester, each focused on different elements of exam writing, students better understand the expected organization and elements of exam writing.

Conclusion

Writing assignments enrich any course. Adapting the Mad Libs format to the law school classroom helps incorporate writing assignments that enrich the students' learning experiences without significantly increasing the grading for professors.

Hillary Burgess
Charlotte School of Law

Karen J. Sneddon
Mercer University School of Law

Chapter 9

Professional Skills Across the Legal Education Curriculum

Thirty years ago the American Bar Association's *MacCrate Report* identified ten fundamental skills and four fundamental values for effective lawyering. Each of these skills and values were further broken down into smaller component parts. More recently, the *Carnegie Report* and *Best Practices for Legal Education* have recommended that students spend more time applying skills, values, and knowledge to the kinds of problems lawyers face in practice. As some law school deans have noted, we should call our institutions "lawyering schools" not "law schools."

The American Bar Association currently requires all accredited law schools to teach "professional skills generally regarded as necessary for effective and responsible participation in the legal profession" (ABA Standard 302(a)(4)); the ABA's interpretation notes that "[t]rial and appellate advocacy, alternative methods of dispute resolution, counseling, interviewing, negotiating, problem solving, factual investigation, organization and management of legal work, and drafting are among the areas of instruction in professional skills that fulfill Standard 302 (a)(4)." (ABA Interpretation 302-2) Legal employers echo this call for students to graduate with more professional lawyering skills; some of these employers will not hire law graduates unless those graduates can do more than read, analyze, and write about legal authorities.

Many schools have embraced this call, requiring students to complete a simulation, externship, clinic, or pro bono requirement, or take a number of required skills courses. Other schools have decided to require more skills training in existing courses, such as Legal Analysis, Research, and Writing. Recognizing the role of statutes and regulations, some schools also have started to require additional courses such as Administrative Process, and offer specialized courses in statutory interpretation. Some schools have gone further, seeking to integrate skills and doctrine across an array of courses, recognizing that skills and doctrine are intricately related.

In addition, a few schools have started mapping skills, knowledge, and values across the law school curriculum, looking at where in the curriculum a number of fundamental lawyering skills and values are introduced, practiced, and demonstrated. Law schools at Northeastern, the City University of New York, Washington & Lee, Gonzaga, Washburn, University of New Hampshire, Elon, and Charlotte, among others, have systematically sought to integrate ways to prepare students more effectively for practice. In addition, many schools promote and champion students developing professional skills and values through a wide variety of public service and pro bono programs, as well as extracurricular activities such as intramural competitions. We encourage you to visit these law school's websites—as well as learning about the programs at your own school—to learn more about how schools are addressing teaching skills and values.

In addition to helping students to be more prepared to practice law upon graduation, engaging students in practicing fundamental lawyering skills and values helps them learn important substance and develop their identity as members of the legal profession. As many of the contributors to this chapter note, having students engage in drafting and negotiating contracts, prepare a factual investigation plan, collaborate in designing a professional oath, resolve ethical dilemmas, and analyze statutes helps them gain a much deeper understanding of the relevant law, whether it is the law of employment, property, real estate, commercial transactions, or professional responsibility. Teaching lawyering skills and values is not separate from teaching law. Teaching lawyering skills and values teaches students about what lawyers *do*, who lawyers *are*, and helps them consider who they want to *be*.

Much like teaching doctrine, teaching professional skills involves identifying, cataloguing, and assessing these skills and values, whether these skills are taught in traditional doctrinal courses, such as Torts, Contracts, and Constitutional Law, or experiential electives, such as Wills Drafting and Street Law. As with learning doctrine or analysis, students learn professional skills effectively by engaging in active learning and using methods such as simulation and role-playing. The contributions that follow show a variety of ways in which schools and teachers have helped students learn skills and values.

A. What Are Lawyering Skills?

A number of studies, reports, and surveys have identified important lawyering skills, including *Best Practices for Legal Education*, the *MacCrate Report* and studies conducted by professors and members of the bar. Professional lawyering skills refer to a plethora of cognitive and affective practices that promote lawyering excellence. These skills include collaboration skills involved in working with colleagues at law firms, government organizations, and nonprofit groups. Professional skills also include affective skills, such as those lawyers use in interacting with colleagues, staff, opposing lawyers, judges, decision makers, and clients. Skills common to legal education include negotiating, litigating, interviewing, and counseling.

Having reviewed a number of statements of effective lawyering skills, *Best Practices for Legal Education* adopted the Law Society of England and Wales's statement of the important attributes of competent lawyers. They are:

1. Demonstrate appropriate behavior and integrity in a range of situations, including contentious and noncontentious areas of work.
2. Demonstrate the capacity to deal sensitively and effectively with clients, colleagues and others from a range of social, economic and ethnic backgrounds, identifying and responding positively and appropriately to issues of culture and disability that might affect communication techniques and influence a client's objectives.
3. Apply techniques to communicate effectively with clients, colleagues and members of other professions.
4. Recognize clients' financial, commercial and personal constraints and priorities.
5. Effectively approach problem-solving.
6. Effectively use current technologies and strategies to store, retrieve and analyze information and to undertake factual and legal research.

7. Demonstrate an appreciation of the commercial environment of legal practice, including the market for legal services.
8. Recognize and resolve ethical dilemmas.
9. Use risk management skills.
10. Recognize personal and professional strengths and weaknesses, to identify the limits of personal knowledge and skill and to develop strategies that will enhance their personal performance.
11. Manage their personal workload and manage efficiently and concurrently a number of client matters.
12. Work as part of a team.

Roy Stuckey et al., Best Practices for Legal Writing: A Vision and A Road Map 54 (2007).

In addition to the core competencies above, other educators, such as Dr. Roland Smith, of the Center for Creative Leadership of Greensboro and Colorado Springs, have been attempting to bridge the gap between law school and effective law practice by gathering data on what good lawyers do and how they do it. Smith and others are applying that knowledge to design ways law students and practitioners can identify the relevant skill sets and then improve those skill sets, so they are practice-ready, and understand what it takes to develop skills helpful for the next stage of their professional lives. This approach is predicated on the belief that, regardless of practice setting, very experienced lawyers need different skills than somewhat experienced lawyers, and somewhat experienced lawyers need different skills than entering lawyers.

While students might not achieve competence in all these skills in law school, they benefit from being introduced to and practicing as many skills as possible so that they can be prepared for their chosen profession.

B. How Do We Teach Lawyering Skills in Law School?

Almost all law schools have courses where students learn important skills and values, such as in clinics or externships. They also have stand-alone upper-level elective skills courses, such as Trial Advocacy, Interviewing, Counseling and Negotiation, and Transactional Drafting. Some schools have an array of such courses, like Pre-trial Advocacy, Expert Witnesses, Licensing, Trademark Registration, Will Drafting, Mediation, Alternative Dispute Resolution, Law Practice Management, and Patent Prosecution. Schools often limit enrollments in these courses to 20 students or fewer, allowing all students to actively engage in repeatedly practicing lawyering skills and values.

In addition to learning skills in these smaller skills-intensive courses, a number of law teachers have incorporated teaching skills and values into traditional doctrinal classes. Incorporating teaching skills and values in larger courses does not substitute for the in-depth learning that occurs when students are part of clinics or externships, work as law clerks, or participate in community service and other programs, but it provides a way for more students to get more practice in using lawyering skills. In teaching skills and values, we highly recommend you seek out and learn from colleagues who teach the skills-intensive courses above. These colleagues are experts in teaching skills and values. Their approaches to course design—including how they identify learning objectives, select teaching methods, provide feedback and assess their students—can provide valuable ideas and insights on integrating skills and values into other courses. Most of them will be honored and happy to help you do so.

Because practicing law is complex, students learn lawyering skills and values by practicing them in a variety of ways in a number of contexts throughout their legal education. Requiring all students to take a clinic or externship provides them with skills and values learning. Having every law student also engage in a variety of different lawyering skills at least once a semester would provide them with an even greater opportunity to be prepared for the demands of law practice.

Identify Concrete, Measurable Learning Objectives for Lawyering Skills and Values

As with any teaching experience, it is helpful to determine what students should be able to *do* in terms of lawyering skills and values by the end of the course, tailoring the learning objectives to the course and what lawyers do in practice. A stand-alone course such as Interviewing and Counseling should have more sophisticated objectives and those objectives should include a higher level of performance or mastery than a course that integrates the same skills of interviewing and counseling clients as part of a course on business transactions. For example, by the end of the stand-alone course, students should be able to effectively interview and counsel a range of diverse clients with a variety of issues. In an integrated course, students might more appropriately be able to conduct an initial interview of a client presenting a basic business issue.

Lawyering values are ineffable and consequently most teachers have a harder time identifying measurable learning objectives. The values themselves have been identified by those who study the profession—they include values such as acting with integrity, treating colleagues with respect, engaging in reflection and self-regulated learning, contributing to the community, promoting justice, and acknowledging errors and mistakes—but these are considerably harder to measure. In this area, teachers benefit from learning from colleagues who teach simulations, clinical, legal writing, other skills courses, as well as colleagues from other disciplines who have identified effective and efficient ways to teach and assess skills and values.

If you are new to teaching skills and values, we recommend you start small and make incremental changes. Focusing on one or two skills or values, or parts of them, is more likely to be manageable and productive than striving for mastery of a wide array of those skills and values. We also recommend that you talk to your colleagues about where else in the curriculum students are learning skills and values. If many other courses engage students in conducting initial client interviews, you may want to choose a different skill or value, such as investigating facts, developing confidence, or engaging in self-reflection. A Torts course can ask students to advise a client about a potential negligence claim. In Civil Procedure students can work as a team to prepare a discovery plan. A Criminal Procedure course can engage students in arguing a motion to suppress. A Property course can ask students to counsel a client about a potential land sale or take a photograph of an easement.

Provide Context and Relevance

As with any teaching, students benefit from understanding the context of the skills and values they are being asked to learn, and why learning that material matters. Many students come to law school believing that they will be learning "the law." While they learn within the first semester that legal education means more than understanding doctrine and includes applying doctrine to new situations, and writing about that in coherent prose, many do not immediately recognize the value of learning other lawyering skills and values. Without having seen attorneys in practice or having themselves engaged in lawyering tasks, students often have misconceptions about what lawyers do, and what behaviors they need to practice and refine to develop those skills.

Students also benefit from learning about the complexity involved in effective lawyering. Watching an effective lawyer interview a client or negotiate a deal may look easy, but in both situations, the lawyer is likely engaging in a complex array of skills including processing structured legal knowledge, actively listening for explicit and implicit messages, applying questioning techniques, gathering and selecting relevant facts, formulating theories, designing solutions to problems, and evaluating problems and potential solutions. Learning to use these complex arrays of skills effectively—and under pressure—does not come from having watched one interview or negotiation, or heard a lecture on the topic. Lawyers learn these skills over time, with repeat practice and feedback.

Identify Prior Knowledge and Preconceptions

As with the learning of any material, students arrive with a variety of backgrounds and preconceptions when learning lawyering skills. Gathering information about these backgrounds and preconceptions, by surveying students online, or conducting a brief questionnaire in class, can help teachers tailor skills teaching to maximize student learning. If, for example, students believe that understanding the law of wills and trusts is disconnected from the skill of interviewing a client whose parent recently died and who wants to know if he or she will inherit the parent's home, it helps to identify and address that misconception before trying to teach effective client interviewing and counseling. Certainly, empathy and active listening skills are important in interviewing a client whose parent has recently died, but failing to ask about siblings, the existence of a will, or other information crucial to inheriting property can lead to malpractice.

Similarly, students with extensive experience and expertise in skills related to lawyering benefit from a teaching approach that acknowledges their expertise and shows them how to transfer their skills to legal settings. For example, students with investigative, social work, health science, and paralegal backgrounds already may be skilled interviewers and fact gatherers. Asking for their forbearance when introducing the basics of interviewing and factual investigation respects their expertise. Inviting them to help their classmates who have less developed skills also honors their experience and is more likely to inspire them to bring their skills to the next level and collaborate to improve everyone's learning.

Students also benefit when teachers connect their learning to previous learning in law school. In their Legal Research, Analysis, and Writing courses, many students have been introduced to a range of skills, and may have been introduced to additional skills in their required first-year courses. Gathering information about what students have learned in those courses—or other concurrent courses—and then relating it to the skills being practiced in second and third years allows teachers to teach skills more efficiently. For example, having talked to colleagues teaching first-year courses, an Administrative Law teacher learns that almost all first-year students engaged in teamwork skills by working as part of a professional group in one or more first-year courses. The teacher might also learn about the kinds of values students have been exposed to through the school's orientation and pro bono programs. In her upper-level Administrative Law course, that teacher can ask students to build on those experiences to work in a professional group to give a presentation, engage in a simulated deposition, or negotiate a contract.

Choose Appropriate Teaching Techniques for Students to Learn Professional Skills

Whether we teach skills and values as stand-alone courses or as part of an integrated course—and we believe that all law school courses should teach some skills and values in addition to legal analysis—the same principles of effective teaching and learning techniques apply. Using role-plays, experiential learning exercises, simulations and any number of other active learning techniques help students master these skills. For all of these, students need clear directions, expected outcomes, information about resources, adequate time to complete the task, and feedback so that they can improve their learning. All of these techniques can be adapted for short in-class exercises to semester long projects where students practice using a number of different skills and values.

1. Role-plays

Students also can take on the role of a lawyer, client, third party, decision maker, colleague, or other constituent. In many classes, students are often assigned the role of litigators, making arguments for or against issues such as admitting material into evidence, guilt of a criminal defendant, or liability of a party. Teachers can do this instantly and spontaneously in class. They can indicate a line dividing the classroom in half and then ask students sitting on one side of the line to represent plaintiffs or prosecutors, and those on the other to make arguments for the defense.

To expand students' skills and develop their awareness of the complexity of most legal problems, teachers can assign students to a greater array of roles. For example, in an Environmental Law course, in different classes or at different points in the course, students could collaborate in designing effective environmental legislation, serving as the attorneys representing a business client, members of a state or federal environmental agency, lobbyists, public interest advocacy groups, neighborhood groups, and public health officials. Similarly, in a Family Law course, individual students or groups of students could be asked to take on the role of a guardian ad litem, father, mother, and child protective agency representative in trying to collectively resolve a child's placement in a custody proceeding. By researching and taking on different roles, students benefit from considering different perspectives and engaging in negotiating, problem solving, and thinking creatively about legal issues. Within role-plays, students can practice a wide variety of skills and values.

2. Experiential Learning Exercises

Bringing real-life scenarios into the course also helps students appreciate the complexity of what lawyers do and apply a variety of skills and values to diverse practice areas. Students engage in any number of real-life examples or experiences that help them connect abstract concepts to real life. A teacher can easily help students learn about lawyers' skills and values in class by bringing in a guest speaker, showing video clips or photos of material related to the course, or relating course learning to current events. Students can also take field trips, conduct interviews, engage in public service projects, and practice researching law and law-related material to deepen their learning of fundamental skills and values.

Many law students engage in experiential learning from observing court proceedings, such as appellate arguments, or participate in externships, clinics, or service projects. To expand students' learning of skills and values beyond the traditional litigation model, students can observe other processes, such as proceedings at a state or federal agency, a registry of deeds, department of revenue, school board, or technology transfer office. Similarly, in addition to being asked to interview practicing lawyers and judges or having those lawyers as class guest speakers, students can interview people who frequently interact with lawyers, such as members of an accounting firm, school administrators, nongovernmental organization leaders, retailers, police officers, or social workers.

Public service experiences can include working with lawyers to help low income clients obtain tax assistance, volunteer at a domestic violence shelter, or teach high school students about their legal rights. Students may also volunteer and assist lawyers in helping veterans obtain disability benefits, draft legislation, draft public education materials for community members, interview witnesses, investigate facts, and research legal theories and relevant documents. Whether engaging in real-world research as part of a public service project or for a class, researching laws, regulations, public disclosure documents, or training manuals provides students with valuable hands-on skills training. As with other instructional techniques, using real-life experiences can be included with other exercises to engage students in learning a variety of lawyering skills and values.

3. Simulations

As with experiential learning, engaging students in simulations can lead to deep learning of lawyering skills and values. Simulations are particularly effective for some students; students who struggle with learning through verbal discussion and reading and writing often excel when they engage in an effective simulation. Simulations can involve a wide range of skills and values learning, including problem solving, making professional judgments, taking appropriate risks, engaging in self-monitoring and reflection, and organizing and managing legal work.

In contrast to experiential learning, simulations have the value of controlling what students learn. The teacher can design a simulation to focus on particular skills and values, eliminating the distractions and vagaries of real life. Simulations' disadvantages are that they lack the authenticity of practice and misinform students about the messiness and unpredictability of practicing law.

Designing effective simulations, like designing effective writing exercises, takes energy and practice. As with any new teaching approach, we recommend you start small, ask for help from your colleagues, pay attention to and capture a simulation's successes and problems, invite feedback from students, and seek to improve the simulation every time you use it.

Assess Students' Skills and Values

As the saying goes, "students pay attention to what you *inspect*, not what you expect." If you tell students that you will grade them on a client interviewing exercise, or that they must demonstrate competence in collaborating in a small group to pass the course, students will pay attention to the skill or value to be assessed. To do this fairly, students need to know the assessment criteria, and have an opportunity to practice and get feedback on the skill or value before they must show competence. (For more on assessment, see Chapter 12). Again, collaborating and learning from colleagues who are already experienced in teaching skills and values will provide you with valuable material.

C. Address Barriers to Teaching Lawyering Skills

Some faculty members are concerned that teaching lawyering skills and values will take too much time and rob the course of learning important knowledge. They may also need to be persuaded that teaching skills and values is worth the time and effort, especially if teaching them takes more time than other preparation or is outside of their teaching comfort zone. In addition, faculty members may be concerned that spending the time to teach skills and values detracts from their own scholarship, service or other teaching.

Teachers who teach skills and values can show colleagues how to balance teaching skills, values, and knowledge, and provide concrete suggestions about how to teach them effectively and efficiently. Law schools who seek to promote having graduates who are closer to being "practice ready" can support teachers in a variety of ways, such as by providing course release time, offering stipends to develop materials for teaching skills and values, paying for research assistants to help with developing new materials, subsidizing teachers to attend related conferences, sponsoring faculty development workshops, and encouraging teachers to visit and learn from colleagues at other law schools. In addition, law school administrators can reward faculty who teach students skills and values. Administrators can value that work in promotion, retention and annual reviews, publicly praise and acknowledge teachers' efforts in teaching skills and values, include skills and values as part of student evaluations, and provide those who teach skills and values with their preferred schedules and classrooms.

Contributions in this chapter suggest ways to identify, teach, and assess lawyering values.

References

- RELATIONSHIP-CENTERED LAWYERING: SOCIAL SCIENCE THEORY FOR TRANSFORMING LEGAL PRACTICE (Susan L. Brooks & Robert G. Madden eds., 2010).
- RONALD BENTON BROWN & SHARON JACOBS BROWN, STATUTORY INTERPRETATION: THE SEARCH FOR LEGISLATIVE INTENT (2010).
- BARBARA GROSS DAVIS, TOOLS FOR TEACHING (1993).
- Jay Feinman, *Simulations: An Introduction,* 45 J. LEGAL EDUC. 469 (1995).
- Gerry Hess, *Listening to Our Students: Obstructing and Enhancing Learning in Law School*, 31 U.S.F. L. REV. 941 (1997).
- LINDA D. JELLUM & DAVID CHARLES HRICIK, MODERN STATUTORY INTERPRETATION: PROBLEMS, THEORIES, AND LAWYERING STRATEGIES (2006).
- Robert MacCrate, *Report of the Task Force on Law Schools and the Profession: Narrowing the Gap*, 1992 A.B.A. SEC. LEGAL EDUC. & PROF. DEV. (1992).
- MICHAEL HUNTER SCHWARTZ, SOPHIE SPARROW & GERALD F. HESS, TEACHING LAW BY DESIGN: ENGAGING STUDENTS FROM THE SYLLABUS TO THE FINAL EXAM (2009).
- Marjorie M. Shultz & Sheldon Zedeck, *Predicting Lawyer Effectiveness: A New Assessment for Use in Law School Admission Decisions* (CELS 4th Annual Conference on Empirical Legal Studies, Working Paper July 31, 2009).
- ROY STUCKEY ET AL., BEST PRACTICES FOR LEGAL EDUCATION: A VISION AND A ROAD MAP (2007).
- WILLIAM SULLIVAN ET AL., EDUCATING LAWYERS: PREPARATION FOR THE PROFESSION OF LAW 115 (2007).
- MARYELLEN WEIMER, IMPROVING YOUR CLASSROOM TEACHING (SURVIVAL SKILLS FOR SCHOOLS) (1993).

The Real Estate Transaction as a Teaching Tool

Much of the teaching and learning in law school is focused on the litigation perspective. There are fewer opportunities to discuss deal-making and transactional practice, particularly negotiating techniques, contract drafting, and contract analysis. However, a significant percentage of law students do not become litigators. They become transactional lawyers, and it is important to provide teaching that focuses on their needs. The *MacCrate Report* stressed the need for law schools to better prepare students for law practice while they are still in law school. I wanted to find ways to integrate practical training for transactional practice into the substantive curriculum.

Several years ago, I designed and began teaching Real Estate Development and Finance. This course presented a perfect opportunity to integrate transactional practice into a more traditional curriculum.

The most interesting and fun aspect of the course, for me and my students, was the transactional teaching tool that I developed. During the term we planned and built (hypothetically of course) a commercial office building. We leased it to tenants and by the end of the term began to formulate plans to sell the completed project. Almost all of the theory and documents in the course were discussed in the framework of our simulated project.

A piece of land was presented to the students. It had a realistic, if hypothetical, street address in our city and a legal description. A renowned tax attorney made a presentation on the formation of entities to hold title. We chose an appropriate type of entity and the students named it. We studied option contracts and purchase contracts and their specific provisions. We read and discussed contracts of varying levels of sophistication. I provided a draft contract for our project that contained internal inconsistencies. The students were required to spot the inconsistencies and draft language to correct them to best meet the needs of the project.

This experience showed students the importance of careful reading and drafting. It provided the perfect opportunity to teach students about the relationship between, and need for consistency among, all of the documents in a transaction. We learned that every provision and every word is important. We also learned why certain provisions are included, how to go about deciding what provisions are needed in a particular transaction, and how to draft provisions. Unfortunately, time constraints limited the opportunity for extensive drafting experiences; mostly, we had to talk about drafting and then draft specific, narrow provisions.

We covered negotiating on behalf of buyer and seller and did problem-solving for various types of situations. The next phase of our real transaction was the due diligence for our project. Based on a hypothetical feasibility study (several feasibility studies for actual projects were placed on reserve in the library for students to read), we learned that the building had to be a certain size to be optimally profitable. I invited a highly regarded zoning and land use attorney to class. He covered the basics of zoning and land use as they relate to a project, and we learned about variances, height restrictions, lot coverage, setbacks, parking requirements, green space, etc. In the process, we learned that our parcel was not large enough to legally construct the building. With our expert consultant's assistance, we decided that it was not likely we would be successful in obtaining a variance. Fortuitously, an adjacent lot became available at an attractive price, and we could go on with the project. In the course of our due diligence we reviewed a detailed simulated survey, a title commitment and documents comprising the special exceptions. We talked about the standard exceptions. An environmental expert made a presentation on phase I and phase II environmental assessments. He presented an actual phase I study for our site. The students particularly enjoyed working with the survey and the title documents. We learned about the various symbols used on a survey and saw how easements created by legal documents are depicted on a survey.

We closed on our purchase, with a simultaneous closing on the adjacent parcel. The draft closing statement had an error in it that was spotted by one of the students. We struggled over trying to decide if it was really an error. The students' assignment for the next class was to prepare corrected buyer's and seller's closing statements. Once again, the "error" stimulated particularly effective learning.

An engineer spoke to the class about problems that can be encountered in a construction project. We discussed how problems might be addressed via careful drafting in the construction or architect's contract, and negotiating resolutions of construction problems. We also reviewed a construction loan agreement and mortgage and learned how construction loan transactions differ from traditional mortgage situations.

Next, with our building nearing completion, we studied and discussed office building leases, including the tenant work letter. The relation of leases to a sale of the building was also discussed as we briefly explored whether we might want to sell our building upon completion.

Our development project was, of course, a complete success. Nevertheless, we needed to consider projects that were not successful. We spent the last portion of the course looking at a troubled project, specifically loan workouts, foreclosures, and deeds in lieu of foreclosure. The last class provided a brief discussion of bankruptcy.

The students reported that they especially enjoyed this class and that it should be taught on a continuing basis at least once each year. The vast majority said the real transaction model improved their understanding of the material. Some said they felt that the real transaction model was essential to their understanding. Others suggested that the course would be even better if the simulated project were further developed and incorporated into the lessons. All agreed that the course reviewed and solidified their understanding of the first year courses in Property and Contracts. Many felt better prepared to enter the practice of law because of the course.

The following bibliography lists a few sources that inspired me to try this approach:

- Christian C. Day, *Teaching Students How to Become In-House Counsel*, 51 J. Legal Educ. 503 (2001).
- Daniel B. Bogart, *The Right Way to Teach Transactional Lawyers: Commercial Leasing and the Forgotten "Dirt Lawyer,"* 62 U. Pitt. L. Rev. 335 (2000).
- Greg Sergienko, *Procedure Students "Discover" Exams*, The Law Teacher (Institute for Law Teaching & Learning, Spokane, WA), Spring 1997, at 10.
- Robert MacCrate, *Report of the Task Force on Law Schools and the Profession: Narrowing the Gap*, 1992 A.B.A. Sec. Legal Educ. & Prof. Dev. (1992).

Carol Zeiner
St. Thomas University School of Law

Do Tell: Informal Communication about the Law

Through a series of interviews with a wide range of practicing lawyers when I was an associate dean, I learned that lawyers spend much of their time communicating about the law in less formal ways than law school would have students believe. Thus, when I recently taught Employment Law, I opted to focus less on what the law says (which is complex and changes often) and more on what employment lawyers do. I organized the course around a number of projects. Three of the projects were designed to promote informal legal communication. These projects revolved around a transactional setting, a mild antidote to a curriculum that generally focuses on litigation.

- Students worked in a large firm and were assigned to write two descriptions of a new federal statute on genetic information in the workplace. One description was to be sent to clients via the firm's electronic updating service. The other was written on a pro bono basis for the local legal aid organization that posts descriptions of major employment laws for the general public.
- Students worked in-house at a grocery store chain and were assigned to train the various store managers on a state wage law governing deductions from wages or last paychecks. This project included writing an outline of the law and preparing a handout for the managers as well as delivering a training session, with the rest of the class serving as the managers.
- Students worked in a mid-sized firm and were assigned to develop a policy on the use of private cell phones by drivers for a courier service. The students wrote a letter drawing on legal rules and also on statistical studies of the danger of cell phone use while driving. In addition, the students met with the assigning partner, me, to explain the work before it was sent to the client.

I embedded a series of teachable moments in the various projects. For the first project, we worked on the difference between their reading abilities and the literacy of the average person. For the second, students experienced being on the receiving end of a legal presentation and critiqued their peers, providing a kudo and a suggestion. For the third, the information was delivered to the students in a few emails that they had to piece together. In addition, I intentionally asked a question none of the students would be able to answer, so they could learn to say, "I don't know."

Each project required some level of skills instruction. Because I coordinate our first-year skills course and know its follow-up very well, I could base the instruction on what students already knew. For example, I used the evaluation criteria they had already seen for advice letters and contracts (which are taught in the spring of the first year). A reference librarian taught students how to use various employment law resources. I provided sample statutory summaries and employment policies. I conducted a bad training session and a good one, including handouts. Experiencing poor instruction can very quickly demonstrate the importance of attending to teaching methods, not just the content of a presentation. Every piece of a project was evaluated against a pre-set list of criteria, which I talked through as I assigned the project.

Happily, all of the projects were well received by students who readily saw the relevance of the projects to their future careers, enjoyed the interactions, and welcomed the opportunity to exercise creativity. I believe that students learned the various legal topics much better than they would have in a more traditional class. More important, given the focus of the course, they steadily developed their capacity to communicate about the law as they received my feedback, shifted settings, and tackled more demanding projects throughout the semester.

When I asked students to write at the semester's end what they learned from the course about being an employment lawyer, I was pleased to see their comments about the counseling function. The students recognized that lawyers help the client do the right thing, offer options, serve as a liaison role between workers and management, keep up-to-date, teach clients about the law and risks, understand public policy and the intention behind the law, manage responsibilities to both employers and employees, and keep ethical considerations in mind.

Deborah Schmedemann
William Mitchell College of Law

Professional Development Obligation

One of my core goals as a law teacher is to facilitate my students' development of a commitment to lifelong learning ("the will") and their abilities to engage in independent, self-regulated learning ("the skill"). Students, however, do not naturally develop either the will or the skill. Consequently, I have created a requirement I call the "Professional Development Obligation" (PDO) for my Contracts students.

On the first day of class, I let students know my goals for the requirement and how they can satisfy it, and I try to remind the students of the requirement periodically throughout the semester. Over the years, I have come to realize more and more how much students value and benefit from having control over their own learning processes; consequently, every year or so, I expand the number of alternative ways students can satisfy the PDO.

Although I have the occasional student who concludes the entire requirement is "busy work," most regard it as a helpful tool in their learning process in my Contracts course. Below I explain how I articulate the requirement to my students, the benefits of the requirement, and a few of the pitfalls.

How I Articulate the PDO to My Students

The PDO is fully addressed in my syllabus. The portion of my syllabus that addresses the PDO follows. (My syllabus also explains that the PDO counts for 10% of each student's grade in the course.)

Mandatory Professional Development Work and Essay

- Like most law professors around the country, one of my goals is to give you the skills, knowledge, and values you need to be able to learn and grow as a professional. I therefore have chosen to make these skills an explicit and graded part of my course.
- I also have serious doubts about the common law school practice of evaluating students using a system that gives no credit to motivation, effort, and creativity and in which your entire course grade depends upon a single examination.
- All students who complete the work described below will get at least 70% of the points available for this portion of your grade. I am reserving the last 30% of your score to reward students who write insightful essays, who do more than the minimum, and whose insights and efforts are excellent.
- Because you are in the best position to evaluate what you need to grow as a professional in the context of my course, I have decided to give you several options to meet this course requirement and to allow you to choose how to do so. No matter which option you choose, you must hand in, on the last day of class before the final: (1) evidence of your efforts; and (2) a two-page essay in which you identify which option(s) you have chosen, the bases for your choice(s), and what you have learned from your efforts.

Options:

1. **Keeping a Professional Development Journal.** You may satisfy your Professional Development Obligation by continuing to keep a journal, making at least one entry every week responding to the "Professional Development Reflection Questions" in *Contracts: A Context and Practice Casebook*. You may answer as many or as few questions as you like as long as each entry is at least 500 words. Your evidence must include your journal and a statement that your entries are all 500 or more in length.

2. **Taking The Optional Multiple-Choice Quizzes and Reflecting on Your Results.** Each week or two, I will be posting optional multiple-choice quizzes to the course webpage. The quizzes will be designed to test whether you have learned the skills, knowledge, and values that are the subject of that week's assignments and class discussions. To satisfy your Professional Development Obligation in this way, you must take every quiz, evaluate, for each question you answered incorrectly on each quiz, why your answer was wrong and why the correct answer was correct, and decide how you will use your results on each quiz to improve your learning in this and your other classes.
3. **Course Webpage Postings.** You also can meet your Professional Development Obligation by posting at least ten significant comments to the course webpage for this class. (See below for a definition of "significant comments"). With 75 or so students, I cannot always meet the needs of every one of you. Postings give me an additional teaching resource, especially because students can meet the requirement by asking or answering questions. In fact, if you understand something well enough to clearly explain it to someone else, you have mastered it. Additionally, because I can resolve some student confusion outside the classroom, I can devote more classroom time to building your analytical skills and the other learning goals for the class. I also believe some students learn better from reading and writing, and the posting requirement supports that need. Finally, I want to try to promote collaboration and peer-help because, in my opinion, law school is too competitive.

   What is a "significant comment"? You have considerable flexibility to decide what types of comments you wish to make. Significant comments include: (1) original statements about the cases and rules of law we are studying, the policies that underlie those rules and cases, and how to apply the rules and apply and distinguish the cases; (2) original examples or nonexamples of any of the legal concepts we are studying; (3) questions about any of the materials we are studying (so long as the question does not reflect a failure to attempt course work); (4) original exam-like hypotheticals raising any of the issues we are studying; (5) answers of any other student's question or hypothetical; (6) critiques of another student's answer to a question or hypothetical; (7) reflections on your use of the self-regulated learning cycle for your work in this class; (8) reflections on the use, applicability and effectiveness of any learning strategy you have used in this class or in any other class; and (9) outlines, flowcharts, and practice hypos you have created in preparing for the midterm and final in this class.
4. **Making It Real.** Adult learners benefit from seeing the real-world implications of what they are learning. Consequently, I want to reward those of you who stay current on the news, enjoy scouring the Internet, and find applications of the concepts you are learning in real-life news stories or in contracts you have seen or signed. I also greatly appreciate students who take the time to figure out the relevant rule of law in the state where they intend to practice law. To meet this obligation, you need to bring the newspaper article, Internet posting, contract, statute or court opinion within one week of our study of the concept to which your submission relates and submit a one paragraph explanation of how your submission relates to the concept we are learning/ have learned.
5. **A Combination of the Choices.** Finally, to meet your Professional Development Obligation, you may do a combination of the other four options. If you choose this option, you are responsible for determining whether the portion of each option you have done, when combined with the other options you have chosen, reflects the required quantity of work. (For example, you can meet the requirement by completing all the requirements for three of the six quizzes (50%), by doing three of the required 14 journal

entries (~21%), and by making three of the required ten substantial postings to the course webpage (30%).)

The Benefits of the PDO Requirement

As my explanation to my students makes clear, the PDO is designed to help students develop their self-regulated learning skills and take control over their own learning. It also adds an additional assessment to my assessment package, engages students in activities that help them develop as Contracts students and as professionals, and rewards students who are willing to work hard and manage their time.

Pitfalls of the PDO Requirement

In the past, I had disclosed the obligation at the beginning of the semester in class and in my syllabus and never mentioned it again. I have found that I get better submissions and students learn more when I remind them of the requirement throughout the semester. Rushed, end-of-the-semester submissions end up becoming little more than busy-work. I also learned that I had to make the percentage of the final grade a significant enough number to give students an incentive not to blow off the PDO and live with the grade consequences; 10% seems to be sufficient.

Michael Hunter Schwartz
Washburn University School of Law

Marisa Tomei Talks about Teaching Law

In the movie *My Cousin Vinnie,* actress Marisa Tomei indicted law school teaching with this question to her rookie lawyer boyfriend: "They didn't teach you that in law school either?"

So how should law schools answer her accusation? Of course, one way is to make sure the students are prepared in substantive areas, especially those on the state bar exams. A second way is to ask lawyers what should be taught in law schools about the fundamentals of law practice. A third way is to research the literature, and a fourth is to review law school curricula.

My review of the literature showed that lawyers treasure several skills—in addition to "thinking like a lawyer"—such as business savvy, communication skills, ability to work in groups and teams, managerial talent, and creativity. I recently surveyed electronically several thousand California Western Law School graduates. The survey responses revealed that marketing and business development skills, client care techniques, and methods of funding and managing a law practice were also important. A review of the websites of about 175 ABA-accredited law schools showed that only about one in five offer courses on the fundamentals of the "practice of law."

Is it possible to develop these skills in law school and meet these perceived needs, including Ms. Tomei's, by using pedagogical techniques? The answer is "yes," especially if active learning techniques are emphasized. Such techniques are already used in several settings, including seminar presentations, moot court arguments, and mock trials. Practical experience can be gained in clinical programs (named after the medical school model) and from internship, externship, and clerkship courses.

As an adjunct law professor for the past 14 years I have attempted to combine features of all of these fundamentals into a two-unit, 14-week course entitled, "Practicing Law: Successful Strategies." There are 21 different topics (vetted through practicing lawyers) including client care, marketing, funding, managing, hiring staff, practice forms, Rules of Court, and so on. The students are divided into seven teams, and the teams present the topics in 30-minute chunks over the term. I back up those presentations with experiences and cases from 30 years of law practice, with handouts, and with short lectures. The only other limitation placed on the students' creativity is the general one of decency. And then the fun, and the learning, starts.

Random assignment to teams forces them to manage and overcome many of the frustrations of group work, which is a fundamental legal practice skill in and of itself. The students are critiqued (privately), especially when they use legalese rather than the plain speaking that juries and clients find useful and persuasive. They are commended when their creativity soars, including presentations by home videos, mock game shows, skits, a Dave Letterman-type "Top 10" list, parodies of slick marketing seminars, and even a field trip, to name a few.

But how do game shows teach these fundamental legal skills? That depends on the definition of legal skills, doesn't it? If fundamental legal skills are the ones lawyers described in the literature and in the survey responses, then this pedagogy and course design measure up pretty well. For instance, creative muscles are stretched and worked. Granted, a game show or a skit in law school might not have a place in a later murder trial. Creativity always does, though. And by observing 21 different presentations, the students begin to appreciate what communication styles are effective and what styles might not work. In addition, the journals handed in at the end of the course show that, despite the varied presentations, the fundamentals of each topic were successfully transferred. Also, collaborative skills are developed, and the students must design and implement their own lesson plans for their assigned topics. Further, the topics address what lawyers tell us are important for students to know.

To those who admire the pedagogy displayed in the book and movie, *The Paper Chase*, this method of student-led active learning is probably heresy. Indeed, many of us ex-law students recall (though not with fondness usually) the humiliation the Socratic Method visited upon us and our classmates as we attempted to guess what the professor was thinking and our responses were invariably found lacking. Learning did occur, despite the terror. However, measured against the skill sets lawyers tell us are needed, it is difficult to see how the case method can deliver the goods.

The alumni (now in practice) of my Practicing Law course spoke strongly in favor of this type of course (71% "strongly agreed" this type of course should be mandatory in law school, plus another 21% "moderately agreed"). As for the pedagogy, a total of 71% agreed ("strong" and "moderate" combined) with the importance of student-led active learning.

Of course, our next humbling moment in law practice is never more than a phone call or letter away, at which point Ms. Tomei's opening question can arise once again. However, law schools can reduce the number of opportunities for her indictment if we do a better job of designing our courses and our pedagogies to deliver the fundamentals that lawyers tell us are needed to enable students to succeed in the legal profession.

James Eckmann
California Western School of Law

Factual Investigation — First Exposure

Conducting a factual investigation is a core professional skill for lawyers. Both the *MacCrate Report* and *Best Practices for Legal Education* include performing a factual investigation as a lawyering skill that should be taught in the law school curriculum.

The following exercise was designed to introduce students to fact investigation. Although this exercise originated in the context of a first-year Civil Litigation course, it could be adapted easily to any course in which fact investigation plays a role.

The Exercise

> Yesterday you were contacted by Pat Grimes. You had a short conversation with Pat and agreed to meet with Pat next week.
>
> Pat owns a Moomba ski boat, manufactured by Skier's Choice, Inc. Last summer, Pat's ten year-old son, Bo, was injured during a family outing on Lake Coeur d'Alene in Idaho. Bo was swimming near the boat. Bo passed out from carbon monoxide poisoning and nearly drowned. He sustained serious cognitive injuries.
>
> Each member of your firm should spend one hour this week investigating Skier's Choice, Moomba, and carbon monoxide poisoning. Then prepare a firm memo that:
>
> 1. summarizes what you learned about Skier's Choice, Moomba, and carbon monoxide poisoning that is relevant to a possible negligence claim against Skier's Choice and/or Moomba and
> 2. sets out a plan for further investigation, identifying the types of information you would attempt to obtain and the potential sources of that information.
>
> See your textbook for a discussion of fact investigation. Your investigation is taking place before any lawsuit is filed; therefore, your investigation plan should not include any of the discovery devices (interrogatories, depositions, subpoenas, etc) available under the Federal Rules of Civil Procedure. The firm memo is limited to 2 pages, single spaced, Times New Roman, size14 font.

Students complete this exercise in "firms" of four students. During the one-hour investigation, every student relies exclusively on the Internet. In class, I ask a firm to report two things they learned about Moomba, Skier's Choice (both real entities), or carbon monoxide poisoning. I then have every other firm report two different things they learned during their investigations. Students learn a tremendous amount about the entities and carbon monoxide poisoning from a one-hour, online search.

The fact investigation plan serves a different purpose. While most students are very comfortable conducting an Internet search, most are novices at other forms of fact investigation. In class we brainstorm non-Internet means of investigating facts, including interviews, observations in the field, document requests from public agencies, etc. Items on our list come as a revelation for most students. For example, although by the time students complete this exercise they have read a recent case involving carbon monoxide poisoning, Skier's Choice, and Moomba, it is rare for any student to suggest that an appropriate investigative step would be to call the plaintiff's lawyers from that case.

The skill of conducting an effective, efficient fact investigation is much more sophisticated than doing a one-hour Internet search and generating an initial investigation plan. However, this simple exercise actively engages students in conducting an investigation and thinking about how to structure an investigation plan, which are important steps toward developing this important professional skill.

Gerry Hess
Gonzaga University School of Law

Integrating Interviewing Skills Seamlessly into Doctrinal Classes

Interviewing skills can be effectively integrated into doctrinal courses as shown in the exercises below. These exercises illustrate the applicability and importance of a variety of component skills, from how questions are posed to clients, to the value of active listening, to the role of emotion in the lawyering process.

A Ten-Minute Exercise on Asking Questions

The first part of this exercise involves informing the students that they will be interviewing a client who has an issue related to their reading in the next class session. Then, ask for volunteers to act as clients (or recruit volunteers) and prepare a short hypothetical for them that integrates some doctrinal theory you wish to explore.

When class begins, divide the students into groups, assigning each a client. Instruct half of the groups that they have five minutes to ask as many questions as they want, but they can only ask questions that ask for a "yes or no" response. Instruct the clients that they may answer more than "yes or no" to these questions, but only if it would seem natural for them to do so. For the other half of the class, instruct the groups that they should first take two minutes to formulate one question and that this will be the only question they can ask. (You may want to limit the question to one that can be asked in one breath or within a certain number of words, to avoid an interrogatory-type multiple-part monstrosity of a question). The students are then to ask the question and let the client talk for up to three minutes without interruption. The clients of this half of the class should be instructed to answer as fully as the question seems to require.

When five minutes is up, ask each group, "Why did your client come to see you, what does he want, and what issues do you see in representing this client?" Begin with the closed question groups. Obviously, these black-box questioners will have very incomplete information. They often will have more inaccurate information as well because they will have filled in the blanks with their own assumptions. Then ask the open-ended question groups each what questions they asked. Finally ask these groups about the information they gathered. In ten minutes, the students will have come to realize the power of an open-ended question and silence in gathering information.

A Ten Minute Exercise on Listening

A similar exercise can be used to teach students about the value of active listening. Have the students interview you or a volunteer client for three to five minutes. Then give the students a quiz over what they heard or ask them to write a client letter memorializing the conversation. To reinforce the power of checking for accuracy, allow one half of the class to only ask only open-ended questions, while the other half of the class is allowed to restate and check information or ask closed-ended follow up questions. Debrief the exercise by comparing reports of depth and accuracy of information collected from each group. Discuss the techniques they can use to improve their listening habits.

Interviewing as a Case-Briefing Technique

Instead of asking students to state the facts of a case, pretend to be the client in a case they have read for class and ask them to interview the client to present those facts. Choose a particular point in time in the case history (the initial request for representation interview, the interview after a judgment at the trial court level, etc.). If this class follows the open-ended questioning class, the student may simply be called upon to recite the facts of the case. However, the professor can extend this exercise to teach lessons about client facts as well. Choose a case in which there are important facts that do not appear in the opinion, facts about which any good attorney would be asking a client. Then briefly discuss with the students the reasons why clients may not be able or willing to provide the whole picture. Alternately, choose a case in which the client presents a challenge to communication in some way (for example, a client who appears to be lying, or who has limited competency). Finally, choose a case in which the emotional content of the facts would present a significant challenge to gaining information, establishing rapport, or facilitating decision making. This is easier in some courses than others—with criminal defendants and family law clients, for example—but in some senses the lesson is more powerful in classes in which the students are likely to believe emotion plays no role, like contracts or corporations. You will need good role playing by the clients for the students to learn how emotion interacts with client decisions and affects factual reconstruction, so for this exercise it is especially helpful for you to recruit (or be) a good actor.

You can repeat this exercise several times during the semester to extend lessons on interviewing and bring more reality to the case reading exercise.

Incorporating Interviewing into Final Examinations

Obviously, the best way to assess student progress in learning about interviewing is to watch the student interview, but this may be impractical in large classes, even with video recording technology. You can, however, incorporate interviewing into a final exam by testing discrete skills. To test questioning, give the students a brief fact scenario and ask the students to formulate the questions they would ask the client. Be sure to instruct the students that you do not want them to simply list the topics about which they would question, but to draft the language of the questions they would use. This will test not only a student's ability to spot issues and elements in the doctrine, but also to phrase questions that will elicit complete and accurate information. To test listening, provide a portion of your exam as a video of the client talking about his or her case. By recording the statement, the professor can proof and edit and provide control over what the input is for the students to work with.

Interviewing clients, witnesses, and others is an important part of the attorney's skill repertoire but is one of the skills taught least systematically in the curriculum. By incorporating lessons throughout doctrinal courses, students will be aware of the importance of the skill and gain some preliminary instruction into some of the components of effective interviewing.

Barbara Glesner Fines
University of Missouri–Kansas City School of Law

Integrating a Workshop on Negotiation and Drafting into a Contracts Course

In my second-semester Contracts course, I included a "negotiation and drafting workshop" for the last four class sessions. The purpose of the workshop was to provide an opportunity for students to learn how to apply their substantive knowledge to the skills of negotiation, collaboration, and drafting. Each of the four class periods was scheduled for one hour and 25 minutes. Fifty-eight students were enrolled in the course.

First Class Session

Prior to the first workshop class, the students researched an article, treatise, book, or online resource on the subject of negotiation. I asked each student to prepare to share with the class five things of importance in the negotiating process.

The first workshop class began with a brief discussion on contract drafting and how it differs from other types of legal writing. One of the key concepts was that the drafting of the contract begins during the negotiation process. The discussion then shifted to the "negotiated contract" as distinguished from the "adhesion contract." During this phase, students shared their findings on the principles of negotiation from their research assignment.

Second Class Session

Before the second workshop class, the class was divided in half. One-half of the class was to represent a property owner who wanted to build a cabin in the mountains. The remaining half of the class was to represent the building contractor. Each student was randomly paired with another student to form a lawyer team to represent one of the clients. Each lawyer team was sent a "confidential memorandum" from the client authorizing the team to negotiate a contract for the building of the cabin, within the parameters of the client's desires. The property owner and building contractor memoranda differed regarding each client's desires with respect to the construction cost, payment terms, remedy for a delay in completion, dispute resolution, change orders, and indemnification in the event of injury to third persons. Students were to formulate their strategies and proposals before class and be fully prepared to negotiate toward reaching a resolution on the legal and factual issues.

The second class period was devoted entirely to the negotiation process. Student lawyer teams representing the contractor were paired with student lawyer teams representing the property owner. Two employees of the law school were enlisted to play the role of the general contractor and the property owner. The employee-role players attended class and were available to student lawyers who needed to "consult with their client" regarding any issue that was beyond the authority granted in the memoranda.

Third Class Session

Before the third class, each student team drafted a proposed agreement based on the results of the negotiations. Resources available to the students included a monograph written by Joseph Kimble of the Thomas Cooley Law School entitled, "A Brief Introduction to Drafting Contracts" and online resources on contracts drafting, such as the AdamsDrafting website, www.adamsdrafting.com.

The first part of the third class period involved a review of the types of contracts that are in common use, including: (1) a real estate sales agreement; (2) a landlord-tenant rental agreement; (3) an employment agreement; (4) a publication agreement; and, (5) a construction loan agreement. Students noted the differences in length, style, and contents of the contracts.

During the remainder of the class period the student teams collaborated in the drafting process and worked on wording, clarity, and style. By the end of class, students were close to having a final draft to present to their client for approval and signature.

Fourth Class Session

The homework assignment for the fourth class was to complete the final draft of the contract in collaboration with the other team. The final agreements were then sent to me electronically before class.

In the fourth class period, we reviewed each of the contracts on the overhead projector. Students compared the results of their negotiations and the wording, clarity, and completeness of each team's contract. During the remainder of the period, students provided feedback on the workshop and completed an anonymous questionnaire.

Assessment

The workshop is a valuable and worthwhile learning experience for students. It allows the students to learn and practice the skills that are a necessary adjunct to the learning of contract principles and analysis. Most importantly, it provides the students with the confidence that comes with knowing that what they learn in their substantive course has real and useful application in the practice of law. This confidence is reflected in the following student comments:

- "I really enjoyed this group assignment because it showed us the practical application of what we learned throughout the semester."
- "I believe the practical experience provided in this exercise is important to my becoming practice ready."
- "I enjoyed the experience of working with fellow students I didn't know very well."
- "It made me feel like a real lawyer."

Stephen A. Gerst
Phoenix School of Law

Incorporating Skills Training in a Torts Course

I have long thought that students could benefit from a significant hands-on skills experience in a first-year doctrinal course. Ideally such an experience would promote collaborative learning, not only among the first-year students, but also between first-year and upper-level students. It also would be low-tech and low-cost. With those goals in mind, here are the results of an experiment I tried with my first-year Torts students last year.

The Exercise

Last fall I told the students that by the start of spring semester they should have read *Damages* by Barry Werth (Simon & Schuster 1998). *Damages* tells the captivating story of a lawsuit brought against a doctor and a hospital for severe disabilities stemming from the birth of Tony Sabia. I told students this would be their "record" when they and a partner represented a client and arbitrated this case after spring break.

In January I began to use the Sabia case in class to illustrate different negligence principles. This "record" enriched our class discussions, especially concerning the standard of care and causation. It also inspired examination of aspects of trying a tort case that otherwise might not have arisen. (One example involved the ethical issues, coupled with the role of insurance, in directing litigation.) In February the rubber hit the road when students began to prepare their cases. They were most concerned about two things: (1) they didn't know how to try a case and were concerned they would do it "wrong;" and (2) this exercise was too much work.

In response to concerns of doing it wrong, I repeatedly emphasized that this wasn't a trial advocacy experience. Rather, this was an opportunity to apply the law we were studying to *Damages*'s rich factual record. The only way students could do it wrong would be if they prepared poorly and missed the boat on the law and the facts. Rules of evidence would be so relaxed as to be nonexistent.

As for the workload, I considered those concerns and relaxed the extent to which they could utilize each other's work. This also promoted the goal of collaborative learning. Anxieties further diminished when I set aside a 50-minute class session for the teams to caucus privately. This was probably the single best feature of the exercise. Leaders quickly emerged and each group (especially the plaintiffs) caught fire as they plotted strategy and divvied up tasks (e.g., researching specific areas of law, writing expert witness affidavits, and writing portions of a model post-hearing brief).

Students could select their own partner, client (Plaintiff Tony Sabia, Defendant Dr., or Defendant Hospital), and/or date of hearing. When asked questions, I always posted detailed answers on the class website so everyone had the same information.

Students in Advanced ADR served as arbitrators. I emphasized that this was an exceptional opportunity to consider a legal dispute from a neutral perspective. Most students took the arbitration very seriously.

By trading one class hour I created a three-hour time block during regular class time for students to present their cases. Groups could also schedule mutually convenient alternative times. Many hearings lasted longer than three hours.

Students were keenly interested in the results. Arbitrators' decisions were due one week after receipt of post-hearing briefs. Arbitrators emailed their awards directly to me and to each student. I collated the results (without identifying teams by name). They were fascinating. Awards varied widely. Moreover, students were startled that multiple arbitrators who had heard the same case (we had more arbitrators than cases) sometimes reached quite different results. Although the doctor in the actual case had settled for a substantial amount, no arbitrator in our cases assessed any damages against her.

How would I evaluate performance? Each student had to submit one written work product related to the case—and to attest that it was solely his or her effort. The quality of that written assignment would tip final exam grades that were on the cusp either way, and many of my grades are on the cusp. Note: The criticism I received concerning grading was that I was too lenient. Good students wanted more credit for the work they put into this exercise.

Student Feedback

Immediately after the arbitrations I asked all Torts students to provide feedback, anonymously or otherwise. Almost one-half of the class responded, all of them via email and by name. Opinion was divided. Several students said this was a lot of work with little apparent benefit. Others said it was one of the best experiences of their first year (e.g., "This is why I came to law school."). One student said she'd initially been skeptical but, when the attorneys in her office reacted to the exercise so enthusiastically, she threw herself into it and thought it was great.

Conclusion

I believe this exercise provided a valuable learning experience in Torts in several ways:

- It forced all of the students to participate in an alternative learning experience, especially given my belief that all students can benefit from a complex and intense nonwriting skills experience in a first-year doctrinal course, even if they have not had evidence or trial advocacy;
- Working from an actual case permitted consideration of many aspects of a tort lawsuit that would not have arisen in class discussion or wouldn't have made such an impression in a different context (e.g., how plaintiffs' attorneys screen cases, what an insurance company's role is in controlling litigation, etc.); and
- The exercise brought students together.

The arbitration also was valuable for the Advanced ADR students. To the best of my knowledge this was the only educational experience in which they had been a judge, decided a case, and been forced to explain their decisions in detail, in writing.

Despite a few rough spots resulting from my designing and implementing this exercise for the first time, I will make beneficial changes the next time through. I will provide more detailed instructions at the outset. I will drop the doctor as a defendant, since students never understood why she was in the case in the first place and sympathized with her dilemma. Finally, I hope to obtain the assistance of four experienced personal injury attorneys—two plaintiff and two defense—to serve as advisors to Team Tony and Team Hospital. Their perspectives can only enhance the experience.

Christine Ver Ploeg
William Mitchell College of Law

Teaching Statutory Construction through Reverse Problems and "Why" Problems

Many students struggle with statutory interpretation and most find statutes more difficult to analyze than judicial opinions. This is not surprising. After all, in many law schools the bulk of the first-year curriculum consists of common-law subjects, and thus students tend to have more experience with cases than with statutes. Beyond that, cases provide more information than statutes do. Most cases contain three basic components: a story (the facts); a moral or conclusion (the holding); and the reasons supporting that conclusion (the analysis). In other words, they give you a factual context and then tell you what the court is doing and why. Statutes, in contrast, give students only one-third of that: the what. Statutes typically do not either illustrate the facts to which they apply or expressly indicate the reasons underlying their provisions. Yet students do not—and cannot—fully understand a statutory provision until they supply the other two components for themselves. Reverse problems and "why" problems compel students to do this and thus demonstrate to them what they should be doing whenever they must analyze a statute.

Reverse problems do not ask students to determine how the statute applies to a factual pattern. Instead, students are given the statutory text and are asked to provide an example of the facts to which it might apply. In other words, reverse problems ask students to come up with one of the missing components to understanding: the factual context.

Let me illustrate with some examples. Section 2-719 of the Uniform Commercial Code provides that parties are free to alter the normal remedies provided for in the Code, but that if the parties limit remedies and then circumstances cause the limited remedy to "fail of its essential purpose," the Code's normal remedies become available. When we get to this provision, I ask students to come up with an illustration of when a limited remedy would fail its essential purpose. Sometimes I give the assignment in class, and then provide students a few minutes either to think about it or to discuss it with a classmate. More commonly, I give the assignment as part of their homework before class, and in fact have included several reverse problems in the course books I have co-written. Students occasionally flounder in their attempts to respond to these problems but most of the time they come up with a reasonable answer and even have a bit of fun. Here are some more examples, all involving the Uniform Commercial Code.

- Section 2-719(3) provides that an exclusion of consequential damages is presumptively, but not conclusively, unconscionable with respect to personal injury from consumer goods. I ask students to come up with an illustration of when such exclusion would not be unconscionable.
- The definition of "inventory" in § 9-102(a) (48) includes "materials used or consumed in a business." I give them a traditional problem involving a bank's supply of stationery, toner cartridges, and deposit slips. After they realize that this is inventory despite the fact that it is not held for sale, I ask them for an example of inventory not held for sale that would be far more valuable.
- Article 9 deals with a variety of situations in which tangible collateral can be transformed. Some generate "proceeds," some involve "commingled goods," and some involve "accessions." All of these terms are defined in the Code. I like to identify for students a hypothetical debtor's business and the collateral the debtor has offered, then ask the students for an example of each of these types of property.

Reverse problems help students decipher the text of a statute for themselves. The reverse problems thus help students learn to deal with statutes and become more comfortable with them.

"Why" problems work similarly. These problems ask students to identify the reason or reasons underlying a provision. In other words, the problems ask why a statute does or does not do something or why it distinguishes between two different situations. As with reverse problems, "why" problems compel students to supply one of the critical missing pieces of information they need to truly understand a provision.

I tend not to use "why" problems when the answer is obvious. I thus would not inquire why environmental laws prohibit dumping hazardous waste or why criminal codes treat murder differently from manslaughter. When I do use the problems, therefore, they can be very difficult.

For example, Article 9 of the Uniform Commercial Code has many rules on how to perfect a security interest and how to maintain perfection once it is established. One of those rules, §9-315(d)(2), treats second-generation proceeds differently from first-generation proceeds. To illustrate, if Bank has a perfected security interest in Debtor's forklift and Debtor trades the forklift for an elephant, Bank's interest will attach to the elephant and will be perfected. If, however, Debtor had sold the forklift for cash and used the cash to buy an elephant, Bank's interest would attach to the elephant but would likely become unperfected 20 days after Debtor received it. I ask students why the Code creates this dichotomy. The Code itself does not give the reason and neither do the official comments. However, the answer is discernable if the students take the time to think through the issue from the perspective of the relevant party (in this case, the relevant party is not the Bank or the Debtor, it is someone seeking to acquire rights in the elephant from Debtor).

Here are some more examples, again from the U.C.C.:

- Section 9-615(a) provides that junior lienors can be paid out of the proceeds of a foreclosure sale but makes no provision for payment of senior liens. I ask students whether this is an oversight.
- I ask why Article 9 does not indicate that junior liens are discharged when a senior secured party collects on the collateral (such as when the collateral is accounts receivable), as opposed to when the senior sells the collateral.
- Pursuant to §9-615(g), a junior secured party who sells collateral takes the cash proceeds of the sale free of any claim of a senior secured party. I ask students to explain why Article 9 does not provide a similar rule for when a junior secured party collects on the collateral.

"Why" problems work well only if the students already understand both what the statute does and to what it applies. Such problems should therefore be used last in statutory analysis. They do not provide the last word, however. I always follow them up by reminding students that the specific answer is less important than the process we used to obtain it. The students should routinely take the time to identify the reasons that underlie statutory rules because only after students have isolated the rationale will they truly understand the rule. As a bonus, knowing the why makes it easier to remember the rule.

Stephen L. Sepinuck
Gonzaga University School of Law

Teaching the Same Course a Different Way

At Nova Southeastern University Law Center, substantive courses are offered in basically three formats: classes; seminars; and workshops. Classes may contain as many as 100 students and students' grades are typically determined by their performance on an exam. Seminars are generally capped at 18 students, and students are evaluated on a substantial research paper and class participation. Workshops are capped at 20 students, and professors are free to design both the classroom component and the evaluation mechanism as they deem fit.

In the traditional Nonprofit Organizations class we cover issues of state law relating to the formation, operation, and dissolution of nonprofit organizations and charitable solicitation. In addition, we discuss federal tax law concerning the organization and operation of several different types of exempt organizations, particularly charitable, social welfare, and social–recreational organizations. To make room for in-class assignments, I limited the coverage of exempt organizations to public charitable organizations, commonly referred to as 501(c)(3) public charities.

Last year, after having taught a Nonprofit Organizations course as a traditional class several times, I offered the course as a workshop. Because I wanted the workshop to incorporate the learning of both substantive law and practical skills, I pared down the syllabus to allow time for in-class projects and presentations by the students. I had four major goals for the workshop. I wanted the students to:

- Learn what it means to represent charitable organizations as a practicing attorney;
- Become familiar with the substantive law concerning charitable organizations;
- Develop and practice skills that attorneys representing charitable organizations use while representing their clients; and
- Have fun.

During the third week of the workshop, I invited an attorney to speak to the students about representing charitable organizations. By this point in the semester the students had an overview of this area of the law and were able to ask informed questions of the speaker. This accomplished my first goal.

It was important to me that the students learn about the relationships between common law, constitutional law, state statutes and the Internal Revenue Code in the regulation of charitable organizations. The text for the course was Fishman and Schwarz, *Nonprofit Organizations: Cases and Materials* (Foundation Press 2d Ed. 2000), which I supplemented with problems and exercises that I had drafted. During the first part of most of the workshop sessions we covered the material in fairly traditional ways with me at the front of the room. During the second part of the session, the students would divide into small groups to work on problems and other exercises involving the material we had earlier discussed. This gave the students the opportunity to work with their colleagues applying the law to hypothetical fact patterns. In addition, the students were required to write a research paper. This assignment gave the students the opportunity to explore in depth an issue related to charitable organizations that was of particular interest to the student. These three teaching techniques accomplished my second goal.

Providing the students with practical experience was my third goal. I devised two drafting assignments for the workshop. The first assignment was an individual project, the second a group project.

The individual assignment required the students to draft a contract. One complaint that I have often heard uttered by students is that they graduate from law school without having ever drafted a contract, so I decided to include such a project in the workshop. This project required each student to hire an executive director for the organization their group had created, according to the directions set forth in the assignment.

For the group assignment, I had the students divide into self-selected groups of no more than four. Each group was required to form a charitable organization under state law. I did not give the students much more direction than that, although in class we had discussed formation issues and the purposes for which nonprofit organizations can be formed. This exercise required the students to study the Florida statutes to determine which documents were necessary for formation, the filing fees, and where to file. To help the students understand the connection between state nonprofit law regarding formation and federal law regarding qualification as a 501(c)(3) organization, the students were required to draft a memorandum discussing why their organization would be entitled to exemption under 501(c)(3) of the Internal Revenue Code.

The most difficult project to devise for the workshop was the public speaking assignment. In addition to forming a charitable organization, each group was also directed to create some sort of resource tool for the s organization. Some of the examples given to the students included a manual for directors describing their legal duties to the corporation or a guide discussing charitable solicitation. The public speaking assignment required each group to present its organization and resource tool to the class.

The students' projects exceeded my expectations. They developed PowerPoint slides, websites, newsletters, brochures and overhead presentations designed to introduce their organizations to their relevant communities, beneficiaries, and potential donors. While some of the resource tools were not technically legal resources, they were descriptive and informative.

The benefits of offering a course as a workshop are many. Among them are small class size, greater interaction with and between the students, and time during the semester to evaluate assignments and provide feedback to the students. While I will do some tinkering with the workshop based on my evaluations and student comments, I believe that the goals that I had for the course were met. And yes, the students and I had fun.

Angela Gilmore
Nova Southeastern University, Shepard Broad Law Center

Ninety Second Oral Argument Game

To help students think through their arguments in my legal writing class, we do a 90-second oral argument game. I adapted this from my colleague Carol Wallinger, who holds in-class three-minute practice oral arguments, called "lightning rounds." Each student stands up at the podium and answers tough questions posed by the teacher, until a kitchen timer goes off.

I adapted Carol's technique into a kind of game. A couple of weeks before students turn in their briefs, students give me one tough question for each side, Appellant and Appellee. I edit questions to avoid duplication and often add a few key questions. In class, questions for Appellants are in one hat and questions for Appellees are in another. A pair of students draws a question out of the hat, runs into the hall to confer for a minute, then returns, with one student playing the Judge and one student up at the podium on behalf of the Appellant. The Appellant launches into the usual moot court opening, only to be interrupted by the Judge, who poses the question drawn out of the hat (and therefore also has to speak in front of the class), and the lawyer answers. The entire oral exchange is 90 seconds. I ring a bell, everyone applauds, and the next pair is up. The students then switch judge/litigant roles, draw a question from the hat for the Appellee, and repeat the process.

These oral arguments require the students to grapple with a tough question but are low pressure because the opportunity to brainstorm with a partner eliminates the "deer in the headlights" response, and because of the game-like atmosphere of picking questions from a hat, the bell-ringing, applause, and the fast-pace of the short arguments.

Shortly after students turn in their briefs, we do the 90-second oral argument game again. This time, students have read the briefs of their opponents in the upcoming oral argument and, in lieu of a reply brief, students draft three tough questions for the judges to ask their opponents at oral argument. I limit questions to those likely to be relevant to most briefs and then drop questions into hats. We do the 90-second oral argument game again, this time with tougher questions drafted by students more familiar with the law and facts.

Students appreciate the opportunity to briefly simulate the experience of responding to a judge's question at oral argument. Student evaluation comments include:

- "I find that these 90-second arguments reduced my stress in preparation for the real Oral Argument."
- "[C]ollaborating on the 90-second arguments also guided me in my own argument and forced me to confront issues in my brief."
- "The 90-second [arguments] were very helpful because they helped stimulate the quickness of a real oral argument."
- "At the time, I did not like doing the 90-second oral arguments in front of the class. But it had one of the most positive effects on me and subconsciously prepared me for my oral argument."
- "The 90-second practice oral arguments in front of the class did a good job of mimicking the kind of questions in a real oral argument along with the pressure you feel."
- "All of the practice oral arguments were unbelievably helpful. It allowed me and others to overcome any fears of public speaking and also gave us a chance to hear other people discuss the law and the cases out loud."

[An earlier version of this essay appeared as Sarah E. Ricks, *Some Strategies to Encourage Reluctant Talkers to Talk About Law*, 54 J. LEGAL EDUC. 570 (2004).]

Sarah Ricks
Rutgers School of Law–Camden

Chapter 10

Professional Values and Identity

> "Many of life's circumstances are created by three basic choices: the disciplines you choose to keep; the people you choose to be with; and the laws you choose to obey." — Charles Millhuff

Professional values and identity for lawyers stem from an understanding of lawyering in a public responsibility context, setting them apart from the obligations of a private business. Even if lawyering does have characteristics of a business, it is one whose shareholders are all members of society. Therefore, the contract is not simply between lawyer and client, but between lawyer and society.

A. The Need For Professionalism in the Legal Profession

In recent years, the legal profession has paid closer attention to the subjects of professional values and identity. These subjects, sometimes grouped under the rubric of professionalism, have been thrust to the forefront by an increasing public awareness of criminal and unethical behavior by lawyers. Bar associations and inns of court have welcomed the opportunity to explore how to promote and maintain values and identity in the profession.

Within legal education, however, the commitment to studying the professionalism on a systematic basis has faced several obstacles. Traditionally, the discussion of professionalism was largely done on an ad hoc basis, through guest speakers, or designated as part of a self-contained legal ethics course. The traditional ethics course was taught in the latter part of law school and revolved around the Model Code of Professional Responsibility. In many schools the course became a preparatory program for the Multistate Professional Responsibility Examination (MPRE), one of the requirements for admission to the bar, serving to minimize the focus on professionalism independent of the Code and its interpretation. Also, it is difficult to engage students in discussions of professionalism prior to their becoming attorneys and understanding day-to-day life as an attorney. While ethical modeling by professors in their daily discourse can occur, that modeling may not connect to what attorneys do and why they do it.

As the mass media conveys attorney transgressions and criminality to millions of people in an instant, there appears to be a growing demand for instilling in students a commitment to the values and conduct of a professional — and not simply adherence to the statutory minimums set by legislatures through professional ethics codifications. The diverse curricula at many law schools, however, reflect the struggle to reach consensus on how to treat the moral imperative of professional values and identity.

Consequently, while there is agreement that law schools should undertake a greater role in inculcating students in a culture of professionalism, there is no clear path regarding how to achieve this objective. Several approaches to teaching professional values and identity have arisen and will be discussed below. The approaches often turn on how the concept of professionalism is articulated.

B. Defining Professionalism

The concept of professionalism has several different definitions. Some forms of self-conceptualization involve creating a distinctive professional persona, one which adopts internal values and external symbols, such as the formality of dress of the professional culture. A professional person, alternatively, might layer professional attributes over his or her authentic self, so that the professional persona is merely an extension of his or her personal self.

Others believe the basic characteristics of professional lawyers can be understood in terms of a skill set developed as a habitual practice, just like any other skill set. Professor Tom Morgan has developed six "essential characteristics" of professional attorneys that law faculty should model: (1) learned knowledge; (2) skill in applying the relevant law to the facts; (3) thorough preparation; (4) practical and prudential wisdom; (5) ethical conduct and integrity; and (6) dedication to justice and the public good.

The Carnegie Report describes professionalism more as a fiduciary duty lawyers owe to society as a whole:

> Professions operate within ... explicit contract[s] with society.... The basis of these contracts is a set of common goals shared by the public and for which ... professions take responsibility. These are public values, and the core of professional privilege is based on the professions' willingness to commit to them. (21).

This conceptualization places lawyering in the public responsibility context, setting it apart from the obligations of other private business.

Commentators note that aspiring to engage in professional conduct is preferable not just intrinsically, but also instrumentally. The intrinsic value of acting professionally is the reward that comes from doing the right thing. The instrumental benefit is that being a moral actor and ethical attorney promotes efficacy in practice.

C. Teaching Professionalism in Law School

In earlier times, the law school curriculum did not systematically and explicitly teach students about professionalism. In some ways, this made perfect sense, given that law students were just beginning the arc of their professional careers and many students did not understand what lawyers do or the nature of a professional obligation. Instead, it was assumed that nascent lawyers would come to understand through assimilation what it meant to be a professional. Consequently, professionalism was not taught in structured courses next to Torts and Contracts because teaching students to become professionals was premature and would have taken up valuable time which could have been used to teach substantive legal doctrine. Instead, law schools reminded students about professionalism in subtle ways. Schools often had honor codes, a professionalism oath, and guest lecturers from the local or state bar to provide ethical narratives about law practice.

In recent times, professionalism has attained a more explicit status within the law school curriculum. A more critical eye has been cast on the impact of legal education on professional values and identity.

Over the past several decades, sociologists and lawyers have studied the affective domains of legal education and lawyering. The emotive impact of legal education on students has become an important subject to a growing number of professors. Professor Daisy Hurst Floyd, for example, found that negativity in legal education resulted from a variety of factors, including: (1) immersion in a highly competitive environment; (2) increased feelings of failure and inadequacy among most students in the "middle of the pack;" (3) significant focus on short-term goals; (4) devaluation of emotional matters; (5) feelings of isolation; (6) a loss of purpose; (7) reduced expectations of meaning in employment; (8) isolation from classmates; (9) pressure to hide a lack of confidence; (10) overemphasis on learning legal analysis. Professor Floyd has noted, "law school causes students to lose the sense of purpose that made them want to be lawyers. The loss is not only harmful to individual students, but it also has enormous negative consequences for the profession and for those served by the profession." See "Reclaiming Purpose: Our Students and Our Own" in this chapter. Further, Elizabeth Mertz has explored the causes of stress and negativity of law school in *The Language of Law School: Learning to Think Like a Lawyer.*

A growing appreciation of the possible adverse effects of legal education on students led concerned professors to promote humanism in legal education, including the formation of the AALS group, the Section on Balance in Legal Education. (AALS Section on Balance in Legal Education, www.law.fsu.edu/academic_programs/humanizing_lawschool (last visited Mar. 01, 2011)). Recent scholarship explores both theory and practical ideas to further humanism, professionalism, and professional identity in legal education. (Symposium, *Humanizing Legal Education*, 47 Washburn L. J. 235 (2008). See also Rhonda Magee, *Legal Education and the Formation of Professional Identity: A Critical Spirituo-Humanistic—"Humanity Consciousness"—Perspective*, 31 N.Y.U. Rev. L. & Soc. Change 467 (2007)).

Professional identity and professionalism, even when considered significant, can be challenging to teach. Below are a variety of approaches to incorporating professional values and identity throughout the law school education.

1. *Modeling*

One way to instill professional behavior in students is to model it, so that it is "evident in the words and conduct of the faculty, administration, and staff, especially the faculty." (*Best Practices for Legal Education* at 129). Modeling concerns the measurable, from being on time to class and office hours, to the subjective, such as how a professor responds to student questions or technology glitches in class.

2. *Placing Students in a Professional Role*

The term "role playing" can understate the value and importance of students acting as lawyers in the classroom. While students in traditional classroom settings learn how to act as law students, from answering questions and taking notes, this learning does not directly serve them in other settings, such as law practice. By allowing students to experience the role of a professional in class, students gain appreciation for the skills required, the elements of professionalism, and the process and pace of lawyering. Realistic simulations of law practice also help students to understand how their grades on exams might not accurately reflect their skill level for lawyering in real life.

3. *A Narrative Technique*

Some professors have utilized a narrative technique, storytelling, to teach professionalism. This approach allows a much broader and contextual analysis of lawyer behavior; far beyond the cognitive "thinking like a lawyer" that is the core of much of legal education. Storytelling allows students who have not experienced lawyering to get a glimpse of it on many levels: cognitive, affective and kinesthetic. It allows them to better appreciate how certain types of behaviors occur. For example, Professor Hank Shea, of St. Thomas University in Minnesota, has interviewed and recorded former lawyers who have engaged in significant criminality, generally in the area of white collar crime. Shea, a former Assistant United States Attorney, asks these individuals on video how they ended up on the path that led them to prison, which can teach powerful lessons to law students.

4. Professionalism Centers

Several schools have created centers for ethics and professionalism. These centers have opened pathways for a dialogue about professionalism as part of the lawyering role. Further, the centers elevate the importance of professionalism relative to the other subjects students are studying. These centers have different orientations and descriptions, but all attempt to forward the discourse about professional lawyering. These centers include: The Halloran Center of Leadership at the St. Thomas University School of Law in Minnesota; the Center for Ethics, Service and Professionalism at Thomas Cooley Law School; and the Nelson, Mullins, Riley & Scarborough Center on Professionalism at the University of South Carolina School of Law, to name a few.

5. Professionalism Oaths

Many schools ask students to take professionalism oaths, fashioned after the oath taken by students in medical schools. For example, Texas Tech Law School offers the oath in the context of a ceremony at the beginning of law school. Co-author Michael Schwartz suggests later in this chapter that the relevancy and meaningfulness of these oaths can be promoted by asking students to craft their own professionalism oaths.

References

- Daisy Hurst Floyd, *The Development of Professional Identity in Law Students*, (June 2002) (unpublished manuscript), http://www.law.fsu.edu/academic_programs/humanizing_lawschool/images/daisy.pdf (last visited Mar. 1, 2011).
- Neil Hamilton & Verna Monson, *The Empirical Relationship of Professionalism to Effectiveness in the Practice of Law*, 24 Geo. J. of Legal Ethics 137 (2010).
- Ruth Ann McKinney, *Depression and Anxiety in Law Students: Are We Part of the Problem and Can We Be Part of the Solution?*, 8 J. Legal Writing Inst. 229 (2002).
- Elizabeth Mertz, The Language of Law School: Learning to "Think Like a Lawyer"(2007).
- Thomas D. Morgan, *Law Faculty as Role Models*, in A.B.A. Section of Leg. Ed. & Admissions to the Bar, Teaching & Learning Professionalism, Symposium Proceedings (1997).
- Edmund Rostran, *Tech Law School Hosts Annual Pledge of Professionalism*, The Daily Toreador, Aug. 26, 2010, http://www.dailytoreador.com/search.
- Roy Stuckey et al., Best Practices for Legal Education: A Vision and a Road Map (2007).

- William M. Sullivan et al., Educating Lawyers: Preparation for the Profession of Law (2007).
- Symposium, *Humanizing Legal Education*, 47 Washburn L. J. 235 (2008).
- Mark Weisberg & Jacalyn Duffin, *Evoking the Moral Imagination: Using Stories to Teach Ethics and Professionalism to Nursing, Medical and Law Students*, 16 J. of Medical Humanities 247 (1995).

Getting Students to Invest in Professionalism Oaths

A number of law schools have begun requiring their students to swear to oaths of professionalism during the students' law school orientation experiences. The schools bring in judges or even justices of their state supreme courts, have the students raise their right hands, and, then, swear to the oath. Typically, these oaths include promises to act honestly and professionally, to respect others and themselves, and to serve the profession, and their communities. This wonderful idea, however, has one important and challenging limitation; how do you get the students to see the words they are speaking as meaningful?

At Washburn, we have put what we believe to be an important spin on this idea. All entering students are placed in small, structured study groups led by closely-supervised, upper-division, second- and third-year students. These groups meet several times throughout orientation and twice per week throughout their first semester of law school. Accordingly, team-building is a crucial enterprise.

Consequently, each group's first project is to research the notion of professionalism, particularly in the legal profession, and to collaboratively draft its own oath of professionalism. The dean of the law school and the judge who will be administering the oath select the best oath and the students are sworn in using that oath.

This process has several decided advantages. First, it forces students to reflect on their own understandings of professionalism and to expand their understandings of the idea by collaborating with their peers. To complete the exercise, the groups must inscribe themselves in the concept of professionalism. Second, the process of collaborating serves as an icebreaker. It causes the groups to work together, to exchange ideas, and to begin developing camaraderie. Third, it creates excitement; students really hope their group's oath is selected. Finally, it converts what could be a superficial experience into one that is truly meaningful.

So far, the winning oaths have been at least as good, if not better, than anything a faculty committee could have authored. By way of example, this year's winning oath was:

> I, _______________, hereby commit to myself and to those who came before me to uphold the traditions and values the legal profession exemplifies. In addition, it is my responsibility to assist in paving the way for the legal professionals of the future. I will demonstrate the values of Washburn by acting with integrity, focusing on the betterment of my community, and continuing to pursue my learning beyond graduation. This oath is more than a ceremony. I, as a legal professional to be, recognize that it is both a duty and privilege and commit to uphold this oath from this day forward.

Michael Hunter Schwartz
Washburn University School of Law

Teaching Values and Lawyering Skills

Teachers of law school classes can effectively teach how values influence policy decisions and communicate the role of values in the management of law as a profession. I will describe an exercise I have used in an interviewing and counseling course that, along with other lessons, demonstrates how students' personal values will influence the character and quality of their representation of their clients. I developed the exercise to serve as a vehicle for teaching students about the importance of client decision making in the counseling process. In using the exercise, I have found that it may be useful in a wide variety of skills courses, clinical courses, professional responsibility offerings, and other courses in which the instructor is interested in teaching about the effect of values upon lawyering skills.

The Exercise

At the beginning of the exercise, I tell the students they will need to play two roles. For one role I ask them to imagine they are all partners in a small law firm looking for a *pro bono* project. As partners, they will listen to potential clients present their cases. They will not be able to ask the clients questions, but, after hearing the clients' stories, they, as the firm's partners, will have to decide upon one client to represent. They are to assume that none of the clients can afford an attorney or arrange to have the case handled on a contingency basis.

In addition to having the students play firm partners, I assign each student to a client group. In a class of about twenty students, the groups are usually made up of two or three students, and the students in each group are to plan how best to present the client's case to the firm. The students must also choose one or more students in the group to role play the client before the firm. Each client group is given a written description of less than a page outlining their client's problem.

A wide variety of client cases may be developed for the simulation, and faculty members might create some in their areas of substantive law interest. In my simulation, one client is a married couple with a young child. A neighbor made an abuse complaint to the state's child protection agency and a social worker from that agency removed the child. The agency has not yet held or scheduled a hearing. The clients want to require the state to hold an immediate hearing and they wish to get the child back. Another client is a single mother with three young children. She and her children receive public assistance. In the past, the father of two of the children has given her some money, but he no longer does. The department of public welfare, apparently aware of the father's past contributions, is terminating the family's public assistance. The client's only income now is public assistance and she doesn't know how she'll get by without it. Other clients I have included in the exercise in the past are a man who has been charged with battering his wife and needs representation, researchers who have come up with a drug they believe will block the development of AIDS but cannot afford to fight the Food and Drug Administration on licensing, and a group of women who have been discriminated against in hiring and promotion by a large local employer.

During class, I call upon the various client groups to present their clients' cases before the firm (the full class). After all of the groups have presented their client's cases, I ask the full class to decide which client the firm will represent.

Observations and Lessons Learned

While the class decides upon a client to represent, I take copious notes on the decision-making process, focusing on how students who have played various clients behave when their clients' cases are discussed. Following the role play, I make some observations about student behavior during the exercise and the effect of values on that behavior. I try to do much of this through questions, but I resort to comments when appropriate or needed.

Although the order in which I handle topics will vary from class to class, I usually try to cover points on client behavior, advocacy, decision making, and how the students' values affected their behavior in the exercise. I consider the observations and conclusions about how values affect advocacy to be the most important lesson that students can learn. Students whose values support taking the case of the client that they have played in the exercise will most often be a strong advocate for that client after switching to the role of firm partner. Those students whose values would oppose taking the case of the client they played will disassociate from that client in the firm role. A student, for example, might yell out during the decision process, "Get rid of the child abusers." The association and disassociation that occur in the exercise mirror that of the practicing bar. Real-life lawyer–client identification and disassociation are often more subtle than that of my students', but it is no less real.

Many of us who have practiced law have seen lawyers sabotage the cases of the clients where the lawyer's views of right and wrong conflicted with a positive outcome for the client. We also have seen the lawyer blinded to opposing positions by myopic allegiance to the client's cause. My main hope for the exercise is that students, having experientially come to understand the effects values can have on a lawyer's performance, will be able to see the effects of values in their own practices and correct for them. There are other lessons as well.

One very positive aspect of the exercise is that an instructor neither needs to nor should make judgments about the relative importance of the values expressed. An implicit lesson is that it is important to respect, within certain limits, others' values and not be overly critical because of these differences.

Another lesson for the students is in understanding client motivations and behavior. The students, in having to put themselves in the roles of clients, are in a better position to understand client behavior in the interview process. Some students, in playing the client roles, omit facts that may result in their cases not being accepted by the firm. Others exaggerate the facts to ensure that their cases get accepted. In general, this form of advocacy mostly exists with students who sympathize with their assigned client. I hope that by seeing how some students playing clients will stretch the truth, the class members overall will have more understanding of their own future clients' willingness to do the same thing. Students also may find that simply having played the client may cause a student to develop a loyalty through the association, albeit a fictional one. This behavior mirrors that of the practicing attorney, who, having spent time with a client, will begin to develop a similar kind of loyalty.

Another lesson concerns the types of arguments lawyers make. This fundamental lesson is an implicit part of many law school classes. The exercise's lesson on the types of arguments provides an explicit lesson on how the students, as clients, appealed to the law firm decision-makers and how, as law firm partners, they advocated having the firm accept a particular client. Students may discuss advocacy points, including the need to evaluate the decision-maker and the use of emotional appeal, detail, posture, and self-interest. Taking detailed notes, including quotations, during both parts of the exercise, one will be able to lead a discussion on the types of arguments students made, specific examples of them, and their effectiveness.

During the decision-making process, students may discuss the appropriate role of *pro bono* cases and factors attorneys should consider in deciding whether or not to take the cases. Occasionally, students weigh in heavily with points about how a case will require minimal effort, might bring the firm helpful publicity, or not be troublingly controversial. Other students invariably argue against considering these factors and some will even declare the factors inappropriate.

During the decision-making process, students inevitably make assumptions about the clients and the clients' cases. For example, students have suggested that the welfare termination case will be easy. They have suggested that both the man accused of domestic violence and the couple whose child was removed are culpable. Another point one might raise during the discussion of the decision-making process is about our willingness to make unwarranted assumptions. While working hypotheses are needed, relying upon untested assumptions causes incorrect decisions and poor advocacy.

Applications in the Law School Curriculum

The exercise highlights in an interviewing and counseling course why attorneys need to foster client-centered decision-making. As students discern how their values have affected the ways they select a particular *pro bono* case, they become more aware that attorneys must not impose decisions upon clients who may have different values. In alternative dispute resolution courses, the simulation can help mediation students see both why they need to determine what is of value to the parties and why the outcome they, as mediators, might want to impose may not be best for the parties involved.

Professional responsibility is another course in which the exercise might be used to foster the lesson of client-centered decision-making. The simulation could lead to a discussion of how dissonance between a professional responsibility requirement and attorney values may affect behavior.

The exercise could easily become a part of the classroom component for a clinical course. Having taken students through the simulation, a clinical professor could more easily address with students issues raised in the simulation when they arise in clinic cases; for example, a student's failure to pursue a client's case aggressively when that student's values are in conflict with the client's behavior or desired remedy.

The exercise may help some of our students avoid the flaw Gerald Brenan ascribed to intellectuals. "Intellectuals are people who believe that ideas are of more importance than values. That is to say, their own ideas and other people's values." (GERALD BRENAN, THOUGHTS IN A DRY SEASON, (1978)).

John Capowski
Widener University School of Law

Developing Students' Professional Interpersonal Skills

"Being willing to admit when you are wrong." A 3L named this as one of the most important attributes of people who were good at working with their classmates. She'd been surprised to find that the ability to admit mistakes and apologize were more important qualities than academic prowess or hard work. Having a solid work ethic, competence, and integrity were certainly important for professional collaboration, but these she considered minimum standards. What made her classmates truly desirable as collaborators was their humility.

We know from surveys of the bench and bar that the ability to work with others is important for practice. One large international law firm names "Citizenship—developing self and others, teamwork and collaboration" as one of the four most important skills associates should develop. Most students know how to behave as professionals. We can help our students learn and practice professionalism skills by harnessing their experiences and knowledge. Below is one way I have facilitated the development of these skills.

Method

In each course I teach, whether large, small, required, or elective, I enlist students' collective wisdom in identifying the attributes of professionalism and the ways to promote it. During the course, students get feedback on their performance as professionals, and "professional engagement" becomes a portion of their grade for the course, usually 10 to 20%. Attaching a grade to the professionalism component is important for two reasons. First, I want students to understand that this is an important part of their learning in the course, and second, I want students to pay attention to professionalism. As others have said, "people pay attention to what you *inspect*, not what you *expect*."

Setting Professionalism Goals and Consequences

Within the first two weeks of the semester, students have three minutes to work in small groups to identify at least three important professional behaviors they want their classmates to use. Calling on one group at a time, I elicit one new attribute until all are listed on the board. The students almost always identify everything that I consider important professional behavior. Their classmates should show respect, listen, contribute, not dominate, be prepared and on time, and communicate well. As a class, we agree that these behaviors are the criteria for evaluating their professional engagement. I explain that every letter of recommendation I write will include information about a student's ability to act as a professional.

Working again in small groups, students have three minutes to identify a consequence for a student who fails to engage as a professional. Some groups recommend that students should lose professional engagement points, but others come up with creative alternatives. As a class, we agree on the consequences. One semester, for example, we adopted a student's suggestion that students arriving late to class had to dance to their seats, which resulted in very few students being late that term. Perfection is not the goal. As in practice, there are times when we get in stuck in traffic or are less prepared than usual because of conflicting demands. If these are rare events, they are forgiven, particularly if we communicate and take responsibility for our lapses. Students receive full professionalism points at the beginning of the course; these points are theirs to lose.

Promoting Professional Engagement During the Semester

During the semester, I publicly thank students for being well prepared and engaging in the identified professional behaviors. In doing so, I note how students' positive interactions are connected to practicing law effectively. Pointing out when students are acting professionally usually helps their classmates who aren't. For example, after I noted in class how well one small group had worked together—they had all moved close together, took turns speaking, made eye contact, encouraged each other, and referred to authorities—all the other small groups adopted the same behaviors. When those cues don't work, or when students' behavior is extremely unprofessional, I have talked to them in private, asking them to tell me about their experience in class. Every student has started by apologizing for the unprofessional behavior before I have said anything. Usually a student has tremendous regrets and we discuss ways to remedy any problem or prevent its recurrence. In class, we talk about stress and how it hinders our ability to act our best.

I keep notes on students' highly professional interactions and their lapses throughout the semester. When students have been in class for about one-third to one-half of the semester, they get feedback on how well they are doing as professionals. Based on the professionalism criteria identified at the beginning of the course, I will let them know of any lapses that threaten their ability to earn full professionalism points. Alternatively, when students have been working within the same small groups, those in their groups provide them with feedback. This feedback is not graded. It is designed to help them see how well they are meeting professional criteria and to provide notice of areas they need to improve. It also serves to open a discussion if their professionalism self-assessment differs from their classmates' or mine. The goal is that everyone who has received constructive feedback will improve; the assumption is that everyone can still earn full professionalism points.

Evaluating Professionalism

As with mid-semester feedback, at the end of the semester I review my notes on students' performance in class and allocate points. The vast majority of students earn full professionalism points. All of the students who earn lower scores have had feedback and multiple opportunities to improve. While it is disappointing when students do not act professionally, it is important to remember that this is part of their development, and it is heartening to hear later when they have learned from their mistakes. As a 3L student said, "I regret nothing as much as the way I behaved my first semester. I acted like a jerk and have been working for two years to get over that reputation." I was happy to be listed as a reference for him.

Sophie Sparrow
University of New Hampshire School of Law

Teaching Students about the Role of Lawyer as Counselor: Winning Isn't Always Everything

When I first started teaching a course on contract drafting, I was taken aback by my students' attitudes towards client representation: they believed that a lawyer's role was to "win," even if it encouraged lawsuits in the process. "Why draft a contract to avoid the need for litigation when you can represent your client in the lawsuit?" and, "Why not make yourself look good to your client by winning the lawsuit based on a favorable contract interpretation?" were some of the sentiments that I heard. Having practiced law for more than ten years before entering the teaching profession, I knew that such attitudes were impractical, improbable, and bordering on the unethical.

Should I really have been surprised by my students' reactions? From the very first day of law school, in all of their first-year required courses, students learn about the law through the lens of litigated cases and through the eyes of a lawyer in the role of advocate—a lawyer that is supposed to argue for a particular position or a cause. For example, in their Contracts class, my students had learned about the principles of contract law by reading the courts' opinions in litigated cases. The classroom discussion most likely centered on the types of arguments that can be made for or against any particular issue. Their exams probably asked them to play the role of a judge evaluating arguments or a lawyer arguing for or against a particular outcome. In other words, law school classes generally portray lawyers as advocates and teach students "to think like a lawyer" by teaching them to argue.

Even for those of our students who will be future litigators, I believe that we have a duty to teach them about the role of the lawyer as counselor, and not only devote our time and efforts on the lawyer's role as advocate. A lawyer fills the role of counselor when she gives advice and represents her client, but unlike the lawyer as advocate, she does so without necessarily arguing for a particular position or cause. Lawyers serve crucial roles that do not focus on making arguments or "winning", but on planning, advising, and counseling their clients on a wide variety of matters, such as risk assessment, avoidance of potential legal problems, and the resolution of disputes without resorting to litigation.

To a client, the lawyer's role certainly is not always about winning a case; it is generally in a client's best interests to avoid litigation. As stated by President Lincoln in his Notes for Law Lecture in 1850 (and quoted by Chief Justice Warren E. Burger in his Forward to the American Law Institute's Study on Paths to a "Better Way"): "Discourage litigation. Persuade your neighbors to compromise whenever you can. Point out to them how the nominal winner is often a real loser—in fees, expenses and waste of time." Since clients do not want to spend time and money to litigate matters unnecessarily, a better client relationship (and thus an enhanced lawyer's reputation) is often based on the ability to avoid, not necessarily win, litigation. This is true for many different types of lawyers, but especially for the transactional lawyer who negotiates and drafts contracts. The goal of the transactional lawyer is to effectuate the client's needs and desires; namely, to draft a contract that protects his client's rights, but that will likely be performed by both parties to the transaction and thus not end up in litigation.

While practicing lawyers know that they often represent their clients without ever arguing or advocating on their behalf, many law students do not. When I developed my contract drafting course, I consciously decided to focus on introducing my students to the role of lawyer as counselor. We extensively discuss how a lawyer can best represent her client in the various stages of contract drafting and negotiating, by planning, advising, and counseling clients. I structure the course using the case file method so that my students represent a particular client throughout the semester. The contract drafting assignments require them to draft contracts that protect their client's interests, but are fair and not so one-sided that they will be rejected by the other party. We also discuss ways to protect a client's interests by drafting a contract that is easily understood by the lay parties to the contract, in an effort to avoid the need for court intervention and interpretation. At first, some of my students struggled with these concepts. Some students still drafted contracts that were so biased towards their clients' position that they would likely be summarily rejected by the other party. Other students went to the opposite extreme and drafted contracts that did not adequately protect their clients' interests. Fortunately, after engaging in role-playing exercises where the students were paired up and represented their respective clients to negotiate and jointly draft contract terms, the students began to better understand, and appreciate, the role of lawyer as counselor.

Thus, while most traditional law school courses will continue to teach students through the use of litigated cases and to emphasize the lawyering skills of argument and advocacy, I think that we should also at least aim to teach them about the role of lawyer as counselor. For starters, we need to expose law students to the role of lawyer as counselor in many of their courses, side by side with teaching them about the role of lawyer as advocate.

After reviewing cases in class, professors can ask their students not only about the arguments that each side could have made, but about *whether* the lawyers should have advised their clients to take this case to trial in the first place. The resulting discussion is likely to be the same, but with a slightly different focus to the question, law students can begin to realize the importance of the role of the lawyer as counselor. Law professors should also consider asking their students to think about *why* a particular case ended up in litigation; was it the result of any misconception or error on the part of the lawyer that might have been resolved without resorting to litigation? For example, many, if not most, breach of contract cases result from poor drafting of the contract's language, which could have been rectified by the lawyers in the planning and drafting phases. Similarly, risk assessment and risk reduction advice from lawyers could limit the number of tort cases that are litigated. Lawyers have a duty to counsel their clients on ways to avoid potential legal disputes as much as they have a duty to strongly advocate on behalf of their clients if those disputes arise.

Therefore, I advocate for professors to start teaching students about the role of the lawyer as counselor throughout their law school experience, since winning isn't always everything.

Susan M. Chesler
Arizona State University, Sandra Day O'Connor College of Law

Is God on Your Seating Chart? Discussing Religious Beliefs in Class

Visit any law school class and one thing will quickly become apparent. Logic rules. Arguments are raised and dissected, weaknesses laid bare under the cool white light of legal analysis. What is a penumbra, and what does it have to do with the U.S. Constitution? How do we find these penumbras? Are they visible only during a full moon? This sort of tongue-in-cheek questioning always brings a knowing chuckle from the students. Reasoning this way—the banter of linguistic logic—is comfortable, fun.

On top of logic (or perhaps underneath it) there is experience. We owe this to the legal realists, who taught us to pay attention to the goings-on of the real world, where the rubber meets the road, so to speak. Today in class we'll discuss the death penalty. Let's start with a few studies from the social sciences, check out what sociologists say about the racial imbalance on death row, or how social psychologists score the deterrent effect of the death penalty. Hopefully experience and logic will align, and the students will leave class with a beginner's level of understanding of the area of law covered.

But what about belief? What about God?

Belief is generally not subject to logical scrutiny. At its simplest, belief merely exists in the mind of the person holding that belief. Anyone who has taught in a law school for a year or two will have come across a student who, when pressed to back up an argument with logic, will reply with a frustrated, "I'm sorry, that's just the way I feel!" That is belief. When confronted with a statement of belief, most of us law teachers will give a figurative shrug by saying little or nothing. We turn the page, starting a new volley with another student.

Belief comes from many sources; bias, ignorance, personal experience, parental teachings. Belief also comes from religion. This is a special category of belief, deserving special attention in the law school classroom. The reason for this special attention begins with the first amendment to the Constitution, where religious expression is provided with clear legal protection. The law—and by extension legal education—must accommodate this particular form of belief.

A second reason for the special treatment of religion in legal education is that religious belief usually isn't a knee-jerk, "that's just the way I feel" belief, but is more sophisticated, part of a whole-world view of how to decide right and wrong and, more broadly, how to live life. Often, adding religion to the mix in discussing the policy and social implications of a given legal doctrine will add significant depth to that discussion, and the discussion will resonate with more of the students. In this regard, numbers count. The student who says, "that's just the way I feel," probably stands alone in a classroom in his or her belief. A student who speaks from religious principle may speak for many others in the class.

A colleague of mine who teaches professional responsibility asks students each year to analyze a moral problem based on (1) the Golden Rule; (2) Rule Utilitarianism; or (3) some other value system with which the given student feels comfortable. The responses are written out and handed in. In each class, at least 10% of the students base their answers on religious beliefs. I expect the actual percentage of students with deeply held religious values is greater than that, but some students feel constrained to use Rule Utilitarianism or the Golden Rule because they seem more lawyerly. The point is, like it or not, our students bring God to class.

Despite the fact that many of our students are religious, their beliefs often stay far below the surface, in part because religious concepts are not readily applicable to much of the law school curriculum. Contracts, Property, tax courses, Business Organizations, and Civil Procedure fall into this category. The substance of these courses seems so far removed from religious doctrine that religion is rarely an issue. At the other end of the spectrum, religion is at the heart of some courses: First Amendment, International Human Rights, and Legal History, to name a few. In these courses, religion is usually treated as an abstraction, a "right." This takes much of the edge off the conversation. Religious and nonreligious students alike can speak freely, using the logic of "rights talk."

The trickier courses are those that demand subtle comparative moral/policy judgments from the students. To make these judgments, many students rely on beliefs as well as logic and experience. I have observed this firsthand in teaching courses such as Feminist Jurisprudence, Wealth Redistribution, and, currently, Law & Anthropology. The difference is profound. Whereas logic is a cool white light, religious belief can be red hot. Emotions run high. Voices rise and quake. Tempers flare. At its worst, religion can become oddly profane in a class, a taboo subject. To avoid this, I have tried a number of things over the years and have settled on a few rules of thumb.

Suppose in the middle of a discussion of same-sex marriage (or some other controversial subject) a student says, "I'm a Lutheran, and we believe...." My first rule of thumb is that such a comment is not inappropriate. Still, the comment probably will land with a thud. The other students are simply not equipped to handle it. But handle it we will. I let the student finish, and then, with as little fanfare as possible, I point out that this is a religious belief. I might say something like, "So this comes from your church?" After the student assents (usually with a tight nod), I will say, "Okay. Not everyone here is Lutheran. What can those people learn from this?" Often—usually, in fact—the student will compare the Lutheran view with some other aspect of our course, something with which the others feel more comfortable. Students begin to nod, or shake their heads, and the conversation moves on. We have succeeded in drawing the religious belief into the fold of the day's discussion.

If the above doesn't work, if our putative Lutheran cannot tell us how non-Lutherans can learn from his or her comment, I will ask one further question: "If we hold with the doctrine of separation of church and state, how can your belief properly inform the law?" Many religiously inclined students will take a stab at this by pointing out, for example, that voters carry their religious beliefs into the voting booth, and so we need to understand their beliefs if we are fully to understand the way the law is shaped. If no one else has a comment, I will let the subject drop there, passing on to the next argument, the next student. Meanwhile, our Lutheran is likely satisfied, having had his or her day before the court of classroom opinion. Keep in mind that this is belief we are discussing. It cannot be challenged with logic: to do so would be illogical. All we can do with belief is know it for what it is and add it to our repository of experience.

That is my positive spin on religious belief in the classroom. I also have two negative rules, two never-evers. I never let a demeaning comment about a religion or a religious group pass without comment from me. I usually keep it low key, such as, "That's a pretty sweeping generalization." Or, "I'd want to see some proof before I went further with that line of reasoning." The students learn quickly that religious put-downs are not going to win any converts.

My second negative rule is that I never give any indication of my own religious views. To do so would be distracting and overreaching, and would cause concern even to those students who hold the same beliefs as I. This does present a neat post-modernist quandary. My beliefs inevitably will shape my classroom conduct, so why hide them? To maintain my power position vis-a-vis the class, goes the post-modernist argument. To this I plead not guilty. My goal as a law teacher is to convey the material in any given course, including policy, philosophy, black-letter rules, background facts and all else that is reasonably relevant. Expressing my beliefs would only get in the way of that goal. On the other hand, student beliefs, particularly religious beliefs, can be informative and bring us all to a deeper level of understanding.

Robert L. Palmer
George Washington University Law School

The Real World: Teaching Professionalism in Virtual Dialogue to the Google Generation

Current law students are accustomed to virtual communication. Indeed, virtual communication in the form of email and Internet dialogue is the primary means of written communication for the younger Generation X and Millennial Generation students. Moreover, a cursory review of the latest trends in toddler and preschool age toys and educational directives suggests that subsequent generations will be characterized by a proficiency in virtual dialogue. While this may bode well for the efficiency of law practice in the future, certain aspects of virtual communication give rise to subtle and, at times, remarkable, lapses in professionalism. In fact, certain attributes of virtual communication, including its immediacy, lack of intimacy, and lack of nonverbal visual cues, can create an impression of unprofessional behavior, particularly when viewed through the lens of a reader who is a member of a generation less accustomed to virtual dialogue. This sometimes becomes apparent in virtual communication by law students which is either directed at, or viewed by, professors and/or professionals in practice.

In this context we have, in recent years, been disappointed by lapses in professionalism by our students in email dialogue and web communication, such as on blogs and social network sites (e.g., Facebook, MySpace). Some lapses are readily apparent—demanding or dismissive tone, clearly inappropriate content—while others are far more subtle and in all likelihood unintentional. Because lapses in communication have a detrimental effect on legal education and law practice, we decided that the pedagogy of legal rhetoric should include a focused analysis of professionalism in communication, particularly virtual communication. We deemed this essential to educating our students about all types of communication that lend themselves to advocacy, the goal of good lawyering. We sensed, however, that the biggest obstacle to the success of our objective would be to identify lapses in professionalism that professors and professionals would acknowledge, but that might be less apparent and therefore potentially insulting to students. We therefore elected to discuss these issues in a workshop environment. We also deliberately focused on the presentation method, opting to illustrate the concepts in a virtual presentation format, (i.e., an actual email dialogue and realistic web communication) to link the teaching methodology with the perceived problem (and solution). The realistic presentation methodology would not only reinforce the concepts, but would resonate with the students' reality, and therefore reveal the consequences of unprofessional communication. The corresponding impact on efficacy of advocacy, we felt, would similarly be clear.

Our workshop focused on two types of virtual communication: email and personal web pages. Because our students regularly use their laptops in class, we devised a PowerPoint that had integrated links to a fictitious email exchange and some fictitious personal web pages. The email exchange reflected a hypothetical dialogue between lawyers in a law firm; the personal web pages depicted two of the law firm associates who had engaged in the email dialogue. Both categories included exaggerated as well as subtle lapses in professionalism.

Prior to directing students to the email exchange, we discussed some specific attributes of virtual communication that give rise to lapses in professionalism. For example, because virtual communication is less formal than other types of communication and because it is instantaneous, it leads students to believe that they do not need to incorporate the conventions of professionalism common in other forms of written correspondence. Moreover, the personal nature of email correspondence, web pages, and blogs gives writers a sense of privacy that does not actually exist. Following the identification of these attributes, we discussed current news stories illustrating the serious repercussions that may flow from the failure to adhere to conventions of professionalism in virtual communication.

We then directed the students' attention to the fictitious email exchange that illustrated communication between associate and associate, associate and senior associate, and associate and partner. Current research suggests that both Generation X and Millennials are skeptical of authority and therefore less cognizant of professionalism concerns relating to a hierarchy of authority. (*At A Glance: Employee Groups by Generation*, HEALTHCARE REGISTRATION, Jan. 2007, at 6, noting that Generation X employees tend to be "resourceful; tech-savvy; selective in terms of seeking opportunities that allow them to enjoy working with friends; selective in terms of seeking opportunities based on the expectation that work will be purposeful; and skeptical of institutions."). The email exchange between various actors in this fictitious scenario was therefore intended to illustrate the very real hierarchy of authority that exists in the practice of law. The email exchange focused on assigning associates to work on a client matter and was designed to reinforce concepts of professionalism relating to respect for colleagues, clients and client matters, and legal processes.

Incorporating the links to the email exchanges and web pages not only presented the information in a manner that more closely mirrors reality, but also allowed us to take advantage of technology in our presentation. For example, it allowed us to provide the students with direction via projected slides while they turned their attention to the web links.

When we turned our students' attention to the email exchanges, we asked them to break into smaller groups and work through the exchanges together to identify lapses of professionalism. We also directed them to identify instances where the communicators exhibited the type of professionalism one would hope to see in a law practice. We then came back together as a class to focus on respect for authority, respect for business and legal processes, and respect for issues of privacy and/or confidentiality. The teaching process was a collaboration with the students that allowed them to make conclusions about professionalism and take ownership of the solutions identified. Students enjoyed the informal atmosphere and limited humorous content we incorporated, but they took examination of the material seriously and were able to identify both intentional and unintentional lapses in professionalism. Moreover, they were able to offer suggestions as to how the communication could be modified to meet expectations about professional dialogue.

Our workshop has several attributes that made it an ideal tool for teaching students the boundaries of professionalism in informal virtual communication. The workshop not only presented some of the information through humorous and entertaining examples, but was also both informal and collaborative. It proved to be an effective method of highlighting for students what professionalism is and how it impacts their virtual communication in and out of the workplace, as well as how it impacts their ability to be effective and satisfied lawyers.

Melissa H. Weresh
Drake University Law School

Lisa Penland
Drake University Law School

Teaching Restorative Justice Practices

Restorative justice is an integral part of the Community Justice Project's core curriculum. The Community Justice Project ("CJP") is a civil rights legal clinic where law students are trained to become not just lawyers, but engineers of social change. During the clinic experience, CJP students explore the historical roots of restorative justice and practical implementation of restorative principles, while drawing upon principles of community-building, reconciliation and peacemaking.

A restorative justice curriculum should combine reflective learning, introduction of theoretical perspectives and experiential learning. The restorative justice component of the CJP curriculum includes readings related to the philosophy of restorative justice and practical application of restorative justice principles. These readings are: *The Little Book on Restorative Justice* (Howard Zehr, 2002) and "Restoring Community: The Process of Circle Sentencing" (Kay Pranis, 1997). CJP students are challenged to reflect upon the meaning of restorative justice during their reading by comparing and contrasting the traditional criminal justice system with restorative justice principles. This discussion combines intellectual stimulation and aesthetic values as students seek to draw upon metaphors related to restorative justice. These metaphors include: flower (representing an organic process); wheel (representing the significance of "putting right wrongs and harms"); and river (representing change in landscape, course and interconnectedness of community). CJP students have also created their own metaphors to add to the restorative justice discourse. These metaphors include: community garden, bridges, spiral of interactions, dove and butterfly.

In subsequent class lectures and discussions, CJP students continue to reflect upon the principles of restorative justice and seek opportunities to explore the transformative power of restorative justice. These reflections have a lasting impact as law students begin to identify key values that they seek to espouse as future legal professionals.

CJP students also discuss ways to build restorative communities. In class discussions, students share their definitions of community and identify core values of restorative communities. This discussion aids students in identifying their active, participatory role as community members by building communities that value hope, respect and interrelatedness. Further, students explore the history of restorative justice in other cultural contexts, which aids in the development of cross-cultural competency. Students are challenged to explore the historical roots of restorative justice, which extend far beyond Western influences. This includes exploration of the Sub-Saharan ideology of "ubuntu," by which a lawyer has the responsibility to uphold justice and equity for all. The 1997 South African Governmental White Paper for Social Welfare highlights that:

> Each individual's humanity is ideally expressed through his or her relationship with others and theirs in turn through recognition of the individual's humanity. Ubuntu means that peoples are people through other people. It also acknowledges both the rights and responsibilities of every citizen on promoting individual and societal well-being.

Further, Native American faith traditions also embody values of restorative justice of "living in balance with self, community, and the creator". (*Circle Sentencing*, ACFNewsource (July 4, 2000), http://www.acfnewsource.org/religion/circle_sentencing.html). Additionally, early roots of restorative justice are evidenced in Liberian cultural practices of "coming to the Palava Hut" to resolve conflicts in a community centric model. "Come to the Palava Hut: A Place for Mediation in Liberia." Dr. Duessippina Bonner.

Reflective exercises are an integral part of defining restorative justice and community building, and imagining change in the justice system. Following the teachings of renowned philosophers, it is important to "know thyself" (Socrates) and foster your "moral imagination" (Dewey). By allowing time for deep reflection and internalizing themes of justice, fairness and community, CJP students deepen their knowledge and moral development. This is a key step in moral development—and a lifetime commitment to the service of others—as students explore their moral compass as a guide to resolving and managing conflicts. Throughout the semester, the students complete reflective exercises, which include drafting of reflective essays, journaling and participating in small group discussions. Sample quotes related to the concept of justice include those by Charles Dickens: "Charity begins at home and justice begins next door;" Henry Louis Mencken: "If you want peace, work for justice;" Socrates: "Nothing is to be preferred before justice;" and Dr. Howard Zehr: "I have a dream that we won't have to talk about 'restorative justice', because it will be understood that true justice is about restoration, and about transformation." These quotes lay the foundation for engaging discussions on the future of restorative justice and community-building.

Storytelling is also an important component in reflective learning and restorative justice education. Howard Zehr's *Transcending: Reflections of Crime Victims* (2001), is used to illuminate the vivid accounts of victims of crime. This book is used in class to highlight the importance of a victim-centered model in the context of restorative justice. During class, a student may read and introduce a victim's account to create a space for a restorative dialogue.

The CJP curriculum provides a model for the development of a restorative justice curriculum. In replicating the model for a more general restorative justice curriculum, there are several key components that should be incorporated. As highlighted above, the curriculum should cultivate human connections. This may include reflective forms of art, such as storytelling, poetry, songs and faith perspectives. Also, restorative language should be adopted. This language would include the use of positive and inclusive language by establishing shared values, expressing care and commitment to others.

In conclusion, through the adoption of a restorative justice curriculum, students will be challenged to explore the essence of justice and create ways to build more restorative justice.

Artika Tyner
University of Saint Thomas School of Law

Professionalism, Integrity and Reputation: Providing Opportunities in Simulation Courses

Simulation courses are an ideal place to portray and play out concepts of professionalism, and to experience how personal and professional integrity interact. Starting with the first class of my intensive negotiations course, interwoven throughout and culminating in our final activity, I focus on how professional reputations are built and spread. The themes that recur are:

- Your reputation matters;
- You start building your professional reputation while you are still in law school;
- Professional communities are small and people within your practice community will know your reputation; and
- You need to understand the messages others take away from your behavior in professional interactions.

I'm pretty certain the themes get through to at least some students. They comment that the "reputation" messages hit home and have an effect on their ethical development.

On the first day, we play a variant of a "prisoner's dilemma" (Win as Much as You Can), following an approach described in Gerald Williams' 1983 instructor's manual. (Gerald R. Williams, Teacher's Manual, Legal Negotiation and Settlement 78–79 (1983)). When debriefing, we specifically talk about how people felt about being "betrayed" by others seeking to maximize their own gain, and whether they'll trust those people again soon. We talk about what it takes to rebuild trust and some ways to do that. And, in that first class, I introduce the reputation index that is a weekly feature of the course.

The reputation index, as it exists within our four-hour, 14-week class with weekly negotiations, provides a sheltered environment where students can experience how their conduct is perceived by others, whatever their intentions might have been. The concept of the dichotomy between intent and effect is a new one to many students (in those words at least), but resonates fairly quickly. Students seem to learn a lot from the reputation index even before I've taught them much of anything about negotiating.

I use a variation of business professor and negotiation guru Roy Lewicki's reputation index, in which students comment weekly (my modification) and then cumulatively

(Lewicki's method) at the end of the semester about their interactions with the others in the class with whom they negotiate. (ROY LEWICKI ET AL., TEACHER'S MANUAL, NEGOTIATION: READINGS, EXERCISES, AND CASES (4th ed. 2003)). After every negotiation is completed and we have debriefed the negotiations in class, students are asked three questions, in writing, about each of those with whom they interacted in the negotiation, partners and counterparts alike: (1) did the others in the negotiation follow the Model Rules; (2) did they contribute to the learning; and (3) was it a good or bad professional experience?

Each answer is given a numerical value (+1 for positive, +1 for ethical, +1 for "contributed to my learning," 0 for neutral, and −1 for the negative) and is added to an individual's running total. Twice during the semester, in the middle and at the end, I give individuals their own numbers and all comments that have been written about them (if scoring someone else negatively, you must give a reason), and also report the class maximum, minimum, and average scores. For reasons I don't fully understand and am exploring with social psychologists who do research in this area, students typically score each other more harshly cumulatively than immediately during the week in which they actually had a bad experience. (This is exactly contrary to the research that says you have the strongest memory of a bad experience when it first happens, and then it attenuates over time.) The most common negative comments have to do with perceived misrepresentations and hardball interactions where participants feel abused or misused by the tactics used by another. These comments are generally received with initial mystification by students who only see themselves as being zealous advocates or, interestingly on more than one occasion, students who see themselves as pushovers for competitive advocates and thus need to be "tough."

In addition to providing the cumulative numerical tally at the end of the semester, I use Lewicki's form asking students to select no more than seven people who have "bad" reputations, "good" reputations, and who contributed directly to their learning. Again, any negative scoring requires a comment. This form is also filled out in class, and the results are tallied and returned during the final class of the semester.

Somewhere in the first third or so of the semester, we also do a quick exercise in which students are asked to imagine overhearing others discussing them at their retirement dinner in the restaurant's restroom, when the others do not know they are being overheard. I ask students what they want others to say about them in that circumstance and ask them to write it down (privately, not to turn in). I use this exercise to suggest that we build up to the summary comments others make about us, and should have in mind the desired comments as the "superordinate goal" of our careers. I do not ask students to say out loud what they have written down, but some students always volunteer: "fair," "wise," and "made a difference," are some typical comments. Of course, there's always the student like the one who said his goal was to be known as a "ruthless winner" at the end of his career. At the end of class, he learned that not one person in the class would voluntarily negotiate with him again, and that no one would trust anything he said. Maybe he left re-thinking his tactics for getting there (or maybe not!)

The question of "what kind of lawyer do you want all your moments to add up to?" then leads naturally to the concept of *choosing* how one presents to others in various professional circumstances. Here is where I introduce the idea of what kind of lawyer do you need to be in this interaction? Is the goal to build relationship? To intimidate the other party? Make that person angry? Make a deal? How does this choice relate to your reputation and your strategy for your negotiation/interaction?

My overall message is that the goal is to layer a set of professional skills *on top* of one's "authentic" self (I'm not sure what that is, but my students use the term a lot). I point out that no one pays you to act out your fight with your life partner or your sister in your professional interactions, so you need to have a professional persona that is layered over your own personal reactions and emotions. This plays out in a lot of different ways: you may need a different persona for different situations, but they all layer over who you are, so who you are is always the foundation—and you'd better know what that is and where your boundaries are before you get into a difficult situation. This means, establish early what employers and clients can expect in terms of how you will utilize your professional skills.

I work on the concept that if you intend to build a relationship or make a deal in any given interaction (or even if your goal is to intimidate the other party) then each and every moment of your interaction should support that goal. (We use the theater analogy of beat-scene-act-play, where each beat (a single movement in a scene) should support each scene, which supports ... you get the idea.) But all of it loops back around again to who you are and what you stand for. In negotiations that present ethical dilemmas (which are numerous), I point out that anticipation is better than reaction. When students tell me they crossed the line because being a zealous advocate required them to do so, and they were just doing what their clients hired them to do, we talk about how lawyers compromise their ability to represent other clients in the future. I point out that there is a profession—older than lawyering—in which the professional does whatever the client pays for, but it's not called lawyering, it is called something else.

Students take the reputation index seriously, both by filling it out, and by considering the feedback they receive about their own conduct. I hope they take the lessons with them into their careers and that these experiences help them to be better lawyers—and maybe better people, too.

C. K. Gunsalus
University of Illinois Colleges of Business and Medicine

Attorney Trust Accounts: Teaching the Basics Using a Classroom Simulation

In recent years the legal profession has increasingly called upon legal educators to better prepare students for their entry into the active practice of law. In particular, the bar has been urging law schools to devote more attention to an assortment of skills and the development of professionalism in students who will soon be lawyers. Legal academics have responded, providing skills training in a wide variety of areas, including trial and appellate practice, legal research and writing, and interviewing, counseling, and negotiation.

The project described here focuses on a skill and body of knowledge that is central to the practice of law, that every lawyer should be conversant with, yet receives little attention in most law school curricula: the technical ins and outs of maintaining the lawyer's trust account in accordance with the specific requirements of the jurisdiction's version of Model Rule 1.15 or Disciplinary Rule 9-102. Even the lawyers who never actually have to run a trust account in a lifetime of practicing law—such as partners or associates in large law firms—are responsible for properly safekeeping clients' funds and should be conversant with the mechanical operation of these accounts. Moreover, in these days of increased lawyer mobility, a large-firm lawyer who was heretofore insulated from the day-to-day operation of the trust account may suddenly become a sole practitioner, who by necessity must run his or her own account.

Law schools usually incorporate the subject of trust accounts into Professional Responsibility courses. Typically, this coverage involves a single class review of the pertinent sections of the Model Rules and Model Code. From this short lesson, most law students learn that as lawyers they must have a trust account, must not ever commingle their own money with that of their clients, and must never steal or even borrow money from the trust account.

The typical law school class, however, using popular professional responsibility materials, entirely neglects extremely significant questions for the student about to be a lawyer: (1) exactly how am I supposed to carry out the mandate of the Rules or the Code? (2) what books and records do I need to set up and maintain? and (3) how do I go about entering each specific transaction?

Two factors may account for the lack of such specifics in typical law school curricula. First, many law students have little experience in business, financial or accounting matters and have difficulty with these concepts. In an informal poll of one of my own classes, about half of the students claimed to reconcile their own checking accounts on a monthly basis; a significant number did not know what it meant to reconcile a bank account. Second, the subject matter may seem obvious, both to those who are knowledgeable and those who are ignorant.

This exercise, especially if computerized, would be suitable for an advanced Professional Responsibility seminar. It is probably too much for the basic Professional Responsibility course and too time-consuming for the Clinic. This suggests a small seminar enrollment, say 15 students, each working individually.

The Trust Account Simulation

With this background in mind, I devised a semester-long simulation exercise to teach students how to operate a lawyer's trust account on a daily basis. The simulation has two goals. The first is to explicate the basic mechanics of running a trust account. These mechanics include identifying what books and records are necessary and how to enter various transactions into them, as well as learning how to reconcile the books to the monthly bank statement. To give the simulation even a rough resemblance to real life, the exercise requires a large number of transactions. Various problem transactions, such as how to deal with a returned settlement check, supplement the more mundane items.

The second goal of the simulation is to convey to students the importance of timely and accurate record keeping in their trust accounts. Since many busy law students tend to procrastinate, this attempt to inculcate values rests on a system of grading penalties intended to motivate prompt handling of transactions. My hope is that the lesson will carry over to actual practice.

Although I originally conceived of this simulation as just a trust account exercise, it soon became clear that to learn the lesson of "no commingling," students would have to maintain not only a trust account, but a business account as well. A side benefit of introducing the business account is that it prompts a discussion of the business side of the practice of law, as well as doubling the number of opportunities for learning to reconcile bank statements.

How the Simulation Works

At the beginning of the semester, the students receive an introductory handout describing the goals of the exercise and introducing them to the Rules or Code provisions that apply to trust accounts. The handout also includes all of the forms needed for setting up the necessary books and records and detailed instructions on how to do so. Each student creates a notebook containing both a business account and a trust account. Each account includes a check register with a running balance, checks, deposit slips, and a place to file bank statements. In addition, the trust account records include blank forms to be used for each client—these are sub-accounts of the master trust account. This preliminary handout also reviews the class rules regarding record keeping and the submission of student work and stresses the stringent penalties that may be imposed for failing to make the necessary entries accurately and promptly.

Once the students have set up their books, they begin to receive transactions. A "transaction" is a piece of paper that describes an event requiring some entry in one or more of the student-attorney's records. It may include an incoming check described in the transaction. For example, a typical business account transaction might be, "Pay the phone bill. You owe the phone company $197.55." A typical trust account transaction might be, "You settled a case for Charlene Client for $150,000; attached below is the insurance company's check in settlement. You had this case on a one-third contingent-fee basis and have advanced the expenses listed below." This transaction would include a mock check for the mentioned amount, together with a list of expenses advanced on behalf of the client.

For each transaction, the student must decide what to do next. The transactions do not reveal which account they are intended to affect, nor what the student's appropriate action should be. In the examples given above, the student would need to draw a check for the phone bill, posting it in the business account check register. The insurance check would have to be deposited in the trust account with entries made in that account's check register and in Charlene Client's sub-account. This action would be followed by a calculation and disbursal of the settlement to the client and the lawyer by drawing the appropriate checks out of the trust account, with the concomitant entries. This settlement transaction provides an opportunity to discuss in class the problem of how to deal with the disbursal of uncollected funds: how long must the lawyer wait before disbursing that settlement? Students must also obtain the client's endorsement (provided, upon request, by the professor) and draft a letter to the client explaining the final settlement and accounting in the case. Some of the more complex transactions raise a host of additional ethical issues.

Virtually every transaction requires some action regarding either an incoming or outgoing check. In addition to the book entries, the students must also actually process the checks and deposit slips. The professor acts as the bank or banks involved: students drop off their incoming and outgoing checks, with appropriate paperwork attached, in the simulated "banking system" (actually a box outside the professor's office). With the aid of an assistant, the professor processes the checks, just as depositary and payor banks would in the real world. At one-month intervals, students receive bank statements with cancelled checks for each of their accounts and then must reconcile their books to their bank statements.

The professor collects the students' books of account in class at unannounced intervals and checks them for the promptness and accuracy of the entries. The exercise runs for approximately 8 to 10 weeks out of a 14-week semester, allowing time for class discussion and for down time while the books are out of the students' hands.

Conclusion

The trust account simulation exercise can work well in a variety of law school settings, such as a course in professional responsibility or lawyering skills, or a live client clinic.

This exercise involves a lot of work, both for faculty and for students. I believe, however, that it is probably the best way to teach this essential skill to law students who do not have a prior grounding in the subject.

Steven Wechsler
Syracuse University College of Law

Reclaiming Purpose: Our Students' and Our Own

Over the last three years, I have asked law students to help me discover the ways in which legal education affects their transformation into lawyers. My goal is to better understand the ways in which law students develop their professional identities. This objective is in part motivated by the current crisis of meaning in the profession. What seeds do we sow in law school that are manifested, both positively and negatively, in the profession? To the extent that we are sowing the seeds for negative professional experiences, what can we do to mitigate that effect?

The most revealing—and most troubling—answer is that law school causes students to lose the sense of purpose that made them want to be lawyers. The loss is not only harmful to individual students, but it also has enormous negative consequences for the profession and for those served by the profession.

This realization was first brought home to me during a class discussion about the third year of law school. Third-year students described feeling apathetic, even paralyzed, about their legal studies and their futures as lawyers. Several described their journey from excitement about beginning law school to their disappointment with the reality of law school and their resulting perception of law practice. A second-year student, who had been listening attentively, suddenly spoke up: "It's like the grief process," she said. "Hearing their stories is like listening to the ways in which one moves through the stages of the grief process: there is loss, then denial, then mourning, then anger, then acceptance. The third-years have arrived at the acceptance stage. They have accepted that what they thought this was all about is not accurate. It's turned out to be different from what they hoped." As she spoke, there were murmurs of recognition and assent, along with some laughter at such a grim metaphor for the law school experience. We pursued her construct: If the students thought she was accurate about the grief process, what was the loss they had experienced? What loss had been grieved and now accepted as gone? What had they had at one point that was now dead?

Over time, my students have offered an answer: they recount losing the sense of purpose—their visions of what it means to be a lawyer—that brought them to law school. Not only have students been able to articulate the loss of this vision, but they have repeatedly described the loss as quick and traumatic, very much akin to a death, reinforcing the aptness of the grief metaphor.

Students come to law school with an idea that being a lawyer is something meaningful, something important and valuable. They are drawn to a vision that includes a job undertaken in relationship with and on behalf of other people, helping clients to solve problems or to move through difficult times. While they may not have a detailed or even realistic picture of what lawyers do, students envision themselves engaged in professional work that is intellectually challenging and that has value and meaning. They arrive at law school with hope and expectation that their work as lawyers will have a positive impact for society as a whole. For many, the external rewards may also provide an incentive, but those are the only incentives for very few. It has become quite clear to me that my students want to feel good about what they do professionally, which requires that their work give them something beyond the superficial benefits of money and prestige.

Upon beginning law school, students quickly learn that law school values rational, objective analysis to the exclusion of other qualities, such as self-awareness and interpersonal relationships. They also learn that winning—as measured by the prizes of grades, law review membership, and certain jobs—is the most important goal. They believe that they must adopt those values as part of their changing professional identities. They believe that their personal visions of lawyering are naïve and unrealistic. As a result, students replace their hopeful expectations for their work lives with minimal expectations for finding meaning and purpose in their work. They will accept unfulfilling work environments because they think that there is no other option.

These reduced expectations impose a terrible burden on new lawyers as they begin their professional lives. If we as legal educators are contributing to that burden, we are failing our students and our profession. We must find a way to correct that failure.

The question, of course, is how to do so. My students have helped me begin to see some possible ways.

The first is that students are helped by strengthening or developing skills of self-awareness and reflection. I have used a variety of techniques to stimulate reflection. They include written essays, brief in-class reflective exercises, participation in a web-based discussion board, class discussion, and longer experiential or research papers. I have also used the Myers–Briggs Personality Type Indicator as one method of discussing the importance of self-awareness and understanding of others. Some students come to law school with these skills of self-awareness and reflection; others do not. The time demands of law school, the competitive environment, and the emphasis on analytical reasoning devalue self-awareness and prevent reflection. Yet, these are essential skills for finding meaning and purpose in law practice, as well as for forming and sustaining relationships.

Similarly, students report positive outcomes from opportunities to develop connections with each other and with lawyers and other professionals. In some classes, I have hosted weekend retreats with students and between five and eight professionals, lawyers, and others (e.g., a doctor, journalist, ethicist, and psychologist).The retreats have offered time for intensive discussion on a variety of topics as well as for informal interaction. Additionally, lawyers and others have participated as guest speakers and brought lawyers into the classroom vicariously through fiction and nonfiction works, including biographies. Because many law students feel isolated, students report surprise and relief upon learning that their reactions to law school are similar to those of other students. This realization was particularly helpful in demonstrating to students that anxieties and even fear are normal parts of becoming and being a professional and not indicative of incompetence, as many had perceived in their isolation.

Additionally, students are reassured by hearing lawyers discuss their own successful searches for meaning in their professional lives, and for achieving balance and integration of their professional and personal lives. They are relieved to hear professionals talk of dealing with fear and of making mistakes and correcting them. We have had intensive and energetic discussions of whether it is realistic to view work as a calling, as defined by Frederick Buechner: "The place where your deep gladness and the world's deep hunger meet." One student's comment about the interactions with professionals is illustrative. They offered, the student said, "insight to people starving for guidance, hope, and reassurance."

A number of students report a reclaimed sense of purpose from these experiences. From one student: "I walked away ... feeling as though I did make the right decision by choosing this as a career path." From another: "I want to be the same person at work that I am within myself. I don't want to sacrifice my values or passions because my job requires it ... I now have more pride to enter the legal profession and to defend the profession. I also feel more optimistic about the practice of law."

As so often happens when we teach, my efforts to help students learn have resulted in my own learning. In setting out to understand lawyers' development of professional identity, my own professional identity has changed. I learned about myself, engaged in reflection about the appropriate role of legal education and educators, and connected in new ways with my students and with professionals who were brought into the teaching enterprise. As I truly listened to students' reflections about their learning, their inner lives, and their professional and personal concerns, I developed a greater appreciation for the depth and complexity of their lives. I see them differently, which has broadened my vision of what it means to be a law professor, just as I was attempting to broaden their visions of what it means to be a lawyer. Thanks to my students, I have reclaimed my purpose as a teacher.

Daisy Hurst Floyd
Mercer University School of Law

Encouraging Continued Personal Assessment Within the Framework of Skills Courses

In my course on negotiation, I want to encourage student thoughtfulness about understanding the process of the continued development of lawyering skills not just in the fourteen weeks of a school term, but throughout their careers. In a recent version of the course, I added the following to my usual writing and performance assignments:

Personal Assessment

> During the first week of the term, look over the syllabus and note the various topics we will be examining. (The first few pages of each chapter will help you if the topic is not clear from the syllabus.) Write a short note: one to two pages is fine, about an aspect of negotiation you anticipate that you will find challenging to perform, and what you think you will find relatively easy, among these topics. Do not turn this assignment in; save it for future reference. At the end of the term, you will retrieve it and add a page assessing your predictions, and describing what you plan to continue to work to improve as you practice law. (You may wish to improve what you perceive as a weakness, or you may wish to concentrate on becoming excellent at some aspect of negotiation that you have decided you have a good feel for. You can decide this later.) These papers will be turned in at the end of the term. You will also be encouraged, but not required, to post these on the course webpage, and may get some helpful feedback from your classmates.

The resulting papers were, I would have to say, amazing. Student "prediction" comments reflected confidence, anxiety, and curiosity. They were candid about the discomfort they anticipated, for example, in using power or in carefully measuring what information would be revealed or concealed. Several students, noticing that the course will cover "fairness" and "social norms in bargaining," were sure they would find it easy to be fair, while wondering if others would be. Some noticed the topic "misrepresentation" and wondered how they would react to professional ethical norms that they anticipated would contradict their personal standards of behavior.

Student insights met the explicit goal of encouraging a receptive attitude toward examining individual values and skills. Almost equally important, student predictions served to accomplish an implicit objective as well. Judging by their written comments, most of the students had read the syllabus through and even looked at the referenced chapters at the outset of the class in order to complete the assignments. My unplanned success in getting students to read ahead likely explains how frequently student comments in discussions during the term involved concepts in chapters not yet assigned. Bear in mind that I did not read the prediction statements when first written; instead I collected the completed assignment at the end of the term.

Students' final "assessment and goals" statements comparing their early predictions to their actual performance in the course simulations commented on how accurate their early predictions were, and identified strengths and challenges for future focus. Some also reflected on negotiation experiences outside the course.

One student reconstructed negotiations from his work experience, appreciating that he had used integrative bargaining to successfully reduce costs for his company by breaking down a contract into constituent parts and dealing with several vendors. One compared integrative bargaining and fairness norms and related each to her future employment in construction litigation, identifying strengths that she would continue to develop. Several noted how challenging it is to keep in mind the nonmonetary concerns of a client so that the true bargaining zone is identified. Some identified a need to get over a fear of math when figuring out whether a client's requirements have been met. Some insights were a surprise; others reinforced the student's earlier hunches. Paper after paper showed the effort and careful reflection I had hoped for.

I have several thoughts about why this assignment succeeded. I had tried to establish an expectation of reflective thinking in other assignments. For a simulation illustrating lawyer–client issues in which some students were clients, students who were "clients" were assigned to write their reflection paper on the question "How did the lawyer help or hinder the progress of this negotiation?" For a problem involving information that the parties wish to conceal, "What ethical or contractual concerns would you have about concealing X in a real negotiation?"

I also taught this particular class in the evening, and therefore had a number of older students. Like many faculty members, I have a sense of greater maturity and practical wisdom among our second career students, which may actually inspire the younger students, as well. In short, we had rapport, experience, and shared efforts at critical application of negotiation ideas.

Overall, I believe this assignment can be a regular part of a variety of skills courses. In fact, it could quite possibly work in doctrinal courses, as well.

Harriet N. Katz
Rutgers School of Law–Camden

Preparing Law Students to Serve and Lead

"Servant leadership begins with the natural feeling that one wants to serve, to serve first. Then conscious choice brings one to aspire to lead."—Robert Greenleaf

Servant leadership is a part of the course curriculum in the Community Justice Project ("CJP"), a civil rights legal clinic. An integral step in preparing law students to become "servant leaders" is to incorporate principles of leadership development into the law school curriculum. The law school curriculum can be used to train law students in identifying and combating social injustice, enabling law students to envision themselves as protectors of those without power and the creators of transformation in the legal system. Legal educators can aid in this training by teaching theoretical perspectives of servant leadership and providing opportunities for students to develop their leadership skills.

Methods of teaching the principles of servant leadership

A lecture series on servant leadership is a fundamental component of the CJP curriculum. The lecture begins with students defining servant leadership. Students share their definitions and work collaboratively to develop a working definition. For example, servant is characterized as one who expresses submission or debt to another; while a leader offers direction to others and uses influence to create change. A combination of these definitions describes the characteristics of a servant leader.

The textbook used to teach principles of servant leadership is *The Servant as Leader*, by Robert K. Greenleaf (1991). This book provides a framework for exploring servant leadership and core leadership capacities. While in class, students engage in a small group discussion based upon the readings. Particular issues explored are whether a leadership crisis exists, characteristics of the servant leader and methods for serving as a servant leader.

Greenleaf raises the premise that there is a leadership crisis caused by a lack of moral values or ethics; the need for wise counselors, practical visionaries, and creative problem solvers; and a lack of connection with community. Students discuss and analyze this leadership crisis. Students share examples of the leadership crisis in a historical context and present day matters. Students also offer examples of lawyers who currently serve in a servant leadership capacity.

Based upon their reading, students are asked to characterize who is the servant leader. The key characteristics of servant leaders include reflective listening, the ability to work collaboratively with others, the ability to engage in creative problem solving, an interest in promoting social justice, and the ability to inspire others. Additionally, students brainstorm methods for serving as a servant leader during their clinical experience and vocational journey. Students have committed to engaging in community-building, fostering civic engagement, and collaborating with key policy stakeholders to further social justice initiatives. More importantly, many have realized that they have allowed their leadership talent to lay dormant. Greenleaf warns that the challenge facing leaders today is the "strong natural servants who have the potential to lead but do not lead or who choose to follow a nonservant."

Students are also encouraged to continue reflecting upon principles of servant leadership and the role of lawyers as leaders. As part of this reflection, students are introduced to Rev. Dr. Martin Luther King's "The Drum Major Instinct" and listen to the audio version of the speech during class. In this speech, Dr. King characterizes greatness by one's commitment to service. He stated: "by giving that definition of greatness, it means that everybody can be great, because everybody can serve." Other service quotes are introduced as well. "Service is the rent we pay to be living. It is the very purpose of life and not something you do in your spare time." Marian Wright Edelman. "The best way to find yourself is in the service of others." Mohandas Gandhi.

In subsequent class lectures and discussions, CJP students are challenged to identify their leadership strengths and discuss ways that they can serve in the community. Students use a leadership assessment to aid in identifying their servant leadership attributes. This assessment is entitled: *Becoming a Servant Leader: Do You Have What it Takes?* (NEBGUIDE, Oct. 2007, http://www.ianrpubs.unl.edu/epublic/live/g1481/build/g1481.pdf). Following completion of this assessment, students meet with their case team partner to compare and contrast their leadership qualities. They also draft a reflective essay related to their discoveries which provides an opportunity to highlight the leadership strengths of their case team. Further, students are encouraged to complete the Strengthsfinder assessment (MARCUS BUCKINGHAM & DONALD O. CLIFTON, NOW, DISCOVER YOUR STRENGTHS (2001)) which identifies one's top five areas of strength. These leadership assessments aid students in ascertaining their leadership qualities, creating a strategic plan for implementing their strengths and then continuing to enhance their strengths throughout their careers. (Artika Tyner, *Discovering Your Strengths and Reaping the Benefits*, *in* THE 101 PRACTICE SERIES: BREAKING DOWN THE BASICS (A.B.A., Young Lawyers Division, 2008), *available at* http://www.americanbar.org/groups/young_lawyers/publications/the_101_201_practice_series.html.)

Conclusion

The greatest benefit of integrating principles of servant leadership into the law school curriculum is to prepare students to serve and lead in their local communities and globally. Principles of leadership in the law school curriculum can help the next generation of "servant leaders" to emerge. Students will discover new ways to utilize their talents and legal skills to build communities, give a voice to the voiceless, and give power to the oppressed.

Artika Tyner
University of Saint Thomas School of Law

A Humanizing Classroom Exercise

Somewhere in middle of the fall semester or early in the winter semester, when students are feeling oppressed generally and depressed specifically about examination results, I take a break from doctrinal Civil Procedure and spend a class discussing the pitfalls of law school. The primary goals of the class are to:

- Introduce/validate the idea that law school can have negative effects on students;
- Encourage students to think about ways that they can minimize these negative effects;
- Personalize both the professor and fellow students.

The week before the class, I distribute a reading assignment consisting of two law review articles. Many articles would work, but after some trial and error, I have settled on articles by Professor Susan Daicoff and the late Professor Peter Cicchino. (Susan Daicoff, *Lawyer Know Thyself: A Review of Empirical Research on Attorney Attributes Bearing on Professionalism*, 46 AM. U. L. REV. 133 (1997); Peter M. Cicchino, *Defending Humanity*, 9 AM. U. J. GENDER SOC. POL'Y & L. 1 (2001)). The Daicoff piece introduces two concepts to focus on in class: first, her assertion that there are certain lawyer personality traits; and, second, the high rate of depression and substance abuse among lawyers. The Cicchino piece is an essay that employs personal narrative to examine law school and law practice. Both pieces have annoyed students, surprised them, and led to the occasional "Aha!" moment.

I require students to react to the articles before the class by asking them to respond in writing to questions. The two questions I most frequently ask are: (1) identify the most interesting or surprising part of either article; and (2) name two ways you have changed—or ways that others close to you would say you have changed—since beginning law school. Other questions might include: "What are the four words you would like used to describe you as a lawyer?" and "Is there any principle in the defense of which you would be willing to lose your job?" By requiring a written response, I ensure that the students will actually read the assignment and be prepared to talk about it in class. More importantly, the process of thinking about and then writing out the answers enhances the benefit of the assignment to the student.

In the classroom session itself, I start off with some self-disclosure. I may talk for instance, about my law school stress levels or where I fit in Daicoff's taxonomy of lawyer personalities. I then begin the class discussion. Sometimes I ask the students to share their answers to the first question and then let the discussion flow from there. Other times, I break the students into groups to discuss their answers. I may also provide a separate list of questions for the groups.

This class has proven its usefulness in several ways. First, it opens up a topic—law student distress—that most students are probably living, but that generally lurks in the shadows. By introducing this topic to the students, the class validates what they are experiencing. For many students, this is the first time that they realize they are not alone; this new-found knowledge is both powerful and reassuring.

After naming this phenomenon, the class can then move on to allow the students to think about ways to combat the negative effects. One way to do this is to have students write down the name of someone they had offended since starting law school. It could be, for instance, a loved one, a friend to whom they were rude, or someone to whom they did not allot some necessary time. At the end of the class, I urge students to find a way to apologize to that person some time in the next week. This exercise has elicited a very positive response from the students.

Second, the class personalizes their fellow students and their professor. Students see that, although their colleagues may be strutting and preening with the best of them, it is often just a self-protective act. Because law school often alienates and devalues students, this humanizing of the "other" is constructive.

This topic and discussion, even if never formally revisited, remains open throughout the course and, one hopes, throughout the students' law school experience. There are occasions where the readings or discussions will be brought up, either by the students or the professor. It is well worth the missed doctrinal class session.

Justine A. Dunlap
University of Massachusetts School of Law–Dartmouth

Teaching Judgment in Law School

Attorneys are expected to exercise judgment in a wide variety of situations, from holding client money in trust, to limitations on arguing a matter before a court, to negotiating with other attorneys. In a sense, judgment is a significant reason people pay for lawyers' advice.

Judgment can be described as the exercise of decision-making behavior in a particular context. The application of judgment is readily apparent in such activities as driving a car, flying an airplane, and mountain climbing.

While some people believe judgment is simply learned from experience, when viewed as a decision-making skill set, judgment indeed can be taught. Pilots, for example, are taught how to develop their decision-making process with respect to themselves, their aircraft and the external environment. (Harry Kraemer, *Flight School: Can a Flight Instructor Teach Judgment?*, FLYING (Embry-Riddle Aero. U.), Sept. 27, 2010), *available at* .http://www.flyingmag.com/training/learn-fly/flight-school-judgment).

In law school, judgment affects how students direct their attention in classes, make comments on Facebook, perceive legal ethics, and more. Judgment also is a regular factor in how students prepare for and take law school exams. Law student grades in part can be attributed to the way students used judgment to perform on tests under pressure, including whether they spotted legal issues, emphasized the important issues, and allocated time properly.

While judgment and the standards that drive decisions often are fashioned individually or shaped by local culture, legal education can promote the express study of judgment. Some illustrations of how judgment can be studied in law school follow.

1. Real Lawyers, Real Lies

Professor Hank Shea, a former Assistant United States Attorney white-collar crime prosecutor and current Senior Distinguished Fellow at the Holloran Center for Ethical Leadership in the Professions at the University of St. Thomas School of Law, illustrates what can happen with a lack of professional judgment through interviews with attorneys who committed crimes involving lying and deception. These former lawyers are interviewed by Professor Shea, sometimes at law schools with students present, and other times remotely, but captured on video, to impress students with real-life stories of lawyers whose bad judgment lands them in prison—and the step-by-step analysis of how they got there.

2. Examinations

First-year law students, in particular, often need direction to frame their efforts efficiently, from how to organize subject matter, to how they can best prepare for examinations using that subject matter. In particular, students often need assistance in learning to navigate legal "forks in the road." While it is primarily left for academic support or success programs to deal with those types of strategies and tactics, doctrinal professors also can help by discussing meta-cognition and how students can improve their decision making. Professors can ask students who are preparing for a midterm or final examination about their exam preparation strategies and tactics. The professor can discuss outlining, collaborative efforts between students to create team-based learning, and some pitfalls associated with each. The professor in this regard is acting more like a coach than as a teacher of doctrinal material, but this discussion creates a bridge between student learning and performance. This same concept also works with third-year students who are about to graduate and prepare for the bar exam, another journey with which students do not have familiarity and where strategies and tactics also could make a big difference.

3. Directed Questions About Judgment in Class

Students often must make choices in spotting the key issues and then emphasizing that issue. While these choices are discussed in classes, cases often do not discuss why bad choices are bad or why the court emphasized the issues it did. That is why a hypothetical question offering different paths, including poor ones, can be offered to students for the express purpose of discussing those choices. This exercise not only reveals whether students miss the important issues, but whether they are taking short cuts in the logical progression of the analysis and perhaps jumping to conclusions. For example, a state contract favoring a resident business owner over out-of-state owners can trigger a discussion of whether the dormant Commerce Clause or the Privileges and Immunities Clause should be favored in the analysis, leading to an express discussion of judgment.

4. The Twenty-Dollar Dilemma

Sometimes, a question of judgment does not directly relate to lawyering, but can be designed around a practical problem raising ethical and judgmental issues. What would students do if they found $20 sticking out of an ATM late at night with no one around? This question creates an exercise in line-drawing. Most students will respond with a "rule" that permits their desired behavior. Of course, adding or modifying facts, such as making it $2,000 sticking out of the ATM, or that the camera is broken, or that the $20 was found on the floor of the kitchen at their law firm, cause some students to change their perspective and predicted behavior. This problem also illustrates that ethics and judgment—much like legal problems—depend heavily on the relevant facts and how they are presented.

Conclusion

The idea of illuminating judgment as an express subject of discussion can help students significantly and prepare them for the real world. Judgment is a skill that comes with experience—and teaching.

Steven I. Friedland
Elon University School of Law

Chapter 11

Formative Assessment — Feedback to Students During the Course

The focus of this chapter is formative assessment: students apply the skills, values, and knowledge they are learning in the course and receive feedback about their performance. The primary purpose of formative feedback is to improve student learning, not to assign grades. This introduction explores the why, what, who, and how of assessment and feedback during the course.

A. Why Do Students (and Teachers) Need Formative Feedback During the Course?

Research shows that the need for practice and feedback applies to all levels of education and across all disciplines. In fact, educational experts assert that an "assessment-centered" environment, in which students have repeated opportunities to practice and receive feedback, is essential to learning. If we want students to learn, we need to give them multiple opportunities to practice lawyering skills and to get feedback on how they are learning.

Having students complete a variety of assessment instruments during the course will allow them to deepen their understanding of the important knowledge, skills, and values in the course. Prompt feedback has a clear, positive relationship to student achievement and satisfaction. Frequent feedback helps students become self-motivated, independent learners.

Assessing student learning during the course helps teachers be more effective. When we review student performance on formative assessments, we discover how well students are developing the knowledge, skills, and values we want them to learn. We see areas where most students are competent and areas where a significant number of students are struggling. Reflective teachers can then design teaching strategies to help students develop greater competency.

B. How and What Should Teachers Assess During the Course?

Teachers can choose from many types of assessment instruments to provide formative feedback to students. Common assessment tools include essay questions, problems, multiple-choice questions, papers, documents (such as wills, contracts, pleadings, articles of incorporation), simulations (oral arguments, negotiations), journals, and presentations.

Two factors guide the subject of our assessment and feedback to students during the course. First, we should assess and provide feedback on student learning of the important knowledge, skills, and values in the course. In short, our course goals should drive our assessment and feedback. Most teachers hope that students learn a variety of things in their courses, including doctrine, theory, thinking skills, performance skills, and professional values. We can improve the focus of our teaching if we (1) are explicit with ourselves and our students about what we hope students will learn; and (2) assess and provide feedback to students during the course on their level of achievement of the important course goals.

The second factor to guide our choice of formative assessments during the course is to prepare students for the graded assessments. If a paper is a significant portion of students' grades in a course, an appropriate formative assessment would be feedback on a draft of the paper. Likewise, if the final exam is part essay and part multiple-choice, students should have the opportunity to practice and get feedback on both types of questions during the course.

C. Who (or What) Can Provide Feedback During the Course?

Formative feedback to students can come from a variety of sources, including the students themselves, peers, external reviewers, computer programs, and teachers.

Self-assessment

An important skill for lawyers is the ability to monitor their own understanding and performance. Consequently, students need to learn to assess themselves. Teachers can facilitate students' self-assessment by providing students with assessment instruments (such as a practice essay question or a practice oral argument) that include explicit criteria for excellent performance. Rubrics and checklists with detailed performance criteria allow students to measure their own strengths and weaknesses. Further, student journals provide an opportunity for students to engage in self-assessment and reflection on their learning. For example, students could use the rubric shown in Figure 1 on the facing page to assess their own oral argument performance.

Peers

Students often provide feedback on one another's learning when they work in study groups or on collaborative projects. Peers can provide more structured formative feedback on one another's writing and performance of lawyering skills if teachers develop detailed performance criteria. To maximize the effectiveness of peer feedback, we can spend a bit of time in class training the students in the art of critique.

External Reviewers

Lawyers, judges, and other professionals from the community are a valuable resource for providing feedback on student skills such as counseling, mediating, negotiating, oral advocacy, and drafting. They greatly expand the teacher's capacity to provide feedback. Teachers can help external reviewers by providing them with explicit criteria for the performance and guidelines for giving formative feedback.

Computer Programs

Computer lessons allow students to learn at their own pace and provide continuous feedback as students respond to questions.

Figure 1. Sample Self-Assessment Rubric

Structure and Substance Introduction: roadmap Substance Law: elements Policy Application of facts Conclusion: relief requested	
Communication Verbal (clarity, pace, passion, respectful tone) Nonverbal (eye contact, posture Gestures)	
Responding to Questions Listen to question Answer directly Transition to argument	
Overall Reflections What you learned Assessment of performance Value of assignment Other	

Teachers

Many types of formative feedback are available for teachers to use with their students. Feedback can be given to an individual or to groups of students, during class or outside of it, in writing or orally. Although individual, written feedback to each student is valuable, it is quite time consuming for the teacher. Fortunately, there are many alternatives that provide significant formative feedback to students.

D. How Can Teachers Provide Students with Effective and Efficient Formative Feedback?

Effective, formative feedback is specific, positive, corrective, and timely. Jon Garon's "The Seven Principles of Effective Assessment" in this Chapter provides additional characteristics of good formative assessment.

Specific

Student learning is enhanced when they get information about specific criteria they have or have not met. General statements, such "Good job!" or "Needs work" do not tell students much if they lack supporting details. To develop specific criteria, take the assessment yourself, analyze your response, and then make a list of the important elements of an excellent performance on the assessment. Think about what students are supposed to learn and how they will show that to you. Start thinking in categories: Are you looking for rules? Exceptions? Factual applications? Policy? Creativity? Articulate the important components within each category and create a checklist or rubric with the criteria. For example, if an essay question addresses a motion to dismiss for lack of personal jurisdiction and asks students to identify issues, articulate the relevant law and policy, apply the facts to the law and policy, and make a recommendation regarding the disposition of the motion, a portion of the checklist could be:

- ❑ Issue …
- ❑ Due Process analysis
  - ❑ Language of 14th Amendment
  - ❑ Policy: functions of personal jurisdiction limits
  - ❑ Minimum Contacts test from *International Shoe et. al.*
    - ❑ Purposeful availment
      - ❑ law
      - ❑ policy
      - ❑ application
    - ❑ Foreseeability
      - ❑ law
      - ❑ policy
      - ❑ application
    - ❑ Stream of Commerce
      - ❑ law
      - ❑ policy
      - ❑ application
    - ❑ Fairness/Reasonableness
      - ❑ law
      - ❑ policy
      - ❑ application
- ❑ Recommendation

Positive

Formative feedback should tell students what they are doing well. Law school trains students to become skilled at critical analysis and some students love the thrill of being critiqued and challenged. But for many students, hearing only about what they need to do to improve can get tiresome and depressing. Research shows that most learners do best in an environment where they are challenged and affirmed.

As a general rule, begin formative feedback by explaining what students are doing well. Even when students perform poorly, there is almost always some aspect of the assessment that the student has done well. If the student has done excellent work, it helps to identify *what* is excellent so the student can build upon that success. As novices, students are not often aware of what they are doing well.

Corrective

Formative assessment should give students feedback about their weaknesses and provide strategies to improve them. Sandwich the specific corrective feedback in between the positive feedback. Limit the corrective feedback to one to three areas; a list of a dozen aspects that need fixing is overwhelming and counterproductive for most students. Be honest and direct, but also compassionate—it is not easy for most students to hear that their work was ineffective.

In addition to being specific, corrective feedback is more likely to help students learn when it:

- Focuses on the work, not the person;
- Avoids making normative judgments;
- Encourages students to become responsible for their learning; and
- Provides strategies to improve.

Providing feedback on a student's performance is very different from providing feedback on the student herself. The focus should be on the student's work and learning rather than on the student or her abilities. Frame corrective feedback in terms of what is effective and ineffective. For example, "Your mock client interview would have been more effective if you had stated your advice in simpler language." Getting feedback that a performance is "poor" or "bad" or "unprofessional" is not helpful. Those words are loaded. Giving students specific feedback about their weaknesses is only half the process. The other half is to provide them with concrete strategies they can use to improve their performance.

Prompt

Students should get feedback while the assessment is fresh and in time for the next assessment. The best feedback is immediate. Students remember what they just did, get results, and can adjust accordingly. Completing an assessment and getting feedback three weeks later has the opposite effect. Students may not recall what they did on the assessment and have a hard time processing the feedback. As a general guideline, the shorter the assessment, the sooner students should receive feedback. In addition, the fewer the students in the course, the sooner they should receive feedback. Giving prompt feedback does not need to be onerous. The goal is make formative assessment ongoing, effective, and sustainable. It is easier to give feedback promptly if you have prepared for it in advance by identifying exactly what you are trying to assess, providing clear directions for the assessment, and preparing a checklist or rubric with specific criteria.

E. Examples of Formative Feedback

Individual Written Comments

Teachers can provide detailed, written comments on students' writing, such as drafts of research papers, briefs, contracts, and practice exams. Written comments should be a mix of positive and negative feedback, include suggestions and encouragement for improvement, and be specific without being so encyclopedic that the student is overwhelmed.

Individual Oral Critique

This type of feedback is appropriate for student performance of lawyering skills. Critique will be most effective if students have detailed performance criteria in advance and the critique centers on those criteria. Additional guidelines for teachers include: start with a positive comment, focus on one or two points, and model excellent communication skills (eye contact, active listening, plain English) during the critique.

Individual Feedback in Class

Teachers can give frequent feedback to individual students in class. When students make an insightful comment, perform clear legal analysis, or ask a perceptive question, teachers should give positive reinforcement. When student comments miss the point or their analysis is confused, they need to know that they are off track.

Individual Feedback out of Class

A great deal of student learning and teacher feedback takes place outside of the classroom. Teachers can provide detailed feedback on student work (such as a student's response to a practice exam) in individual conferences. However, individual feedback can be much less formal. Teachers can give feedback to students in a brief conversation in the hallway, a short written note, or an email message.

Group Feedback of In-class Writing and Quizzes

Multiple-choice questions are an excellent vehicle for in-class quizzes that assess issue-spotting, comprehension, and application of legal rules. Short in-class writing exercises, such as the identification of issues in a fact pattern or an analysis of a problem, are also excellent sources of feedback. Teachers can give immediate feedback through class discussion or can collect the student responses and provide feedback to the entire class in the next session or on the course website.

Group Feedback on Practice Exams

Practice exams that follow a format similar to the graded exams are an excellent learning tool for students. Teachers can give group feedback by discussing in class how the teacher would have approached the exam. Teachers can facilitate students' self-assessment of practice exams by posting a score sheet, rubric, model answer, or sample student answers on reserve in the library or on the course website.

References

- How People Learn: Brain, Mind, Experience, and School (John Bransford et al. eds., 2000).
- Gerald F. Hess & Steven I. Friedland, Techniques for Teaching Law (1999).
- Gerald F. Hess, *Heads and Hearts: The Teaching and Learning Environment in Law School,* 52 J. Legal Educ. 75 (2002).
- Gregory S. Munro, Outcomes Assessment for Law Schools 57 (2000).
- Michael Schwartz, Sophie Sparrow & Gerald Hess, Teaching Law By Design: Engaging Students from the Syllabus to the Final Exam (2009).
- Sophie Sparrow, *Describing the Ball: Improve Teaching by Using Rubrics—Explicit Grading Criteria,* Mich. St. L. Rev. 1 (2004).
- Roy Stuckey et al., Best Practices for Legal Education: A Vision and a Road Map (2007).
- Barbara E. Walvrood & Virginia Johnson Anderson, Effective Grading: A Tool for Learning and Assessment (2d ed. 2010).

The Seven Principles of Effective Feedback

"I hear and forget. I see and remember. I do and understand."—Chinese Proverb

The Seven Principles of Good Practice in Undergraduate Education emphasize the following: active learning, time management, student-faculty contact, prompt feedback, high expectations, diverse learning styles, and cooperation among students. While all these principles have validity in the law school setting, one of the most important is effective feedback.

In law school, faculty members provide students with feedback every day. The Socratic Method stresses active student participation, instant feedback and reinforcement by the professor, and the student's subsequent effort to improve, with the loop repeating until the student learns the new skill. In a one-on-one setting, this model could be ideal; in larger groups, however, student participation tends to lessen.

To reach the entire class, the professor should create an opportunity for full participation. Professors must involve students at a level sufficient to provide feedback and reinforcement until each pupil has acquired the intended skill or knowledge. Frequent written assignments, quizzes, labs, and client projects all serve this function. The form of the activity is less important than the quality of the interaction it generates.

The key to successful instruction, then, is effective feedback and reinforcement. Feedback provides students with information about their performance they can then use to improve their skills. Reinforcement provides positive or negative rewards to promote better student responses. Students often read only those portions of assignments covered in class because there is no reinforcement for doing more. In this way, reinforcement can interfere with feedback. Students will be given the best opportunity to meet the instructor's objectives if the instructor provides both good information, upon which the students can reflect as part of their learning, and explicit, positive reinforcement for demonstrating the skills the instructor is attempting to instill.

I have identified seven principles for effective feedback in legal education. While these techniques have already been implemented in many legal writing and professional skills courses, they apply equally to all law school subjects.

1. Effective feedback should be clearly understood by the student. Furthermore, the student must see the feedback as useful. Students clearly cannot reflect on information they do not understand. Instructors should provide information that builds on what the student knows. This approach provides students the cognitive tools needed to use the feedback effectively.
2. Effective feedback should be timely. It must closely follow the students' work to better help them reflect on what they did and why they did it. Reinforcement, too, must closely follow student behavior to be effective. Exams reviewed months later have far less effect than those returned the next day.
3. Effective feedback should be immediately usable by the student. If students put the feedback into practice immediately, they are more likely to permanently change their behavior. Because students improve in small successive steps, feedback should come to the students in sequence. If feedback comes out of sequence, students often end up confused. The result can be frustration and negativity.
4. Effective feedback should be consistent. The feedback must build on the same themes and correct the same mistakes each time. Students compare the feedback they receive to try to synthesize the lessons. Students also use each incidence of

feedback to build toward the next project. Effective feedback is consistent both from student to student and project to project.

5. Effective feedback should be comprehensive. The feedback must cover each of the criteria set out for grading. An instructor must give value to each skill he or she wishes to improve. Grading only for analysis reinforces poor writing skills. Students will not invest time or effort in activities that are not valued—and hence reinforced—by the instructor. The more explicit the criteria, the more they are reinforced. Further, explicit criteria help students know what to study.
6. Effective feedback should be supportive. It should encourage the student to attempt to improve. Punishments may help discourage particular behaviors, but they can also reduce motivation and disrupt the learning process. This principle does not mean ignoring mistakes. Instead, the instructor should identify both the weak and strong aspects of the student's performance, and stress what the student can do to continue to improve.
7. Effective feedback should be valued. Students must recognize the value in the feedback and treat it as meaningful. When students discount feedback for any reason, its importance diminishes and so does the effect it will have. Student dislike of the subject matter, confusion about the assignment, or delays in feedback will all result in lowering the lesson's effectiveness. Students who are motivated to value feedback will engage in the learning process more intensively and utilize the information with greater effectiveness.

I implemented my seven principles of effective feedback while teaching Professional Skills. The students' success in the skills course led me to use this approach in my subject matter courses as well.

My method of teaching Professional Skills has three features. First, we discuss each skill explicitly in class. Course materials and discussions explore each of the component skills step-by-step. I emphasize the steps that make up writing, editing, analysis and synthesis, client counseling, negotiating, and learning. Second, I present the discussions of each step in the context of the other steps. I use client counseling as a broad paradigm through which the student/lawyer demonstrates every other skill. By using a single broad paradigm, the students have a common framework that they can use to organize all their skills and techniques as lawyers. Third, course materials provide the students with written statements on each criteria used for grading. Neither the criteria nor the numerical valuations change during the semester, so students can compare their competence on each exercise. The reward system attempts to value the reflective learning as well as the substantive projects, so that students invest the necessary time in learning about their own thought processes.

By applying the seven principles of effective feedback as a guideline for designing new course problems and grading systems, instructors have the opportunity to identify the skills, values, and knowledge they truly seek to help their students learn. Students benefit because they understand what is expected in much greater detail, and they can measure their progress toward the goals. This practice also provides reinforcement and feedback to the instructor. The feedback loop is continuous. The reflective process shapes not only our students, but ourselves. For me, at least, this approach has become a very good way to learn.

Jon Garon
Hamline University School of Law

Prompt Feedback and Multiple Forms of Assessment

Students may wonder whether they are adequately absorbing legal concepts if their performance is assessed only in an end-of-semester exam. To give my Civil Rights students multiple opportunities to gauge their own understanding of the legal doctrine, I use all of the following techniques at intervals throughout the semester.

1. Multiple choice questions. Giving the students advance warning that we would have an in-class multiple choice self-assessment of particular doctrines, I distribute a handful of questions and students electronically submit answers. Fifteen minutes later the class as a whole walks through each question. The quiz counts for a tiny percentage of the grade; the purpose is to promptly diagnose student difficulty in absorbing the doctrine. For many students, the multiple choice quiz is a low risk, wake-up call.
2. In-class short essays. Giving the students advance warning that we would have an in-class essay on particular doctrines, I distribute a written hypothetical. Twenty minutes later, students electronically submit essay answers. Immediately afterwards, before reading any of the essays, I walk the class through the key points I am looking for in their responses. The in-class essay is a useful self-assessment whether or not the essay counts toward the grade and even if the experience ends there. However, in addition, within a few days after class, I skim the essays and select four or five good ones to post on our electronic course webpage. The opportunity for students to compare their own answers to the sample good answers is another form of prompt professor feedback but does not take as much teacher time as a full-blown midterm exam and can be repeated more than once during the semester.
3. In-class short, written law practice simulations. These are realistic writing experiences that help reinforce doctrine and also help students appreciate the law practice context in which the doctrines arise.
    a. After discussing a case introducing a new doctrine, I ask students to spend ten minutes of class time jotting down what documents might help the plaintiff in the case we've just read to prove the claim. We then go around the room asking students to share different document requests they drafted.
    b. To reinforce a new doctrine, I orally describe a short law practice scenario in which the doctrine might apply and ask students to spend eight minutes of class time drafting questions to ask the client. We then discuss the questions as a whole class. An example: To reinforce understanding of what conditions create a property interest in a government job and what procedures must be followed in order to fire that employee consistent with due process, I cast students as a lawyer for the Mayor. The Mayor is on the phone, delivering the news that he has just fired an employee. What questions should the lawyer ask the Mayor to determine whether the firing complied with procedural due process?
    c. After discussing several cases fleshing out a doctrine, I ask students to watch a short YouTube video of a situation in which the doctrine might apply (e.g., did an off-duty police officer act under color of law in assaulting a bartender?). I tell students the bartender is now their client and ask students to spend ten minutes of class time jotting down questions to ask the client, focused solely on eliciting information about the doctrine I've just introduced, differentiating

private action from action under color of law. Students then share their different client interview questions with the class.

d. We revisit the same YouTube video later in the semester, when I ask students to view it with an eye toward helping the plaintiff bartender prove a different theory of liability—that the local government should be liable for the police officer's assault—and students spend 15 minutes of class time drafting and discussing document requests to the local government.

4. In-class, 40-minute law practice simulations. In my Civil Rights class, I run ten lengthy law practice simulations. The simulations involve a range of law practice situations: jury charge conference before a district court judge; interoffice meeting among lawyers for the same side to discuss settlement; briefing the client on next steps in the litigation following an adverse district court ruling; settlement conference before a mediator; testimony before the state legislature; appellate oral argument, etc.

   Each simulation is a role play involving about five students, generally two teams of two students advocating opposing positions and one student in a neutral, questioning role. I position the role players in a triangle that encompasses the whole classroom to make every student feel physically included in the simulation. After the first 15 to 20 minutes, I open questioning up to the entire class but require the student in the neutral questioning role to call on classmates. To maximize class involvement, every student must draft and turn in two questions before every simulation and must try to ask a question during the simulation. Further, to maximize student attention, and as a courtesy to fellow students, I require students to close their laptops during simulations. Finally, to ensure that the simulation stays focused on the key doctrines they are intended to reinforce, I occasionally ask questions and occasionally interrupt answers that have gone off track. But, after the first simulation, I rarely have to interrupt. The knowledge that I might intercede is sufficient to keep the simulations focused.

   The in-class law practice simulations give students the opportunity to demonstrate understanding of legal doctrine through oral performance, whether the students are asking or answering questions. The simulations help students to develop their professional identities, not only because they demonstrate their legal skill in class but also because students often choose to collaborate as a team outside of class, in advance of the performance. While the simulations would be useful as self-assessment whether or not they count toward the grade, in my Civil Rights class each student performs two simulations and each simulation is 20% of the course grade.

Sarah Ricks
Rutgers School of Law–Camden

Educating Students about the Critiquing Process

Recently, I held a series of 20-minute appointments during which I diagnosed problems and proposed a treatment plan. No, I am not a physician, and the recipients of this information are not patients. I am a teacher of lawyering skills, and the recipients of the plans are first-year law students to whom I recently returned a memorandum-writing assignment. The range and content of the students' reactions was fascinating: some seem perplexed that their work was not among the best I have ever seen; some seem dismayed that, for the first time, their work had been judged to be merely average; and others seem delighted that they need not seek a tuition refund. Whatever the reaction, though, providing a critical assessment of another's work is never simple.

Many law students have informed me that prior to law school they rarely, if ever, had their actual writing critiqued extensively. Indeed, for most law students (depending on their undergraduate specialty), their teachers' past comments were primarily addressed to the substance of the paper rather than to the words used to present the information. Not only would a stray comma or a misplaced modifier usually go undisturbed, but even the substantive comments were often merely a terse notation in the margin, such as "good point." The extreme performance anxiety of first-year law students along with the alien experience of receiving copious comments on their writing creates a potent, and potentially paralyzing, potion for stress.

With that as a backdrop, lawyering-skills teachers ought to educate students about the process of critiquing they will experience in a lawyering skills course. Because of the importance that attorneys be detail-oriented, students need to understand at the outset of the course that they will receive comments that may appear to an untrained learner to be minutia. It may be helpful for the teacher to give concrete illustrations about how the improper placement of a word within a sentence may obfuscate the meaning of the sentence and may even spawn litigation. It may also be helpful to relate your own experience with receiving feedback. For example, I have reported to students that, when I was a junior attorney, the length of my supervisor's comments on my work product sometimes rivaled the length of that product. Also beneficial may be having one's teaching assistants speak to their students about their own responses to receiving voluminous comments; students can thereby see that successful, upper-class students have undergone the same process. Finally, students seem comforted to hear that the work of all students in the course, whether strong or weak, will receive thorough comment.

I also ask my students to try to develop a healthy, nonantagonistic relationship with the process of critiquing. As a teacher, I view the uncovering of students' writing difficulties as teaching opportunities, and I encourage students to view these revelations likewise as learning opportunities. After all, both teacher and student would agree that it is best that a student's weaknesses be exposed and addressed during law school rather than when one begins working as an attorney. Of course, to improve the chances that students will appreciate, rather than fight, the critiquing process, a teacher must be sensitive to the cumulative and potentially harmful effect of even constructive criticism and be sure to both note students' strengths and to praise their improvement.

Joel Atlas
Cornell University Law School

Self-Editing Workshops

Every year, students make similar mistakes in drafting their memos and briefs. Whether they are writing for a first-year legal writing class, an externship, a clinic, an upper-level writing class, or some other purpose, students can benefit by learning techniques to self-edit their own work. I train students to become their own editors by teaching them some simple self-editing steps that focus on basic analytical writing skills. I teach students to identify and correct their own glaring mistakes before turning in the document for review by a teaching assistant, professor—or worse—by a supervising attorney in an externship or a potential or current legal employer. Moreover, if students correct their own glaring errors before submitting the document to me, my review can focus on aspects of the document that are less visible to a beginning law student.

Here is one way to move students toward becoming independent self-editors. About a week before my legal writing students turn in a final draft, I conduct a full hour, in-class, self-editing workshop. In front of every student is an electronic or hard copy of the student's own current draft. I encourage students to bring hard copies because I frequently ask them to flip to different parts of the document. One goal of the workshop is to help the student slip loose of the author's perspective and empathize with the reader, and examining isolated parts of the hard copy document out of sequence can help students mimic the perspective of the reader and gain critical distance from their own writing.

I stand at the front of the room and direct students to perform discrete editing steps on their own documents, giving them a few minutes for each step. For example, to help students ensure that the brief is organized around legal principles, rather than a case-by-case discussion, I ask students to flip to the Argument section of the brief:

> Please look at the whole Argument section. Using a highlighter, please take seven minutes to highlight ALL the thesis sentences in the whole Argument—both in the explanation of the law and in the application/analysis of how the law applies to your client's facts.
>
> 1. Please read through just the highlighted sentences.
> 2. Read in isolation, do the highlighted sentences outline your client's entire argument?
> 3. Do any paragraphs explaining law begin "In Case A"? If so, will it be easy for the Reader to grasp what legal rule that paragraph will prove?

To ensure that students have persuasively stated the law in a brief, I ask students to look at one part of the Argument section:

> Turn to one of the sections where you've proved the rules for the 8th Amendment law.
>
> 1. Choose one rule sentence.
> 2. Looking at that rule sentence in isolation, will it be obvious to the Reader which side this brief represents?
> 3. Does the phrasing of that legal rule foreshadow how the brief will apply the law to your client's facts?

If a brief or memo requires students to reason by analogy, to ensure that students have drawn explicit analogies between the key facts of a decided case and their own client's facts, I ask students to turn to a section where they have applied the law to the client's facts:

> Look only at the Application/Analysis of the 8th Amendment section where you have applied the law to your client's facts. If you analogized your client's facts to the facts of a decided case,
>
> 1. Please turn to an important analogy you drew.
> 2. Highlight that analogy only.
> 3. Does the analogy specify what fact in the decided case is being compared to a fact in your client's case and why the two facts are similar?
> 4. Does the analogy give the reader enough information to independently evaluate whether the fact from the decided case really is similar to the fact in your client's case?
> 5. If you have no case names in the Application/Analysis, will the reader easily grasp what legal principles are being applied and what their sources are?

After the full class hour spent on self-editing, I post a document with each of the editing steps for students to repeat as necessary, outside of class. Putting the editing steps into the students' hands has the added benefit of clarifying my basic expectations and how I will evaluate the final document.

Sarah Ricks
Rutgers School of Law–Camden

Developing a Student's "Thought Monitor"

Some students find answering multiple choice questions more challenging than writing essay exams; at least there's some leeway with essays. When the questions are multiple choice, you're either right or you're wrong. Because multiple choice questions are such an integral part of the bar exam and have come to figure more prominently in law school exams, students must learn to master them.

Students arrive at an incorrect answer for a number of reasons. The most obvious is that they do not know the law. A superficial or general understanding of a rule is insufficient to distinguish between answer choices. Still, students commit a number of errors that have nothing to do with "knowing the law" and everything to do with answering a question correctly.

- Reading comprehension: Students often misread the question—either the question asked, or the facts in the problem, or both. Sometimes they mischaracterize the facts. These are essentially reading comprehension problems where students do not correctly interpret what they have read.
- Adding facts: Students read into the facts and sometimes add their own which, of course, alters the nature of the problem. Some students do not "add" facts but see implications that have no basis in the facts but which lead them astray in their analysis.
- Failure to identify the issue: Students ignore the specific question that they are asked to address in the question stem and then allow all the presented facts in the problem to lead them astray. Because they have failed to identify the "issue" in the problem, they have no means by which to identify the correct answer choice.

It is essential that students learn to detect the errors in their own thinking and reading processes and correct them. I developed a method to help students cultivate this type of self-awareness when I worked with a bar candidate to improve her Multistate Bar Exam performance. She consistently made incorrect answer choices on the MBE, yet responded correctly whenever asked a question about the law, so apparently she "knew the rules." I realized that to help her and for her to help herself, we needed to figure out what was leading her astray. We tried an experiment. I asked her to read a sentence and tell me exactly what she thought when she finished reading it. We proceeded sentence by sentence. In this way, I could follow her line of reasoning and detect any flaws—whether she misread a word, made an inappropriate inference, or ignored critical language. I could also tell if something was missing from her analysis.

Happily, this exercise in directed reading led to an immediate improvement in her multiple choice exam taking skills and she passed the bar exam on its next administration. Once she learned how to monitor what she was thinking, she was in control of the question and not the other way around.

The following is a process you can use to help students cultivate the skills of active reading and self-awareness and thereby improve students' multiple choice scores.

The Process

What follows is a guide to show students how to engage in an internal, ongoing conversation with themselves when they read. I've addressed it directly to the student so it's as if we were sitting and working together.

Let's get started by reading a real problem. An example from a past MBE will work nicely. Here is what you will do:

1. Begin by reading the interrogatory and proceed to the fact pattern.
2. As you read, pause after each sentence and write down exactly what you think. Don't stop to censor your thoughts; write them as you have them. To borrow an old phrase, "go with the flow."

   Note: By committing your thoughts to specific words, you are forced to be aware of what you are thinking. This approach allows you to backtrack and find the errors in your thought process should you select an incorrect answer choice.
3. After you finish reading the fact pattern, form your own answer in response to the call of the question.
4. Read each of the answer choices and once again write down exactly what you think. Translate your "answer" to fit one of the available answer choices.
5. Now read my thoughts on the problem and compare them to what you've written. Don't expect them to be the same, but your thinking should parallel mine. After all, the same problem should elicit a similar analysis. What I found important, you should have found important. What I questioned, you should have questioned. How I responded to each of the issues raised in the facts, you should have responded to as well.

Here's the problem:

Peavey was walking peacefully along a public street when he encountered Dorwin, whom he had never seen before. Without provocation or warning, Dorwin picked up a rock and struck Peavey with it. It was later established that Dorwin was mentally ill and suffered recurrent hallucinations.

If Peavey asserts a claim against Dorwin based on battery, which of the following, if supported by evidence, will be Dorwin's best defense?

A. Dorwin did not understand that his act was wrongful.

B. Dorwin did not desire to cause harm to Peavey.

C. Dorwin did not know that he was striking a person.

D. Dorwin thought Peavey was about to attack him.

Here's what I thought as I read this problem, sentence by sentence (my thoughts are in italics in the parentheses):

(First, I'll check the interrogatory.) If Peavey asserts a claim against Dorwin based on battery, which of the following, if supported by evidence, will be Dorwin's best defense? *(Since a person is bringing the suit and not the state, it's a civil suit and not a criminal case. I'm looking for Dorwin's best defense to battery, so I'd better keep the rule in mind as I go through this: "a battery is the intent to cause harmful or offensive contact with the person of another." I'll be*

looking for something that negates an element of battery or possibly self-defense.) Peavey was walking peacefully along a public street when he encountered Dorwin, whom he had never seen before. *(Nothing has happened yet, but it may be important that this was a "public" and not a "private" street, but maybe not because the question stem tells me that Peavey brought the action against Dorwin in battery so the state is not involved and it's not a constitutional issue. Maybe "peacefully" goes to provocation and since Peavey never saw Dorwin before, there's no past history between them.)* Without provocation or warning, Dorwin picked up a rock and struck Peavey with it. *(Here's the act required for the battery and I was right about the lack of provocation. Now the issue is one of intent. The facts say that Dorwin "picked up" a rock. This sounds like he acted with purpose. The intent element is satisfied not only when the actor intends harmful or wrongful behavior, but if he acts with purpose or knowledge to a "substantial certainty." Dorwin need not have understood his act to be "wrongful" to have formed the requisite intent: he need only to know what would be the likely consequence of striking Peavey with a rock.)* It was later established that Dorwin was mentally ill and suffered recurrent hallucinations. *(What's the relevance of this? The majority view is that insane persons are liable for their intentional torts. So if Dorwin made a choice to pick up the rock and hit Peavey with it, it doesn't matter if it was an irrational or crazy choice.)*

(On to the answer choices. I'm looking for Dorwin's best defense to battery. I know the act occurred, so any defense will have to negate the intent element or provide for self-defense, which doesn't seem likely since Dorwin wasn't provoked or even knew Peavey.) Choice A: Dorwin did not understand that his act was wrongful. *(This one isn't right because Dorwin doesn't have to understand his act to be wrongful to commit battery; he only has to act with purpose or knowledge to a "substantial certainty." He need only know what would be the likely consequence of hitting Peavey with a rock.)* Choice B: Dorwin did not desire to cause harm to Peavey. *(This is just a variation of A. Even though a battery is the intentional, harmful or offensive touching of another, Dorwin need not have intended harm to be found liable in battery.)* Choice C: Dorwin did not know that he was striking a person. *(This sounds funny, but if Dorwin had no idea—no "knowledge"—he was striking a person, then he could not have formed the requisite intent to do the act. This one may be it but I need to read D.)* Choice D: Dorwin thought Peavey was about to attack him. *(This sounds like self-defense, which is a defense but there's nothing in the facts to lead Dorwin to believe Peavey was about to attack him. Even assuming Dorwin believed he was about to be attacked and needed to defend himself, this still admits that he committed the battery. The question asks for the "best" defense and that's one that says he never committed the battery. I'll go with C.)*

Choice C is the correct answer.

It probably seems as if it would take a long time to think through this problem, but it really doesn't. Just a couple of minutes. It takes much longer to write it, and for you to read it, than it actually takes to do it. That's because what I think as I read is so mechanical it happens automatically. It takes practice, but the process can become automatic for you as well.

I've given you the guidelines and shown you how I go about it. Now you need to practice. I realize it won't be practical to write down your thoughts each time you answer a multiple choice question. But now that you know what should be going on in your head as you work your way through a problem, your task is to be conscious and deliberate during each step of the process. That way you'll remember what you thought and can go back and revisit it should you arrive at an incorrect answer choice. If you make the effort to put your thoughts into some concrete form—even if it's just articulated in your head—you will remember what you thought. Words give form to thoughts. And once there's form, there's something to remember.

Suzanne Darrow-Kleinhaus
Touro College Jacob D. Fuchsberg Law Center

Modeling and Teacher Feedback to Teach IRAC in Substantive Courses

Unlike legal writing teachers, those who teach substantive courses to 1Ls typically don't focus explicitly on teaching the traditional syllogistic method of presenting arguments, or IRAC. Nonetheless, we often complain about our students' inability to analyze our exam questions and compose their answers. To help my students perform better in Civil Procedure, I developed a technique for teaching IRAC that requires virtually no class time and helps almost all my students use it on their first exams. I explicitly modeled Rule-Application-Conclusion in answers posted on my website for web-based problem sets, and I provided feedback to students on their use of it.

My Civil Procedure casebook has numerous "right answer" problems for working students through the basics of the black letter law. I set up these problems as online problem sets using my university's WebQ, a teaching tool similar to the quizzes one can create in TWEN or in the Lexis-Nexis Blackboard Webcourse. Students accessed the problems from my course website and were asked to work through them before class. Originally, I did not post answers on the website until after the deadline for students to submit their responses, but eventually because of student requests, I decided to keep the answers visible even as the students were doing the assignments, on the theory that prompt feedback is educationally desirable.

I structured the answers to make each of the analytical steps required to answer the problem more visible. I set up the answers in very structured Rule-Application-Conclusion format with each section of the answer so labeled. In addition, I asked students to respond in Rule-Application-Conclusion format, and in the space for students' answers to the online problems I inserted prompts to do so.

By itself, this modeling affected some students' presentation of their answers. But I took an additional step. In the third week of the term, I provided email feedback to students either praising them for following the format or encouraging them to do so. The feedback made an impact—one of the students joked before class that he had received an "evil" email from me, but I also received many emails expressing appreciation—and most students began using the IRAC format at least some of the time. I continued to monitor students' use of IRAC and nudged the students who were not using it to do so.

Teaching IRAC this way required lots of up-front work on my part. Now that the problem sets and answers are completed, however, maintenance is required only as the law or the casebook changes. I thought the effort was well worth it, and the students agreed. When asked for their course evaluations to list three class activities that worked, almost all the students included the problem sets in their list.

Deborah Maranville
University of Washington School of Law

Teaching Issue-Spotting Explicitly

Common knowledge has it that the bar exam is, at heart, an exercise in issue-spotting. Probably the same could be said of law school exams, especially those in the first-year. Of course, both exams are based on more than just issue-spotting—they require students to have memorized significant amounts of doctrine, understand the process of application, be able to organize an analysis quickly and cogently (usually in IRAC format) and maintain some level of standard writing form, all in a very tight timeframe. But missed issues receive no points on an exam; likewise analysis of issues that the professor thinks are not triggered gets no points. At the same time, issue-spotting is possibly the least-taught aspect of the law school curriculum. Indeed, law school course syllabi, casebook tables of contents, and commercial bar reviews, by organizing doctrine and opinions by issue, all take issue-spotting off the table.

The key to issue-spotting is the ability to see connections between authority (including policy) and facts in complex settings. In other words, issues live in the interaction among law, policy, and facts. For many students, that interaction is not readily apparent. We believe the teacher has the responsibility—or at least an opportunity—to teach the skill of issue-spotting explicitly. We have identified several aspects of issue-spotting that teachers can help students with, including the baseline ability to recognize instances of facts triggering issues, dealing with complicated sub-rules, spotting hidden issues, and seeing connections among doctrines.

Facts Triggering Issues

Students need to hear explicitly that facts trigger issues. It gives them a way to begin to develop a technique of issue-spotting. For many students, the very notion that facts trigger issues is revelatory. This is due to a number of factors. First, students tend to view the assigned opinions as monolithic narratives, without realizing that the facts as found (and subsequently reproduced in the casebook) were really the product of vigorous argument. Second, the opinion is likely to identify or set out the issue in some way that ostensibly relieves students of the need to do so themselves. Finally, the casebook itself, by labeling chapters and sections so clearly, makes it unnecessary for students to grapple with what the issue is. Students therefore are likely to miss the organic connection between facts and rules that create the issues.

Consider a simple exercise about working with facts: assign a case that has a rule with elements. In class, break the students into small groups. Assign each group one element or sub-rule. Have the groups identify the facts from the case that implicate the element they have been assigned (whether highlighted by the court or not). Does the court focus on any particular element(s), and if so, which one(s) and why? Have the class add or modify facts that trigger their assigned element or sub-rule in a way that might change the analysis and outcome. The key here is pointing out that this exercise will help with issue-spotting. It teaches students to pay attention to the role of facts in triggering issues and satisfying or not satisfying elements.

Connections Among Doctrines

Another tricky aspect of issue-spotting is the ability to recognize some of the less obvious connections among doctrines and use those connections to surface issues on an exam. After studying various doctrines in discrete units, it is important to remind students to step back and look at the big picture: how might these different doctrines fit together in analyzing a hypothetical? After all the doctrine has been covered, you can point out issues that are likely to arise from the same set of facts. For example, in contract law, whenever there is a question about contract interpretation (i.e., the meaning of a disputed term in a contract), there is likely to also be a question about the admissibility of evidence, requiring consideration of the parol evidence rule. Other times, claims will naturally be raised in the alternative. For example, again from contract law, whenever there is a question about whether the requirement of consideration has been satisfied, students should also consider whether the plaintiff could bring a claim under promissory estoppel, an alternate theory of recovery. Making these connections explicit will help with issue-spotting—if you remember to *consider the possibility*, you will be more likely to recognize the presence or absence of facts that trigger the alternate doctrine. Linking these doctrines can be done in review sessions, but should be done at various junctures through the course as well.

Relationships Among Sub-Issues

Students also have trouble when the question tests the articulation and application of "sub-rules." Although the relationship between rules and sub-rules may be clear to teachers intimately familiar with the structure and organization of the doctrine they have been teaching for many years, first-year students often do not make the connections as clearly as they need to in order to be able to spot issues involving a sub-rule. Some doctrines are taught over the course of several class periods and students can miss the connection between the rules learned at the end of that time with what came before. Those connections may be essential for issue-spotting.

Have the class take a minute to answer a question about the link between a sub-rule and the overarching rule. For example: "what is the relationship between option contract and acceptance?" The connection between these two concepts can be obscured by the many layers of rules regarding acceptance, including the objective test (whether a reasonable person would consider the offeree's words or conduct to constitute assent), revocation (whether the offeree even has the right to accept), UCC § 2-207 and battle of the forms (whether the attempted acceptance was valid), and the mailbox rule (whether the timing of the attempted acceptance was sufficient), among other things. Within each of those issues is a complex web of sub-rules, not the least of which is whether the UCC applies. Taking one of those rules to the next level, the rule for revocation includes sub-rules relating to the process of revoking, as well as option contracts and whether the offeror has the right to revoke. Then there are a variety of ways to make an offer irrevocable, each of which has its own set of rules. By the time students learn about an offeree's reliance on an offer creating an option contract, they may lose sight completely of the relevance of that rule in the bigger picture of contract formation. So, to answer the question posed in the exercise, the relationship between option contract and acceptance is: in some cases, whether there's a valid option contract will determine whether an offer is revocable, which may determine whether an attempted acceptance is valid, and ultimately whether a contract has been formed.

Although doing this exercise as a minute paper, which the teacher would collect and read through quickly, provides some feedback about where the students are, the major value of the exercise is to set up a discussion of the issue-spotting aspects of the relationship between what may appear to some students to be unconnected doctrines. It also provides an opportunity to talk with students about how they outline. Their outlines, which on a good day contain accurate doctrine, should in addition, alert them to the kinds of facts that trigger issues. This approach is especially useful with sub-rules like irrevocable offers.

Spotting "Hidden" Issues

Another aspect of effective issue-spotting is that certain issues are likely to be hidden, with no obvious clues in the fact pattern that the issue is triggered. An example of a hidden issue in contracts involves the statute of frauds. The fact pattern might never mention whether there was a writing, so there may be nothing in the fact pattern to remind the student to consider whether a writing was necessary (of course there will always be some fact to trigger an issue, such as, in the case of the statute of frauds, the contract being for a sale of goods over $500 or for the sale of real property, but these facts may be too indirect to trigger the issue for a student who is not paying close attention). Similarly, parol evidence rule issues can be hidden where the call of the question does not refer to a fact as "evidence" or use the word "admissible." A cohesive collapsed outline (i.e., an outline reduced to a checklist) can be critical for spotting hidden issues, reminding the students of all the issues they should consider on the exam. Teachers might suggest to students that they annotate their outlines and checklists with a note to themselves reminding them to consider where the exam might include hidden issues triggered by the absence of facts.

Of course, issue-spotting is not the only skill that students need to succeed in law school and as lawyers. Students in the first year of law school should learn key academic skills (e.g., case reading and briefing, note-taking, outlining, and study skills) and legal reasoning skills (e.g., fact identification and analysis, rule identification and synthesis, and application of rules to facts, as well as issue-spotting) throughout the curriculum explicitly, rather than by intuition, so that they are better prepared in their second and third years to focus on the denser doctrines and more practice-oriented skills. The reason to make academic and legal reasoning skills explicit in the study of doctrine is that students do better when they are aware of their own thinking and learning processes. The process of learning is too often left to intuition and happenstance. Many more students can succeed at greater levels of competence if the process of learning itself becomes the subject under discussion

David Nadvorney
City University of New York School of Law

Deborah Zalesne
City University of New York School of Law

Second- and Third-Year Students as Exam Preparation Experts

I teach a year-long, first-year course in Civil Procedure. Like most first-year professors, I get questions from students about exam preparation starting very early in the semester—sometimes on the first day. The questions are familiar: Do I have to memorize all of the rules? Do I have to remember case names? What about the notes and questions in the casebook? What is the best way to learn the rules? How do I know which rules are the most important? How can I outline Civil Procedure? Will commercial study guides or other students' outlines help me?

I set aside time during the fall semester to address these questions and to talk to the class generally about how to study Civil Procedure and how to prepare for the final exam. Every fall, I tell them that they need to learn the Federal Rules of Civil Procedure, understand the cases interpreting and applying them, and be able to use the rules to answer questions and solve problems based on new facts. Every fall I assure them that although it seems dark at the beginning, if they work diligently the light bulb will turn on toward the end of the semester. And every fall, they stare back at me with skepticism, particularly about the light bulb thing.

A few years back I tried something different. I contacted a small group of second- and third-year students who had earned top grades in my class, and I invited them to come to my class for a day to talk to the students about their techniques for learning Civil

Procedure and preparing for the exam. I scheduled my panel for an entire class period in the fourth week, figuring that date was well enough into the semester for the students to appreciate the advice but not too late to make some changes. I let my first-year class know about my plan, and they were very eager to hear the "real" story about how to survive—and even master—Civil Procedure.

When the day came, the room was packed. The panelists introduced themselves and commented for a few minutes on their experiences studying, learning, and using Civil Procedure. Then they moved into a question-and-answer session. They shared a wealth of approaches and techniques, underscoring that there is no one right way to learn the material. For example, I give a closed-book exam, so learning the key language of the rules is critical. Some panelists made a flashcard for each new rule and went through the flashcards every day, some wrote out the rules until they had them down cold, some listened to recordings every day in the car, some diagrammed the rules to get a visual image, and some recited the rules back and forth in their study groups. When all of the panelists reached consensus—such as on the importance of arguing the facts in an exam—the impact was much greater than I could have achieved alone. They even got through to the students on one of my favorite points, the practical importance of Civil Procedure, by telling stories of how exciting it was to be able to use Civil Procedure knowledge in their summer jobs at firms or in chambers.

I was impressed by the panelists' candor in sharing techniques that did not work. One student warned that there was "bad information out there" and that they should make their own outline rather than rely on a canned or commercial outline. Another student confessed that she had slipped into book briefing in the second semester and had to go back over all those cases later when she realized that she was not really learning the material.

I was also touched by their desire to support and encourage the first-year students. They shared all their secrets and reassured them that the potent mixture of fear, exhaustion, and mental overload that many of them were feeling was typical. In the words of one of the panelists: "You can do it. It is not impossible.... If you study hard, good things will happen for you." And yes, they said that although they struggled during the semester the light bulb did turn on for them toward the end.

The class ended with enthusiastic applause, so I knew it was a hit. At the beginning of the next class, I asked each of my students to identify one thing that they heard at the panel that they would try to incorporate into their routine. Not surprisingly, they remembered the different panelists' contributions in great detail, and many had already incorporated a new strategy or two into their own study routines.

I will definitely be using a second- and third-year student panel on studying and exam preparation again next fall. I recommend it to anyone who is looking for an entertaining and effective way to reach a range of first-year students, as well as to recognize and include former students who have worked hard and succeeded in your classroom.

Elizabeth Pendo
Saint Louis University School of Law

Taking a Small Step Toward More Assessments

Experts on learning tell us that the most effective learning environments are "assessment centered." In those environments, students know what they are expected to learn, understand the criteria used to evaluate their performance, have multiple and varied opportunities to practice meeting performance criteria, and receive feedback on meeting those criteria. They also learn how to use the feedback to improve their learning. While writing and providing feedback on problems, quizzes, essays, and presentations can take time, you can take some small manageable steps towards making your classes more "assessment- and learner-centered" Here's one suggestion.

1. Reuse a question from last year's final exam as a writing exercise.
2. Modify the question so that it is limited to the topics students have been studying to date.
3. Assign students to write the answer as homework. Have them bring in the assignment in electronic or paper form that they can show to classmates. You might want to suggest a time limit for completing the answer, simulating exam conditions.
4. During class, have them pair up or form groups of three or four and first read through each other's answers. Notice similarities and differences. They are often surprised at how differently they respond to the same material.
5. Give students a checklist: your scoring sheet or list of material you were expecting to see in last year's exams. Have them use the checklist to review another person's answer in greater depth.
6. Walk them through the checklist, (e.g., "Find the issue of duty in your neighbor's essay. Identify the standard of care. Compare it to the checklist. Here's what I was looking for and why it is important ...")
7. As you do this, you can use the students' writing to give you feedback on their learning. For example, you could ask "how many of you read essays that included ... ?" A show of hands (or using "clickers") can give you feedback on areas students are struggling with and areas most seem to grasp.
8. Continue through the essay, taking questions.
9. If you have one available, provide one or more examples of a good answer (if you get permission from your former students, you can use their exam answers).
10. At the end of the session, ask students to complete the prompt at the bottom of the checklist: "What advice would you give yourself to improve your performance?" Give them up to five minutes to take the time to reflect on their learning. Invite them to use their advice to improve their learning.
11. Invite students who want to go over the essay to bring their essay to your office during your office hours. Ask them to review the checklist and sample answer and bring those with them when they meet with you.

Time needed: In class: 30 to 55 minutes, depending on the question and depth of detail. Outside of class: one to two hours to prepare the question and checklist, less if you have some from last year you can use. Office hours: one to two hours. My experience, and that of colleagues who use this approach, is that around 10% of your students will come to meet with you. And those conversations last about ten minutes, because the students already have the checklist, feedback from the class discussion, a sample answer, and the experience of observing someone else's work. By the time they meet with you, they have pretty focused questions about the assignment.

Value: By preparing the exam answer in advance, students gain practice applying the material in writing. Committing words to the page is very different from "knowing it in your head" or being able to talk through an answer, which tends to be significantly less precise. Reviewing their classmates' work, applying a checklist, and reviewing a sample answer provides students with immediate feedback on how well they are performing in the course. By doing the exercise in class and providing class-wide feedback, you do not need to read and comment upon each student's work, and a lot of learning still happens.

Sophie Sparrow
University of New Hampshire School of Law

Using Multiple-Choice Quizzes for Formative Assessment

As a reader of this book, you are probably already sold on the idea of formative assessment. That is, you understand that student performance will likely be enhanced if students are provided with frequent information about how well they understand the course material or how well they have mastered the skills being taught. If you are not sold on that idea, please accept it on faith for the next few pages.

Unfortunately, one of the difficulties in providing law students with formative assessment that is timely, meaningful, and individualized is the size of most classes. Reviewing and commenting upon students answers to an essay question or research paper takes an enormous amount of effort and a great deal of time. Teachers with two classes, each with several dozen students, often find that a daunting task. Few instructors are likely to offer it more than once per semester, even though formative assessment works best when it is frequent.

What follows is one possible solution to this problem: multiple-choice quizzes, each administered multiple times. Multiple times? Yes, multiple times. Not only that, I administer them as take-home exams and allow students to work alone or with one classmate. Now before you recoil in horror or regard this as heretical, let me explain. Remember too, the primary purpose is *formative* assessment, not *summative* assessment. The purpose is to help the students learn, not to determine to what extent they have learned.

Format

Each quiz consists of five to eight questions. Students are provided with the quiz and given a day or two to complete it outside of class. They submit it to me for scoring. I indicate which responses are correct and which are not. Each correct response on the first submission counts one point. Students then have another day or two to submit a different answer to those questions they initially got wrong. I re-score the quizzes and each correct response on the second submission is worth three-quarters of a point. Along with their revised scores, I distribute the correct answers. For each wrong answer on the second submission, students may submit a written explanation of why the correct answer is correct. A satisfactory explanation is worth one-half point. The whole process of administering a quiz takes about a week.

I give three or four of these quizzes in each one-semester course. Each quiz counts as a specified fraction in computing students' course grades. That fraction is usually 10 to 17%. Sometimes I specify what the percentage is; sometimes I allow the students to select the percentage at the beginning of the course.

Crafting the Questions

This process would, of course, not work if the questions were easy. In fact, they are often wicked hard (if you're from Boston, you understand the usage of "wicked" here). The key is to provide numerous plausible wrong answers. That goal can be challenging if the question asks about only one thing. So, I tend to have questions that, either on their face or through the possible answers, ask about several things simultaneously. Here is an example:

> In which one of the following situations is the security interest in the identified collateral most likely to be perfected?
>
> 1. The filed financing statement identifies the collateral as "general intangibles" instead of "payment intangibles."
> 2. After perfecting a security interest in accounts by filing a proper financing statement, the secured party mistakenly filed a termination statement when it meant to file an amendment changing its address.
> 3. The filing office in Connecticut rejected a financing statement describing the collateral as equipment because the financing identified as debtor a corporation incorporated in Massachusetts.
> 4. The filing office rejected an amendment adding collateral because the amendment did not provide the file number of the initial financing statement to which it relates.
> 5. In a consumer transaction in which the security agreement describes the collateralized securities account with specificity, the financing statement identifies the collateral as "investment property."

Each of the responses deals with a different section of Article 9 of the Uniform Commercial Code. Consequently, to get the question correct—that is, to pick the best answer—they need to identify each of those provisions and fully understand them all. Another way to make the questions challenging is put reasoning into the optional answers, so that the students have to pick the right answer for the right reason.

Experience

Writing the quizzes takes a very long time. But grading them is very quick. I can return the quizzes within an hour of when they are due, thus giving students very timely feedback on their performance.

To date, student reaction to these quizzes has been extremely positive. Although the students occasionally get a bit frustrated, they do put in an amazing amount of effort and thought. You might think that there would be a problem with cheating on the second submission. After all, if students compared their performance on the first submission with classmates, it would be rather easy to identify all the correct answer to each question. But judging by the number of students whose second answers are still wrong, cheating is not significant.

The quizzes have definitely helped—or forced—students to learn the course material. By the end of the third submission, the whole class knows the answer to each question and why the answer is correct. And that is the goal: not to *measure* their understanding but to *raise* the level of understanding. Judging by their performance on the final essay exam, it works.

Stephen L. Sepinuck
Gonzaga University School of Law

Effective Feedback on Graded Midterm Assignments

Law teachers who use graded midterm assignments sometimes encounter difficulty with some students' unwillingness to accept feedback on midterm graded assignments. Their response can negatively affect the learning environment for the rest of the course.

Three experienced law teachers offer ideas to maximize the effectiveness of feedback on midterm assignments.

It helps first to understand where the students are coming from. Most law students have been very successful in previous educational settings, regardless of the amount of work they put in. So they are shocked to not earn an A or even a B+. Many also struggle with the new skill of applying knowledge to new situations. They may "know" the subject at an A level, but analyze and apply it less proficiently. I find it helps to:

1. Give them an ungraded practice assignment first. Then explain how you grade and why. Show them the process. Make it an option outside of class if you don't have time in class.
2. Early in the semester explain that you have high expectations, believe that students can reach them, and will do what you can to help them succeed. Repeat several times during the semester.
3. Tell them that in law school, students who learn from the feedback they get on their midterms can do much better on their finals.
4. Make sure that your grading expectations are realistic. If the exam is scored based on the way an experienced professor would answer the question, for example, it may not be realistic for a 1L. You may want to show other professors or research assistants your exam and get their take on what is reasonable.

Sophie Sparrow
University of New Hampshire School of Law

To the extent that "feedback" means grade (rather than comments), I find that the problem often comes from the fact that many law schools and law school teachers use a grading scale with less grade inflation than most students experienced in their undergraduate programs. One way to lessen the anxiety about this fact on scored assignments and midterm exams is to give each student his or her score and the median score, but not to convert the score into a letter grade. The score is what gives students a sense of their relative performance and it's the letter grade that produces most of the anxiety.

To the extent that "feedback" means critical comments, be sure to incorporate praise. Telling students what they did correctly or well is just as important as telling them what they did incorrectly or poorly.

Stephen L. Sepinuck
Gonzaga University School of Law

With guidance, students can understand their analytical and writing strengths and weaknesses before you give them direct feedback. I use an exercise in which I first make a copy of each student's exam and I grade/comment on the original. In class, before handing back their exams, I ask students to critique two sample student answers. We go line by line, identifying if the sentence is an issue, rule, application, or conclusion. We debrief. Then I return the clean copies of their exams and ask them to perform the same exercise line by line on their own exams. A lot of groans and laughter. We debrief. Students articulate patterns. Many lights bulbs and "Aha!"s. Then, I ask them to engage in free writing on what they learned about their own analysis/writing by doing this exercise. Finally, I hand out my graded version, which confirms what the students already have identified.

Laurie Zimet
University of California, Hastings College of Law

Fast Formative Feedback

A significant impediment to providing students with prompt and effective formative feedback during a course is the commitment of significant time and resources, especially in large core classes. Consequently, teachers generally end up providing only a summative evaluation of students in the form of a final examination, which only occasionally serves as a formative feedback aid. Yet, the value of formative feedback to improvement and development is widely known. Like a "30-minute meal" by the chef, Rachael Ray, quick and effective formative feedback events are prized by all involved. Fast feedback provides students with time appropriate responses and faculty members are likewise afforded the opportunity to better understand student advancement during the course, while still having the time to meet service and scholarship commitments. The following methods have been tried in law school classes and have weathered the heat of the law school kitchen.

The Five-Minute Extended Class Podcast

This type of podcast is used not only to review recent classes, but to extend the intellectual work of the classes as well. The podcast is consequently divided up into several components: (1) a brief review or discussion of a rule or doctrine covered in a recent class; (2) a problem or hypothetical relating to the doctrine; and (3) a recitation of strategies, protocols, rules and application in answering that problem. The podcast and problem within it can be assigned, but can just as well be offered as an add-on, to help explicate and advance the students' knowledge of the subject area. Students can be expressly informed they can pause the recording after the problem and answer it on their own, only to turn it back on later and hear how the professor might approach a response. Further, students can do the problems and listen to these podcasts at their own pace and on their own MP3 players. Thus, the podcasts promote portable learning and give the students more control over the learning process.

The Post-Class Observational Email or Meeting

Students often do not know how they appear to the professor in class. They may be a few minutes late, add a salient thought in the middle of a long discussion, or demonstrate thorough preparation when called upon. A quick email sent after class to one or several students observing how they are performing in the class can be of great benefit if done constructively. The emails can go beyond observation to judgment, such as commending a student for a particular insight or contribution. I have found students to be generally appreciative of my interest, saying things like, "I am glad you noticed."

If a matter is more involved, an email request to meet briefly with a student to follow up on the student's classroom behavior can be of significant benefit as well. Many times, students who appear distracted or present uneven results in class have issues beyond the classroom that are affecting their performance. A brief direct discussion about it with the student in question can develop a plan for future classes that accommodates the student and encourages better performance at the same time.

The Half-Hour Optional Problem Session

Students often want to assess their performance during a course. Such an assessment can occur through a midterm examination, although that often involves a great deal of resources. Another way to offer student self-assessment, as well as to provide feedback to the teacher on the level of understanding by the class, is to hold an optional problem session before or after a class for a half-hour or so. (I generally offer two or three optional sessions a course.) Students can be given in advance a hard copy of the problems or access to the problems online to afford them the opportunity to work through them in advance if they want to do so. The teacher's analysis of the problems—with the student's contributions—can deepen the students' understanding of the problems and give students a better idea of how they are to approach problem-solving. Potential problems for the optional session could come from a variety of sources, such as old exam questions, released bar exam questions, questions from students, questions extracted from various cases, or problems presented in the course book.

Using Final Examinations to Create Development Plans

Students often use final exams in the same manner as professors—as an indicator of performance. That's where the value of the exam often ends. Students and schools use grades to create a hierarchy for employers, for calculating honors, and for other benefits. Students generally do not use a final exam, however, as formative feedback for improvement purposes, if only because the legal education culture does not promote such use. When a course concludes, the incentive to review the exam is small.

While students can be given detailed answer keys and assess their own performance, exams can be utilized institutionally to stimulate the development of important exam-taking skills. Students can be asked by a professor—or better yet, as part of the school's curriculum—to review their exams, especially after their first semester of law school. The exam review can be to create a development plan to improve exam-taking skills and minimize weak exam-taking habits. The vehicle for such a development plan can be a brief questionnaire filled out and handed in by students after reviewing at least one exam. The questionnaire can ask students to identify their exam-taking weaknesses, exam-taking strengths, and how they will improve their exam-taking skills in the future. This effort focuses the student on self-management and conveys the idea that exam-taking skills can be improved through reflection.

Steven I. Friedland
Elon University School of Law

Chapter 12

Summative Assessment— Evaluating and Grading Students

The primary purpose of summative assessment is to evaluate students to assign grades. Law school grades can greatly affect students' opportunities in school and afterwards. Consequently, summative assessment is stressful for most students. On the other hand, summative assessment can maximize student motivation and learning.

Regardless of the grading system our law schools employ (pass/fail, letter grades, number grades, required median grades, forced curves), students deserve graded assessments that are effective and fair. Summative assessment schemes with integrity share a number of attributes:

- Multiple and varied assessments;
- Congruence between course goals, teaching methods, and assessments;
- Grading criteria given to students before the graded assessments;
- Opportunities for students to practice meeting the criteria before the graded assessments;
- Explicit criteria used to ensure consistent grading; and
- Productive meetings with students after the assessments.

Multiple and Varied Assessments

Many forms of assessments are available to assess students' learning, including exams (essay, multiple-choice, short answer, etc.), research papers, document drafting (contracts, wills, pleadings, etc.), participation, presentations, and performances (interviewing, counseling, advocacy, etc.). Not all students demonstrate proficiency in the same way. While some students do well on traditional essay exam questions, others do better if they are asked to use the course content and skills to deliver an oral argument or draft a document. Ideally, we give students a variety of opportunities to show us their success in learning what we have tried to teach them.

Any combination of assessment forms could be used to determine students' grades. For example, students' grades for a course could be based on: (1) participation in and out of class (20%); (2) research paper (40%); and (3) final exam (part essay and part multiple-choice) (40%). Multiple and varied summative assessments should help us achieve two important results—enhance student learning and fairly measure student achievement.

Congruence Between Course Goals, Teaching Methods, and Assessments

When designing courses, we should articulate our learning objectives—the key knowledge, skills, and values that the students should learn in the course. As we plan individual class sessions, those learning objectives should drive our choice of teaching and learning methods. Likewise, our summative assessments should reflect our learning objectives and the methods we employ throughout the course. In short, we should test what we teach.

Different types of summative assessments are appropriate to measure different types of learning. Essay and multiple-choice exams can effectively test students' understanding of legal doctrine and analytical skills. Drafting papers and documents can assess students' understanding and research, writing, and analysis skills. Graded performances can assess students' skills in such areas as interviewing, counseling, advocacy, and negotiation.

Grading Criteria Given to Students Before the Graded Assessment

Learning and fairness are both furthered when teachers evaluate students on explicit criteria that students receive before the graded assessment. For example, grading criteria for a paper in an Environmental Law course could be framed as follows:

- Writing (20%). This includes punctuation, spelling, organization, sentences, paragraphs, readability, and professional presentation.
- Problem definition (10%). At the beginning of the paper, you must define the issue(s) you will address and your goal(s).
- Analysis. The purpose of the paper is to assess your ability to critically analyze a real-world situation based on the content and skills you learned in this course. You must choose a subject related to the coverage of this course. The specific analysis criteria are as follows:
    - Whether you addressed the issues you identified and whether you met your goals (10%).
    - Clarity (15%).
    - Appropriate use of authority. This means citing to authority to support all statements you make that are not your opinion. (10%).
    - Quality of discussion (depth of analysis, insights, coherence) (15%).
    - Level of understanding of Environmental Law demonstrated (20%).

Another way to communicate evaluation criteria is through a rubric. The sample rubric shown in Figure 1 helps students understand what is expected of them on a Torts exam.

The process of articulating the criteria in writing helps teachers clarify in their own minds the components of excellent performance on an assessment. By communicating criteria to students in writing before the assessment, teachers demystify the assessment process and help students focus on developing the requisite knowledge and skills to perform well.

Opportunities for Students to Practice Meeting the Criteria Before the Graded Assessment

A tremendous amount of learning can take place when students practice meeting the evaluation criteria before the graded assessment. Practice exams, quizzes, paper drafts, and mock performances, coupled with feedback, promote student learning and allow them to be fully prepared for graded assignments. Grading students on their performance

Figure 1 Sample rubric

	Exemplary	**Competent**	**Developing**
Law (25%)	Accurately identifies all elements/factors and sub-issues	Accurately identifies all elements 1 factor or sub-issue missing	Accurately identifies all elements 2 factors or sub-issues missing
Applying facts to law (65%)	Thoroughly applies specific facts and makes reasonable inferences from facts to legal elements, factors and sub-issues	Applies facts and reasonable inferences from facts to legal elements, factors and sub-issues A few minor areas are not thorough	Applies facts and reasonable inferences from facts to legal elements, factors and sub-issues 2 or more areas are not are thorough
Writing and format (10%)	Writing is clear, concise, and precise. Paragraphing and sentence structure coherent. Follows requested format.	Writing has minimal minor errors or may have minor organization or format errors	Has a few minor errors or 1 to 2 major errors with formatting, organization, or writing

when they have had no opportunities to practice is not fair. (See Chapter 11 for ideas on how to provide students with effective practice and feedback.)

Use Explicit Criteria to Ensure Consistent Grading

Grading without explicit criteria can be unfair and inefficient. Teachers in every discipline are inconsistent in grading complex student performances when they lack criteria. A single teacher might score the same test differently at different times and teachers who verbally agree on standards often widely fluctuate in their evaluations of student work. In contrast, when teachers use explicit criteria, such as checklists and rubrics, they grade consistently and reliably. A rubric, checklist, or scoring guideline also makes grading far more efficient. Teachers who have explicit criteria know what they are looking for when they grade an exam, paper, or performance.

The following example is a portion of a score sheet/rubric for a Torts exam question.

Damien's Duty to Patrick—20

- ❑ **Conclusion.** Damien's definitely owes a duty to Patrick as either a business or public invitee. Exact status as invitee unknown without more facts.
- ❑ Business relationship. Patrick could be a business invitee because he is a customer or potential customer of Damien's skating rink. Assumes that Damien's is a privately owned business.
- ❑ Statute § 343 and § 343(a) refer to public places, with skating rinks being a kind of public place. Patrick's status would then be a public invitee. In addition, Damien's could be an enterprise that public officials lease to provide recreation.
- ❑ Accurate facts, e.g. unknown if Patrick paid fee, if Damien's private

Damien's breach of care—45

Conclusion

- ❑ Statute has been violated by Damien's but not relevant so not proof of breach
  May be other ways to prove breach—would need additional evidence
- ❑ **Relevance of statutory breach—ID statute and language.** Montshire Criminal Code§ 343(a): prohibits children under 16 years to be unaccompanied by a parent or adult at public places, including skating rinks.
- ❑ **Damien's violated** statute by allowing Patrick, age 15, into skating rink without adult supervision.
  Apply 2 part test:
  - ❑ **Is Patrick in the group of people meant to be protected by the statute?** Group identified in § 343(a) is children under 16.
    - ❑ Yes, Patrick, a 15-year-old is in the group meant to be protected.
  - ❑ **Is Patrick's broken ankle's kind of harm the kind of harm that was meant to be prevented by § 343 and § 343(a)?**
    - ❑ NO. § 343 and § 343(a) are focused on "protecting children's morals and good habits" and engaging in certain "public activities at late hours" because of the potential harm to children's school work.
    - ❑ While the statute relates to harm to children as a result of being out late, Patrick has a broken ankle, which is unrelated to his school work, morals, or good habits.

Damien's breach being the factual cause of Patrick's injury—10

Conclusion

- ❑ Need additional evidence of breach to determine whether Patrick has a valid claim for causation.
- ❑ Assuming some kind of breach; liquid on the floor or other dangerous condition. Patrick would have to prove that Damien's factually caused Patrick's broken ankle. Patrick would have to prove that "but for" the dangerous condition on Damien's premises Patrick would not have broken his ankle, or that Damien's breach otherwise contributed to Patrick breaking his ankle.

Policy—5

- ❑ Can be woven into the analysis in different places.

Writing and organization—10

- ❑ Organization overall. Separates headings or uses signposts to convey different areas.
- ❑ Concise. Very few extra words.
- ❑ Precise. Accurate grammar, punctuation and word choice.
- ❑ Paragraph structure. Coherent and organized.
- ❑ Format. Follows all directions.

Productive Meetings With Students After the Assessment

Some teachers dread meeting with students after they receive their grades on summative assessments. Students may be upset, frustrated, and angry. However, these meetings can be excellent teaching and learning opportunities. The key is to focus the meeting on the strengths and weaknesses of the student's performance and on how the student can improve in the future, rather than on the teacher's justification for the grade. These suggestions may help make post-assessment meetings with students more productive.

1. Meet with students in person. It is easier to read body language, empathize, and try to help students learn when you meet with them in person, rather than talking about grades via email or the phone.
2. The 24-hour rule. Talk to students only after they have had their graded assessment for 24 hours, which gives students time to cool off and gain a bit of perspective.
3. Have students review all materials before meeting with you individually. Asking students to review their exam or other graded performance, the scoring criteria, the rubric or score sheet, excellent student responses, and any other feedback before they meet with you makes the experience much more manageable and specific.
4. Limit the number of weeks in which students can talk to you about a graded assessment. Meetings about assessments are more effective if they take place when the assessment is fresh in the minds of the teacher and student. The sooner students review the graded assessment, the greater its potential as a learning exercise.
5. Focus the meeting on future performance. Teachers can encourage students to self-assess their studying and exam preparation process in advance of the meeting. Teachers can explicitly set one goal of the meeting as helping the student discover ways to improve preparation and performance on future exams.

References

- Gregory S. Munro, Outcomes Assessment for Law Schools 57 (2000).
- Michael Schwartz, Sophie Sparrow & Gerald Hess, Teaching Law By Design: Engaging Students from the Syllabus to the Final Exam (2009).
- Sophie Sparrow, *Describing the Ball: Improve Teaching by Using Rubrics—Explicit Grading Criteria*, Mich. St. L. Rev. 1 (2004).
- Roy Stuckey et al., Best Practices for Legal Education: A Vision and a Road Map (2007).
- Barbara E. Walvrood & Virginia Johnson Anderson, Effective Grading: A Tool for Learning and Assessment (2d ed. 2010).

Multiple-Choice Test Building

Perhaps the high and low points of a semester for a law teacher coincide. It is the last day of classes, when the culmination of all the professor has tried to accomplish often produces a burst of goodwill and nostalgia on the part of both teacher and students. But the goodwill too often subsides as students anxiously look ahead to the exam, and the teacher realizes that an exam must be produced and, even worse, graded. For teachers, the river of satisfaction has hit the dam of understanding: "We teach for free and grade for pay."

In most American law schools, the evaluation of students occurs in the form of a single, end-of-the-semester, multiple-hour, essay exam. The current essay orthodoxy can be augmented, however, by alternative evaluations. In fact, legal academe discovered other evaluation forms long ago. The alternatives range from the time-consuming (midterm exams and papers) to the ephemeral (quizzes and short writing exercises).

One staple in the alternative evaluation constellation is the selected-response question, better known as the "multiple-choice" item type. These questions present particular problems: they offer credit only for a "best" answer; and they encourage guessing.

On the other hand, such questions offer great versatility, both on a final examination and as part of the in-class learning process. As a testing tool, these questions provide uniform grading and the opportunity for expansive coverage. As a learning tool, multiple-choice item types can be used as a feedback mechanism to facilitate students' self-assessment and promote active interest in the subject matter.

Building Selected-Response Questions

Selected-response questions contain three parts: facts—the body of the question; call—the stem of the question; and selected responses—the answer choices. Two recurring forms of raw materials stand at the core of most selected-response questions: (1) the element of a legal rule or principle and (2) a related fact or facts. In criminal law, the mental state element required for depraved heart murder, for example, might combine with the fact that the defendant shot another mistakenly believing the gun was not loaded. The relationship between legal elements and facts is dissected every day in class in the form of hypothetical questions and appellate case reports. In the context of legal problem solving, the element-fact relationship is central to the outcome.

Selected-response questions can be constructed through a four-step process.

Step 1: Combine Element and Fact

The first step in the process of constructing selected-response questions is to combine a legal element and a fact. The combination of law and fact is not only important for the body of the question (the fact pattern), but also imperative for the selected responses (the answer choices). Illustrations include:

Element	Fact
Mental state for arson	Falling asleep with a lit cigarette in someone else's house.
Termination of a joint tenancy	Secretly selling a share of a joint tenancy.
Free exercise of religion	State law regulating the size of religious symbols in public burial grounds.
Impeachment of a witness	Questioning a witness on whether she had been charged with perjury.

Step 2: Build a Narrative Around the Element-Fact Pairing

The narrative provides the context for the basic element-fact combination. A question without a fleshed-out story is less realistic and far less interesting. Story lines from books, movies, television shows, or everyday incidents are popular. The story commences and generally ends in the body of the question, although sometimes it is continued in the answer choices. Continuations are reflected by facts in the answer choices added through such statements as "If X occurred, then ..." or "T will win if ...".

Thus, if a law-fact combination is "impeachment—cross-examination of the witness about a perjury charge," a story may be created, as it was in the film *My Cousin Vinnie,* about a trial involving two youths from the northern U.S. charged with murder in a small town in the southern U.S. A witness for the defense testifies that he saw the youths near the murder scene while making his morning grits. Can the witness be asked on cross-examination whether he had been charged with perjury before? In the answer choices, the story can be embellished with different facts, such as the perjury charge was three years old, the witness had been tried and acquitted on the perjury charges, and so on.

Step 3: Select an Objective for the Question

The objective of a question is crucial to how it is analyzed. The differing objectives give multiple-choice questions versatility. Objectives include:

1. The best solution to the problem;
2. The best/worst argument by a party to the dispute; and
3. The legal and/or policy rationale for the best answer.

When the objective of the question is communicated to the test-taker, it becomes the call (or stem) of the question. A call of the question should be a complete or nearly complete sentence that has the test-taker resolve an issue (e.g., Who is most likely to prevail?), evaluate an argument (e.g., What is the most effective argument for X?), or explain an underlying rationale (e.g., What policy best supports the court's conclusion?). Underline or italicize the call to make it stand out.

Step 4: Create Answer Choices

The construction of short-answer or essay questions effectively ends after Step 3. Selected-response questions require an additional step—the creation of answer choices. Usually four choices will do; additional choices do not significantly reduce the odds of guessing and make questions more difficult to construct.

The most common framework for answer choices is a dichotomy, in which the first two answer choices answer the call in the affirmative and then the next two answer choices provide negative responses. This construct might look like the following:

A. Yes, because ... [facts/law]
B. Yes, because ... [facts/law]
C. No, because ... [facts/law]
D. No, because ... [facts/law]

Answer choices usually contain an element-fact pairing, although sometimes the answer contains only facts or law. The contents of the answer choices depend on the call of the question. Thus, a call asking the test-taker to identify the most likely type of crime committed in the fact pattern may yield answers providing a choice of crimes. A call asking for the best argument by a party likely will include the law combined with facts. A call asking for which situation is most likely negligence might have only facts in the answer choices.

Incorrect answer choices can be created essentially in one of three ways, by describing (1) correct but irrelevant rules of law; (2) correct but incomplete rules of law; and (3) incorrect rules of law. An irrelevant rule will not help students answer the particular issue and requires issue identification. An incomplete answer choice might contain a single element or a partially correct response, with a more accurate answer provided by another answer choice. An incorrect answer might state a rule inaccurately, which could derive from overruled precedent, the minority view of a rule, or simply an improper statement of the law.

When creating answer choices, create one answer choice that is definitely preferable to the others, not one that is marginally better. The distracters—incorrect choices—should be of a similar length and construction to the best answer choice and plausible to the weaker test-takers. The goal is to have questions that the more knowledgeable and skilled test-takers will answer correctly and the less skilled will miss, not to have questions that everyone misses. Those types of questions effectively do not count in ranking and ordering the test-takers. Also, avoid "none of the above" answer choices.

An Example

In property law, a form of multiple ownership is the joint tenancy, which is distinguished by how it is created and its right of survivorship. One issue that arises in joint tenancy doctrine is how a secret sale affects a joint tenancy. Essentially, such a sale destroys the joint tenancy as to the transferring party. Further, a judicial partition may sever the joint tenancy, but the mere initiation of partition proceedings does not.

Step 1: The Element-Fact Pair: Terminating a joint tenancy—a secret sale of a joint tenant's share.

Step 2: The Story Line: Siblings Alice, Bonnie, and Charles (A, B, and C) were deeded the Palace estate by their parents "as joint tenants with the right of survivorship." Months later, the siblings began to argue and Alice initiated partition proceedings. At about the same time, Bonnie secretly conveyed her share of the property to Dana (D). Charles did nothing. When Charles learned about the partition proceedings, which were still pending, he drove in a furious state to see Alice. On the way, Charles died in an auto accident.

Step 3: The Objective: Which of the following is the most likely outcome?

Step 4: The Answer Choices:

A. Dana and Alice now own the property as tenants in common because the secret conveyance severed the joint tenancy only as to Bonnie. (Best Answer).

B. Bonnie owns all of the property because the secret conveyance was invalid and Alice lost her share of the property by initiating partition proceedings. (Incorrect conclusion and incorrect statement of law).

C. Bonnie still owns part of the property because a tenancy by the entirety cannot be destroyed by a secret conveyance. (Incorrect conclusion and irrelevant statement of law).

D. Dana and Alice own the property as tenants in common because the four unities are required at common law to create the joint tenancy. (Correct conclusion but irrelevant statement of law).

While creating selective response questions requires considerable effort, the investment is generally worthwhile. These versatile questions can serve dual purposes, as both assessment instruments and learning tools.

Steven I. Friedland
Elon University School of Law

Skills Evaluation with Multiple-Choice Questions

Skills evaluation and multiple-choice questions are often thought to be inconsistent. Certainly, multiple-choice questions cannot easily test writing skills. However, multiple-choice questions can evaluate many skills used for legal analysis, and they have some advantages over essay questions for this purpose. Multiple-choice questions can ask about only the facts, pinpointing students' difficulties in reading facts, or they can include a rule of law, pinpointing students' difficulties in applying rules. Moreover, multiple-choice questions provide fast feedback and statistical verification of their reliability. This essay explains some of the uses of multiple-choice questions to evaluate skills, starting with an analysis of the limitations of the essay and traditional multiple-choice exams.

The Limits of Complex Questions in Identifying Student Mistakes

Essay questions can test students' ability to identify relevant facts, apply the law to them, and organize and write an answer. Unfortunately, the very complexity of essay questions limits their usefulness in identifying where students make mistakes. The thought process in writing an exam answer is a chain with many links: reading the question, framing the issue, recalling the rule, applying the rule, and writing the answer. When the chain breaks, it is often impossible to tell which link failed. Failure to address an issue can result from careless reading, which caused the student to miss a relevant fact; from not knowing the applicable legal rule, which caused the student to miss the significance of a fact that the student did read; or from inability to interpret the language of a memorized rule, which caused the student to miss the applicability of the rule.

The traditional multiple-choice exam tests knowledge of the law by asking questions about the legal rule and forcing the student to select among alternative statements of the law or by providing a fact pattern and alternative answers that apply the law to fact. This seems to be the exclusive mode of examination in law schools and on the bar. Multiple-choice questions requiring reading, recall, and application share the defects of essay questions. A wrong answer to a traditional multiple-choice question does not reveal where the student went wrong.

Skills-Oriented Multiple-Choice Questions

The limitations of essay exams and traditional multiple-choice questions have led me to develop skills-oriented multiple-choice questions. These questions examine separately students' abilities to read facts and to apply an unfamiliar rule of law.

Skills-oriented multiple-choice questions have important features for diagnosing students' difficulties and assessing students' skills. Frequent multiple-choice exams for testing skills during the semester allow the instructor to evaluate the success of instruction and provide students with the chance to evaluate their own progress. In addition, multiple-choice tests allow the teacher to provide students with quick feedback, which vastly increases its effectiveness.

The information about where students are going wrong is often a surprise to them. Two aspects of this have especially come to my attention. First, students tend to overestimate how carefully they read questions. Quantifying exactly how often they are missing relevant facts appears to be far more effective in encouraging careful reading than just telling them to read carefully. Second, students who make errors are often genuinely unsure about whether those errors came from their misremembering the words of the rule or from their inability to apply those words. Breaking down the process into rule knowledge and rule application provides them this information.

Examples of This Approach

Questions one through four refer to the *Lamson* case. The correct answers have been *italicized.*

> *Lamson v. American Ax & Tool Co.*, 177 Mass. 144, 58 N.E. 585 (1900).
>
> Holmes, C. J.
>
> This is an action for personal injuries caused by the fall of a hatchet from a rack in front of which it was the plaintiff's business to work at painting hatchets, and upon which the hatchets were to be placed to dry when painted. The plaintiff had been in the defendant's employment for many years.
>
> About a year before the accident new racks had been substituted for those previously in use, and it may be assumed that they were less safe, and were not proper, but were dangerous, on account of the liability of the hatchets to fall from the pegs upon the plaintiff when the racks were jarred by the motion of machinery nearby. The plaintiff complained to the superintendent that the hatchets were more likely to drop off than when the old racks were in use, and that now they might fall upon him, which they could not have done from the old racks. He was answered, in substance, that he would have to use the racks or leave. The accident which he feared happened, and he brought this suit.
>
> The plaintiff, on his own evidence, appreciated the danger more than anyone else. He perfectly understood what was likely to happen. That likelihood did not depend upon the doing of some negligent act by people in another branch of employment, but solely on the permanent conditions of the racks and their surroundings and the plaintiff's continuing to work where he did. He complained, and was notified that he could go if he would not face the chance. He stayed and took the risk. He did so none the less that the fear of losing his place was one of his motives.
>
> Exceptions overruled.

1. Who won in this case?
   A. *The defendant won in the trial court and on appeal.*
   B. The plaintiff won in the trial court and on appeal.
   C. The defendant won in the trial court, and the plaintiff won on appeal.
   D. The plaintiff won in the trial court, and the defendant won on appeal.
2. Which of the following facts is most significant to the court's result?
   A. The plaintiff signed a contract assuming the risk that axes would fall off.
   B. *The plaintiff knew that the axes were likely to fall off.*
   C. The accident happened as a result of negligence by people in another branch of the employment.
   D. The new racks made the drying process less safe.

3. In what situation would the *Lamson* precedent be most relevant?
   A. *The plaintiff smelled alcohol on the breath of the defendant, but allowed the defendant to drive him anyway, and was injured in an accident caused by the intoxication of the driver.*
   B. The plaintiff was an employee and was injured as a result of a defect in the defendant's flooring, which was unknown to the employee and caused an axe to fall on the employee from a higher floor.
   C. The plaintiff was an employee in the painting department, and the defendant was an employee in the axe-head installing department, who injured the plaintiff by throwing an axe head at his supervisor and hitting the plaintiff by mistake.
   D. The plaintiff was a minor employed by the defendant, and was suing for loss of brain function suffered as a result of continued exposure to paint fumes in the defendant's factory.

4. Which change in the law would be most likely to change the outcome of this case?
   A. *Different rules on assumption of risk in negligence cases.*
   B. Different rules on battery and other intentional torts.
   C. Different rules on extreme and outrageous conduct (intentional infliction of emotional distress).
   D. Different rules on the damages recoverable for personal injury.

5. Assume that the intent to accomplish a result exists if the actor desires the result or believes that the result is substantially certain to occur as a result of his acts. In which of the following situations does the intent to make contact exist?
   I. Calvin has thrown 100 slushballs at Susie, but because of his rotten aim he has missed each time. He realizes the odds are strongly against him, but he desperately wants to hit Susie, so he throws another slushball, which hits Susie.
   II. Calvin was outside a stadium testing his new slingshot for propelling slushballs. He aimed his slushballs to fall inside the stadium. Signs outside the stadium advertised the sell-out crowd, but Calvin did not read the signs. Calvin hit someone inside the stadium, as was substantially certain to happen.
   A. Neither I nor II.
   B. I only.
   C. II only.
   D. I and II.

Question 1, which asks who won the case, addresses procedural knowledge and case reading. The "exceptions overruled" at the end demonstrates that the same person who lost in the trial court lost on appeal. From the opinion, it is clear that the plaintiff loses, although the opinion nowhere states that directly.

Question 2, which asks which facts are most significant, assesses reading skills. Its incorrect choices combine possibilities for missed facts and erroneous understanding of the court's opinion. The first option, the signed contract assuming the risk, is legally plausible but factually erroneous. Someone with a correct understanding of the law but poor reading skills would be tempted to pick that. The second option is correct. The third option, that the accident was caused by people in another department, is factually incorrect and would support an outcome different from the courts. The fourth option, that the new racks are less safe, is factually correct, but not important for the court's assumption of risk argument.

Question 3 asks the reader to select the most analogous case. This tests the ability to transfer knowledge from one case to another. To do this, readers must understand the salient features of the plaintiff's decision to encounter a known risk and give that more weight than scenarios that have facts that are superficially similar to those of the *Lamson* case.

Question 4 asks the reader to classify this case by selecting the area where changes would most likely alter the result in this case. The question is quite easy, because there is no hint of intentional torts, emotional distress, or damages rules in the case. A student who cannot correctly classify the case is likely to have weak knowledge of general tort law or extreme problems in identifying the facts.

Question 5 asks the reader to apply a rule based on the standard definition of intent in torts. The correct answer is (B). Intent exists in I because Calvin hopes to hit Susie, even though he expects not to hit Susie. Intent doesn't exist in II, because Calvin did not believe that he was substantially certain to hit someone, although it was substantially certain in reality. Here, providing the student the rule to work through means that the student learns it is his or her ability to apply the rule that needs improvement, not rule memorization.

Concluding Thoughts

I began using skills-oriented multiple-choice questions in a project to improve students' skills and their success on the bar exam. Most students are receptive to these questions and willing to learn from the feedback they receive. The only substantial disadvantage is that drafting these questions is even more time-consuming than drafting ordinary multiple-choice questions. However, the benefits so far are worth it, and I am optimistic about the long-term results.

Greg Sergienko
Western State University College of Law

Weekly Quizzes

Administrative Process is a required class at University of New Hampshire School of Law, and students often find the subject matter difficult. Because the material is cumulative, difficulty increases if they do not keep up. Hoping to encourage good, consistent preparation, I began to give frequent quizzes. I soon appreciated that these quizzes enabled me to know if the students were confused (and about what) as soon as possible, and I began using quizzes in my Intellectual Property course as well.

To make grading the quizzes manageable, the format must be either a very brief essay question or it must be objective questions, particularly if enrollment is high. I favor the latter, because it permits a more comprehensive evaluation and avoids the need for anonymity. I have tried several formats, including fill-in-the-blank, true/false, and multiple-choice, but I find that matching requires the least amount of time in order to compose quizzes of minimal ambiguity.

I try not to hide the ball. My goal is for each student to match ten items correctly within ten minutes. Class averages are often above nine, but students may need coaching. For example, a student who got seven, eight, and six, respectively, on her first three quizzes in September consistently scored tens after a brief discussion. On the flip side, students with a string of tens sometimes get threes or fours, confirming that my quizzes are not too easy.

Beginning students are generally required to match case names with one-sentence descriptions that echo something stressed in class. Although quizzes ordinarily follow the cases as they are presented in the book, I may combine cases if there are more than ten. If there are fewer than ten, I use something like a statutory provision. Because the students are seated close together, I prepare at least three versions of the quiz. Beginning the second week I give 13 weekly quizzes.

I started off giving the quizzes during the first ten minutes of class, mostly to encourage prompt attendance. But I soon moved them to the end of class and allowed students to leave early. However, I had a student complain about the distraction this caused, so I require students to stay for the first ten minutes of the quiz (or until it is clear that everyone is finished). Once the bustle of the departing students dies down, I allow an extra five minutes for those remaining. This accommodates students who need more time, English as a Second Language (ESL) students for example; however, those students who are simply less prepared than they should be do not seem to benefit from the extra time.

I post the quiz scores immediately after class, and my faculty assistant grades the quizzes, usually within an hour or two. After I've checked the papers, I email the average scores and my thoughts about common errors to the students. The quizzes are weighted as 30% of the students' final grade. I minimize the risk of students unduly diverting attention from other courses by averaging the best ten scores for each student, giving frequent quizzes, and by dropping low scores.

Prompt, frequent feedback can provide both students and instructors with timely notice of misunderstandings and knowledge gaps. It also reduces anxiety about finals. Moreover, ignoring a few scores lessens the students' stress and accommodates varying demands on their time.

I have provided syllabi and links to sample quizzes at:

- http://law.unh.edu/thomasfield/courses/admin-pro.php; and
- http://law.unh.edu/thomasfield/courses/fundamentals-of-ip.php.

Thomas Field
University of New Hampshire School of Law

The Document Package Exam

Two facts seem obvious about law school exams: professors dread preparing them and students dread taking them. These propositions seem like incontrovertible facts, but as Ira Gershwin once said, "It ain't necessarily so...." For instance, when I was a new teacher I did not dread writing exams. I found them to be a somewhat fun, if obscure, genre of short story writing. Nevertheless, even if I did not dread writing exams, my students dreaded taking my exams, especially when I got carried away and made my fact patterns too rich in detail.

When I was first assigned to teach Corporate Finance, it dawned on me that my penchant for writing detailed exams could be put to good use by creating realistic hypothetical corporations to illustrate the concepts in the course and to test on the material. My fact scenarios developed into mini-simulations in which my students could participate. These mini-simulations are fun for me to create and more enjoyable for the students to complete. In addition, the technique helps me achieve important pedagogical goals.

In Corporate Finance, an upper-level elective class, students generally come to the class without having had any exposure to the transactions discussed in the cases or to the documentation at the heart of the legal controversies. When I planned my course, it occurred to me that my students' understanding of the subject likely would be highly distorted and abstracted if they learned it solely through the medium of appellate cases. To counter the inherent problem of teaching a transaction-based subject through a litigation-based book, I supplemented my casebook heavily with financial material, articles, and documents.

Because many of my students are "hands-on" learners, I decided to address their lack of context by creating and using hypothetical corporations throughout the course. I use those hypothetical corporations to illustrate the accounting, valuation, and financial aspects of the course. The class's contact with the hypothetical companies culminates in an exam that I have conceived to be a simulation of an actual corporate finance matter that an associate attorney in a law firm might be assigned to work on.

The simulation starts with a detailed fact pattern about two businesses that were originally family owned but that merged and went public. I call the resulting corporation Consolidated Corn and Tobacco, Inc. (COCOTO). I based it on a now de-listed corporation I worked on in practice, American Corn and Tobacco. Toward the end of the term I give my students a document package composed of corporate articles of incorporation, bylaws, SEC filings, a Standard & Poor's Company report, financial statements, and a trust indenture. Happily, I was able to download almost all of this material for free from the SEC's EDGAR website. Students have a few weeks before the end of the term to digest the material. They understand that in order to answer the take-home exam questions completely they will have to master the documents.

Obviously, before I distribute the document package, I know what I am going to ask the students on the exam. The exam questions almost always turn on some corporate finance development that has been in the news during the term. I plant appropriate language and numbers in the documents to raise the issues that will be on the exam.

I give students about two weeks to review the documents and to ask questions either in class or during office hours. This serves at least two purposes: (1) it allows the students to learn about the documents; and (2) it ferrets out the mistakes I made in preparing the document package (I have discovered that the most enthusiastic students quickly focus on inconsistencies in the presentation). I once tried this testing technique without the two-week review period and the students felt overwhelmed. It is an essential part of the learning experience that the students have a chance to digest this information and ask questions in class. I encourage the students to work together during this phase of the project.

On the last day of class, I give the students the "exam," which consists of additional facts that supplement the already well-developed story of COCOTO, along with perhaps some additional documents or newspaper articles and the questions that need to be addressed. Usually the students will not be able to answer the questions fully without using some data from every included document—including the financial statements. Once the exam questions have been distributed the students must work on their own.

This examination technique appeals to many students. Although I started using this technique in Corporate Finance, an upper-level elective, I have since used it in Secured Transactions (a widely subscribed elective) and Contracts (a first-year course). Even though this method of testing makes the students work hard, I have had positive feedback about it every time—except one time in Contracts. That time I did not give the students the two-week period to digest the materials but instead handed out the document package on the last day of class with the examination questions to be administered ten days later in a timed examination setting. I solicited feedback from the exam takers and realized that I had not prepared them adequately for the new type of testing and had scared them when they saw the case files. I learned from that unsuccessful experience to make the file more manageable when testing first-year students and to give the students more information about the examination technique and the goals I am trying to achieve.

The year following the unsuccessful Contracts exam, I administered a case file exam as part of the Contracts midterm. I simplified the transaction significantly. I gave the students three weeks before the end of the term to digest the documents. When I polled the students about the exam it received overwhelmingly positive reviews. After the exam I used the same examination materials as an ongoing hypothetical in the second semester of Contracts to illustrate the ideas that are presented.

There are pros and cons to this testing approach. On the positive side, I perceive the following benefits:

- An involved, role-playing exam can be a lot of fun to prepare and, I believe, to answer.
- It allows students to engage the problem in a manner more like the way in which lawyers work to solve problems.
- If given as a take-home exam, the document package format allows testing on detailed technical subjects, such as accounting and valuation, which might otherwise be inappropriate for timed traditional exams.
- It gives the students the incentive to read and digest deal documents in a way that merely assigning sample documents as a part of a reading assignment never will.
- It allows a degree of collaboration, but ultimately it produces a work product specific to the individual student.
- It permits testing on how well students separate the wheat from the chaff.
- For students interested in the real world of lawyering, the simulation aspect helps them place the material in context and makes it more intelligible. Some students have informed me that applying the law to the information in the exam and the document package allowed them to pull all the course material together and really understand it.

On the down side I see the following:

- It takes a lot of energy and creativity to prepare the document package.
- The level of detail involved invites some mistakes that can cause trouble (e.g., the financials must all work out and be consistent with the other documents in the document package).
- The technique works best in upper-level electives where the students are self-selected and will enjoy being put through the paces in a simulated transaction. I have used this technique in first-year Contracts, but it must be done with a much lighter touch.
- Of course, if given as a take-home exam there will be concerns about honor code violations.
- The exam materials can be recycled, but they require extensive reworking every year to avoid the possibility that students hand down the answers from year to year.

As mentioned above, I have used this testing technique in Corporate Finance, Secured Transactions, and Contracts. Anyone who would like a complete package of one of my exams should contact me at egouvin@law.wnec.edu and I will send you a hard copy of a recent exam and document package.

Eric J. Gouvin
Western New England College School of Law

Performance Testing

There is a disconnect between law school curriculum and bar examination preparation. This gulf benefits only the bar review courses, not our students. Bar review courses will never be rendered obsolete; they are a necessary component to focus study in the final months before the bar. However, there seems to be no compelling reason for law school professors to avoid including some bar examination preparation skills in the law school curriculum.

For example, the majority of bar examinations in the United States now include a "performance test" component. Yet, performance testing is an unknown format to many law professors in the United States because they took a bar examination that consisted only of essay questions and the Multistate Bar Examination (MBE). Humans tend to avoid things they do not understand. Law professors are human. Therefore, law professors tend to avoid performance test issues.

My own firsthand experience with performance testing comes from sitting for the California bar after practicing for over a decade and teaching law school, as both an adjunct and a full-time professor. Within weeks of having graded Property exams in another state, I found myself sitting in a bar review classroom in west Los Angeles surrounded by hundreds of anxious, recent graduates listening to a Torts lecture. Assault, battery, and conversion ... the experience was surreal. Besides grappling with the potential karmic implications of being a student again, I determined to learn more from the experience than just how to pass the bar. The simple lesson learned was that law professors have opportunities to incorporate some basic bar preparation information in every course in law school.

After practicing for a couple of years, I returned to teaching and taught a section of Legal Analysis and Writing (LAW). The course involves student preparation of a closed research memorandum and an open research memorandum. The LAW course also includes a final examination, which is a performance test that requires the student to write an objective legal memorandum. Requiring students to write a legal memorandum as a final examination is appropriate because the class had spent an entire semester on the topic. And, as an actual performance test experience, the students are given an opportunity to assess their time management, reading comprehension, analysis, and writing skills years before sitting for the bar examination.

The task of writing an objective legal memorandum is only one of the tasks that can appear on performance tests. Fact gathering, persuasive brief writing, and factual analysis are other skills commonly tested. The testing materials include a task memo, a file, and a library. The "task memo" gives some facts and direction. The "file" includes factual materials such as letters, depositions, or affidavits. The "library" consists of the cases, statutes, regulations, or other legal resource material that the student must read, synthesize, and apply to the facts. To review examination formats, a useful resource is the National Council of Bar Examiners website (www.ncbex.org), which provides sample multistate performance tests. By reviewing these and other samples available from your jurisdiction's bar examiners, one can quickly get a sense of how to structure such an examination.

One of the more difficult aspects of preparing the LAW examination was to make it feasible for first-year students to complete within the two-hour time frame available for the class. For my first-semester, first-year class, the examination included three very short cases and provided the "question presented." The "file" section was abbreviated so that relevant facts were given in the task memo.

During an optional examination review class, I reviewed performance test skills with the students. I circulated an example of a recent California performance test. By familiarizing the students with the format, I hoped that they would not panic at the sight of a different type of examination. Also, it demonstrated to students that the work they were doing even in the first year of law school was relevant to their common ultimate goal of practicing law. Judging from the final results, the students were able to handle the examination format and performed about the same as they did on their memoranda assignments.

Law schools should never teach bar examination preparation only. However, practical bar examination preparation should not be wholly excluded from law school classes. Law professors can incorporate some skills and methods in the standard course curriculum that will prepare students for the bar examination. With just a little extra effort, professors can create connections to the bar examination experience that result in tremendous added value for the students.

Teresa Buchheit Klinkner

The Lure of Extra-Credit Projects

While teaching Contracts, it occurred to me that the students would learn the material better if they used it in a different way than the traditional classroom experience. What I had in mind was getting them to try to draft a contract that dealt with the situation they were experiencing. In short, I wanted them to try drafting an educational contract.

I had assigned extra work before and it was always greeted with shrugs and groans. What, more work! They thought they were being subjected to busywork and a waste of time. Approached with that mind-set, most students did their best to get the least possible out of the exercise. The teacher pushes, and the students push back. How could that cycle be broken? How could I get them to want to engage in this learning experience?

Then a student asked, "Is there any way I could earn extra credit?" What? That had not occurred to me. They wanted an opportunity to earn extra credit? When I asked other students, the answer overwhelmingly was, "Yes." So I packaged the contracts drafting exercise as an extra-credit opportunity, which I have described in detail in THE LAW TEACHER, Spring 2001 at 5 (reprinted in FRIEDLAND & HESS, TEACHING THE LAW SCHOOL CURRICULUM (2004).)

Not every student took advantage of the extra-credit opportunity, but most did. And not everyone who did the project put in sufficient effort to earn the credit or reap the educational benefits. But most did. But what was most interesting was that the attitude toward the project was so positive even among the students who did not do it.

Students in my other classes started asking if they could have extra-credit projects like the one I had offered in Contracts. So I devised a project for my Property class that involved a detailed analysis of a standard real estate purchase and sales contract and one for my Real Estate Finance Law class that involved a detailed analysis of a note and mortgage. These projects stimulated the students who were willing to work. They liked having the choice about whether to do the project. Any return of control to them, especially during their otherwise out-of-control first year, was appreciated. Students also liked the opportunity to alleviate some of the law school anxiety about grades by knowing that a good-faith effort on the project would provide this extra credit, which would be judged not by a traditional exam but on a project they could work on gradually over a long time period.

I enjoyed not having to struggle with students to get them to try learning this way. I enjoyed alleviating some of their stress from uncertainty over grades. And I have enjoyed hearing later on how much some of them learned from the experience. The trick, of course, is to design the right project: challenging enough but not overwhelming; a big enough grade reward, but not so large as to make the grading scale unreasonable once the extra credit is added in; and obviously beneficial to them so they can see that the experience is worthwhile and not just busywork.

Ronald Benton Brown
Nova Southeastern University, Shepard Broad Law Center

Collaboration on Examinations

During the past 20 years, in most of my exams, I have used a process designed to make examinations a learning experience as well as a means of evaluating performance. Some time before classes end, I distribute to students a document titled "Information on Facts and Law." This document, typically 5 to 20 pages in length, presents a story involving a fair amount of detail with the potential for numerous legal problems and disputes relevant to the subject matter of the course. The document also contains a variety of statements about the relevant law and usually a number of pertinent statutes. I inform students that most of the examination problems will be based on the facts and legal doctrine presented in that document and encourage them to study it in preparation for the exam and to ponder what legal questions and problems could arise under the circumstances presented. Students take this advice seriously and often become very much engaged in the process, preparing for the task of addressing real examination problems in a meaningful way. In studying and discussing this material with other members of the class, students often create and work through their own hypothetical problems, individually and in groups, and thereby gain a better sense of the subjects they have studied. Many students, I believe, find this focused and creative review the most valuable learning experience of the semester, one that takes them far beyond what I can cover in a three-hour examination.

In the past 15 years, going a step beyond this "focused and creative review," I have given examinations in which students have been allowed to collaborate with other students not only in reviewing the course and preparing for the exam, but also in composing their responses to the exam problems. On two occasions, I set no limits on the number of students who were permitted to work together in composing their answers to the exam problems. In most of my exams, however, I have limited the size of the groups, usually allowing three, four, or five students to work together. In no case have I *required* students to work with others on the exam, although some colleagues have suggested I should do so.

Concerns about Collaboration on Exams

The prospect of allowing law students to collaborate on final examinations presents some issues for both the professor and the students. My primary concern has been that the process presumably compromises, to some degree, the evaluative function of exams. When groups of individuals are graded on the basis of a collaborative effort, some students' grades will certainly be different from the grades those individuals would have received working alone. This criticism, usually stated in terms of a free-rider problem, is the main one voiced by students. I assume that it is not a one-way street. Some students have probably received better grades because of the collaboration but others almost certainly would have received higher grades if they had worked alone. This is a significant concern and it is one reason I have, on a few occasions, combined collaboration and individual work on the exam. Based on conversations with a few students after one exam, however, I am concerned that the combination of collaboration and individual work might create an undesirable group dynamic. In recent years, I have not used the combination of collaborative and individual work in my exams. In most of my courses in the past ten years, I have permitted, but not required, collaboration on the whole exam.

Another issue that has occasionally surfaced concerns "group failure." I have sometimes heard reports about groups which have broken up during the examination period. I don't have many details about those occasions and I don't think it has happened very often. It has probably been the result of disagreements concerning some aspect of the exam or a group's inability to reach a consensus. Although this can certainly be viewed in some respects as a failure, or as a strike against the use of collaboration in exams, it might also be seen as life as usual. In any event, it has not in any way diminished my belief in the value of collaboration in examinations.

I don't know whether there is any way to establish empirically the effect of collaboration on grades, but I have gathered some pertinent and interesting information. For the fall semester exam in 2000, for example, I compared the Property grades of each of my students with the grades they received in three other first-year courses. Of 156 students (two sections), I identified 14 examples of "potentially significant deviation" between the grades students received in Property compared with the grades they received in other courses. The test I used for "potentially significant deviation" was this: The Property grade in these examples was at least three grade levels lower or higher than any grade the student received in the three other courses. (At that time, my school used a ten-grade system from "A" to "F". There were no "A+" grades and no pluses or minuses on grades of "F" or "D".) A Property grade of "B" and all other grades of "C" or below would represent a potentially significant deviation. In six cases the Property grade was at least three grade levels higher, and in eight cases it was much lower than the students' other grades. Twelve of these students worked with others on the exam and two worked alone.

I also have concerns about various dilemmas students might face because of the opportunity to collaborate. The students are free to choose those they will work with on the exam. I worry that a few students might not successfully find collaborators even though they would like to do so. Some colleagues have suggested that I should assign the groups, but I've resisted doing that. On the other hand, some students seem to feel compelled to collaborate because they assume a group will have an advantage over an individual. Based on my experience, as suggested above, this is a mistaken assumption and I always say something to that effect to the students. The grades of individual exam-takers have consistently followed essentially the same pattern as those of groups.

Benefits of Collaboration on Exams

Whatever the drawbacks of permitting collaboration on examinations, my impressions at this point are that the advantages outweigh any disadvantages. Based on student response and my own evaluation of the process, I have come to the conclusion that collaborative exams can be a valuable tool in legal education. The primary benefit of collaboration on exams is that they seem to help many students learn legal theory and doctrine and begin to develop the personal skills of practicing law more effectively than ordinary course work and traditional examinations. I have almost always asked students to evaluate the process in writing and most of those evaluations have been very positive. Similar evidence has surfaced in conversations I have had with students.

The most memorable example of student reaction to the process involved three first-year students who had vigorously sought to persuade me not to allow collaboration on the exam. I think they thought that collaboration essentially defeated the basic purpose of exams, which they presumably thought was measuring and ranking individual performance in the course. I had several good conversations with these students during the time I was deciding whether to allow collaboration in that course. I thought they raised some good points but ultimately decided to allow collaboration on that exam. Sometime after the exam, I had another conversation with one of the three students. I had assumed that they would not collaborate, but he informed me that he and the other two students decided to work together on the exam, which was administered over a three-day weekend. They had access to a cabin in the Texas hill country north of San Antonio and they spent the three days working together on the exam in that cabin. Based on that experience, he reported that he and his colleagues had changed their minds about collaboration on exams, describing those three days as the best educational experience he had ever had.

Overall, I think it is clear that student opinion on collaboration in examinations has been favorable. Consider the responses given by the students in one of my Property courses to a request that they rate the collaborative exam as a teaching/learning device:

- Excellent: 46 students;
- Good: 63 students;
- Neutral: 17 students;
- Poor: 7 students;
- Very Poor: 3 students.

In other words, 80% of the students thought the collaborative exam was either excellent or good as a learning experience, and only 7% thought it was poor or very poor. These numbers are typical; there has not been much variation in student response over the years or from course to course. Based on these surveys, which I have taken in almost all of my courses, and numerous conversations with students over the past 20 years, I believe that collaboration on examinations can produce very beneficial learning experiences for many law students.

A more detailed article on my experiment with collaboration in law school exams is found in *Collaborative Examinations: A Way to Help Students Learn,* 54 J. LEGAL EDUC. 533 (2004).

Douglas R. Haddock
St. Mary's University School of Law

The Five Stages of Grading

After surviving the emotional roller coaster of exam grading, I identified in myself the following five stages of grading:

- Pleasant anticipation;
- Shock and disbelief;
- Anger;

- Depression; and
- Acceptance.

I first approach my exams in a pleasant state of anticipation. It was such a *good* class, with in-depth and widely participatory discussions. Surely, the learning I observed in the classroom will be evident on the exams. In fact, I think, the exam was probably too easy and I'll have trouble separating the good from the less good and applying the mandatory curve.

After grading the first set of essays, I am in a state of shock and disbelief. Where were these students all semester? They had to have been in the classroom since we have a mandatory attendance policy. Didn't they hear anything I said? Didn't they *read?* I'll be lucky to be able to pass a single student.

Next, I become angry. What a waste of my time. Why do I need to read their entire outline in the exam answer? Do they think I don't have anything better to do? Just answer the question asked! I specifically said answer A, B, and C. How could this student have left out B entirely? Don't they *read?*

This is so depressing. I spent hours and hours planning and preparing for each class. I used new technology to help them learn better. I gave ungraded quizzes so they could assess their progress. I encouraged them to ask questions. Am I such an awful teacher that this is all they learned? Maybe it's my fault. Maybe my instructions weren't clear. Maybe I left out a crucial fact. I go back and re-read my essay question and instructions. No, it's all there.

Finally, acceptance. A few students actually correctly identified most of the issues. A few not only stated the correct legal test, but applied it and supported their analysis with relevant facts. Someone was listening. These few bright spots sustain me and give me hope. I re-read all the answers and decide, on the whole, that they may not be what I had hoped for, but they are acceptable. I will try again next year.

Cindy G. Buys
Southern Illinois University School of Law

Grading Techniques

I know of no colleague who enjoys grading. But there are ways to make it more manageable. Below are some practices that work for me when faced with a stack of papers or exams.

1. Start early. Grading doesn't get easier with time. Even if it is only 30 minutes the day you received the students' work, plunge in and at least read a few.
2. Get comfortable. Wear what feels good. Sometimes this means sweats.
3. Sit for only 15 minutes at a time. Even when my back doesn't ache, I try to follow my osteopath's advice: get out of the chair at least every 15 minutes, even if only to stand, take a breath, and raise your arms.
4. Map out a schedule. Work backwards from when you will submit the grades. Figure out how much time you have and when you will grade. Sometimes I do nothing else for a few long days; other times I steadily chip away at the exams over a week or so.
5. Build a buffer into the schedule. When it is time to grade, stuff happens. I either get a cold, the car needs repair, the dog has to go to the vet, or we get an ice

storm and the electricity goes out. Plan on being disrupted. If you're not, you're done early! Reward yourself by spending time doing something delightful.

6. Set time, not task goals. "Grading 85 exams" is overwhelming. "Scoring questions for six hours" is doable.
7. Make realistic daily goals. If I have seven hours to grade, I'll plan for five, and then break that down into five one-hour increments. Plan on it taking longer than you think.
8. Put your grading goals in writing. When I put something on a written list, I am likely to do it. When grading, I draw little squares next to each goal—15 minutes to revise a rubric, scoring a short answer question—and color it in when I am done. Filling in the square makes me ridiculously happy.
9. Reward achievements. I reward myself each time I meet a goal with something simple, like five minutes of checking email, reading, or making a nice cup of tea. When I exceed my goal, the reward gets better.
10. Pay attention to your emotional and energy levels. I find the hardest part of grading to be encountering poor student performance. When that happens, I feel like I have failed as a teacher, lose all energy, and recognize it's futile to plow on. I take an unscheduled break. Writing about the experience helps, as does exercising or doing something completely different. Then back to the task. Later I go back and look for trends in student performance; student performance is valuable data that helps me plan the course next time.
11. Track what works. I've tried listening to music, grading in the local coffee shop, chewing gum, and wearing my favorite slippers. Music and the coffee shop don't work for me; gum and slippers do. The best strategies have come from paying attention to what works.
12. Reorient yourself the next time you grade. I am tired at the end of the semester, and I tend to forget what worked in the past. Rereading my grading strategy notes helps me get jump started the next time around. In fact, I can even put it on the list and color in a box.

Sophie Sparrow
University of New Hampshire School of Law

Chapter 13

Teacher Development and Inspiration

The final chapter in this book addresses sustaining our teaching practice throughout our careers. Many contributions that follow are reflections on the topic "Why I Teach." The reflections are warm, touching, and inspiring. Themes that emerge include the rewards of mentoring, helping students learn and grow, and teachers learning and growing with their students. Other teachers relish the opportunity to change society and further justice by helping students learn skills and values in law school and then apply those skills and values in real life. Many teachers express the pure joy that teaching can bring.

The other contributions in this chapter concern our continued development as teachers. Although continued professional development as teachers can be rewarding, it is not easy. As we learn more about teaching and learning, we may uncover shortcomings in our current philosophy and practice. We may struggle as we try new methods. Sustained development in teaching requires hard work and perseverance.

Teaching Development Stages

Continued teaching development often cycles through several stages: (1) instructional awareness; (2) formative feedback; (3) pedagogical knowledge; (4) implementation; and (5) assessment.

Instructional awareness is the first step in the process of improving teaching. Self-reflection can increase our understanding of our own teaching philosophy and practices. What do we believe are the core purposes of legal education? What are our roles as teachers? What assumptions do we make about teaching and learning? What behaviors do we exhibit when we interact with students? Are our teaching methods consistent with our educational philosophy?

Formative feedback is critical to improving teaching and learning. To make effective changes in teaching, we need to know the strengths and weaknesses of our current practices and their effect on students' learning. We can gather that information from ourselves, students, and colleagues.

Pedagogical knowledge can help us put the feedback we receive in context. We can gain valuable insights from scholarship about teaching and learning. As we deepen our understanding of learning theory, student motivation, teaching methods, instructional design, and assessment, we can appropriately adjust our teaching.

Implementing changes in our teaching philosophy, attitudes, and practices should be incremental, not wholesale. A good start in teaching improvement would be to implement one or two small changes throughout a course.

Assessment occurs when we evaluate the effectiveness of our teaching improvement efforts. Did our changes in philosophy, attitudes, and practices improve our teaching and our students' learning? This information forms the basis for our next development cycle.

Teaching Development Activities

Many types of teaching development activities are available for teachers who want to increase their effectiveness. The dozen development activities discussed below fall in four categories: (1) self-assessment, reflection, and study; (2) formative feedback from students; (3) collaborating with colleagues; and (4) workshops or conferences on teaching and learning.

Teaching Development Activities

Self-Assessment, Reflection, and Study

- Thinking about effective teaching methods before and after class
- Reading books and articles on teaching and learning
- Completing inventories on teaching practices
- Reviewing a video recording of your own teaching
- Keeping a teaching journal

Formative Feedback from Students

- Reviewing student evaluations of your teaching after the course
- Gathering feedback from students on your teaching during the course

Collaborating with Colleagues

- Talking with colleagues about teaching and learning
- Observing a colleague's class and providing feedback
- Having a colleague observe your class and provide feedback

Teaching Workshops and Conferences

- Attending a national or regional conference on teaching and learning
- Attending a workshop at your institution on teaching and learning

Self-Assessment, Reflection, and Study

Many faculty members provide their own teaching development through individual assessment, reflection, and study. Self-study and reflection can help us to become more aware of our teaching assumptions and behaviors, to articulate a coherent teaching rationale, and to make informed changes in our instructional practices. Most teachers have deeply ingrained assumptions about teaching and learning, which affect teaching behavior. To develop as teachers, we must identify our current assumptions and behaviors that may hinder our effectiveness. Reflective teachers can explain the rationale behind their teaching. That rationale can give us confidence and serve as the foundation for our pedagogical choices. As a result of examining assumptions and developing a rationale, reflective teachers modify their plans, attitudes, and actions in the classroom.

Evaluation forms and inventories can help teachers engage in self-assessment. We can analyze our teaching by completing the same course evaluation form that the students fill out at the end of the term. Most teachers' self-assessments of their strengths and weaknesses agree with their students' assessments.

Inventories help teachers assess the presence, absence, and extent of instructional behaviors. Inventories adapted to legal education allow us assess our teaching in the context of seven empirically derived principles for enhancing learning: encouraging student-faculty contact; fostering cooperation among students; encouraging active learning; giving prompt feedback; emphasizing time on task; communicating high expectations; and respecting diverse talents and ways of learning. These inventories are available in *Teaching Law by Design* (2009) and at http://lawteaching.org/resources/books/teachinglawbydesign/teachinglawbydesign-appendices.pdf.

An excellent tool for reflection is a teaching journal. The process of keeping a professional journal promotes reflection. Journal writing helps us create a comprehensive account of our experience. The journal is a place to record problems, successes, strategies for improvement, and ideas for subsequent classes. Because journal entries are made close in time to our experiences, they are often more accurate than our recollections months later. Journal writing helps us clarify our assumptions and theories about teaching and learning, evaluate the effectiveness of instructional practices, and identify alternative methods to try in the future. Further, teaching journals are tools for setting goals, planning class sessions, and restructuring courses. We can use journals to analyze problems and work through the strong emotions that accompany teaching. Finally, journal writing can be a vehicle for us to integrate our personal and professional selves.

Numerous print and electronic resources facilitate teaching development. Articles, books, newsletters, videos, and websites address the theory and practice of teaching and learning. These resources can help us improve our teaching by causing us to reflect on our instructional practices, giving us ideas, and inspiring us to take reasonable risks and exert the effort needed to improve teaching and learning. Introductory lists of these resources are available at the end of each chapter in this book, in *Teaching Law By Design* (2009), and at the Institute for Law Teaching and Learning website, www.lawteaching.org.

Video recording can be a particularly powerful device for assessing and improving our classroom communication skills. A video of a class provides accurate, reliable, audio and visual feedback of several areas of our classroom performance:

- Verbal communication: clarity of speech, volume, verbal ticks;
- Visual aids: legibility of board work, visual impact of computer presentations;
- Nonverbal behavior: eye contact, movement, gestures;
- Questioning: types of questions we ask and how we handle student responses; and
- Other presentation skills, including organization, flow, and pacing.

Despite the value of video recording in teaching development, many teachers are reluctant to be recorded due to anxiety about the recording and review, which can reveal communication glitches and dramatically illustrate the disparity between teachers' self-image and the behavior they see on the video. Several techniques can minimize the anxiety and maximize the value of video recording and review.

1. Select a class to be recorded. Explain to students that the purpose of the video is to provide feedback on your teaching, not to record their performance.
2. View the video soon after the class, while it is fresh in your mind. View the recording once to get over the natural tendency to focus on minor distractions (e.g., Do I really sound like that? Look like that? Have those mannerisms?).

3. View the video a second time with a supportive colleague who can provide perspective and can help you focus on significant strengths and weaknesses rather than the minor distractions (voice, appearance) that have little to do with effective teaching.
4. Use the video to generate detailed data on aspects of your teaching. For example, record every question you ask and analyze the clarity and depth of each question. Or keep track of what is happening at minute intervals: Is the teacher talking? Is a student asking a question? Is a student commenting? Are the students engaged in an exercise?
5. Choose one or two aspects of your teaching to address in response to the feedback you gathered from the video.

Formative Feedback from Students

We can get helpful feedback from students about our teaching and their learning. Most teachers review student evaluations after the course. In addition, many teachers gather feedback from students about teaching effectiveness during the course.

Extensive empirical research in higher education demonstrates the value of student evaluations for teaching development (independent of any role student evaluations play in retention, promotion, and tenure decisions). Written student comments can provide us with suggestions regarding our clarity, delivery, organization, punctuality, fairness, demeanor, and availability outside of class. Dozens of studies reveal a persistent positive effect of written feedback from students on subsequent teaching effectiveness.

Despite the potential benefits of end-of-the-term student evaluations for teaching development, some law teachers are reluctant to use them. Their reluctance may come from a lack of confidence in the value of student evaluations and the pain that comes from reviewing negative comments. Stewart Harris provides excellent advice on how we can maximize the benefits and minimize the pain when reviewing our student evaluations (see below, "Sometimes, We Really Do Suck").

Gathering formative feedback from students can help us improve our teaching during the course. Teachers can design short written or online questionnaires to obtain detailed feedback from students to improve teaching. Keep the questionnaire simple—three to five questions. Explain to students the purpose of the questionnaire: to gather feedback to make your teaching and their learning more effective. Distribute the form in class or online. Have your students respond anonymously. Review the responses, looking for prevalent themes and then report briefly to the class about common responses to the questions. Inform students of at least one suggestion that you intend to implement.

Teachers who use questionnaires during the course can experience several types of benefits. First, students' responses provide specific feedback and suggestions to improve teaching and learning. Further, the process of seeking student feedback and implementing their reasonable suggestions shows our deep respect for students. Finally, the questionnaire process demonstrates an important professional skill—welcoming and profiting from constructive feedback.

Collaborating with Colleagues

Our colleagues are valuable teaching development resources. Talking with colleagues about teaching and learning is a common and effective type of development activity. These discussions can further several important dimensions of teaching development:

- Increasing our awareness of our own teaching practice and philosophy;
- Increasing our knowledge of teaching and learning principles;
- Improving our level of confidence in our teaching;
- Increasing our enthusiasm or passion for teaching; and
- Making changes in our teaching practices.

Discussions among colleagues about teaching and learning can be private conversations between two teachers in a faculty office. These conversations between trusted colleagues can uncover common fears and problems, bolster our morale, and motivate appropriate changes in teaching practices. It is especially important for junior faculty members to feel comfortable having these conversations with more senior colleagues. Productive interchanges about pedagogy can occur in small groups, for example, during a brown bag lunch discussion. Discussion groups are more likely to lead to instructional improvement if they focus on a particular topic, such as ways to facilitate active student participation in class or how to motivate students to make use of the course website, rather than on teaching in general.

Colleagues can provide teaching development for one another by observing classes. Peer observations can be especially valuable if they are reciprocal; for example, three colleagues each agree to observe one another's classes. The reciprocal nature of the observations creates mutual vulnerability and shared responsibility. The colleagues can follow a three-step process. First, the colleagues meet for a pre-observation conference. They discuss their approaches to teaching, goals for the class to be observed, material for the class, expectations for student preparation, what students will do during the class, and the teaching methods to be used. Most importantly, they tell one another the specific types of feedback they would like to receive. Areas for feedback could include the teacher's organization, clarity, use of visual aids, types of questions, handling student responses, verbal and nonverbal communication, and level of student engagement during class. Second, the pairs visit each other's classes and gather the requested feedback. Third, the colleagues meet for a post-observation conference. Those discussions should include the specific feedback requested in the pre-observation conference, positive and negative reactions to the class, and the extent to which the goals for the class were accomplished. Sophie Sparrow explores the power of reciprocal peer observations in "Are We the Teachers We Think We Are? Observing Others Teach—Lessons for the Teacher" below.

Teaching Workshops and Conferences

Teaching effectiveness conferences and workshops are popular faculty development activities. High-quality teaching conferences are sponsored by organizations such as the Association of American Law Schools, CALI, the Legal Writing Institute, the Society of American Law Teachers, and the Institute for Law Teaching and Learning. Many law schools provide teaching development workshops for the full-time and adjunct faculty.

Many faculty members find attending a national, regional, or local conference or workshop to be among the most effective faculty development activities. For example, a survey of participants five years after an AALS teaching conference, found that attendance at the conference increased attendees' reflection on teaching methods (97%), knowledge of teaching and learning principles (96%), awareness of their own teaching philosophy (95%), confidence (71%), and enthusiasm for teaching (70%). In addition, 93% of the respondents implemented changes in their teaching practices as a result of the conference.

References

- Thomas A. Angelo & K. Patricia Cross, Classroom Assessment Techniques: A Handbook for College Teachers 3(2d ed. 1993).
- Barbara Gross Davis, Tools for Teaching (2d ed. 2009).
- Gerald F. Hess, *Improving Teaching and Learning in Law School: Faculty Development Research, Principles, and Programs*, 12 Widener L. Rev. 443 (2006).
- Gerald F. Hess, *Learning to Think Like a Teacher: Reflective Journals for Legal Educators*, 38 Gonz. L. Rev. 129 (2003).
- Gerald F. Hess & Sophie M. Sparrow, *What Helps Law Professors Develop as Teachers?—An Empirical Study*, 14 Widener L. Rev. 149 (2008).
- Larry Keig & Michael D. Waggoner, Collaborative Peer Review: The Role of Faculty in Improving College Teaching (1994).
- James B. Levy, *As a Last Resort, Ask the Students: What They Say Makes Someone an Effective Law Teacher*, 58 Me. L. Rev. 49 (2006).
- Michael Hunter Schwartz, Sophie Sparrow & Gerald F. Hess, Teaching Law By Design: Engaging Students from the Syllabus to the Final Exam (2009).
- Maryellen Weimer, Improving College Teaching: Strategies for Developing Instructional Effectiveness (1990).
- Maryellen Weimer, Improving Your Classroom Teaching: Survival Skills for Scholars (1993).

Sometimes, We Really Do Suck

While I don't try to influence my written student evaluations—other than by teaching well—I have occasionally told my classes that cryptically negative comments, such as, "You suck," while perhaps true, are not particularly helpful. I have then clarified that it's perfectly all right for them to write that I suck, but that if they want me to stop sucking, they had better tell me, with some degree of specificity, just how I suck.

This is the starting point of my primary method of pedagogical self-improvement. I begin with the sobering recognition that, sometimes, my performance is less than perfect. I further recognize that my colleagues will not be available, most days, to sit through my classes and gently guide me along the path to enlightenment. That leaves my students. They are the only other people in my classroom, day in and day out. Accordingly, I must look to them to tell me when, and how, I have gone off the rails.

But this is only the starting point. Once my students have penned their love-epistles, I must decide how best to use them. I describe my methodology below, for whatever its value to others.

1. Set aside adequate time for review. The time needed will depend, of course, on the number of evaluation forms, but, whatever the total number, I try to set aside enough time to examine each evaluation carefully, looking for important trends and tidbits. A quick flip-through won't do it.
2. Remember the 3% rule. I teach mostly large classes, of approximately 100 students, so percentages are easy to calculate. Over the past decade, I've noticed a trend: no matter what I'm teaching, no matter how I do it, between 1 to 3% of my

students hate me. I'm not talking constructive criticism here, but abject hatred—of my personality, the pitch of my voice, even my choice of neckties. It took me a year or two to figure out that such visceral antipathy had nothing at all to do with my teaching. It is rather, I believe, a reflection of whatever personal demons the students in question happen to be fighting on the day they are asked to fill out their evaluation forms. I give such evaluations the credence they deserve: I disregard them.

3. Separate the evaluation forms into three physical piles. One pile is the aforementioned "haters" pile. The second, comprising (blessedly) most of the remaining 97%, is the "generally positive" pile.

   The third is the most troubling: the "legitimate criticism" pile. You know what I mean. Legitimate criticisms are the ones that keep cropping up, over and over. The complaints that give me pause. The specific comments that make me ask myself, "Did I really keep the class over the allotted time that often?" or "Did I really waste too much time at the beginning of the semester and make up for it by rushing during the final weeks?" Ouch.

4. Evaluate the legitimate criticisms and develop strategies to address them. Sometimes this is straightforward. I might simply resolve that, "I'll get a new watch and keep better track of class time," or, "I'll make sure to stick to the schedule in the syllabus." Other times, it's not so easy. When my students once complained—legitimately—that I assigned too much "background" and "historical" reading in Constitutional Law, I had to redesign my syllabus to assign only what was truly relevant to a general, introductory course. It was a painful process—I will miss the lively class discussions of mid-19th-Century Commerce Clause analysis—and it took time, but it was ultimately worthwhile.

5. Do it all over again the following semester. One good thing about frequent evaluations is that I can assess, pretty quickly, whether I've actually corrected legitimate problems, or whether new strategies are in order. I can also nip any new problems in the bud. I try to take a page from Henry Ford and strive for continuous improvement. Henry sold a lot of cars.

That's it. Conceptually, it's all rather simple. The difficulty, of course, is implementation. I know some colleagues who never read their student evaluations, unless forced to by an impending promotion or tenure decision. Others do it as perfunctorily as possible, disregarding (or, worse, obsessing over) anything that is remotely negative. Few, if any, of the colleagues with whom I have spoken go through a methodical process similar to the one that I have described.

But it's worth the pain and the effort. I am pleased to report that, over the years, as I have worked my way through my share of rookie mistakes (and quite a few others) my pile of "legitimate criticisms" has gradually shrunk. Now, I receive perhaps one or two a semester. I've yet to achieve classroom nirvana, but I have a process in place that keeps me moving, at least incrementally, in that direction. Perhaps, on some fine spring morning, decades hence, I'll face only two piles of student evaluation forms on my desk: "generally positive" and "haters." Then I'll revel in the former, disregard the latter, and take the summer off.

Stewart Harris
Appalachian School of Law

Are We the Teachers We Think We Are? Observing Others Teach — Lessons for the Teacher

Having strongly believed in the importance of reflection, and having taught students to be reflective about their own learning for the last several years, I have tried to apply the same principles to my teaching. I have usually done so in a limited way, such as by writing notes to myself about a class after teaching it, or talking to a few colleagues on an ad hoc basis. These conversations usually happened when I felt that a class went particularly poorly or well, and I wanted to share the pain or joy. I felt that I knew who I was as a teacher.

Several years ago, I had an opportunity to think much more deeply about my role and about the role of teachers in general. This happened when two of my colleagues and I engaged in a project we called "Teaching Triangles." We adapted this from materials we had read about in the Tomorrow's Professor listserv, and from The National Teaching & Learning Forum newsletter. Each of these sources talked about "Teaching Squares," an alternative to peer teaching evaluations. Developed by St. Louis Community College, Teaching Squares was a way to get faculty to talk about teaching without triggering defensiveness. The college's handbook is available at http://www.ntlf.com/html/lib/suppmat/ts/tsparticipanthandbook.pdf.

Following the process described in the Teaching Squares material, the three of us agreed with the fundamental principles of nonevaluative teaching observations: showing each other respect and appreciation, sharing responsibility, and above all, focusing on what we observed as it related to our own teaching. Over the next few weeks, we would each observe at least one of each other's classes, and then we would meet to discuss our observations. We were not out to evaluate each other, we were out to learn.

And we did so. My two colleagues observed me teach first-year students Persuasive Writing and Oral Advocacy; two of us observed a colleague teach an Ethics Seminar and an Employment Law Practice course. We observed our third colleague teach Criminal Procedure. As observers, we sought to pay attention to our reactions to what was going on in the class, and to think about how it affected us as teachers. Much like Peter Elbow's "reader-based feedback" where a reader responds to writing by noting the reader's reactions, we were providing "observer-based feedback." After observing or being observed, the two of us in those roles would talk about what we noticed and what it made us think about our own teaching.

Once we had all visited each other's classes, my Teaching Triangle partners and I spent one lunch talking about what we had learned. These were not all happy observations. For example, though the three of us do not perceive ourselves as Kingsfield-type-law professors, we all noticed how much power each of us seemed to wield in the class, and how oblivious we were about it. Though we thought we were student-centered and strived not to be the voice of the expert on the stage, our voices dominated the classroom. While we all see our teaching as a priority, and devote a great deal of time to preparing for class, we noticed that our off-hand remarks, less than well-phrased or well-timed questions, and unclear directions caused us to be less than effective in promoting student learning. And though we each believed in having students learn from each other, and treat their classmates with respect and dignity, in all of our classes students first and foremost looked to us as their source of learning, their source of approval.

Before we started our Teaching Triangles project, I anticipated I would learn from it. Each semester I observe at least four classes, and have always learned from the experience;

moreover I enormously value and respect my Teaching Triangle colleagues. I believed I would learn by observing master techniques I could apply. Instead I learned that I didn't truly know who I was as a teacher or how my students perceived me. Was this disconcerting? Yes. Was it valuable? Unquestionably. Would I do it again with these or other colleagues; would I recommend it to others? Yes and yes. Working on being the teacher I want to be has turned out to be much more difficult than I thought; I hope that the next time I engage in teaching observations I am making progress towards that goal.

Sophie Sparrow
University of New Hampshire School of Law

The Law Professor as Student, or National Velvet, I'm Not

Ferri's ears prick forward as we near the jump. My Arabian mare is moving easily, her strides regular as a metronome, judging the take-off point—eager, but not rushing. On her back I am poised correctly in the two-point position: my heels are down, my legs firmly around her sides, my seat just slightly out of the saddle, my chest up, shoulders back, eyes looking straight ahead between her ears. One stride away from the fence I feel Ferri gather herself for the leap; I close my legs to signal her to take off, and move my hands forward in a crest release to give her more rein. She jumps smoothly, arcing over the fence in what feels like just a larger version of her normal canter stride. I move with her in perfect balance, enjoying her soaring strength. We land in harmony and Ferri canters happily on, sensitive to my directions as I turn her toward the next jump in the course.

Well, that's how it happens in my dreams. In real life, this is more like it:

Two strides away from the fence, I start to wonder if this is such a good idea, after all. The fence, an 18" high cross rail which both Ferri and I could step over if necessary, suddenly looks about six feet high. I stiffen in anticipation, clutching at the reins and leaning too far forward. Confused by my mixed signals, Ferri takes off one stride too soon, bounding in a longer arc to clear the fence. The larger leap throws me off balance. My legs come off of her sides, my heels fly upward and I fall first forward onto her neck and then backward into the saddle, hitting her in the mouth with the reins. Annoyed, upon landing Ferri breaks into a rough, jolting trot. I respond by hauling harder on the reins, which she ignores, tossing her head.

At about this point my riding instructor, Karene Cohen, calls out, "BREATHE, Jan!" Breathe? I think indignantly. Here I am practically rigid with terror, trying to keep my heels, legs, chest, hands, and eyes where they're supposed to be—and on top of that to remember where the next jump is on this course—and Karene wants me to breathe?

I have learned to trust Karene, so I follow her instructions. Although my heart is pounding and my mouth is dry, I loosen my death grip on the reins, and take a deep breath. Once I do that, my chest opens up and I uncurl from my fetal crouch over Ferri's neck. As I sit up, my seat bones connect firmly with the saddle, and my legs drop down and around my horse. Feeling my legs close around her, Ferri rounds her back up under me and moves smoothly forward, coming willingly into contact with the reins again. All of a sudden, we're back in balance, and I can think about the next fence. It's a miracle!

This would be a better story if it only happened once, but the embarrassing truth is, it happens in almost every riding lesson. I have to learn the same thing over and over again—as Karene and Ferri can attest. Although there are "natural" riders in the world—

people who have an innate talent for riding, and who progress rapidly to a high level of skill—I am not one of them. National Velvet, the heroine of my childhood reading, was one such rider; although she never had a lesson, she and her beloved Piebald won the Grand National steeplechase.

I am not National Velvet. I am over 50 years old: asthmatic, uncoordinated, chronically exhausted, stiff and sore, and packing more than my share of cellulite. All the things that effective riding demands are terribly hard for me to do. After years of taking lessons, reading books on riding, watching advanced competitors, and practicing hour after hour on my own, I'm still just a marginally competent rider (or, as Karene says when she's feeling generous, "not terrible").

It's pretty embarrassing to have to admit that I'm only marginally competent at anything, especially at something I want to do so badly. Like most law professors, I'm used to success in the role of student—being the class star that sits in the front row and volunteers. It's been a shock to my ego to experience life from the bottom, rather than the top, of my horseback riding class.

I had to accept that I was not a "natural" rider, and that I would likely never be as good a rider as someone with that gift. But I could become a competent rider, step by step, identifying each skill that I needed to develop, making sure I understood it—and then practicing it over and over until, one day I got it right. (And then, of course, losing it again when I tried to combine it with another, more difficult task ...) Over the years I have built one skill upon another and slowly become—not excellent, not very good, but better than I was! And to get where I am as a rider I have had to work harder than I ever did to achieve academically or as a practicing lawyer or a teacher. Perhaps for that reason I take almost more pride in my riding.

Coincidentally, about the time I started riding lessons, I began to co-teach the Legal Process course. This course, part of Loyola's Academic Support Program, is open to second- and third-year students in academic difficulty. By definition, students in Legal Process are not "succeeding" in law school; they have had exceptional difficulty in their first or second year. And certainly many other students, while not on academic probation, also struggle to "get it," to understand what law school requires and to master those skills. For all of them, the reality of law school has fallen short of their dreams.

When they enroll in Legal Process, or come to talk in my office, these students are often embarrassed. They were successful students as undergraduates. Many of them have been successful in careers other than law. All of them have demonstrated strengths and talents in their lives outside of law school. Sometimes they make a point of mentioning these achievements. They want me to know that they really are people worthy of respect, even though they're having a little trouble right now with outlining, or understanding procedural due process.

They are torn between rage and despair. They tell me about the student last year who sat next to them, didn't take any notes, never briefed cases, read the commercial outline the night before the exam, and got a 92 in the course. They briefed every case, never missed a class, lost the love of their life because they insisted on studying so much—and still barely passed. "It's unfair!" they cry. It's so frustrating to watch these fellow students, for whom law school seems to come naturally, succeed with less effort.

I understand, I tell them. I may not have when I first became a law teacher, but I sure do now, after all these years in the saddle. It may not come "naturally" to you, just like riding doesn't come to me, but you can learn how to make it "second nature"—step by step, identifying each skill that you need to develop, making sure you understand it—

and then practicing it over and over until, one day, you get it right. Then you combine it with another skill, and build on it, and build on that—and you will get better. And when you have mastered it in this way, you can take a pride in your achievement that the "natural" legal thinker cannot.

I think perhaps all law professors should try being students again, try learning something which they passionately want to do, but at which they are just not very good. It could be golf, or origami, or playing the violin. It doesn't have to involve a horse. (But for those of my colleagues who are interested, I'd be happy to call your local riding stable for you, and set up a lesson!)

Jan C. Costello
Loyola Law School, Los Angeles

Why I Teach

What follows are reflections from 12 law teachers on the topic "Why I Teach."

Tony Arnold

More than anything, my passion for a model of personalized education that emphasizes mentoring influenced me to select an offer to teach at Chapman University School of Law. Although mentoring each student is unique and multifaceted, I have appreciated several features of my rapport with students at Chapman.

I am available and accessible outside of class. I try to be keenly attuned to the struggles, successes, strengths, and weaknesses of each student. I enjoy supervising student papers, because students choose topics that excite them and I am able to provide them detailed feedback on drafts. I praise intelligent insights and encourage more rigorous thinking, as the students craft their own "masterpieces." I care very much about what a student will do with his or her education. I am an advocate for my students with prospective employers, picking up the phone or offering to write a letter on behalf of a student whenever appropriate.

Finally, I believe that a vastly higher degree of learning occurs when faculty and students come to know each other as humans, not just educational participants. The rewards of mentorship have been tremendous. Along the way, my ideas and values, and even my life have become interwoven with the ideas, values, and lives of those students who in turn will make a difference in the lives of others.

Dozens of students and former students attended my wedding in June 2000, and three former students participated in the wedding. It was a testimony to the privilege of mentoring students—that they are a part of my life and I am a part of theirs. Because we learn not just from books or classes but from life itself, I am confident that they and I have learned more from our shared journeys than we could learn merely by study and lecture.

Tony Arnold
University of Louisville, Louis D. Brandeis School of Law

Steve Coughlan

You can see it in the faces of a choir, when they've sounded that perfect bell-like tone, and they should all be marvelling at how they've achieved something together that no one person could achieve independently, except that they are too enraptured by the music itself to bother forming such a thought.

You can see it in the closed eyes of a musician, saxophone or flute or harmonica in hand, when the music flows like a breeze that could carry you away, and you know that she's not taming this song, isn't wrestling it to the ground, but is just caught up in it like anyone else, not making the music, simply listening to it wash over her as it washes over everyone.

You can see it in the movements of an athlete, a basketball player driving to the net or a figure skater about to do a jump, when he isn't calculating, he isn't planning, he isn't estimating his opponent's likely responses or precisely how much force to push off with, he has simply seen the next few seconds of the future and knows, with crystal clarity, that *this* will work.

You can see it, once you know you should be looking, in the actions of a juggler, when the balls or clubs or rings are flying, twisting and spinning, and they aren't going everywhere, they are going there—and there—and there, just as they should, and objects and hands arrive naturally at the same place and same time, with no seeming need for conscious action, like the gears in some predestined clockwork mechanism.

I don't sing or play an instrument. I'm not a professional athlete, and I don't even juggle as often as I'd like. And I can't *tell* you what "it" is.

But I do teach. And sometimes, when good questions are being asked, and good responses are begin given, and the discussion flows like a raging river, wild and uncontrolled yet following its natural course, and I am a leaf in that river riding it to its end, amazed at the blossoming understanding that is palpable in the air.... In those moments, though I still can't define it, can't describe it, can't put it in words—in those moments I come as close as I get to knowing what "it" is.

And that's why I teach.

Steve Coughlan
Dalhousie University Schulich School of Law

Suzanne Darrow-Kleinhaus

I came to the practice of law after 12 years as a technical writer. After practicing for several years, I jumped at the opportunity to teach at the law school where I had graduated but a few years before. I am now an associate professor of Legal Methods at Touro College, Jacob D. Fuchsberg Law Center. I could tell you about my students and the classroom and how it comes alive with ideas when we connect, but the truth is that my father said it better in a letter he wrote to me. I consider it one of the most precious gifts I have ever received. My father, Albert Darrow, wrote:

"The Teacher"

> Dear Suzanne,
>
> Harry Truman once said "it makes not much difference what sort of a building you're in when you're after knowledge, but it does count entirely on who teaches you."
>
> Many teachers are bright, quick, intelligent and articulate—and yet they are not good teachers. Why is this so? It's not very difficult to answer once you pause a bit and think. They lack the other attributes that make a teacher a success. To

succeed you must be a complete person. In addition to being smart and articulate, you need to have wit and charm. You have to be able to teach the subject matter in such a way as to make the student interested and motivated to learn what you are trying to teach.

In the end, what the teacher must have most of all is dedication. The teacher has to say, "I can, I will, I must—teaching is not everything, teaching is the only thing." Such a teacher is worth all of the gold in Fort Knox.

Never let go of your dream to teach and to write. It is who you are.

I remember 55 and 60 years later many of the teachers who motivated me. Mr. Wechsler and Mrs. Jerome in English, Mrs. Calabria in Spanish, Mr. Berkowitz in History, my sixth grade teacher Mrs. Keenan, and my music teacher Miss O'Hara. I and others like me are their legacy.

"Knowledge is the lamp that never goes out" and the torchbearers are the great teachers, who by their dedication to service instill in us the idea that we all have value.

Love, Dad

Suzanne Darrow-Kleinhaus
Touro College Jacob D. Fuchsberg Law Center

Chris Johnson

So why do I teach? The question frightens me a little, for though I spend so much time teaching, in different moods I have many different answers. And thinking back to when I started teaching, I find reasons now already abandoned. As with so many of life's great interpersonal adventures—college, friendship, marriage, fatherhood—I embarked on my teaching career with hopes and expectations in which I am already deeply grateful to have been disappointed. I offer here two examples, neither very profound. True to my pattern of learning about fatherhood, marriage, etc., in learning to teach I have been astonished by discoveries of the obvious.

First, I expected that to teach I would need, and soon have, encyclopedic knowledge of criminal law and procedure. To survive the lag between my first class and my awaited epiphany of sublime knowledge, I would simply fake it. I now know that I will not soon master every puzzle of criminal law. For years to come, my students will find mysteries I had never noticed, much less resolved. Furthermore, if complete mastery is to be a consequence of teaching, it will also be, for me, the end of teaching. If a time comes when I stop learning in the classroom, I should stop teaching there. I teach in order to learn.

Second, I expected to find in teaching a purely intellectual respite from the real human consequences of my criminal defense practice. Nobody's life or freedom could depend on my classroom performance. That expectation, which I did not at first even recognize as divisible, soon proved wrong in two different ways.

The illusion that one could meaningfully study the topics of criminal law in a dispassionately abstract spirit did not survive the first day of class discussion on the law of rape. One student, reacting to a classmate's comment with raised voice and with a thundering slam of her casebook, reminded us all that the puzzles of criminal law are moral and emotional, as well as intellectual. Conflict and tension remain, and belong, in the classroom as well as in practice.

It took only a little longer to find the second flaw in the expectation. With graduation and criminal practice looming in their futures, many students stubbornly insist on the immediate relevance of their education. When the dilemmas of conscience that we read and talk about in class happen in life, what, they ask, does the honorable criminal practitioner do? In teaching, I participate in the acquisition by students of great power over other human lives. Their future clients have much at risk in their education, and demand that as the students acquire power, power does not acquire the students. When I can find no improving link between today's classroom and tomorrow's justice, I should stop teaching. I teach not to escape the high human stakes of criminal practice, but to engage them more fully.

Chris Johnson
University of New Hampshire School of Law

Danne L. Johnson

I teach because I am a teacher, a student, and a believer in the textures of life.

I have spent most of my adult life teaching—teaching others about women, race, class, culture, syntax, working hard, perseverance, and overcoming. These life lessons and experiences, which I continue to learn, are among my tools for the classroom. These tools and my experience in legal practice enable me to contextualize legal education for all students.

Before joining the academy, I was an ad hoc teacher. Classes, in the form of talk shows, were held in the car, on the subway, and in the kitchen. My listeners were friends and colleagues, and often strangers passing by my heated discussions. My husband titled the broadcast "Sisters with Views," and the name has stuck. In addition to my "broadcasts," I supervised attorneys in the area of securities regulation. I was called upon to teach young attorneys history, writing, organization, public speaking, and ethics, among other topics relevant to the practice of law at the U.S. Securities and Exchange Commission. As a result, I have a practice-based view of teaching and learning.

I insert the discussion of alternative dispute resolution, drafting (including grammar), ethics, current events, and client interviewing into my courses. These are tools which transcend the substantive law, and their use allows for distinctions to be drawn between excellent and mediocre attorneys.

I approach legal education from a holistic point of view, recognizing that legal theory and history are the underpinnings of the doctrines we teach, and that the intersection of these topics with the common use of the law, is the end result of our educational process. Students must be able to see the law from the foundation to its ultimate use.

So what do I get out of it? I get to see the faces of students as they grasp the subtle nuances between doctrine and practice. I learn and grow through each class. I get a warm feeling knowing that my students are prepared to get their cases before a judge and to keep them there, or to use the art of negotiation to avoid litigation. I look forward to the one or two students who come back from a summer experience and proudly report that, "I had to teach them civil procedure" or "I had to explain that this instrument was a security." These students recognize that learning has taken place.

I teach for fulfillment as a teacher, a student, and a believer in the textures of life.

Danne L. Johnson
Oklahoma City University School of Law

Angela Mae Kupenda

Those Who Can't, Teach?

I'm sure you've heard the saying, "Those who can't, teach." While it is usually meant to disparage teachers, it can be taken as expressing a meaningful calling. Now, before you become outraged thinking that one in the academy is admitting lawyerly incompetence, let me explain. Let's face it. Although I desire to be, I can't be a congressional representative, trial lawyer, lobbyist, school principal, judge, law clerk, corporate lawyer, social activist, grassroots organizer, etc.—all in one lifetime.

So I teach. And, as I teach others who later make a positive difference in the halls of congress, politics, grassroots communities, corporations, elementary schools, etc., I get to indirectly affect many arenas in my lifetime. I teach, therefore, to make a positive impact on society in a way broader than one person normally can in a single lifetime.

My niece, Monica, was trying hard to learn how to ride her bicycle without training wheels. One afternoon, Monica left me a voicemail, saying, "Auntie, hurry to Nana's after work. She's taught me how to ride my bike." Now, Nana is my mother and she uses a wheelchair. She probably has not been on a bike in over 60 years. I wondered how she could teach Monica to ride, because Nana can't ride. When I arrived, Monica was racing around, confidently and expertly handling her big bicycle. As I stood with my mouth open, she yelled back that Nana talked to her and explained how to hold her body and balance. I looked over at Nana, who was sitting there in her wheelchair, beaming and looking as proud as Monica. I thought, "Those who can't, teach."

I teach in the way my fifth-grade teacher, the late Mrs. Mary Jane Pace, taught me to have a confident, bounce-back-and-never-give-up attitude, all while I was attending post-*Brown*—but still separate, unequal, and all-black—schools. She taught us to think for ourselves, to explore ideas without fear, to believe in the dignity and worth of all individuals. She taught us that we can do almost anything we set our heart to. Mainly she taught us to be educated and responsible people and not educated fools, to use her language.

Why do I teach? I teach because I can't. I can't do it all and make a difference everywhere. But, maybe one day I will have made a difference in many other arenas, just like Nana and Mrs. Pace made in Monica's and my life.

Angela Mae Kupenda
Mississippi College School of Law

Andrew J. McClurg

Like everyone, I teach for lots of reasons, many of them selfish. Here's my stab at capturing them in 450 words:

1. I teach because teachers changed my life.
2. I teach because no matter how many times I've taught a course, it's still a mystery what's going to happen when I walk into the classroom.
3. I teach because I get to adopt a hundred terrific "kids" every year without having to pay to support them. Law students demand the same things from me as my real child: admonishment, affection, consolation, exhortation, direction, discipline, everything except my Visa card. But they give back some of the same things, too. Certainly, they work much harder for their allowance (final grade).

The labor expended by a law student simply in trying to understand future interests could make a thousand beds and take out a million bags of garbage.

4. I teach because a graduating student who never registered on my radar surprised me with a card that said, "For showing me what a lawyer can be, I thank you."
5. I teach because the energy, intelligence, and inquisitive spirits of law students make them delightful people to be around. What happens to them after they become lawyers, I can't say and disclaim responsibility for.
6. I teach because when I was sweating out 70 hours a week as a disillusioned litigation associate, my father sat in my living room and said with regret, "The worst thing in life is to look back and realize you never made the best of it." I filled out the AALS Faculty Register form a few weeks later.
7. I teach because of my admiration for the student who will never get the top paper, never be on law review, and never land a job at a silk-stocking law firm, but who works harder than those who do.
8. I teach because I love to laugh and few things are more hilarious than first-year law students. Bless their anxiety-ridden hearts. In 1987, the very first student I ever called on as a Torts professor became distraught when, after stating the facts, I said, "That's the case in a nutshell." She thought I was accusing her of being unprepared and stealing the facts from a West *Nutshell* book. It's been a laugh a minute ever since.
9. I teach because I learn.
10. I teach because, every once in a while, I change a person's life.

Andrew J. McClurg
University of Memphis, Cecil C. Humphreys School of Law

Marjorie A. Silver

Thirty Touro law students went down to New Orleans over the 2007 spring break to help with the Katrina recovery efforts. When they returned, several made a presentation about the work they had done, accompanied by a slide show.

Some of the students made extraordinary efforts to contact homeowners living elsewhere who had fled New Orleans in the wake of Katrina, to notify them that official pink signs posted on their houses threatened demolition unless they took immediate action. Others, upon learning how incredibly complex the requirements were for obtaining a permit to rebuild, decided to prepare a step-by-step instruction manual in easily understood plain English. After they completed drafting, they took the manual to City Hall to verify that the information in it was correct. The official who examined it was so impressed that he asked whether he could make copies to distribute.

When I heard this presentation I kvelled (To *kvell:* Yiddish *kveln* to be delighted, from Middle High German *quellen* to well, gush, swell; to be extraordinarily proud; rejoice (from http://www.m-w.com/dictionary/kvell) "This is why I teach," I thought.

In early May of that same year, I was in New Orleans for the AALS Clinical Teachers Workshop. On Saturday morning, a colleague and I hired a taxi, and had the driver take us down to the Lower Ninth, to personally witness the devastation. After driving around for about an hour and a half, we turned a corner and there were the headquarters for Common Ground. I recognized the sign from the students' slides that said something like: "Shame on you tourist for just driving by and not stopping to hear about our pain."

So of course there was no way we weren't going to stop! I got out of the taxi and walked up to a big, shirtless man with long dreadlocks (it was *very* hot!), and introduced myself: "Hi, I'm Marjorie Silver. I'm a law professor from New York." And just to make conversation, I added: "In fact, some of our students were down here a couple of weeks ago ..." The man shouted "Touro!" I—quite taken aback, knowing that many students from many schools had been in New Orleans at the same time—said "Yes!" And he said, "Come here and let me give you a big hug! Your students were *wonderful!* They were *amazing!* They made a difference in the lives of at least 60 people!"

It was one of the most wonderful, most incredible moments of my life.

I am so proud of these students. They demonstrated outstanding problem-solving skills. They didn't wait for someone to tell them what to do. They identified real needs, and took meaningful action, using their legal training *and* their wealth of life experience.

This is why I teach.

Marjorie A. Silver
Touro College Jacob D. Fuchsberg Law Center

Amanda L. Smith

I knew that I wanted to be a lawyer after I read *To Kill a Mockingbird* in the ninth grade. The judge appointed Atticus Finch to represent Tom Robinson, an African American accused of raping a Caucasian woman in Alabama in the 1930s. The judge picked Atticus based upon Atticus' reputation. Despite threats to himself, his client, and his family, Atticus remained a lawyer of integrity, who did his job even when it was not easy. I have always aspired to be a lawyer like Atticus Finch and expect other lawyers to be the same.

When I entered practice, I had a wonderful mentor who taught me the importance of reputation in legal practice. In navigating sometimes murky ethical waters, I knew my mentor would not always direct me toward the easiest or quickest route, but I knew he would steer me toward an ethically sound course that would best serve my clients. I came to value my reputation as an attorney of integrity.

I teach because I want our profession to be infused with integrity. I want my students to learn to use professionalism as the everyday lenses through which they view their legal practices, rather than to compartmentalize ethics into just another class or bar exam topic. I model the behavior that I want them to carry into practice: I deliver on promises that I make; I show up on time; I promptly respond to emails and voicemails; and I treat everyone with respect. Fortunately, I also teach as part of a writing program that has incorporated professionalism as part of students' grades. Students are expected to act like the professionals that they are training to become and, like in the real world, there are penalties for the failure to do so.

Out in practice, my students will face tremendous pressures to win. I teach because I want my students to win like Atticus Finch did in *To Kill a Mockingbird*. While Atticus lost the case, Tom Robinson's friends and family stood to show their respect and gratitude as Atticus walked out of the courtroom after the verdict. I teach because I want my students to win their cases in a similar way, by representing their clients to the best of their abilities and with the utmost of integrity. I teach so that our profession will never lose its professionalism.

Amanda L. Smith
Widener University School of Law

Sophie Sparrow

I teach because I am awed and fascinated by the power in learning. Witnessing this is a true joy. This gift—seeing students grow—is why I teach. On the days when work presents its toughest challenges, I gather strength by envisioning students gaining confidence. Like fledglings, some students soar farther and higher than others. But almost all fly. It is such a pleasure to witness them going from tumbling around in dazed confusion to owning the strength of their wings.

This happens each semester. Science majors who studiously avoided every college writing course begin law school convinced that the ability to write fluidly is reserved for the chosen few. Later I see these students apply for clerkships, seek positions on journals, and sign up for advanced writing classes. I know they now believe in the power of their words.

Other students infectiously rejoice in their new strengths. Students who never thought they could speak in public emerge from oral arguments exclaiming, "I want to be a litigator!" Standing tall in their suits, shoulders back, faces beaming, they look like professionals. More importantly, they see this in themselves. They are going to be lawyers.

Regardless of how ready students are to study law, my goal is to coach each of them to a new level. Some progress from having little understanding of the law to actually being able to apply a rule to a set of facts. Others move from seeing discrete doctrinal details to understanding the broader principles that weave them together. The joy is in seeing this growth.

Sometimes learning comes with sadness. It hurts to receive low grades and to go from believing that law school isn't too hard to painfully realizing that something crucial is missing. But when, upon reviewing their work, students can start to diagnose the problems and suggest ways to address them, I know that they are developing skills that can last them a lifetime.

Ultimately, this is the best gift of all. It is when students know that they can fly without me. Then they own the power in their own learning.

Sophie Sparrow
University of New Hampshire School of Law

Diane Sullivan

I am the daughter of a mill worker from the City of Fitchburg.

When I was seven years old, I knew I wanted to be an attorney. At that very young age, I noticed that when neighbors had serious problems or tragedies, they called upon lawyers for help, even though most couldn't afford them. It seemed to me, even then, that lawyers were the advocates, leaders, and defenders of many of those in the community who were poor or struggling to provide for their families.

I remember thinking then that I needed to become a lawyer to help out people like my mother and father, both of whom were denied educational opportunity and the power that comes with it.

After I graduated from Fitchburg High School, I went to work as a bank teller making $60 a week. My boss, a man in a pinstripe suit, told me that I would get a raise for my superior performance, and I did. It was an additional $3 per week. It was at that moment that I realized I had better find a way to get an education. I'd be damned if I would settle for annual raises of $156.00. I knew then that getting a college education was crucial for me in order to be able to help the people I cared about. So I became the first ever in my family to attend college. But I had to do it the hard way—at night, initially one course at a time. I remember clearly that when I had saved enough money to enroll for my first college course, I signed up for business law. I was thinking, somehow, some way, some day I would get to law school. But was the law—the profession I dreamed of—available to someone from the working class like me? I wasn't sure.

That first college business law class confirmed my passion for the law. The professor told us, "I am going to treat you like law students." While others in my class groaned, I was elated. "That's why I'm here," I thought. On my final examination, he wrote on my paper that I belonged in law school. "Yeah," I muttered to myself, "Easier said than done."

But I saved my pennies (literally in a jar) and continued to take one course at a time because that was all I could afford. Eventually, as my income rose, I was able to take more classes until I was on a schedule of four night courses a semester. It took me nearly a decade to receive my B.A. from Fitchburg State College. All the while I remained focused on going to law school.

Finally, in 1988 at age 32, when the Massachusetts School of Law opened its doors, I applied, was accepted, received my degree, and passed the Massachusetts bar examination. I had fulfilled my dream (which often seemed impossible); I had become an attorney.

Today, I am a professor of law at MSL and my students have backgrounds similar to mine. Many of them are also the first in their families to go to college and then to law school, and have had to work while going to school. But they have persevered because they want to live a more fulfilling life and to control their own destinies.

Their commitment inspires me to strive hard to be a role model for our students, and to teach them that with hard work, dreams *can* come true.

Diane Sullivan
Massachusetts School of Law

Kathleen Elliott Vinson

I teach because of my love of learning. When learning is talked about in the context of academia, most people think of students learning from a teacher. While it is exciting for a teacher to see the light bulb go on for a student, other great teaching moments occur when a teacher reflects on what she has learned from the other side of the podium, from student to teacher. Teaching is not a one-way linear approach, but rather recursive and reflective for both student and teacher.

I have taught for more than a decade; but whether I have taught for ten years, ten months, or ten days, I am just as eager to learn from my students as I am to impart my knowledge to them. While it is important to be knowledgeable and experienced in one's field, when teachers feel they already know everything about their course and its pedagogy, or that they could not gain any knowledge from their students, teaching and learning ends on the part of both the teacher and the students. My best teaching occurs when I am confident in my abilities, yet open to learning from my students.

Teaching is challenging, exciting, inspiring, and rewarding. It provides a great opportunity for the teacher to learn. Teaching is challenging when I need to use creative, different ways to introduce information to the class because students have different learning styles and bring different perspectives, assumptions, values, and skills to the classroom. Teaching is exciting when I realize that students have understood a difficult concept, which could help establish the foundation for their future learning and success. Teaching is inspiring when I learn the challenges some students have had to face and what they have overcome through persistence and perseverance. Finally, teaching is rewarding when I talk to the students instead of talking at them and listen patiently to them, which can have a lasting effect on their educational experience and their life.

In the end, I hope the knowledge that I have shared with my students is as great as the knowledge that I have gained from them.

Kathleen Elliott Vinson
Suffolk University Law School